Studies in Disorders of Communication

General Editors:

Language of the Elderly:
A Clinical Perspective

Jane Maxim and Karen Bryan

National Hospital's College of Speech Sciences, London

With contributions from Ian Thompson, Monash Medical Centre, Australia

W

Whurr Publishers Ltd
London

First published 1994 by
Whurr Publishers Ltd
19b Compton Terrace, London N1 2UN, England

British Library Cataloguing in Publication Data
A catalogue record for this book is available from the British Library.

ISBN 1-870332-35-0

Singular no. 1-565932-54-4

Photoset by Stephen Cary
Printed and bound in the UK by Athenaeum Press Ltd, Newcastle upon Tyne

Preface

When asked about the rehabilitation prospects of a client, most students and many professionals cite old age as a poor prognostic sign. Even our own students, with whom we have (we thought) carefully discussed concepts of ageing, stereotyping and the need to assess other factors such as mental and physical health, have been known to say this. This book is an attempt to redress that balance and to look at what does constitute change as we age. Specifically, we discuss changes that occur in language processing and performance. The beginning of the book presents a very different picture from the second half, which deals with pathological changes in language functioning due to disease processes.

The clinical importance of distinguishing 'normal age-related' change from pathological change cannot be overstated. Health professionals who work with the elderly need to ensure that they are not interpreting all 'normal' changes as pathological: 'she forgets the odd word – must have Alzheimer's disease'; or conversely 'all old people become confused, don't they?'

Age-related changes are sometimes put forward to support the view that elderly people cannot benefit from intervention. In fact, following acute illness such as stroke the elderly usually respond well to therapy: they walk again, communicate and often go home to live. Some evidence suggests that therapeutic intervention can even be of benefit in progressive neurological diseases.

We are involved with the elderly as clinicians, researchers and educators of future professionals. It is evident that there is often a lack of continuity between these areas. Researchers do not always investigate the areas that clinicians work in, research findings may not be followed through to clinical validity, and clinicians' work practices may preclude the incorporation of innovative approaches. We have attempted to show how research findings might influence clinical practice. There is increasing recognition that the elderly do not form a homogeneous group. The effects of education, institutionalisation and social isolation need to be distinguished from actual changes in language processing. The interrelations of normality, pathology, research, clinical practice and service provision to the management of a single elderly individual are all connected. The complexity revealed should be a stimulus for future debate and wider consideration of the needs of the elderly.

In the UK, community-care legislation (irrespective of whether one agrees or disagrees with its philosophy) can be seen as an opportunity to evaluate services for the elderly. In the case of a service such as speech and language therapy, the current picture is of a hospital-based, disease-treatment oriented service. But clinicians could develop an important role in facilitating adaptation to change, in managing change and in maintaining communicative functioning. This may seem unrealistic, but there are increasing numbers of elderly people, and they have increasing spending power and increasing political influence, which may help to bring their needs to greater prominence. At a conference on demographic changes and health care in the elderly population, a health manager (Edwards, 1991) offered the following description of a woman aged 75 in the year 2001 which we have adapted.

Elsie has become a regular visitor to her GP's surgery since her stroke. The surgery has changed in the last decade. The new building houses a physiotherapist, occupational therapist, speech and language therapist, psychologist and dietician and one of the fund holding partners is a nurse. A meeting room can be used by different local groups to discuss health matters. Elsie had a short time in hospital following a stroke but the integrated nursing and rehabilitation team helped a great deal and provided a full care plan for the domiciliary rehabilitation service. She has been encouraged to use a full range of personal aids and has a tailor-made wheelchair which she uses for longer journeys. When she noticed that her hearing was deteriorating, she went along to the speech and language therapist's 'drop-in' clinic and was given an appointment to see the visiting audiologist and subsequently had a hearing aid fitted. She is able to call a help line if any of her aids are giving her difficulty and get instant advice. In her handbag she carries her medical notes on a computer chip health card. In Elsie's area, the elderly have become a force to contend with – demanding and getting special ramps and signs to help their mobility and dietary advice to keep them healthy. She is currently going to a hearing-aid users' group, set up and run by elderly people who are successful users and want to encourage others over the settling-in period. The group calls in professional help when they think it necessary and arrange this through the neighbourhood clinic staff.

So is this an idealised view of health care for the elderly? None of these ideas and services are radically new. They are, in fact, almost all in existence somewhere. Perhaps the only major departures are in the citing of services for the elderly and in the participation of the elderly in their own health care.

Dementia research is at a very exciting stage, where real progress is being made in examining the neuropathology and where old concepts of disease entities are changing. Looking at the older literature, we wondered whether a Pick's patient would now be considered as a progressive aphasic and an Alzheimer's patient as having Pick's disease! It is also demoralising that there remains a dearth of detailed descriptions of language in normal old age, in disease conditions and in the recovery process. Single case study methodology applied to language in the normal elderly and in the elderly who manifest the effects of disease processes are badly needed.

All of the issues mentioned have made the completion of this book rather difficult, and certain decisions on the organisation of the material may reveal a bias or present an impression that we did not originally set out to make. Above all we hope that this book will stimulate more research in this neglected field.

We would like to acknowledge everyone who has helped us in the preparation of this book. In particular, Professors David Crystal, Ruth Lesser and Maggie Snowling for their constructive comments on earlier drafts, and our colleagues at the National Hospital's College of Speech Sciences, especially the librarians.

Jane Maxim would like to acknowledge the Leverhulme Trust, who funded the transcriptions.

Finally, our thanks to Stephen, Islay, Paddy, Max, David and Ruth.

Jane Maxim
Karen Bryan
September 1993

General preface

This series focuses upon disorders of speech language and communication, bringing together the techniques of analysis, assessment and treatment which are pertinent to the area. It aims to cover cognitive, linguistic, social and education aspects of language disability, and therefore has relevance within a number of disciplines. These include speech therapy, the education of children and adults with special needs, teachers of the deaf, teachers of English as a second language and of foreign languages, and educational and clinical psychology. The research and clinical findings from these various areas can usefully inform one another and, therefore, we hope one of the main functions of this series will be to put people within one profession in touch with developments in another. Thus, it is our editorial policy to ask authors to consider the implications of their findings for professions outside their own and for fields with which they have not been primarily concerned. We hope to engender an integrated approach to theory and practice and to produce a much-needed emphasis on the description and analysis of language as such, as well as on the provision of specific techniques of therapy, remediation and rehabilitation

Whilst it has been our aim to restrict the series to the study of language disability, its scope goes considerably beyond this. Many previously neglected topics have been included where these seem to benefit from contemporary research in linguistics, psychology, medicine, sociology, education and English studies. Each volume puts its subject matter in perspective and provides an introductory slant to its presentation. In this way we hope to provide specialised studies which can be used as texts for components of teaching courses at undergraduate and postgraduate levels, as well as material directly applicable to the needs of professional workers.

David Crystal
Ruth Lesser
Margaret Snowling

Contents

Preface v
General preface viii

Chapter 1

Ageing and communication 1
Who are the elderly? 1
Chronological and biological age 2
Senescence and senility 2
Neurocognitive changes 3
What do we know about the elderly? 3
Our expectations of the elderly 4
What is successful ageing? 5
Theoretical frameworks of cognitive ageing 5
Age-related changes that can affect language and communication 7
Communication disorders and disease processes in the elderly 15
Theoretical issues in aphasia, normal and pathological ageing 18
Methodological problems in the assessment of the elderly 24
Summary 27

Chapter 2

Language and language change in the normal elderly population 28
Language processing and language change in the elderly 28
Theoretical backgrounds of language research in the elderly 30
Cognitive parameters of language 31
Language change with increasing age 33
What patterns of language breakdown in Alzheimer's-type dementia and acquired aphasia might suggest about language in the normal, healthy elderly 46
Summary

Chapter 3

The grammatical structure of conversational language in the normal elderly 54
Introduction 54
The elderly group 55
Analysing elderly language 57
Language variation in the elderly 59
What is a sentence? 59
Sentence length: word measures 62
Mean number of sentences per turn 64
Sentence measures summary 65
Sentence types and categories 65
Clause elements 67
Phrasal structure 84
The verb phrase 89
Pronoun use 93
Summary 94

Chapter 4

Complex structures, errors and repair in the normal elderly 95
Introduction 95
Coordinators and coordination, subordinators and subordination 95
Sentences containing disfluencies 102
Sentence repair and filler syllables 111
Summary 112

Chapter 5

Language profiles of the normal elderly 113
Performance variation among the elderly 113
Eight grammatical performance profiles 113
The transcription of intonation 113
Conversational language samples 115
Profile variation among the elderly 141
Conclusions 144

Chapter 6

Language pathology in non-Alzheimer dementias 150
Incidence and prevalence 149
Pick's disease 149
Diffuse Lewy body disease 154
The progressive aphasias 154
Vascular dementias 156
Parkinson's disease 160
Progressive supranuclear palsy 164
Huntington's disease 165

Creutzfeldt–Jakob disease 166
Depression and dementia 166
The AIDS – dementia complex 169
Wernicke's encephalopathy/Korsakoff's psychosis 170
Conclusions 171

Chapter 7

Language pathology in Alzheimer's disease 173
The Alzheimer's disease complex 172
Longitudinal profiles 175
Language research 180
Lexical semantics 180
Semantic and grammatical processes above single-word level 183
Discourse, cohesion and repair 187
Agnosia and Alzheimer's disease 191
Reading, writing and spelling 192
The dyspraxias and Alzheimer's disease 193
Conclusions 194

Chapter 8

Current service provision for the elderly in the UK 196
Introduction 195
Issues in service provision 196
Current provision of care for the elderly 197
Current speech and language therapy provision for the elderly 200

Chapter 9

Speech and language therapy intervention with the elderly 205
Introduction 204
Intervention studies with the elderly 204
What speech and language therapists do with elderly clients 207
Assessment of elderly clients 207
Interventions with elderly clients 214
Working with carers 219

Chapter 10

Future directions 225
Proposed models of care in the UK 225
Care in the USA, Canada, Japan and France 226
Aims for future speech and language therapy provision in the UK 228
Future directions for research 231

Appendix I: Original LARSP chart 233
Appendix II: Modified LARSP chart 234
Appendix III: Glossary of LARSP abbreviations 235

Appendix IV: Means for all structures counted during the 20-minute sampling period 237
Appendix V: Means for all structures per 100 sentences 240
Appendix VI: Hachinski Ischaemia Score 243
Appendix VII: DSM-III-R criteria for diagnosis of dementia 244
Appendix VIII: British Geriatric Society Statement of Intent(1988) 246

References 247

Index 273

Chapter 1 Ageing and communication

The ageing process involves a series of changes in the mental and physical functioning of humans. These changes alter the way in which elderly people communicate. Human communication skills demand the synergy of voice, speech, language and cognition. Voice is a result of the transformation of breath support into acoustic energy by the larynx and the shaping of that energy by supraglottic structures into frequency (pitch), loudness (intensity) and rhythm (intonation). Speech demands the complex balance of phonation, articulation, resonance and prosody, whereas language is the formulation of our thoughts into verbal or written symbols. Communication adds a further dimension to this process and involves the exchange of messages through spoken, written or gestural language. When discussing communication, wc are examining the interaction of cognition and language, a complex interaction between different aspects of memory, attention and language itself.

This chapter will discuss attitudes towards elderly people and aspects of the ageing process that are relevant to communication. It will then present an overview of disease processes in the elderly, and a discussion of the issues involved in differentiating between normal and pathological ageing.

Who are the elderly?

Ask yourself: who is elderly? The answer would probably be 'Someone who is quite a bit older than me!'. If you were to ask the same question of someone considerably younger than yourself they might well think that you are old, whereas your idea of 'old age' might be quite different. Similarly, our perception of age may be culture specific. We have learned expectations of what elderly people can do and how they behave, although these perceptions are not necessarily accurate. One culture may think of old age as beginning at 70 while in another it may be 45, if average life expectancy is 50 years. Therefore, we may not be able to make an accurate guess at the age of someone from a different ethnic background because we do not have the relevant information. Thus the concept of 'old age' appears to be relative rather than absolute.

Currently a chronological age of 65 appears to be the agreed age for commencement of old age. In the UK, 15.8% of the population are over the age of 65, and this is expected to rise to 21.6% by the year 2036 (OPCS, 1988). Furthermore, within this expected rise, in the 1990s the numbers of very elderly people (i.e. those over 85 years) are expected to rise rapidly.

The size of the elderly population is growing in most Western countries. In Australia, estimates suggest that, by the year 2001, 11.7% of the population will be over 65 years of age (Australian Bureau of Statistics, 1982). Estimates from the USA suggest that 17–20% of the population will be over the age of 65 by the year 2030, which represents approximately 51 million people (Schoenberg, 1986).

The use of 65 years as an arbitrary indicator of 'ageing' enables us to gather the type of figures quoted above. However, the concept of 'ageing' involves more than just chronological factors. Ageing is now considered a natural process, part of the developmental lifespan, and can be differentiated from pathological processes, which are more likely to occur in old age.

Chronological and biological age

Chronological age need not be identical to biological age. The physiological processes of ageing may occur prematurely or appear to be delayed: ageing of the voice is an example of this. Both men and women experience changes in their voice because of the effects of hormone changes and calcification (Kahane, 1983). However, the changes in dimensions such as pitch range differ between men and women, and interactions with disease processes such as arthritis may increase the calcification of the laryngeal cartilages. Thus, while research shows that the voice is a good indicator of age, some voices may age faster than others (Ringel and Chodzo-Zajko, 1987).

Similarly, there are known to be age-related changes in the rates of neuronal drop-out in the cerebral cortices of elderly people, which are distinct from the pathological changes associated with disease processes such as Alzheimer's disease (Tomlinson, 1977). However, in some individuals these disease processes are triggered at an earlier stage than might be expected where ageing is both pathological and accelerated.

Senescence and senility

Senescence describes the normal changes that take place in the ageing individual, involving all aspects of body function. The most noticeable changes in relation to communicative abilities are slower response time, word finding difficulties in conversation and changes in the voice. *Senility* describes the abnormal changes that occur as a response to a group of diseases that cause gradual deterioration of communication and cognition.

These terms are useful when we need to describe the specific aspects of communication that differentiate the two states, but the border line between the two groups is indistinct. What we can define are two clearly distinguishable groups of changes, being at opposite ends of a spectrum of change but having a common middle ground:

- changes due to normal heathy ageing;
- changes due to pathological ageing.

Neurocognitive changes

Although maximum human development takes place between birth and adolescence, development continues, albeit at a slower pace, throughout life. New skills can be learned; for example the lexicon continues to expand indefinitely until death or illness intervenes. Many active elderly people use terms such as 'yuppie' and 'lager lout', which came into use only a short time ago and which have been assimilated along with a semantic network. Even if an elderly person does not use these words he or she will probably be able to give a definition of them.

However, the elderly often complain of reduced mental skills such as poor memory, and mental testing confirms this perception (McGlone et al., 1990). Changes occur in the ability to communicate and to coordinate language abilities with cognitive, memory and attention skills. These changes result from a complex interaction of internal senescent processing changes, neurocognitive changes and biological changes. This interaction leads to great variability in the ability of elderly people to function in everyday life. This variability in behaviour and capacity is a constant challenge to clinicians working with the elderly.

Our expectations of performance in the elderly are also important. When a 20 year old forgets a name, this is seen as a 'lapse' of memory, i.e. a temporary state. But when a 75 year old forgets something it is often seen as a 'loss' or a more sinister indication of failing abilities.

What do we know about the elderly?

One of the most striking features of the elderly population is the imbalance between the numbers of men and women. The 1981 National Census in the UK found that the group aged 65–75 years comprised approximately 40% men and 60% women; in the 75+ group this is roughly 30% men and 70% women.

Traditionally the elderly are thought of as needing to be 'looked after', but in the UK 97% of elderly people live in their own homes (although this number is likely to rise as the number of very old people increases). For the 3% who live in residential homes, nursing homes or sheltered accommodation there is a range of disability: 17 in every 100 are severely dependent, 42 moderately dependent and 41 reasonably independent (Midwinter, 1989). The likelihood of living alone increases with age, with 61% of women aged 75 or more living alone.

Most surveys show exponential increases in the prevalence of disability with ageing. The most common causes of disability are the dementias, arthritis and stroke. However, health problems do not necessarily lead to decreased functioning. Throughout life people make unconscious modifications to their behaviour and life style to compensate for degenerative changes and permit a full and high-quality life. Many elderly people accept a degree of impairment that they would have found unacceptable during middle age (Wells and Freer, 1988)

Our expectations of the elderly

In the Middle East, age is seen as a blessing which brings status and prestige to a man (Slater, 1964). Unfortunately, in Western cultures, youth is revered and old age tends to be seen in a negative manner. The stereotyped view of an elderly person as being ill, frail and mentally incapable remains prevalent in society even though there is no evidence to support this view (except for a small minority of the very elderly).

Palmore (1982) states that many of the problems of ageing stem from, or are exacerbated by, prejudice and discrimination against the aged. The term 'ageism' has been coined to denote discrimination against individuals purely on the basis of their chronological age. However, research conducted in the USA suggests that a more positive attitude towards the elderly is developing, especially among young people (Austin, 1985). Nussbaum, Thompson and Robinson (1989) consider that the election of a senior citizen (Ronald Reagan) as President of the USA in 1980 and 1984 was a manifestation of this change of attitude!

In order to communicate effectively with elderly people we need to examine our concepts of 'age' and our resulting expectations and stereotypes. Do we expect to find more problems in elderly clients and therefore give less consideration to causes other than pathology such as depression and anxiety? Anyone working with the elderly needs to ensure that they do not have the following misconceptions:

- Do you expect less from the elderly in the way of response to treatment and therefore consider treatment less justified or justified for a shorter period of time?

- Do you expect less in terms of everyday activities and functioning and therefore lower your expectations for treatment?
- Do you expect to find pathology rather than considering the 'normal' changes associated with ageing?
- Do you accept the personality and behavioural range that we expect to find in the younger age groups or do you put 'eccentricity' down to pathology? (An awkward old person might well have been just as truculent when young.)
- Do you expect elderly people to cope less well with illness or loss of ability? (It is known that the elderly often cope better than middle-aged people with disability and therefore achieve a high level of compensation.)

What is successful ageing?

Successful ageing, in the sense of maintaining independence until close to death, appears to be a realistic goal for the majority of elderly people. But what constitutes successful ageing? Ryff (1986) suggested that there are six criteria for successful ageing:

1. Self-acceptance, i.e. a positive attitude to one's own life.
2. Positive relations with others.
3. Autonomy, i.e. being able to function on one's own.
4. Environmental mastery, i.e. manipulating the environment to fit one's needs.
5. Purpose in life, i.e. feelings of meaningfulness and integration of the various parts of one's life.
6. Personal growth.

When treating elderly people, clinicians need to keep these criteria in mind and to try to ensure that management decisions made with or on behalf of an elderly individual facilitate successful ageing. In their discussion and evaluation of the theories of successful ageing, Nussbaum, Thompson and Robinson (1989) emphasise the importance of communication to successful ageing. They state that, although successful ageing is a very complex phenomenon dependent upon many psychological factors, maintaining communication is of vital importance in achieving successful ageing.

Theoretical frameworks of cognitive ageing

The traditional, long-held view of the effects of ageing on cognitive performance has been largely negative. Studies have shown that performance on measures such as intelligence tests is lower in elderly people than in younger groups (Kaufman, Reynolds and McLean, 1989). This reduction in performance was regarded as representing 'deficits' in cognitive/language performance. The advent of theories of 'lifespan' psychology and the view that development is a process that continues throughout life has allowed age-related changes to be viewed as normal rather than as deficits. This is supported by studies of functioning in the elderly which show that the majority of elderly people cope without difficulty with everyday tasks such as communication, reading, writing, shopping, managing household tasks and travelling.

A much more positive view of the elderly is to regard cognitive processing as changing with age and to separate 'normal' changes from the pathological changes associated with disease. Thus what is 'normal' for a 20 year old is different from what is 'normal' for a 60 year old.

Research into age-related change has sought to produce a theoretical framework to explain how the age-related changes occur. Salthouse (1991) discusses the necessity for a theory of age-related changes and sets out five theoretical frameworks, all of which have some advantages and a number of disadvantages but none of which could be said to be the 'definitive' theory. The theoretical frameworks are interesting to consider because they illustrate the approaches taken by ageing research:

- *Environmental change*: age-related differences in cognitive functioning are related to biological and physical changes occurring outside the individual such as changes in diet, social roles, pollution etc.
- *Disuse*: cognitive abilities decline with time after they are learned and with changes in cognitive needs and expectations as people age, retire etc. This theoretical approach illustrates the need for information on the frequency with which relevant cognitive processes are utilised during the daily lives of people of all ages.
- *Qualitative difference*: styles or modes of processing change with age during a given cognitive task.
- *Localisation*: the goal of many researchers has been to try to identify the specific aspects of processing that are most affected by age.
- *Reduced processing resources*: this theoretical framework attempts to combine features of other theories by postulating that the amount of age-related difference in performance appears to be related to how much processing is required, as well as to the type of processing.

Salthouse points out that these frameworks do not yet convert directly into actual theories of cognitive ageing which could generate specific hypotheses for testing. This is clearly a goal at which continuing research is aimed. However, such theories alone would not explain the age-related changes in cognitive processing. Information also needs to be incorporated on the subject's biological status and health, experiential history and education.

Advances have occurred in neuropsychological research into cognitive processing in the elderly, and in the study of age-related neuropathological changes. The correlation between findings in these two fields is beginning to lend support to neurocognitive theories of age-related change, for example in memory. Moscovitch and Winocur (1992) suggest a theory of memory functioning in which the hippocampus and the posterior neocortex are involved in the encoding, retention, and automatic retrieval of the contents of memory. The hippocampal element is singled out as the element most susceptible to age-related change, which accounts for the decline in consolidation of memory and long-term retention with age. Frontal lobe mediated functions also operate on the input to the hippocampal system and its output. These processes are said to be more susceptible to age-related change. Such a theory of memory processing can be used to explain why certain memory processes are affected by age-related changes and others are not.

Support for this theory comes from neuropathological studies which map the areas of the brain most affected by neuronal loss, amyloid protein deposits and other changes, with the hippocampus being particularly susceptible (Selkoe, 1992).

The need to link neuropathological findings to the study of brain–behaviour relations is now recognised (Chui, 1989; Haxby et al., 1991). Furthermore, some changes revealed in neuropathological studies support the notion of differences in brain structure being compensatory in order to maintain functioning. For example, Coleman and Flood (1987) have reported a net growth of dendrites in some regions of the hippocampus and the cerebral cortex between middle age and early old age (seventies), followed by a decrease in dendrites in late old age. They suggest that the initial increase in dendrites allows the viable neurons to compensate for the loss of neighbouring neurons. This ability to compensate apparently ceases in late old age. Again, these findings support the assertion that age-related changes do not necessarily equal a deficit.

Age-related changes that can affect language and communication

A number of sensory and environmental changes may have secondary effects on an elderly person's ability to communicate. Such changes must be considered when assessing the ability to communicate.

Motor processing

Virtually all aspects of performance have been found to become slower with age (commonly called psychomotor slowing). The exact cause is unknown, but it is thought to be due to processing delays and is particularly apparent in difficult or complex tasks (Hertzhog, 1989).

This slowing should be considered when assessing elderly people. The use of timed tests may penalise the elderly unless allowance is made for psychomotor slowing. Furthermore, the results may be interpreted as representing a disorder (for example in visual perception in a timed recognition test) when they are actually due to the subject having insufficient time to process the test information. It is vital that performance in elderly subjects is compared with that of age-matched controls who may show an equal level of generalised slowing.

Speech production

Respiratory support for speech is less efficient in the elderly because loss of elasticity of the lungs and reduced power of the lung musculature (Lynne-Davis, 1977) results in decreased vital capacity.

Changes in laryngeal functioning contribute to changes in voice pitch in the elderly (Honjo and Isshiki, 1980). The laryngeal musculature becomes biomechanically less efficient with age, probably because of age-related disturbances in the vascular supply to the muscles (Kahane, 1981).

Age-related changes in the temporomandibular joint may restrict or alter the normal patterns of mandibular movement. This can affect some articulatory features during speech production (Kahane, 1981). Some weakening and slowing of function of the facial musculature is considered normal in elderly people, although this can present as a mild motor speech disorder (Ryan and Burk, 1974).

Although the normal elderly are not dysarthric, speed and accuracy of articulation diminishes beyond the sixth decade (Thompson, 1986). A study by Larson, Hayslip and Thomas (1992) showed that delays in voice-onset timing were evident in older men. Ultrasound studies have indicated that tongue thickness and tongue position vary greatly during the production of selected phonemes, even though this produces no perceptible acoustic differences in speech between older and younger subjects. Sonies and Caruso (1990) therefore speculate that in order to achieve normal-sounding speech, elderly speakers may be required to make compensatory tongue movements which are unnecessary for younger people.

Changes in dentition can affect speech production. The most obvious change here is teeth loss and the subsequent need for dentures. The wearing of dentures in itself should not lead to mechanical problems in speech production but age-related changes in the size and shape of the jaw result in many elderly people having ill-fitting dentures. Speech production may be adversely affected because the dentures move while the person is talking. More commonly, movement of the dentures causes mouth soreness and ulcers which ultimately results in some elderly people refusing to wear dentures at all. Speech production without teeth frequently gives rise to mild dysarthria. It is therefore important that dentures are checked regularly.

Decrease in saliva production may cause a dry mouth and tongue (Gioella, 1983). Certain drugs (for example anticholinergic preparations) may have side-effects on the soft tissue of the oral cavity, the most common being dryness of the mouth which can affect speech production. Antidepressant medication, particularly tricyclic antidepressants, can cause dystonic movements of the mouth such as lip licking and continuous, repetitive tongue movements, which may disrupt speech production (Gawel, 1981).

The auditory system

The auditory system undergoes a number of changes with age that may affect the ability to hear. As well as directly affecting communication because the subject is unable to hear what is said, hearing loss can disrupt social functioning and can contribute to isolation and withdrawal from the company of others leading to restricted opportunities for communication.

Hearing problems affect a large proportion of elderly people. In the UK, 35% of the population are estimated to have a hearing loss sufficient to affect daily living. The elderly account for a disproportionately large number of the hearing-disordered population. A study in the USA (National Centre for Health Statistics, 1980) showed that 47% of the 75+ age group have a hearing loss.

Figures for the numbers of people with a hearing loss vary because of differences in criteria for the diagnosis of a 'loss' and the testing methodology (Davis, 1983). However, the results of a specific study of the elderly population in residential homes in South Glamorgan showed that 68% of the residents failed an audiological screening test and that 48% had a hearing loss greater than 45 dB (Hart, 1980). This study also investigated the communicative consequences of hearing loss: 41% of the residents were found to have communication difficulties which could be attributed to difficulty in hearing, compared with 11% of the residents who had communication problems due to confusion or 'senility'.

Weinstein and Amsel (1986) examined the hearing status of a group of thirty institutionalised elderly individuals with a diagnosis of dementia and found that 55% of the subjects had a moderate to severe hearing loss. These subjects were retested on a mental test score with amplification, which resulted in one-third of them being re-classified as having less severe dementia. The authors therefore caution against the use of exclusively verbal tests in diagnosing or classifying dementia.

Given that hearing loss is an important factor in communication difficulty for a large number of elderly people, it is vital that clinicians check on the hearing abilities of their clients and that they are fully aware of the effects of hearing loss on the individual.

The term used to denote deterioration of auditory functioning due to ageing is ***presbyacusis***, which refers to a variety of hearing disorders that affect the elderly due to the cumulative effects of a number of disorders or insults and contribute to the degeneration of the auditory mechanism of the inner ear (Willott, 1991). Presbyacusis is associated with reduced sensitivity to higher frequency sounds and decreased ability to discriminate between adjacent frequencies and between consonants (Corso, 1981). The main audiological features of presbyacusis are:

- decrease in hearing sensitivity;
- reduction in understanding at suprathreshold levels;
- speech audiometric results that are worse than would be predicted from pure-tone thresholds.

These factors have a detrimental effect on speech perception (Jerger et al., 1989). Other auditory problems associated with presbyacusis are:

- reduced understanding of fast rates of speech;
- reduced understanding of speech in noise;
- reduced hearing of higher pitched voices and whispered speech;
- particular difficulty in using the telephone.

The causes of presbyacusis are many and include:

- inherited genetic defects (Nance and McConnel, 1973);
- acute and chronic exposure to noise (Humes, 1984);
- ototoxic drugs (Worthington et al., 1973);
- vascular disease (Kimura, 1973);
- true cellular ageing (Strehler, 1976).

Four types of presbyacusis have been described:

1. *Sensory presbyacusis* results from degeneration and loss of the hair cells of the cochlea and presents as a high-frequency hearing loss.
2. *Neural presbyacusis,* resulting from loss of neural fibres, affects accurate interpretation of complex acoustic stimuli such as speech. This results in greater reduction in speech sound discrimination scores than pure-tone thresholds would predict.
3. *Mechanical presbyacusis* produces reduced pure-tone thresholds with good discrimination due to alterations in the mechanical properties of the cochlea.
4. *Metabolic presbyacusis,* atrophy of the stria vascularis in the inner ear, causes equal loss of thresholds at all frequencies.

Degenerative changes also occur in the middle ear because of stiffness of the joints between the bones of the middle ear, but there is no evidence that this has a significant effect on the hearing system of the elderly (Etholm and Belal, 1974). As with any other age group, elderly people may suffer from conductive or sensory neural hearing losses due to causes other than presbyacusis, such as wax build-up (which is common in the elderly) (Fisch, 1978), middle ear infections, otitus externa (where the skin of the canal becomes irritated and results in inflammation) and otosclerosis (in which an overgrowth of bone in the middle ear gradually prevents transmission of sound to the inner ear). Elderly people are just as likely as younger people to have such problems with hearing and their deafness should not be assumed to be due to 'old-age' and therefore go untreated. Elderly people are potentially able to benefit from referral to ear, nose and throat departments for assessment, for possible treatment of deafness and for the prescription of hearing aids where appropriate.

However, it is estimated that 40% of people who are prescribed a hearing aid do not use it, and the elderly often have physical difficulty in using such an aid (Franks and Beckman, 1985). It is therefore essential that a hearing aid is correctly fitted and is in good working order. Elderly people may need assistance in adjusting small control buttons and in changing batteries. Operations such as cleaning the earmould may also be difficult for people with poor vision or hand control. Staff who work with older people benefit from advice or in-service training on how best to communicate with hearing-impaired patients (Kent, 1989).

The effects of hearing loss on communication are to make conversation more difficult, requiring a louder and slower style (Eisdorfer and Wilkie, 1972), and causing loss of confidence in the ability to hear, resulting in increased requests for repetition of information and contributing to social withdrawal (Falconer, 1986).

A further problem for elderly people with a hearing loss is that people often mistakenly associate deafness with deterioration in mental functioning. This may be due to similarities between the symptoms of hearing impairment and some types of psychiatric disorders (indistinct speech, not answering when spoken to, answering inappropriately or out of context and pitching the voice inappropriately; Herbst, 1983). The relationship between hearing loss and cognitive decline remains unclear. Ivy et al. (1992) state that at least some of the apparent decline in cognitive ability with ageing may be due to decreased sensory input to higher mental processes, but Colsher and Wallace (1990) (who examined the effects of hearing and visual losses on cognition in a non-institutionalised elderly population) found no evidence of a link between level of sensory functioning and level of cognitive functioning, provided that other variables such as depression and poor health were controlled.

The visual system

The visual system also undergoes changes associated with ageing. The aperture of the pupil, which admits light to the structures behind it, reduces with age (Fozard, 1990) so that adaptation to changes in lighting is less efficient. Good lighting is therefore essential when working with the elderly.

Elderly people are also less efficient at focusing on near objects, for example the page of a book, because loss of lens elasticity makes it more difficult for the eye muscles to alter the shape of the lens. This change becomes evident at about 45 years and is perceived as long-sightedness. The medical term for this condition is presbyopia, and it leads to almost everyone needing spectacles by the age of 65.

The ability to perceive depth is affected by the ageing process (Bell, Wolf and Bernholz, 1972), which may cause problems with environmental orientation. There is also a progressive decline in sensitivity to colours with age (Lakowski, 1973). These changes need to be considered if language testing in elderly people involves the use of complex visual stimuli.

A number of disease processes can affect vision in the elderly. About 60 000 people in the UK over the age of 65 are registered blind. The three main causes of slowly progressive loss of vision in the elderly are cataracts, glaucoma and senile degeneration of the macula.

Cataracts

Cataracts appear as an opaque region of the lens of the eye that may block part (or all) of the light passing through the eye. Initially there is a subtle loss of colour appreciation, then increased short-sightedness and, as the cataract thickens, increased deterioration in vision. Cataracts can be treated chemically or surgically (Chylack, 1979).

Glaucoma

Glaucoma is caused by a rise in fluid pressure inside the eyeball, which compresses the optic nerve. When this happens gradually it may be painless or cause aching of the eyes. Sight can be lost irretrievably and it is important that elderly people are checked regularly by an optician because this condition may be detected and treated. There is thought to be a hereditary link to this condition. The incidence of glaucoma increases with age, affecting about 9% of people over the age of 65 (Kahn et al., 1977).

Macular degeneration

Macular degeneration of the retina accounts for about 40% of the cases of blindness in elderly people and is becoming one of the most prevalent causes of blindness in the USA and the UK (Sorsby, 1966). The macula is that part of the retina which is most critical for tasks requiring fine discrimination, such as reading. The only treatment for macular degeneration is strong reading glasses and low-vision aids, giving a poor prognosis for continued vision (Lewis, 1979).

Loss of vision can affect communication directly by causing loss of visual information from the speaker's face and difficulty in coping with visually presented material in reading and writing, and indirectly by increasing isolation and decreasing opportunities for communication.

Restricted mobility

Reduced mobility in elderly people may be caused by a disease process such as arthritis, an unsuitable environment (e.g. one with lots of steps) or lack of motivation (for example if the person is living in a residential home where all needs are catered for and movement of residents is discouraged). Lack of physical activity is thought to be inextricably linked to reduction in mental activity, creating a cycle of decline in everyday functioning (Spiraduso, 1980). This can be prevented by encouraging independence, for example by providing tea- and coffee-making facilities in a residential home which require the residents to walk to a central point.

Attention

This is the ability to concentrate on a stimulus and to apply mental faculties to the task in question. Many assessments of language and cognitive functioning assume that the subject has such skills. However, there is a considerable body of evidence to suggest that elderly people develop deficits in selective attention (Walsh and Prasse, 1980) although more recent studies suggest that this is apparent in divided attention situations and not in focused attention situations. Plude and Hoyer (1985), in their summary of research in this field, conclude that there appears to be a discrepancy between laboratory findings, which generally show an age-related deficit, and evidence from the real world where the vast majority of elderly people continue to function adequately in everyday activities (see pp. 31–32).

Memory

Memory is a multidimensional construct and research has shown that there is a complex relationship between age and memory. Methodological factors such as familiarity of the material being recalled, importance of the material, motivation level, type of task and type of retrieval measurement are known to affect information recall in elderly subjects (Botwinick, 1978). For example, Peterson et al. (1992) found a decrease in verbal learning in a large sample of normal elderly subjects but no decrease in a delayed recall task.

There is also evidence to suggest that different types of memory are differentially affected by the ageing process (Craik and Jennings, 1992). There is a mild decrease in short-term memory in older subjects although this again varies according to factors such as the complexity of the information to be recalled (Craik and Rabinowitz, 1985). The decline in long-term memory with age is more significant and is primarily attributable to encoding or organisational difficulties (Rankin and Collins, 1985). More recent work on memory and comprehension in old age suggests that age has no general effect on levels of conceptual knowledge. Light (1992) states that both younger and older adults appear to access general world knowledge in the same way, although there are age-related differences in the amount of material that can be remembered and older people have more difficulty in remembering contextual information.

Other studies have investigated memory in more functional contexts. A study by Kausler and Hakami (1983) on memory for conversations suggested that in a recognition memory test format the differences in performance between younger and older subjects are greatly reduced. Cavanaugh (1983) reported that there was no age deficit in the recall of information derived from television in subjects with high verbal ability but that there was in subjects with low verbal ability.

Therefore it should not be assumed that the changes in memory that occur with age are necessarily detrimental to the ability to use language effectively. Smith and Fullerton (1981) suggest that the differences in performance of older subjects on memory tasks should be viewed as adaptive change, rather than decreased cognitive ability.

Language and memory are discussed in detail in Chapter 2.

Institutionalisation and social isolation

Standards of self-care and everyday functioning tend to decrease after entry into residential homes (Wilkin, Mashiah and Jolley, 1978). Research to specifically evaluate the level of communication in residential homes has shown that few interpersonal exchanges take place and that relationships rarely develop between residents (Lubinski, Morrison and Rigrodski, 1981). Other studies have shown that the effects of institutionalisation on communication can be partially prevented by encouraging the use of language and cognitive abilities (Barnett-Douglas, 1986; Bryan and Drew, 1987).

Although elderly people who live in their own homes do not suffer from the effects of institutionalisation as such, many have limited contact with the outside world and rarely speak to another person. This can lead to an increasingly reduced communication network and ultimate withdrawal. Treatment of communication disorders can be less effective because the elderly person has no opportunity to utilise language skills. Attendance at a day centre or luncheon club or regular visiting by an appropriate volunteer may be a vital part of the management of the communication disorder.

The direct and indirect effects of sensory changes and environmental conditions on an elderly person's ability to communicate are therefore very important and need to be considered along with the effects of any disease processes. Many elderly people have difficulty with both vision and hearing, thus compounding their problems and reducing the opportunity for compensation.

Communication disorders and disease processes in the elderly

In addition to the social, environmental and physical changes that may affect the ability to communicate, a wide range of disease processes can affect the elderly. Problems in the elderly are often attributed to the dementias. It is important that other possible causes of communication disorder are excluded before a diagnosis of dementia is made. Table 1.1 shows the possible clinical causes of communication disorder in the elderly.

Table 1.1 Differential diagnosis of causes of communication disorder in the elderly

Acute onset	*Associated with impairment of alertness*	*Associated with other neurological deficits*	*Progressive cognitive decline*	*Stepwise decline*
Stroke Head injury	Depression Confusional state Acute psychoses	Parkinson's disease Huntington's disease	Alzheimer's disease Pick's disease	Multi-(infarct) dementia

Acute injury

Head injury or stroke is common in the elderly: indeed, the incidence of stroke increases with age (Kertesz and Sheppard, 1981). Similarly there is a peak in the incidence of closed head injury in the 70+ age group (Walsh, 1978). Wertz and Dronkers (1990) examined the effects of age on aphasia type and concluded that patients with Broca's aphasia are significantly younger than those with Wernicke's aphasia, but that age does not affect the severity of the aphasia or its response to treatment. A study by Wade, Langton-Hewer and Wood (1984) showed that age in itself is not a poor prognostic sign for recovery from aphasia after stroke, although the elderly are more likely to have negative prognostic signs such as hearing loss which may affect recovery.

Psychiatric illness

Elderly people may suffer from the same range of psychiatric illness (such as paranoid disorders, anxiety states, phobias and compulsive disorders) as younger people. However, the incidence of psychiatric disorders increases with age and is estimated to be evident in 40% of over 65 year olds (Kay, Beamish and Roth, 1964). Psychiatric disorders can cause language to change. Gravell and France (1991) have reviewed the relationship between language and psychiatric disorder.

By far the most common form of psychiatric illness in the elderly is depression (Pitt, 1982). In depressed individuals language output can be severely curtailed although linguistic competence is not altered (Roth, 1983). Depression can become so severe that the person's impaired concentration, lack of interest and psychomotor slowing gives rise to such poor performance on cognitive tasks such as memory and calculation that dementia is suspected. This impression is also reinforced by the depressed person's social withdrawal and reduced self-care. The term *depressive pseudodementia* has been used to describe this condition (Kiloh, 1981). Differential diagnosis of dementia and depression is further complicated by depression frequently being evident in the early stages of dementia, particularly in Alzheimer's disease (Cummings et al., 1987). The importance of behavioural observation and a detailed and accurate case history in distinguishing the effects of depression from those of dementia cannot be overstated (Ron, 1990).

Acute confusional state

The characteristics of a confusional state are clouding of consciousness, impairment of attention and concentration, visual misinterpretations and hallucinations, rambling, disjointed or completely incoherent speech, and sleep disturbance (Lipowski, 1983). Confusional states may mimic the symptoms of dementia. Admission to hospital following a fall, which the elderly person does not remember, is one of the most common reasons for acute confusional state. Another common cause is urinary tract infection. The onset of symptoms in confusion will be recent, variable and usually associated with a physical problem.

There are few studies of language in acute confusional state, but these suggest that the structure of language is essentially normal even though the content may be disordered by hallucinations with a tendency to produce misnamings (Weinstein and Kahn, 1952).

The dementias

The term ***dementia*** is used to describe progressive, irreversible brain pathology and its behaviourial sequelae. The most common form of dementia is Alzheimer's disease. The rate of progression in Alzheimer-type dementia and other diseases causing dementia is variable. There are also, fortunately, causes of dementia (e.g. pseudodementia) that are reversible or in which the decline may be halted (Marsden and Harrison, 1972; Grossberg and Nakra, 1988). Although brain function usually changes in dementia, the brain is not always the primary site of the disease but may be affected by other systemic changes (e.g. metabolic disorders).

Some definitions of dementia do not include the concepts of progression or irreversibility but most do use the term 'global'. The Royal College of Physicians Committee on Geriatrics (1981) proposed the following definition:

> The global disturbance of higher cortical functions including memory, the capacity to solve problems of everyday living, the performance of learned perceptuo-motor skills, the correct use of social skills and control of emotional reactions, in the absence of clouding of consciousness.

Some patients may, however, present with specific but progressive aphasia. Their deficits are not global but may become global over time (Poeck and Luzzatti, 1988). For these patients we would want to include the concept of progression, but not the concept of global impairment.

Another definition might be that the dementias are a group of behavioural syndromes related to (but not always synonymous with) diseases affecting brain tissue and which may be global, progressive and irreversible.

One concept crucial to an understanding of dementia is that of difficulty in adapting to changes in higher cerebral functioning. Although there is evidence that some individuals do make useful adaptations to their deficits, most people with dementia are unable to do so. This is in marked contrast to people who have aphasia following a focal lesion and who can make useful adjustments to their language deficit and do manage to communicate.

Dementia therefore describes a clinical syndrome of generalised cognitive impairment in an alert patient (Rossor, 1987). There are a wide variety of causes (see Table 1.2), but the following features are common to them all:

- Progressively acquired cognitive impairment, i.e. there must be evidence of deterioration from a previous level. This should distinguish the dementing process from existing learning difficulties.

- Normal level of alertness as opposed to the person being drowsy or overtly agitated, which may distinguish dementia from a confusional state.
- Acquired cognitive impairment evident across a range of cognitive functions. This may distinguish dementia from focal deficits such as dysphasia.

Exactly what is meant by 'a range of cognitive functions' in the last criterion illustrates one of the difficulties in the differential diagnosis of dementia. The American Psychiatric Association defines dementia in terms of memory dysfunction plus one other aspect of cognitive impairment (McKhann et al., 1984) associated with an organic cause. However, this definition is not universally accepted and is not without diagnostic problems.

To say that a patient has dementia is obviously insufficient. It is essential to describe the cognitive impairment and behavioural sequelae involved and to give an indication of the severity, onset, progression and any fluctuation in the disorder. The underlying cause of the dementia should be diagnosed. The main aetiologies of the dementias are listed in Table 1.2, which is a summary of the causes of the dementias in the adult population. Some of the dementia-producing diseases are not progressive and some may be treatable. The degree to which treatment is effective depends upon the condition, but few treatments lead to completely normal functioning. Perhaps one of the few diseases that can be significantly altered is hypothyroidism. The list does not include all causes of the dementias, and in particular omits those diseases, such as Friedrich's ataxia, which are apparent in childhood and which may progress to speech, language and cognitive dysfunction in young adulthood.

These disorders and their associated language manifestations are discussed in detail in Chapters 6 and 7.

Theoretical issues in aphasia, and normal and pathological ageing

Normal versus abnormal language change

It can be difficult to differentiate normal language changes from abnormal ageing, and indeed many healthy old people display alterations in language on an aphasia test (Walker, 1982). Research into adult language dysfunction has concentrated on dysphasia due to focal lesions while research into dementia has, until recently, focused on

Table 1.2 Main types of dementia

Primary degeneration	
Alzheimer's disease	Predominantly cortical degeneration
Pick's disease	
Parkinson's disease	Dementia associated with other neurological disorders predominantly involving subcortical structures
Lewy body disease	
Steele–Richardson–Olszewski syndrome	
Multisystem atrophy	
Progressive supranuclear palsy	
Huntington's disease	
Wilson's disease	
Spinocerebellar degeneration	
Cerebrovascular disease	
Multi-infarct dementia	
Binswanger's disease (progressive subcortical encephalopathy)	
Subdural haematoma	
Infective and inflammatory disorders	
Neurosyphilis	
Encephalitis (e.g. herpes simplex)	
Subacute sclerosing panencephalitis	
Slow virus dementia (e.g. Creutzfeldt–Jakob disease)	
Multiple sclerosis	
Acquired immune deficiency syndrome	
Metabolic disorders	
Vitamin B_{12} deficiency (Wernicke–Korsakoff syndrome)	
Endocrine disorders (e.g. hypothyroidism, hypercalcaemia, hypocalcaemia)	
Chronic hepatic encephalopathy	
Renal failure and dialysis	
Toxic disorders	
Alcohol toxicity	
Anoxia	
Drug toxicity	
Toxicity due to other poisons (e.g. heavy metals)	
Neoplastic disease	
Meningioma	
Midline tumour	
Metastases	
Paraneoplastic syndromes	
Other causes	
Normal pressure hydrocephalus	
Trauma	

disturbances of memory rather than language. In spite of some current interest in language breakdown in dementia, there are still relatively few single case studies, cross-sectional or longitudinal studies of language in the dementias. Adequate descriptions of language function and progression in the dementias are therefore lacking.

Cortical versus subcortical dementia

An operational division of dementia into cortical and subcortical has been put forward to describe those dementias in which the most prominent pathology is found in the cortex and those in which the pathology is wholly or largely in the subcortical structures of the brain (Albert, 1980). It is a useful division to make at a gross level because different clusters of clinical and behavioural symptoms are produced by different diseases, but the clinical picture reflected in the literature is not so tidy. Albert's (Albert, Feldman and Willis, 1974) seminal paper on progressive nuclear palsy, a subcortical dementia, described the clinical features of emotional changes, memory disorder, difficulty in manipulating acquired knowledge and slow processing; features that were previously ascribed to damage at the cortical level. This description of a subcortical dementia was therefore important because it made clear that behavioural symptoms suggesting cortical damage could be presenting symptoms for conditions in which the pathology was subcortical. Other conditions with subcortical pathology (such as Parkinson's disease and Huntington's disease) were then examined against this new evidence (Iles, 1989). There have been objections to the term 'subcortical dementia' because disorders such as Huntington's and Parkinson's diseases do have associated cortical pathology, and patients with Alzheimer's disease have abnormalities in their subcortical nuclei. The advent of this classification has led to the reappraisal of the relationship between the cortex and subcortex.

The debate on cortical and subcortical dementias is a good example of the state of research into dementia. The concepts of senile (over 65 years) and presenile dementia (under 65 years) were well established until the mid-1970s and, despite neuropathological evidence, these two forms of dementia were considered to be separate. Research has shown this to be an erroneous division as some patients from both age groups have identical disease processes. More recently, clinical reports suggest that there are several subtypes of Alzheimer's disease, some of which may, in time, become recognised as new clinical entities (Rossor, Kennedy and Newman, 1992).

Dementia in the younger and older elderly

Two issues concerning age and dementia are important in our understanding of the dementias. First, certain diseases that cause dementia have peak incidences at different ages. Pick's disease often begins in the 50s, whereas Alzheimer's disease is much more common among the 75+ age group. Secondly, recent evidence suggests that the clinical features of Alzheimer's disease may differ according to age: a 60 year old with Alzheimer's disease may show different deficits to an 80 year old with the same disease. It is not clear how much this is to do with the interaction between the normal decrements of ageing and the abnormal deficits of the dementing process and how much the disease process itself changes with increasing age. If a normal 60 year old and a normal 80 year old with comparable health, education and environment were tested, we would predict some differences in their language and cognitive profiles although these differences might be small and more to do with speed of processing than with qualitative differences. Such differences might well be magnified by the dementing process. Research suggests that younger elderly people with dementia show more specific deficits of cognitive functioning, but this may be disease dependent (Constantinidis, 1978).

Aphasia and language in dementia

Because of the differences in onset, natural history and symptoms of aphasia caused by focal lesions and the language disturbance in dementia, these disorders should be clearly differentiated. However, the use of aphasia syndrome labels to describe the language disturbances in the dementias is pervasive in the literature (Appell, Kertesz and Fisman, 1982; Cummings and Benson, 1992).

Most researchers rightly prefer to retain the term aphasia to describe language pathology from a focal lesion. Bayles, Tomoeda and Caffrey (1982) identified five differences between aphasia and dementia:

1. Aphasia occurs with a sudden onset (e.g. stroke), whereas dementia occurs slowly over time.
2. The deterioration of language in dementia is progressive but this is not so in aphasia.
3. Aphasia is due to focal lesions whereas dementia is accompanied by diffuse brain atrophy.
4. Aphasia has a minimal effect on intellect whereas loss of reasoning abilities is a primary feature of dementing illnesses.
5. Aphasic patients can present with a dissociation between verbal and non-verbal abilities whereas most patients with dementia show simultaneous deterioration of both verbal and non-verbal functions (e.g. visual perception).

This list appears unequivocal at first reading, but patients often present in a much more ambiguous manner. Aphasia may be progressive in nature, and a syndrome of progressive aphasia has been described

(Weintraub, Rubin and Marsel-Mesulam, 1990). Aphasia can also be due to an area of focal degeneration in the brain which does not appear to increase in size (Kirshner et al., 1987). Whether these conditions represent a protracted early stage in a more global dementing process is unclear (Foster and Chase, 1983).

In patients with multi-infarct dementia, language impairment may occur suddenly because a cerebral infarction affects language processing. If this occurs early in the course of the disease, it can appear as a discrete aphasia. However, most patients will show other cognitive problems and the patient will go on to develop other neurological deficits as the vascular disease advances.

Evidence from studies comparing aphasic and dementing language suggest that language breakdown in dementia often reflects the wider progressive impairment of cognition. However, language problems may be the presenting symptom in some dementias in the absence of any significant cognitive impairment. The debate concerning terminology has some theoretical significance but may be far more important in clinical management. In research terms, we still know very little about the incidence, course and prognosis of specific language disturbances in the dementias, with or without cognitive impairment. However, the literature on aphasia caused by focal lesions of sudden onset is extensive and quite clear on prognosis. Most aphasic patients go through a period of spontaneous recovery, are able to make some useful adjustments to their language deficits and show relatively few cognitive changes unrelated to their language deficits. To use the term aphasia for both clinical groups may confuse the families and carers of aphasics and be detrimental to their clinical management.

The differential diagnosis of aphasia due to focal lesions and the language deficit secondary to dementia can also be problematic because both groups share fluently produced language, frequently an absence of hard neurological signs such as hemiparesis and a peak incidence in patients aged 70 or over. Most reports of the incidence of different types of aphasia conclude that sufferers of Wernicke's aphasia, as a group, are older than those with Broca's aphasia (Basso et al., 1980; Code and Rowley, 1987). A number of explanations have been suggested, including an interaction between age and site of lesion (Obler, Mildworf and Albert, 1987) and the increasing left lateralisation of language with age (Brown and Jaffe, 1975) but none stands careful scrutiny. There is evidence that the prevalence of fluent aphasias among older people may result from the increased mortality rate among older global aphasics (Coppens, 1991). There may also be an interaction between damage to the elderly brain and the linguistic and cognitive changes in normal ageing such as difficulty in understanding complex sentence constructions, short-term memory deficits and decreased speed of language processing (Obler et al., 1978; Holland and Bartlett,

1985).

Whatever the reason for the greater age of Wernicke's aphasics, it is not always easy to make the differential diagnosis between Alzheimer's disease and a Wernicke's or transcortical sensory aphasia in the absence of a reliable history of sudden onset that would indicate a cerebrovascular insult or head injury. Brain tumours present a further diagnostic problem because symptom onset may be progressive, but symptomatology is usually different and diagnosis clarified by CT scanning.

Cognition and language in the dementias

There is some discrepancy between linguistics and psychology in the way that each discipline has characterised the language disorder in the dementias. Neuropsychology has tended to view language as part of cognition while linguistics and speech pathology have conceptualised language and cognition as a partnership of systems.

This can most clearly be exemplified if we look at what in psychology is called semantic memory and in linguistics the semantic system. One hypothesis on memory makes a division between episodic and semantic memory (Tulving, 1972) but sees both as part of the memory system. Indeed, it has been argued that language is part of this memory system (Allport, 1985). Therefore, in an information-processing model of single-word processing, each component in the model is a memory store for a certain aspect of language. Linguistics, however, puts forward the concept of language as a dynamic system with different levels. Garman (1990) captures the essential problem:

> does it [the mental lexicon] consist ... of a well defined word-meaning component in systematic relationships with linguistic word forms; or does it consist essentially of just those stored word forms which are directly mapped onto a general knowledge base that is not specifically part of the lexicon itself.
>
> (p. 244)

Research on disordered systems in the dementias has provided some clues to this relationship between language and cognition. Both single case and group studies have produced evidence that certain aspects of language and cognition deteriorate at different rates and do dissociate (Whitaker, 1976; Schwartz, Marin and Saffran, 1979; Bayles, 1982) and that language may be relatively preserved in the face of poor cognition and vice versa (Bayles, 1982; Mesulam, 1982). There is still a need to differentiate between specific language changes and changes in language function which are secondary to cognitive change.

A specific issue for debate is the question of whether the language deficits in dementia represent problems with access or storage. One of the characteristics of focal aphasia is a problem of access to language processes or items within a store. Many aphasics, tested on a naming test, may achieve approximately the same score if tested on two consecutive days but the items they name may vary between the two tests. Similarly, on a picture description task an aphasic may be able to produce approximately the same content on consecutive tests but the sentence structure may vary considerably. Some aphasic patients are able to gain access to stores but items within the store are not specified enough for accurate retrieval and a closely related item may therefore be accessed instead, e.g. fork for spoon or [f ɔ d] for fork. In severe or global aphasia access may be possible only to a small and invariable number of items in a store.

What, then, do we know about the accessibility of language in dementia? The debates in the literature have tended to focus on whether there is a disruption of access to the stores, disruption in the internal organisation of the stores themselves or whether items become, at some stage, irretrievably lost to the person. The most illuminating data have undoubtedly come from single case studies in which extensive testing has shown blurring of semantic boundaries (Schwartz et al., 1979) and irretrievable loss of items (Funnell and Hodges, 1990). In particular, Funnell and Hodges' single case study shows the successive shutting down or inaccessibility of semantic and then phonological output lexicon in a longitudinal study. Studies have usually identified either access or storage problems, suggesting that both deficits can occur in the dementias. A further suggestion has been that it is the effort required in processing that accounts for the variability in findings (Hart and Semple, 1990). What is clear is that only extensive, well constructed and longitudinal testing will help to answer some of the questions about what accounts for the deficits in language performance in the dementias and how they may change as the disease progresses.

Methodological problems in the assessment of the elderly

A number of practical problems are associated with language assessment in the elderly.

Age

The effects of normal ageing have to be distinguished from those due to pathology. Therefore the performance of an elderly person needs to be compared with that of age-matched peers. The boundary between normal ageing and pathology is often described as 'fuzzy', and the clinician needs to take into account the effects of normal ageing.

Unconfirmed diagnosis

Many patients seen in day centres or in the community may not have been referred to a neurologist or geriatrician for confirmation of their medical diagnosis. This is particularly so in cases where Alzheimer's disease is strongly suspected, as diagnosis will not lead to treatment. Lack of firm medical information combined with poor history of the disorder from the client and family can leave the clinician with little information on which to base management. In the early stages of dementia, differential diagnosis between the dementias and dysphasia can be very difficult, but evidence of language disorder, suggestions of increasing disability from the family, evidence of short-term memory disorder and problems with activities of daily living are more likely to suggest a diagnosis of dementia.

Disease progression

Studies of elderly people frequently examine the language of a group of patients with the same type of dementia but not necessarily at the same stage of the disease process. However, we know that language skills vary at different stages of the disease and so a knowledge of the history and time course of the disorder in relation to the patient's language abilities may be lost. Clinicians need to be aware of general language characteristics identified in group studies as well as knowing the effects of disease progression on language processing which may only come from future single case longitudinal studies.

Premorbid abilities

Variation in premorbid language and cognitive skills may be relevant to the speed and course of the deterioration in dementia. Some rather controversial evidence suggests that patients with previously highly developed verbal skills will be slower to lose them (Wilson et al., 1978). This factor may further complicate variations in disease progression. Also, tests for early dementia frequently use complex language skills which some elderly people, particularly those who finished formal education at a very young age, may find difficult irrespective of their deficits.

Assessments not primarily designed for use with the elderly

Very few tests of language and cognitive functioning are specifically designed and validated for use with the elderly. Therefore, when using tests such as aphasia batteries, clinicians need to be aware of test validity, reliability, standardisation and norms. Specifically, a test that involves timed responses will disadvantage the elderly.

Differentiating other effects of testing

Testing may be affected by variables such as fatigue, poor attention, anxiety and background noise. These variables can apply to anyone undergoing any form of testing but are more likely to occur in the elderly, especially in those who are unused to testing or unused to a hospital or clinic setting. These factors are often mentioned by researchers and clinicians, but are not then evaluated in relation to test results. However, these variables can affect performance and therefore need to be appraised. A clear example appears in Chapter 5: Mrs S presented with a rather unusual conversational style, with short phrasing resulting in a much greater than expected mean number of utterances in addition to greatly increased scores on unintelligible utterances. All sorts of linguistic, cognitive and communicative conclusions could be drawn from this. However, the data were collected in the subject's home and the researcher draws our attention to the fact that the subject was being constantly interrupted by the noises of a caged bird! Hence the findings must not necessarily be taken in isolation as reflecting the person's normal mode of communication.

Sensory deficits

Tests that rely on visual or auditory processing may be affected by the decline in sensory acuity that occurs with age, for example difficulty in naming pictures may need to be distinguished from visual problems. Patients may not have their spectacles with them or may not have had their eyesight assessed for many years, and visual perceptual problems may further complicate the test profile. Memory deficits can also compromise results in language tests that involve remembering auditory or written material.

Medication

Elderly people take more drugs than younger people and the effects of the medication are present for longer due to slower metabolic functioning. Test performance can be affected by drugs such as sedatives or anticholinergics. Co-careldopa (Sinemet) may have an 'on/off' effect which causes the performances of patients with Parkinson's disease to vary considerably.

The potential problems discussed in this section may give the impression that language assessment and diagnosis is somewhat difficult with elderly clients. To a certain extent it is, but assessment in different modalities involving a carefully selected range of response requirements should eliminate many of these difficulties. This assessment, combined with taking a detailed case history, skilled observation and a multidisciplinary approach should enable clinicians to accurately describe the language pathology evident in elderly clients.

Summary

Clinicians working with the elderly need to have the following:

- Detailed knowledge of the process of normal ageing particularly in relation to language.
- Detailed knowledge of the effects of both acute and degenerative disease processes on language functioning.
- A detailed profile of the client, their premorbid abilities, lifestyle and personality and their current presentation in these areas.
- An overall profile of the client's everyday functioning.

Having combined these areas of knowledge to form a hypothesis, the clinician needs to test and modify this hypothesis in order to arrive at an accurate diagnosis of the type and severity of language impairment. This information will inform the clinician's management of the elderly client with communication disorder in terms of direct intervention, advice to the client and carers, and assisting other professionals to achieve more effective communication.

This chapter has outlined an approach to elderly people which views age-related change as normal and suggests that elderly clients should be approached in the same way as younger clients with acquired communication disorders. Given that the vast majority of elderly people retain functional language and cognitive abilities, the need to distinguish normal age-related changes from pathological changes due to disease processes has been emphasised.

Age in itself should never mark a client as less important or less rewarding to work with. Because the ageing process may be said to 'complicate' the processes involved in language and communication, there is a particular need for carefully planned and detailed assessment and intervention.

Chapters 2–5 examine language and language change in the normal healthy elderly in more detail. Chapters 6 and 7 examine the effects of brain pathology on communication in the dementias. Chapters 8 and 9 return to the clinical perspective and consider clinical intervention and service provision for the elderly. Finally, Chapter 10 discusses future directions in clinical provision and language research.

Chapter 2
Language and language change in the normal elderly population

Language processing and language change in the elderly

What do we need to know for clinical use about language in the normal elderly population?

- Does language change with age?
- If so, what are these changes?
- Are these changes functionally or clinically relevant, i.e. do they make a difference to the everyday lives of elderly people and does clinical management need to be age adjusted?
- Which cognitive parameters of language show change with age and what are the effects of any interaction with language changes?
- Do the elderly compensate for cognitive or language deficits and, if so, how do they do so?

The information on normal language processes is still relatively sparse compared with the growing literature on language in neurogenic disorders such as cerebrovascular accident and the dementia-producing diseases. The study of language in the normal, healthy elderly is important in setting norms for understanding the language changes that take place in the neurologically impaired. However, such a study is also important in itself because the product is a description of the language used by a particular group of people. Such descriptions of naturally produced language are useful reminders of both the variety and the homogeneity of language.

As the proportion of the population categorised as elderly has risen, there has been a commensurate rise of interest in all aspects of ageing. Research investigating aspects of language in the elderly has mainly focused on whether their language is different from that of younger age groups and, if it is, whether the changes show only increased difficulty or whether different processing strategies are used by the elderly (Light and Burke, 1990). More commonly, the research has contrasted the language breakdown in acquired neurological damage and disease with the more intact language system of the normal, healthy elderly person, often employing a formal testing procedure (Appel, Kertesz and Fisman, 1982; Bayles, 1982).

There are cogent reasons for the neglect of elderly language as a legitimate research topic, the most prominent of which has been the conclusions of psychometric testing of IQ in the 1950s and 1960s that performance on verbal subtests did not change greatly with age (Salthouse, 1990). Cognitive functions, and in particular the ability to learn in the ageing population, have been fertile ground for investigation since the 1940s. Much research has looked at the effects of ageing on performance, particularly in relation to IQ testing (Wechsler, 1958; Eisdorfer, Busse and Cohen, 1959; Jarvik, 1962; Cattell, 1963). The conclusions of almost all this research have been that language-mediated tasks are less likely to deteriorate with age than non-language-mediated tasks, although some research concluded that language tasks did show a small falling off in performance after the age of 60 years (Thorndike and Gallup, 1944). These findings lead to the assertion that language skills do not deteriorate (or even change) with age unless neurological disease intervenes. Jarvik (1962), in a rare longitudinal study, found that his overall population did show language changes with age but, when he divided survivors from non-survivors at the end of the study, a different picture emerged. Those who had survived showed very little or no decline in verbal tasks but those who had died had showed significant reduction in verbal skills in the testing before their deaths. He concluded that cognitive skills were susceptible to conditions such as heart disease and hypertension.

The conclusion that verbal skills do not change with age is highlighted by Wechsler (1958) and Cattell (1963), both of whom divided their IQ batteries into subtests that change with age and those that are relatively resistant to ageing. This division is largely between language-mediated and non-language-mediated tasks. Wechsler called this division 'hold' versus 'non-hold' subtests while Cattell's division was between 'crystallized' and 'fluid' intelligence, the former in each case being investigated by language-mediated tasks that were found to change little with age.

Large-scale studies of intelligence have concluded that language, or at least language-mediated tasks, are more resistant to the effects of ageing. Smaller scale and generally more recent experimental research by psychologists has suggested that parameters of language such as semantic memory organisation (Craik and Lockhart, 1972), information processing (Rabbitt, 1965), speed of verbal processing (Clark, 1980), deep semantic encoding (Craik and Simon, 1980) and passive versus active semantic memory (Botwinnick, West and Storandt, 1975) provide evidence that change does occur with increasing age. These parameters may affect language use and comprehension. As such cognitive functions may be said to support the linguistic system, it is reasonable to suppose that, with a large enough deficit in any or several of these areas, language performance will be changed. These areas of cognition will be briefly noted as relevant only as far as they provide evidence of the kind of linguistic organisation that characterises the elderly person's language.

One perhaps under-researched area is that of test and task familiarity and motivation. Do the differences occur between younger and older populations because of these factors rather than specific language and cognitive differences? Many studies have used task training or elderly groups with task experience, or have matched their groups carefully on education and vocabulary scores. These have either found smaller differences between old and young or have demonstrated greater improvement by the elderly than by the young on the tasks (see p. 33).

Theoretical backgrounds of language research in the elderly

What has motivated research into the language of the normal, healthy elderly? Some impetus for greater interest in the language of the elderly has been provided by two specific linguistic hypotheses.

Jakobson (1968) suggested that the dissolution of the phonological system in adult acquired aphasia is a reversal of the acquisition found in children and that this regression hypothesis might hold for other linguistic levels. There is some evidence against this argument (Caramazza and Zurif, 1978; Goodglass, 1978), particularly the hypothesis regarding levels other than the phonological. However, the normal elderly and the elderly with diagnosed dementia of the Alzheimer type (DAT) have provided some evidence of linguistic regression (Scholes, 1978; Cohen, 1979) at grammatical and semantic levels of language.

Secondly, Chomsky's hypothesised distinction between language competence and language performance has provoked researchers into asking whether this actually exists and, if so, whether competence is lost in both adult-acquired aphasia and various forms of dementia (Chomsky, 1965; de Ajuriaguerra and Tissot, 1975; Caramazza and Zurif, 1978). These studies have generated an interest in the language capabilities of the normal elderly as another source of information for testing these and other hypotheses concerning adaptation to a changing linguistic system (Cohen, 1979; Obler and Albert, 1981).

More recently, theories which attempt to describe the modularity of the language-processing system have added a new impetus to the study of language in dementia, although relatively few studies have been published. An early paper by Schwartz, Marin and Saffran (1979), for example, looked at single-word processing and the semantic system in dementia (see Chapter 7). The language of the normal elderly has also been reconsidered using information processing models (Light and Burke, 1990); these are discussed below.

Having described some of the theoretical backgrounds that have motivated research, we should note that no one coherent theoretical strand has united the work on elderly language, nor has there been a hypothesis that seeks to explain the deficits found within the elderly population or, more saliently, to predict them. An honourable exception to this lack might be Jakobson's regression hypothesis, which predicts decline in a reverse order to development but does not explain why. Salthouse (1990) suggests that information-processing theory needs to

> provide a general framework for understanding the effects of aging. Such a framework must serve both an integrating and a predictive function. That is, it must indicate how age-dependent phenomena are related, by coordinating them under a common theoretical construct. And, presented with new research paradigms, it must predict which will show age effects and which will not.
>
> (pp. 11–12)

Any theory of cognition and language that seeks to explain the deficits in ageing has also to be predictive.

Cognitive parameters of language

Research into areas of cognition that support language points to changes in speed of processing skills (Clark, 1980; Salthouse, 1985; Welford, 1985), auditory perceptual abilities (Maccoby, 1971; Cohen and Faulkner, 1981) and attentional skills (Rabbitt, 1979; Plude and Hoyer, 1985) that all have some part in changing the ability to understand and use spoken language, as well as to read and write. In this section, those areas of cognition supplementary to language will be reviewed and the main conclusions concerning changes with age discussed.

Ageing and attention

The ability to attend is important for both linguistic and cognitive processing, particularly for complex tasks. The elderly show little change in sustained attention (vigilance) that requires attention to one task only (Plude and Doussard-Roosevelt, 1990).

Selective attention (which includes the ability to ignore irrelevant information and attend to a selected task) does show some change with age, although there is no evidence of qualitative differences in performance between young and older groups. The elderly do, however, show greater difficulty in allocating attention to the target task (see Plude and Doussard-Roosevelt, 1990 for a review of ageing and attention).

Early research suggested that the elderly might have modality differences in attention (Plude and Hoye, 1985). On visual tasks requiring selective attention, they have greater difficulty in ignoring irrelevant information; however, more recent research points to visual perceptual deficits in the elderly, which are absent in the younger population and which may account for this finding (Ball et al., 1988). Studies using dichotic listening tasks show no deficits for sustained attention but some difficulty with selective attention tasks that are complex or have a required response speed even when the elderly are screened for age-related hearing loss (Schonfield et al., 1982).

Another aspect of attention is that of processes requiring effort versus automatic processes. If there is finite attentional capacity which reduces with increasing age, then larger attentional demands will lead to larger age-related deficits (Hasher and Zacks, 1979). Elderly people are predicted to do worse than younger people on tasks that require greater attentional capacity, but the research findings are contradictory (Plude and Hoyer, 1985; Salthouse, 1990).

Ageing and memory systems

In the organisation of memory, a division between episodic (autobiographical) and semantic (language and knowledge) memory has been postulated (Tulving, 1972, 1983). Another more recent model of memory as consisting of neural networks has been outlined in which, like neurons and their connecting fibres, a concept is said to be distributed throughout the structure (Rumelhart and McClelland, 1986).

Experimental evidence suggests that several types of memory are compromised in the normal elderly population but these losses rarely do more than inconvenience and annoy the individual in everyday life. Working memory (short-term or primary memory) capacity and retrieval speed probably remain unaffected by normal ageing but the ability to manipulate information in working memory may decline with age (Botwinnick and Storandt, 1974; Dobbs and Rule, 1989; Salthouse et al., 1989). The normal elderly are able, for example, to remember as many digits as younger age groups but have far more difficulty in repeating the same digits in their reverse order. There is some evidence that the elderly find greater difficulty in using short-term memory when the input is visual rather than auditory (Cerella, Poon and Fozard, 1981).

Episodic and semantic memory (long-term or secondary memory) show differential age effects. Episodic memory shows age effects on recall of newly learned material and recall of activities and actions

(Craik, 1984; Kausler, 1989). Recall of events may differ with residential context: Holland and Rabbitt (1991) found that elderly people in residential care recalled and rehearsed more events from their earlier life than more recent events, while elderly people living independent lives recalled more recent than early events.

Semantic memory has generally been thought to be more resistant to ageing. Tasks that require recognition of material show little change with age but active retrieval from semantic memory is slower in older populations (Craik, 1984; Bowles and Poon, 1985; Howard, Shaw and Heisey, 1986). Word fluency tasks, requiring the generation of words in a chosen category or beginning with a specified letter, also show age effects.

Some research suggests that the elderly may be able to compensate for their memory deficits if taught certain strategies such as categorisation of material or visual imagery (Perlmutter, 1979; Yesavage, Rose and Bower, 1983; Rissenberg and Glanzer, 1986; Meyer, Young and Bartlett, 1989). Other research suggests that the context in which information is used may have a significant effect on memory abilities in the elderly population and opens up possibilities for manipulation of memory (Schaffer and Poon, 1982; Holland and Rabbitt, 1991).

For a review of memory changes and ageing see Lovelace (1990).

Ageing, problem solving and classification skills

One common image of an elderly person is that of someone with increased rigidity of views or difficulty in changing set. Studies of age differences in problem-solving ability have often used tasks that require language mediation and have generally shown that, in novel situations, the elderly find it more difficult than younger people to generate the concepts necessary to solve a problem. When given strategies for doing so, the performance of the elderly may match that of the younger group (Hulicka and Grossman, 1967; Meyer, Young and Bartlett, 1989). Longitudinal studies and those that use educationally well matched groups suggest that the age difference may be very small and an artefact of variables such as education, task familiarity and health (Charness, 1985). Salthouse (1984) suggests further that cognitive limitations in the elderly population can be avoided by those who have specific skills because their functional abilities are adaptable.

Language change with increasing age

Research into language and ageing can be divided into two main areas.

- The first area is that of language use and comprehension among the normal elderly and encompasses research into the possible linguistic organisation used by the normal elderly.

- The second strand concerns the nature of the differences between younger and older people in their language-processing abilities and, specifically, whether any differences are quantitative or qualitative. Research suggests that changes occur in both areas (Salthouse, 1991).

A later section will briefly discuss evidence from studies of language disturbance in focal aphasia and Alzheimer-type dementias (DAT) (see pp. 46–52). The rationale for including this information is that a linguistic and neuropathological continuum has been postulated between normal elderly and those with DAT. Therefore conclusions from language research into DAT may point to areas where the normal elderly might have problems in language processing.

Against this background of deficit-based research, another aspect of language is relatively neglected. Language skills develop throughout life and vocabulary may continue to expand indefinitely. New words which come into general usage – such as poll tax (UK), and RVs (recreational vehicles: USA) – are understood and used by the elderly. Other skills reflecting the ability to use different speech registers are also capable of continued development (Obler and Albert, 1985).

Because the literature comes from disparate research areas with different methodologies and conceptual frameworks, some studies will be looked at in detail to illustrate differences in methodology and hypotheses.

How the elderly understand

There is evidence that the ability of the normal elderly to understand language is different from that of younger age groups. Certain linguistic dimensions involved in recognition and comprehension have been investigated only sparsely, but the semantic and grammatical constraints on comprehension and the relationship between these two linguistic levels has been a fruitful area for research into ageing language (Scholes, 1978; Cohen, 1979; Maxim, 1982; Cohen and Faulkner, 1983; Zacks and Hasher, 1990). The tentative conclusions from this research are that the ability to understand may deteriorate with age but different strategies appear to be used in an attempt to compensate for this decline. The ability to coordinate the necessary semantic and grammatical processes may also change with age but, in particular, processing complex syntax shows deficits under experimental conditions.

Understanding sentences and text

Scholes (1978), in an early study of sentence comprchension, looked at comprehension of one type of ambiguous sentence. Citing Bever's (1970) work on the processes involved in understanding a sentence,

Scholes suggested that, in order to understand any sentence, it is necessary to use a set of semantic and lexical hypotheses about linguistic structure together in comprehension. The first few words of the sentence are matched against a 'most popular sentence type' hypothesis. Scholes points out that the use of such a hypothesis can lead to misunderstanding if the sentence is ambiguous in both intonation and syntax (1).

1. He showed her [*the*] baby [*the*] pictures

The sentence can be made unambiguous either by intonation or by inserting the definite article before *baby* or *pictures*.

Using such sentences, spoken with intonation patterns that would not resolve the ambiguity, Scholes tested a college-aged control group and an elderly group (average age 69 years), on a picture recognition task. The elderly group had greater difficulty in understanding even the unambiguous sentences. They also showed a much greater tendency to understand the ambiguous sentences according to the 'most popular sentence type' hypothesis than the younger group. In fact, they interpreted 'He showed her baby pictures' as meaning 'He showed her baby the pictures' 95% of the time. Not only did they appear to have a difficulty with this type of analysis but they also seemed to be less flexible in their ability to use different strategies.

Maxim (1982) compared the comprehension performance of a group of normal elderly and a group of young people on sentences containing one subordinate clause, headed by the adverbial, temporal subordinators *before* and *after*. In children the acquisition of these subordinators in spoken language and in comprehension shows that a child gains complete mastery of the functions of these subordinators only at a relatively late stage in language development, certainly after the age of 4 years and possibly not until the age of 7 (Clark and Clark, 1977). Because this type of sentence is acquired relatively late in language acquisition, it was hypothesised that the elderly might show difficulty in comprehension.

Clark and Clark (1977), in a summary of their research, found two principles operating when children use these structures. Using a grammatical principle, children first assume that the first clause is the main clause. They therefore find it easier to understand sentences where the main clause comes first, followed by a subordinate clause in second position (2).

2. The man aimed carefully	before he shot the president.
main clause	subordinate clause
3. Before he shot the president	the man aimed carefully.
subordinate clause	main clause

Secondly, children assume that the order of mention is the same as the order of occurrence (OM is OC). Therefore sentences that do not violate this principle are easier to understand than those which do. Using this principle (2) is easier to understand than (3). If the subordinate clause begins with *after*, the situation is altered and (4) becomes easier to understand than (5).

4. *OM is OC*: After he buttoned his shirt he put on his jacket.
5. *OM not OC*: She sat down after she had done her shopping.

Maxim tested a normal elderly group of 20 people whose average age was 77 years and a young control group (average age 23 years) on 24 sentences such as (4) and (5). The normal elderly group were tested for ability to repeat sentences longer than test sentences (i.e. of 11–14 words) and were given practice and repetitions when requested. Despite such help, the average number of errors for the elderly group was 16% of the total possible score, whereas the young group scored less than 1% on their average error score. Sentences in which the order of mention was the same as the order of occurrence were significantly easier to understand than sentences where the order of mention was not the order of occurrence. Sentences in which the main clause came before the subordinate clause were not significantly easier to understand than sentences where the main clause appeared second, although more errors in total were made on these sentences. There were also significantly more errors in sentences in which the order of mention was the same as the order of occurrence but the main clause came after the subordinate clause. Therefore, having the main clause in second position appears to complicate comprehension.

It seems likely that the dominant strategy used by the elderly to understand this type of complex sentence is semantic. This is borne out by the fact that sentences containing *before* were found to be significantly easier to understand than *after* sentences. This supports Clark and Clark's (1968) theory of semantic markedness which suggests that pairs of terms such as *before* and *after* have a marked and unmarked form: the unmarked form *before* is acquired earlier than the marked form *after* and is easier for the child to use and understand. Similarly, sentences in which the main clause is in first place or where the order of occurrence is the same as the order of mention are also unmarked. However, the elderly group found complex sentences containing *before* in either position easier to understand than *after* sentences.

Another way of considering complex sentences is to look at left versus right branching sentences (i.e. those in which the subordinate clause is to the right or left of the main clause):

- Left branching: *Because he felt ill*, he went to bed.
- Right branching: He went to bed *because he felt ill.*

Left-branching complex sentences are considered to be more difficult to understand, although the exact nature of the difficulty is open to debate (Frazier and Fodor, 1978; Berwick and Weinberg, 1984). Frazier and Fodor (1978) suggest that their first-stage parser is unable to cope with more than about six words while the second-stage parser has greater ability. The first-stage parser is therefore unable to find the main verb phrase in a left-branching sentence such as (5) because the verb phrase comes after its six word capacity. The second-stage parser therefore has to reparse the first clause. For a discussion of a number of different models of understanding sentences see Garman (1990).

Further evidence from Cohen (1979) and Cohen and Faulkner (1983) showed differences between the young and elderly in extracting certain types of information from spoken text (paragraphs). However, the elderly compensated for their deteriorating ability when decoding by making better use of contextual information. Cohen (1979) looked at comprehension of spoken language in three ways: first she tested the ability of elderly people to answer direct and inferential questions about a passage that they had just heard; secondly, she used a story recall task to look at the kind of information remembered in terms of propositions and certain semantic elements; thirdly, she looked at the ability of the elderly to understand anomalies. Well matched groups of highly educated old (average age 68 years) and young people, as well as less well matched groups of old (average age 79 years) and young people with fewer years of education, took part. Cohen found that both elderly groups had more difficulty in answering inferential questions than the younger groups, although their ability to understand direct questions was no different from that of the younger group. The elderly, highly educated group had greater difficulty than the young when the rate of message delivery was increased. Light, Zelinsky and Moore (1982) corroborated this finding in a later study.

As with the ability to understand direct questions, the semantic complexity of the passages as measured by the ability to utilise pragmatic information did not help to differentiate between the young and old groups. The problems of research design and material are highlighted by Cohen (1979) whose example of a semantically simple passage is more complex grammatically in terms of subordinate clause structure than the example of a semantically complex passage. This fact might have equalised the linguistic differences between the passages, making them equally understandable.

On the story recall task Cohen took account of what was remembered of the story and use of modifiers – e.g. quantifiers (more), temporal modifiers (recently), locatives (in the north) and logical connectives (because). The elderly groups remembered significantly less of these modifiers than the young groups. They did, however, remember specific events in the story but not the link between them as signalled by the logical connectives. Maxim (1982) also remarked on this phenomenon in her study. Her elderly group was heard to repeat the sentences after her but they sometimes replaced the subordinators with a simple coordinator such as *and*. Cohen's findings also suggest that information coded in structures such as prepositional phrases and embedded clauses may be less accessible than that in other structures.

When asked to identify anomalies in a passage, Cohen's elderly subjects made more errors than the younger groups, even though the nature of the task had been clearly shown to them. An example of the kind of anomaly used by Cohen is shown in (6).

6. The Jones family lived near the airport.
   It was quiet and peaceful.

Although the elderly highly educated group made more errors than the young highly educated group, the types of errors made were similar. The elderly subjects with low educational levels gave more value judgements than their young counterparts and made statements about the passage rather than answering the relevant question about it. They also gave significantly more mistaken explanations of the anomalies than the matched young group. Cohen concluded that the elderly had problems with comprehension on the kind of tasks that she gave them because they were unable to coordinate the various processes by which to arrive at a correct conclusion.

Cohen and Faulkner (1983) looked at contextual facilitation effects in a young and old group. Using a visual display unit, they presented sentences with highly predictable endings, low predictability endings and sentences with non-word endings in a context condition. Both groups had to press keys marked *word* or *non-word* to signal what they had read, and their reaction time was monitored. The elderly subjects showed greater facilitation with context on the low predictability endings than did the young group, but there was no difference between the groups on highly predictable endings. Interestingly, the elderly showed facilitation of context (compared with no context) for recognition of non-words but the young group did not. Cohen and Faulkner suggest that they were using the strategy of checking off context-generated possible words against the non-words, rather than searching through the whole lexicon, thus making a decision faster.

Having considered visual presentation, Cohen and Faulkner turned to auditory presentation and context, using white noise as a means of reducing the quality of the stimulus and thus examining the subject's ability to make up for this quality reduction by greater use of context.

The measured variable was the number of words accurately heard. Again the elderly showed greater contextual facilitation than the young, although at high noise levels this facilitation dropped off, perhaps indicating hearing impairment in the elderly group. The researchers argue that these results strengthen the hypothesis of Marslen-Wilson and Welsh (1978) that an acoustic–phonetic signal stimulates associated word cohorts. Sentence context is then used to isolate the appropriate word. If either the acoustic–phonetic signal or the sentence context is not available, then greater use will be made of the more available source of information. The elderly, who have greater difficulty in coping with auditory input for a variety of reasons, compensate by more effective use of context. In a study using similar methodology, Obler et al. (1991) controlled carefully for pure-tone hearing, educational level and verbal IQ. They found an interaction between the ability to predict sentence endings on a variety of sentence types and age. Sentence length did not increase difficulty for the elderly but sentence complexity and low predictability sentence endings did. The elderly showed a much greater preference for using their real world knowledge in predicting sentence endings than the young.

Another method used to study what the elderly remember from text or discourse is to consider whether a levels effect is occurring (i.e. whether main information is more likely to be remembered than detail). Cohen (1979), for example, found that factual information encoded in main sentence constituents was remembered more easily than information coded in other forms such as modifying adjectives and subordinators. Her highly educated elderly subjects showed no levels effect compared with a similar young group but her older less well educated group had a decreased levels effect. Both young and old are more likely to remember main points of information but whether there is a difference in levels effect related to age as such is unclear. Stine and Wingfield (1990), in a useful review of this subject area, found that studies showing a decreased versus same versus increased levels effect were similar in number (see Meyer and Rice, 1981, 1983; Dixon et al., 1982). What is clear from these studies is that variables such as vocabulary, task format, sentence structure and health may all change the ability of the elderly to respond as younger subjects do (which is to recall more main than detail information).

Can research be more specific about the nature of the changes in language processing and, in particular, about the role of memory capacity limitations? Light and Albertson (1990) found that older adults can process inferences as well as younger adults when asked to do so within the constraints of their working memory. They had difficulty with inferential information because they either forgot some aspect crucial to extracting the inference or had difficulty in reorganising the material in working memory. Light and Albertson investigated the ability of old and young groups to understand logical and pragmatic inference, using the distinction from Harris and Monaco (1978) in sentences such as those below, where (8) is a logical implication from (7) but the pragmatic implication in (9) does not imply (10).

7. Neil was forced to fly the plane.
8. Neil flew the plane.
9. Bob was able to climb the ladder.
10. Bob climbed the ladder.

The subjects were asked to respond to sentence pairs such as those above by saying whether the second sentence was true, false or indeterminate. Using complex sentences such as *Bill realised Harrison was sick* they found no difference between young and old groups on logical inferences. For pragmatic inference, the elderly were less likely to respond with an 'indeterminate' answer than the young group but otherwise their performance was similar. The older group had significantly greater difficulty than the young on sentences containing negatives in both clauses. They also performed differently on sentences containing verbs such as *believe* and *say*. Light and Albertson concluded that the elderly have difficulty with inferences when problem-solving and complex linguistic analysis have to be carried out at the same time. On a number of other tasks looking at pragmatic aspects of language, including reference, they found that the elderly group were sensitive to such features but showed greater difficulty if information needed to be retained in order to analyse the sentence fully, and that comprehension failure was due to memory failure. Zelinski (1990), in a review and study of discourse comprehension, found that working memory capacity problems did not cause problems for the elderly in integration of world knowledge and text processing, suggesting that there may be task differences that need to be further investigated.

Perhaps it is worth restating that these age differences are relatively small. Older adults respond correctly most of the time but have greater difficulty than younger groups and, sometimes, the processing constraints appear different for the two groups. Under experimental conditions, differences can be found that are neither functionally visible nor relevant but need to be acknowledged and incorporated into clinical situations when necessary. The context in which language is used, the frequency of use and practice effects are all important variables affecting performance.

It might be tentatively concluded, then, that the elderly are at times forced to rely on a semantic strategy for comprehension when memory load and grammatical complexity of material combine. Although this may seem superficially to suggest deterioration of language-processing abilities, there is a strong argument that the elderly make better use of semantic strategies than do young adults, so that adaptation also seems to take place with ageing. The evidence here is dependent on a relatively small number of studies that look at sentence and text comprehension either as a psycholinguistic process or as part of cognitive function. The material used is often extremely complex linguistically. Much more study is needed on comprehension at other levels, such as phrasal versus clausal complexity, coordination and subordination, and sentence length effects, before any coherent model of change in language comprehension with age can be produced.

Language production by the elderly

In contrast to the growing literature on language comprehension, there are few descriptions of the language that the elderly use. However, some studies look at aspects of language production within a comparative framework. Studying how the elderly produce language compared with younger age groups throws up many methodological problems, however, because it is very difficult to control for important variables such as educational and cultural differences reflected in language styles, dialect and changing language usage. As yet no studies have been published using what might be the best solution: parent/child comparisons.

Most of the comparative research points to an increase in performance errors such as uncompleted utterances, sentence repair etc. While these errors and other disfluencies are often omitted when describing a linguistic system, it has been pointed out that sentence repair, in particular, is systematic and an important sequential aspect of conversation (Schegloff, 1979). McNamara et al. (1992) found that normal healthy elderly subjects corrected between 72% and 92% of their errors on a picture description task. They found no differences between error rate or error correction rate for their five healthy subject groups (30s, 40s, 50s, 60s, 70s) on that particular task.

It has been suggested that the elderly may need more time to process language for production and that therefore certain performance phenomena, such as filler phrases, might be used more frequently by them (Obler and Albert, 1981). Also, if the elderly have greater difficulty in understanding, then their monitoring of their own language might be similarly affected, letting through more errors. Some research has found both predictions to be true. Yairi and Clifton (1972) found that the language of the elderly contained a significantly higher overall number of disfluencies. However, Gordon, Hutchinson and Allen (1976), in a more exhaustive study, compared samples of conversation from elderly (average age 80) and young people for repair, hesitant interjections, fillers, unfinished utterances that were not revised, frequency of pauses and location, and utterance length. The only difference that emerged was in the number of hesitant interjections and fillers, which the elderly group were found to use significantly more than the young group.

Gordon et al. suggested that this might be due to retrieval problems and that language complexity and organisation was well preserved, but it could also be argued that the use of fillers and hesitant interjections reflects the need for more time in processing and organising language output. Indeed, one of the least controversial findings about ageing is that the elderly show reduced psychomotor speed (Welford, 1962). If this slowing is universal in ageing then we would expect to see slowing in both language and cognitive function.

Davis (1979), in a study that went far towards controlling the variables of linguistic comparison, analysed fluent reminiscences and the results of a picture-description task from two groups, of average ages 79 and 58 years. The groups were well matched for educational level, social class and sex distribution and all came from the same area of London. They were asked to describe an incident from the Second World War and the most fluent part of this reminiscence was analysed. The older group used significantly fewer embedded sentences than the younger group and produced more unfinished utterances. The younger group had a longer mean length of utterance than the older group but there was no difference in the number of disfluencies produced by either group. This may be due to the nature of the task, which was to produce fluent, well rehearsed language. The language produced for the picture-completion task was analysed for a word to theme ratio but no difference was found between the groups.

The results from the studies discussed so far indicate that there is an increase in the number of certain types of disfluencies to be found in the language of elderly people. The problem of comparison lies in the definitions of disfluency used by each researcher. Yairi and Clifton (1972) and Davis (1979) appear to have used much the same criteria, and their results are comparable, but Gordon, Hutchinson and Allen (1976) divided dysfluencies into discrete categories. By doing so, they may have isolated the type of disfluency (hesitant interjections and fillers) used significantly more by the elderly population.

Davis also found that her elderly group used fewer embedded clauses than her middle-aged group. Although frequency ratios can often be misleading, the comparability between her two groups is such that the finding strongly suggests some organisational difficulty in language output. In contrast to these results, Obler, Mildworf and Albert (1977) suggest that, in written language, people in their 60s use more embedded sentences than people in their 50s, but that they use fewer sentences and fewer themes when writing about the same picture. The same study also found that a 'telegraphic' writing style was used by younger, healthier people while those in their 60s, some of whom had Parkinson's disease, used full and well constructed sentences. These results are somewhat contradictory and may reflect differing educational standards rather than differences due to an ageing linguistic system.

Some studies have looked at connected discourse in order to describe language in the elderly and have studied communicative competence as an indicator of language ability and cognitive function (Stine and Wingfield, 1990; Zelinski, 1990). Ulatowska et al. (1985) analysed samples of story telling, relating a memorable experience, description of a sequential task and an interview with groups of community-based elderly people, nuns in a teaching order and middle-aged people. They chose reference as a major indicator of discourse integration, because referential difficulties are characteristically found in the dementias and in focal aphasias (Ulatowska, North and Macaluso-Haynes, 1981; Obler, 1983). Their main findings were that discourse competence and cognitive function were closely related in all the contexts sampled. In the sample of nuns (who were educationally well matched) the elderly group showed discourse-processing decrements compared with the middle-aged nuns, but they were also less cognitively competent than the middle-aged group. Ulatowska et al. (1981) reject the conclusion that difficulties with reference in the elderly group are due to short-term memory constraints because the same decrement in discourse competence was found on the memorable experience and sequential task which 'did not constitute short term recall tasks' (p.136) as on narrative retelling. They concluded that multiple factors such as changes in social status and speech styles with age and sensory impairments may cause changes in discourse processing. In contrast, Hultsch and Dixon (1983) found that the elderly benefit from existing knowledge when memory for text is tested and perform similarly to younger groups but do less well on newer information.

An interesting area of research is that of story telling or retelling. Obler (1980) suggested that old, highly experienced story tellers were more likely to communicate their story using elaborated language than younger story tellers. Adams et al. (1991) concluded that the elderly were more likely to both interpret and integrate information in story recall whereas younger people reproduced more of the original text. Although age may produce changes in language comprehension tasks, language output may benefit from practice.

Single-word processing

What evidence is there for changes in single-word processing among the elderly population? An early piece of research by Warren and Warren (1966) throws some light on possible changes in the strategies that the elderly use when listening. Using an experimental methodology different from that so far presented, Warren and Warren used the verbal transformation effect to investigate perceptual changes with increasing age. This effect occurs when a continuous loop tape recording of the same word is played. The listener reports changes in the word form when none are taking place. Warren and Warren found that the number of reported word changes was much lower in the elderly than in a comparable young adult group. A group of children reported a number of changes comparable to those reported by the elderly group but, whereas the children tended to report phonemic changes, sometimes not even corresponding to English phonotactics, the elderly group reported hearing dictionary words. Obler and Albert (1981) comment that, if the verbal transformation effect points to strategies for correcting misprocessed items (as Warren et al. suggest), then the elderly are 'monitoring input at a word by word level'. Obler et al. (1991) found that the elderly were more likely to find a sentence ending plausible than a younger group, again suggesting that not only are the elderly more likely to lexicalise (i.e. to make a dictionary word from a non-word) but they are also more likely to make a sentence ending agree semantically with the preceding sentence. This strategy also seems to match up well with Cohen and Faulkner's suggestion that, for decisions about non-words, the elderly are able to make greater use of context (as opposed to no context) by allowing the context to cut down the choice of lexical items against which the non-word must be checked before it is perceived as a non-word. In the verbal transformation effect, the elderly are using the same type of strategy in only checking off what they hear against items in their lexicon, although here the strategy misfires because it rules out the possibility of non-words being heard.

The elderly are slower than younger age groups on fluency tasks such as producing names within one semantic category in a given period but, given additional time, they achieve the same results in terms of the number of items produced (Obler and Albert, 1981). Earlier work on processing time, expectancy and priming for single words had shown that both old and young subjects show a priming effect and are able to make faster lexical decisions after a semantically related word (Bowles and Poon, 1985). Burke and Harrold (1990), using a word-to-word priming task, found no age effect for time or the strength of priming in on-line (automatic) processing. Older adults were slower on sentence semantics using primed and unprimed material but there was no other difference between them and the younger group. MacKay and Burke (1990) suggest that, although priming remains effective in old age, rate of priming is an underlying cause of processing difficulties.

Obler (1980) reports an unpublished paper written by Kaplan, Veroff and herself, analysing the spoken responses to a delayed recall memory test in which they found that the use of semantically indefnite words increased with age. The problem of word recall is one which the elderly themselves mention frequently and the increased use of pronouns, instead of the appropriate noun, is therefore inevitable with increasing age (Ulatowska et al., 1985). While a decline in the ability to retrieve from the lexicon is probable, passive knowledge of the lexicon remains stable (Botwinnick, West and Storandt, 1975; Till and Walsh, 1980). In an unusual study, Burke, Worthley and Martin (1988) asked young and old adults to record whenever they could not find a word but had 'tip of the tongue' (TOT) information about the word. Older adults recorded more TOT information and also resolved slightly more than the younger group. Any strategy for finding the word was predicted to be similar for both groups, but the older group had more spontaneous resolutions, in which the word came to mind without a strategy being applied. Both age groups had TOT states for place names and people, but the older group had difficulty with common object names not reported by the younger group whereas the younger group had difficulty with more abstract nouns and verbs.

Riegel (1959) showed that some aspects of lexical use may improve with age. A hierarchy of associational tasks, from synonym pairing to analogy pairing, was given to a young group (average age 18;6 years) and a group of people over 65 years. The elderly group gave more correct responses than the young group in the synonym test where the associations were most strongly related and might be expected to have been strengthened with increasing age by continuous use and by the individual's refinement of these associations. In the analogies task, in which the associations are more remote, the elderly group responded only half as well as the younger group. There seem, then, to be two processes involved in ageing here: the strengthening of close associations and the disassociation of the more remote associations. The elderly might therefore find that frequently used words are retrieved with ease while words used infrequently become increasingly difficult to find. This finding is corroborated by Cohen and Faulkner (1983), who discovered that context did not facilitate a sentence-completion task for the elderly any more than for a younger group. As such a task is closer to an analogies task than a synonym task, this result might be expected.

Repair has been discussed as an important aspect of language because it gives some insight into the monitoring processes needed for discourse. McNamara et al. (1992) found a significant relationship between naming ability and the ability to repair errors on a picture-description task. Such results suggest that retrieval and monitoring processes need to be studied in terms of an underlying process which may remain intact with increasing age.

Conclusions from the research on language production and single-word processing can only be tentative because, like the language comprehension research, the research does not form a cohesive body. Some research, such as that by Riegel (1959), can only be tenuously relevant to the conversational language of the elderly but does suggest a difference in lexical semantic organisation or retrieval. The research does have some cohesiveness in that all the studies point to some change taking place with increasing age. More disfluencies may begin to appear in conversational language. The number of 'indefinite' words may increase and reference becomes less competent in older language. Both these aspects of language may be related to the incipient word-finding problems which the elderly report so commonly, but equally may be due to working memory which may be needed for reference in discourse. The use of written and spoken language may diverge, with written language assuming a formality that is not present in spoken language. This is not contradictory and probably reflects the different cognitive skills and educational constraints involved in written and spoken language. Finally, there is evidence that the use of embedded clauses is less frequent in the elderly, which might reflect length constraints but is more likely to be a function of complexity constraints with advancing age.

There is little consensus on why the elderly show these changes in processing strategies. The results could be explained either by limitations on processing capacities or by particular levels of difficulty with specific processes.

What patterns of language breakdown in Alzheimer-type dementia and acquired aphasia might suggest about language in the normal elderly

Recent research into different aspects of aphasic deficits have contributed to hypothetical models of language processing that are equally applicable whether the language-processing system is damaged or intact. While the literature on language in dementia does not have the same underlying theoretical bases, and indeed the research methodology is very varied, it is worthwhile to look briefly at this area in the search for hypotheses about change in normal ageing language processing.

With increasing age, the chance of cerebral disease also increases. The result of most dementias is a progressive deterioration in cognitive function and social behaviour, in which the change in linguistic performance is prominent. The linguistic changes are not uniform but clusters of changes occur in DAT with relative frequency and change with severity. The linguistic breakdown in DAT is distinguishable from that in other types of dementia and that due to cerebrovascular accident or injury, although most dementias share some linguistic changes (see pp. 18–24). There are similarities between DAT and Wernicke's and transcortical sensory aphasias. The breakdown of linguistic performance in DAT is usually of gradual onset with progressive deterioration, whereas after cerebrovascular accident language is disrupted suddenly. The language breakdown in DAT may begin with mild word-finding difficulty, often reported by the people themselves, that are indistinguishable in isolation from the word-finding difficulties experienced by many people from middle age onwards.

This similarity between the normal ageing process and the early stages of dementia as shown in language changes has correlates in neuroanatomical and neurophysiological changes (Wells, 1971; Valenstein, 1981). The fact that this similarity exists has led researchers to compare the normal elderly and those with dementia to evaluate whether gross trends of language change are equivalent for the two groups and to make predictions about the normal ageing process from the results of research on language change in dementia.

From the initial change in language performance there is, as has been stated, a gradual deterioration in the volitional use of language and an increasing amount of language that is stereotyped, often repetitive and unsuccessful in its communicative function. People with DAT may reach a stage where they are neither speaking nor responding to language which is directed towards them. The deterioration in linguistic performance is also variable in several ways. It is variable in time and may cease at a point in its course. More cogently, not all areas of linguistic performance are involved equally and there is evidence that some areas (notably the prosodic, segmental phonological and morphological levels) remain remarkably intact, even at the non-volitional stage that occurs inevitably in the course of DAT (Irigaray, 1973; Whitaker, 1976).

The fluent language found in patients with DAT also has parallels in the language used by people who have Wernicke's aphasia. This is a fluent type of aphasia (Goodglass and Kaplan, 1972) more prevalent in the older population of aphasics (Brown and Jaffe, 1975; Obler et al., 1978). In discussing the changes found in DAT, in which there is pathological, chronic deterioration of language, it is possible to refer to similar documented changes in the language of the normal, healthy elderly. Difficulty in dealing with semantic anomaly and certain complex grammatical constructions are examples of these parallels between the two groups. In the same way, it is also salutary to consider the errors found in aphasic language and 'slips of the tongue' phenomena found in the normal population. If we consider those errors found in both the (mainly elderly) population of Wernicke's aphasics and the normal population, we are likely to have isolated the majority of error types that we may find in the language of the normal, healthy elderly.

Buckingham (1980) carried out just such an analysis and found that several types of errors made by aphasics are also found in the normal population. Lexical selection errors are usually from the same word category as the target in both populations. These selection errors may occur because of semantic or phonological associations between words, but can also occur because of what Buckingham calls 'phrasal blending'. By this he means a blending of two like words or grammatical structures at the preselection level (i.e. at that level where more than one word or structure has been activated but no choice has yet been made) (Buckingham and Kertesz, 1976). Lastly, both populations produce lexical item perseverations and the perseverated item reoccurs only in an appropriate grammatical position. The perseverated item is also likely to have the main stress in the utterance. At the syllable level, perseverations by aphasics are differentiated from those in normals only by the increased span of speech in which they can occur. In aphasia there is an important distinction between content and function words, and the relative percentages of these two classes of words can be an important diagnostic criterion. Garrett (1975) hypothesised that functors would not contain segmental errors because they exist only in their final form and therefore would not be subject to sound exchanges, deletions or substitutions. This hypothesis seems to be true for both Wernicke's aphasics and normal subjects, although Buckingham suggests that stress may play an important role in their intactness. He found that most errors occurring at the segmental level happen on stressed words whereas functors are often unstressed.

Buckingham underlines the fact that the performance errors of both aphasic and normal populations may be similar, but it is difficult to decide whether similarities occur through the same mechanisms. However, he suggests that the same constraints are likely to be operative for both normal and brain-damaged speakers.

It is clear from the literature that no accounts of language in the normal elderly give a broad description of their language; indeed, the literature is also almost exclusively concerned with language change, using comparisons either between groups of differing ages or between the normal elderly and those with neurological disease (see Chapters 6 and 7). For these reasons, any hypotheses about language in the normal elderly must be tentative and also specific. It is not easy to develop a general hypothesis about the language of the normal elderly from such diverse but isolated pieces of research, particularly because most of the research to date has looked at language comprehension and not at aspects of language production in the normal elderly.

Two types of hypothesis can tentatively be made about the language of the normal elderly. Investigations into the language of the elderly with DAT have suggested strongly that a grammatical system is still present, even in severely deteriorated patients (Irigaray, 1973; Whitaker, 1976; Bayles, 1982). This syntactic core seems highly indestructible and the normal elderly may well be using such a core grammatical system*. This syntactic system in DAT works best within sentences, and it might therefore be expected that the within-sentence syntax of the normal elderly would show great consistency at least up to the level that it breaks down in DAT. That level is the division between simple sentences, containing no subordinate clauses, and complex sentences which do contain such clauses.

Secondly, certain areas of grammar do not belong to the core system. Because they do not belong to this stable core system, much greater variation is likely in both the frequency of use and the efficiency with which they are used. Complex sentences belong to this category, as do any grammatical structures that are longer than the simple sentence or clause. In fact, any element of grammar which is optional in the sentence or in a series of sentences may be subject to greater variation. The notion of optionality suggests that any element in a sentence that is not grammatically bound to appear or is semantically redundant is likely to show greater variation than the core grammar. Using this second hypothesis, we will consider some of the research that has been reviewed, and make suggestions about the areas of language that have been investigated and how the findings may be reflected in the use of the grammatical system.

When discussing the system of grammatical organisation used by the normal elderly, it is very difficult to ignore the part played by the semantic system, which includes referential processes, and the changes that seem to be taking place within that system. This change in the semantic system and the change in the relationship between the semantic and grammatical levels appear to have effects for both the normal elderly and those with DAT. The adaptations to a changing semantic system appear to alter the structure at a conversational level in the language used by DAT patients and may do so in the language of the normal elderly. The adaptations are due to both lexical accessing difficulties and semantic structure within the sentence. There are parallels between the word-finding difficulties of the normal elderly and the DAT elderly: both groups are helped by accessing strategies of roughly the same kind (Obler and Albert, 1981; Cohen and Faulkner, 1983), although the DAT group has a far more deteriorated semantic system. If Cohen and Faulkner's research on contextual facilitation is correct,

*The use of the term *core grammatical system* describes only the residual output, in both spontaneous and test conditions, of the person with DAT. This is in contrast to Chomsky's theory of *core grammar*, which is concerned with establishing a core of linguistic principles for natural language (Chomsky, 1980).

then the normal elderly may show relatively few difficulties in word-finding in conversation, although they may show greater numbers of sentence repairs at an early stage in the sentence because contextual facilitation will be greater towards the end of a sentence. Therefore there should be very few sentence repairs towards the end of a simple sentence but more repairs in complex sentences containing embedded clauses.

While the normal elderly appear to rely on the semantic system and knowledge of the world information in comprehending when syntax becomes complex, they, like patients with DAT, have difficulty with comprehension of anomalous sentences (Bayles, 1982). In both groups the semantic system at word level is partially intact but, particularly in the DAT group, is accessible only under certain conditions. Because of the difficulty with anomalous sentence comprehension, similar difficulties in language production may occur, with anomalous or ambiguous sentences passing through any linguistic monitoring system without being detected.

For the DAT group, the grammatical system (at the morphemic level and at the level of agreement between grammatical elements in the simple sentence) may remain intact (Whitaker, 1976). There should therefore be few errors in these areas for the normal elderly, but there is some indication that both groups have difficulty at the level at which syntax makes the semantics of the utterance more complex. The 'automatic' linguistic system of the deteriorated DAT patient breaks down at approximately the same level of sentence complexity as does the volitional language use and understanding of the normal elderly. The DAT patient has difficulty in correcting grammatical errors at the inter-clause level (Tissot, Duval and de Ajuriaguerra, 1967). The normal elderly are, then, also likely to have greater difficulty constructing multiclause sentences.

Replacement of a dual strategy of comprehension, using syntactic and semantic analysis together, by a strategy in which the semantic analysis assumes the dominant role, has implications for language use. If the dominant strategy for comprehension is semantic, it might also influence sentence structure in the normal elderly. Cohen (1979) has shown that the normal elderly have difficulty in using what she terms *modifiers* in a recall task. These modifiers are quantifiers, temporal adjuncts, locative adverbial phrases and adverbial subordinators. Maxim (1982) found that the normal elderly have difficulty in understanding sentences containing adverbial subordinate clauses. Sentences containing such constructions may show a greater propensity to contain errors or to remain unfinished because they increase the grammatical and syntactic complexity of the sentence. Alternatively, they may appear only in small numbers.

Grammatical complexity may also cause a problem related to non-linguistic cognitive decline in the conversational language of the normal elderly. Scholes' (1978) contention that comprehension follows a 'most popular sentence type' strategy could create a situation in conversational language in which more rarely used sentence types were less likely to be used successfully, either because the more rarely used sentence types tend to be more grammatically or semantically complex or because, at points of choice in the sentence (where different syntactic structures are possible), the 'most popular sentence type' strategy reinstates itself, causing the sentence to be abandoned or repaired.

Sentence length is another measure of complexity that has been found in normal elderly groups to decrease in the reminiscence samples of Davis (1979) and to increase in the written language samples cited by Obler et al. (1978), but length does not have an effect on comprehension. Measuring sentence length accurately is not difficult except in the area of subordination and coordination. While subordinate clauses are routinely counted in with the main clause to which they are attached, the relationship between coordinated clauses is an issue of definition. If sentences linked by coordinating conjunctions are considered as separate, any decrease in the number of sentences containing subordinate clauses may cause a drop in mean sentence length. Davis found that her normal elderly group used fewer subordinate clauses than her middle-aged group and that sentence length decreased with increased age. Two points of interest arise from this finding: what part do coordinating conjunctions have in the language of the elderly and, if the use of sentences containing subordinate clauses does decline with age, are there any syntactic structures which compensate for or take the place of the missing subordinate clauses? The reason for suggesting that the use of coordination bears investigation lies in observations by Cohen (1979) and Maxim (1982). When repeating sentences or recalling them, the elderly occasionally replace a subordinator with a simple coordinator. In terms of linguistic processing this is both a simplification and a monitoring failure which might appear in conversational language. However, this failure might remain unnoticed unless the wrong coordinator is used or an utterance appears to be misplaced in a sequence.

The language output of the DAT patient is fluent only in the sense that it is often an unrepaired flow of semantically empty and often anomalous utterances which is given a kind of cohesiveness by the use of prosody. More disfluencies occur in conversational samples of both the normal elderly and the patient with DAT when there is a need to take conversational turns (Hutchinson and Jenson, 1980). When reminiscences or other monologues are allowed, the number of disfluencies may fall. It is necessary, then, to look at the quality of discourse and conversational turn taking so that the extent and variety of these disfluencies can be seen.

The conversational language of the normal elderly has been characterised as having relatively large numbers of disfluencies, which are of several different types. More hesitant interjections and filler phrases occur, which may be a reflection of the changing linguistic system as a whole and the general slowing of psychomotor speed with increasing age. Although such disfluencies occur, they do not necessarily make the language used sound disfluent, rather the opposite. Part of the function of this type of disfluency, whether used by the normal elderly or younger people, is to carry the discourse forward and to mark the fact that the speaker is continuing the turn. These disfluencies also appear in the language of early DAT patients but gradually decrease as deterioration accelerates. It is interesting that, while the normal elderly use more hesitant interjections of the comment phrase type, the DAT patient may develop his or her own idiosyncratic interjection. Williamson and Schwartz (1981) quote one woman as using the phrase *shopping centre* as an interjection. As the disease progresses, the inability to repair may lessen the number of these disfluencies. It could be hypothesised that fillers and interjections are a healthy adaptation to the slowly changing linguistic system, provided that they remain within the normal framework of disfluency types.

Of all the various types of disfluencies, unfinished utterances are of particular interest because they increase with age in the normal elderly population. However, no research has looked closely at the types of unfinished utterances and possible reasons for their uncompleted state, and there is therefore no reason to think that the normal elderly will produce unfinished utterances markedly different from those produced by a younger population. However, the elderly may produce different proportions of types of unfinished utterances from those of a younger population: the normal elderly may produce more unfinished utterances due to lexical accessing problems and syntactic–semantic complexity than the repair type of unfinished utterance found in younger populations. Burke, Worthley and Martin (1988) suggest that this is how the elderly extricate themselves from either lexical-accessing problems or sentences in which the syntactic semantic complexity causes a sentence to be revised or abandoned.

The last area of major importance about which hypotheses can be made is ellipsis. Perhaps because the sparse research available on the normal elderly and DAT populations has been conducted within the domain of psychology, ellipsis has not been investigated. The language produced by people with DAT has been described as elliptical but no attempt has been made to produce evidence for an intact underlying system capable of producing such utterances (Critchley, 1964). Whitaker's (1976) careful study of a possible DAT patient suggests that the grammatical–morphemic system is intact at the most simple levels, but she did not show that her patient was able to produce elliptical utterances, which require both an intact system and deletion rules. The normal elderly will have the same intact core grammatical system and, as they are able to make more volitional use of language, should have little difficulty in producing sentences that have undergone ellipsis, although the contexts in which they produce ellipsis are not known. However, individuals who show difficulty with sentence repair may show a commensurate paucity of ellipsis due to changes in the linguistic monitoring needed with ellipsis.

Summary

Experimental evidence points to some areas of deficit with increasing age, in particular text and sentence processing. One of the crucial topics for further research is the part that processing load and competing functions play in language and cognitive processing. Normal ageing is clearly not a homogeneous phenomenon. There is variation among the elderly population in both the speed and the nature of language changes, and some elderly people exhibit well retained language skills or adaptation to the ageing process.

In Chapters 3–5, the grammatical system of a group of normal elderly people in conversation will be described, including aspects of discourse such as disfluencies and repair which provide additional information on the language processes and adaptations to a changing system.

Chapter 3 The grammatical structure of conversational language in the normal elderly

Introduction

The object of this chapter is to give a grammatical description of language used by the normal healthy elderly. In Chapter 2 we considered what is known about language processing in the elderly population and how the methodology of the studies affects the information to be gained from this area of research. Much of the research reviewed compared the performance of an elderly group and a younger control group on specific language tasks. Such design gives vital information on certain aspects of language under experimental conditions but does not give any feel for how the elderly speak or what processing constraints there may be upon their language production in more naturalistic settings. This chapter sets out to describe how the elderly speak, giving examples of each structure described. More precisely, above-sentence and within-structure and the processing interruptions in the conversational language of elderly people will be described.

There is a need for descriptions of elderly language on a more pragmatic, clinical basis. The clinical use of language samples, produced in conversation, to diagnose different forms of language disorder and to inform therapy for the client is well established, yet clinicians are often left to use their intuitive knowledge of what is normal when making judgements on their clients' language. Below are two categories from the Boston Diagnostic Aphasia Examination (Goodglass and Kaplan, 1983) that reflect the need for the clinician to make such judgements.

1. Minimal discernible speech handicap; patient may have subjective difficulties which are not apparent to the listener.
2. Some obvious loss of fluency in speech or facility of comprehension, without significant limitation on ideas expressed or form of expression.

Such categories make assumptions about the way people speak that are relatively unsupported by any research at a descriptive level. Rating scales are often said to have been based on a normal population but they fail to take into account either human language variation or whether an older population is different from a younger one. In this chapter some of the information about language use by the normal healthy elderly that is needed by clinicians when assessing and developing therapy for elderly people is supplied.

The elderly group

Setting the criteria for choosing the group of elderly people for this study is, in many ways, just as difficult as choosing the linguistic analysis. The notion of a representative cross-section of elderly people in any society is bound by the make-up of that particular society. In most parts of the developed world most people can expect to live to more than 70 years of age. Someone who has already reached their late 60s may well expect to live 15 years or more, depending on familial health and socioeconomic factors. In Europe and North America, the concept of a two-tier elderly society is widely recognised, being divided into the 'young' elderly of up to 75 years and the 'old' elderly of more than 75. A possible criterion for the study might be that the elderly subjects should be living independently in the community but this does not necessarily prevent the inclusion of people with neurological or psychiatric disorders whose language skills would be compromised by their illness. The inclusion of disordered language samples would alter the conclusions about the language of the normal healthy elderly.

Another possibility in selecting the elderly group would be to use only those who are healthy and fit. Such groups have often been used in research on cognitive change with age because the results that they provide are considered to be relatively uncontaminated by the myriad factors reported to be involved in ageing (Jarvik, 1962; Salthouse, 1991). In selecting the group for the study reported here a middle course was taken, the main criteria for inclusion being:

- age over 70 years on the day of interview;
- living independently in the community, without a major part of their care being undertaken by relatives, friends or state agencies;
- no history of neurological or psychiatric disorder (including alcohol or drug abuse);
- English as the first language.

The age range in the sample was 71 – 89, with a mean of just over 78 years for the men and 73–94 years for the women, with a mean of almost 81 years. Table 3.1 gives the comparative figures for age in the study group and the UK elderly population, taken from the National Census (1981).

Table 3.1 Age and sex ratio of sample and the general elderly population in the UK

	Percentage ratio (men:women)
Study sample	
Age range 70–79 years	40:60
80 years and over	32:68
National Census data	
Age range 65–74 years	40:60
75 years and over	30:70

The size of the group to be studied was another important consideration. While it has been suggested that certain aspects of language can be studied using far fewer subjects than others (Labov, 1978), a crucial part of the analysis is the investigation of repair and the types of errors made in naturally produced language samples. For the results of the production error analysis to be valid, a larger group is necessary to allow error patterns to appear and to gain some idea of the frequency of these errors and the structural context in which they are most likely to appear.

It was therefore decided to use a split grouping of elderly people, with 20-minute samples from 20 subjects being fully analysed. Language samples from a further 20 elderly would be used to study those structures that appeared infrequently in the language of the first half of the group and to expand the database for production errors and repairs. The question of whether these subject numbers are great enough to produce a description of elderly language use that can be generalised is not easy to answer but, within the conversational samples of 20 minutes each, a mean of 402 major sentences were used, creating a corpus of over 16 000 sentences. The homogeneity and variation within the language samples are considered in Chapter 5, and how far this description of elderly language can be generalised is discussed there.

Because of the relatively small numbers used, certain objective measures were applied to measure how representative the group was of the elderly population as a whole. The measure most often used in sociolinguistic studies is social class, perhaps more accurately termed socioeconomic grouping. The principal predictor of social class is occupation. In any representative sample of elderly people, the majority are women, and women's social class, if they do not have a job, has traditionally been decided upon by their husband's or father's occupation. Such a classification, although still used, is considered unsatisfactory (Oakley, 1975). Practical difficulties were also encountered in assigning some of the women on this basis. One woman had lost her husband during the First World War; another single woman said that her father had been an ostler, looking after horses for a hotel. The study group was therefore compared with the elderly population as a whole on the following indices:

- proportion of men to women;
- proportion in each 10-year age group from 70 years;
- type of housing;
- marital status;
- cohabitation status;
- contact with social services.

The type of housing in which they were living compared almost exactly with the results of the General Household Survey (1973) for the 70+ age group, with 42.5% living in their own home, 37.5% in local authority housing and 22.5% in private or other rented housing. A few lived in warden-operated accommodation, which allows the elderly person to live independently but to call for help from the warden if necessary. Under the criterion of independent living, the inclusion of this group in the sample might be questioned, but none had been moved to this type of accommodation because they needed care: two of the women required help with their spouses who had had strokes, and the others had been moved from larger local authority houses. None could be differentiated from the rest of the sample on other parameters and they were therefore kept in the group.

Analysing elderly language

The analysis of elderly language described here is based on language samples from 40 normal healthy elderly people, all of whom have English as their first language. Conversational partner and recording environment will obviously have some effect on the amount and style of language produced (Labov, 1978), and to control such factors as much as possible the subjects were recorded in their own homes in conversation with one interviewer who used the same set of question topics for each sample. However, each conversation was allowed to develop within the general topic guidelines.

Choosing a method of linguistic analysis implies a choice of linguistic theory. Such a choice also inevitably means that a selection of the readership will be unfamiliar with that particular analysis or may have well founded reasons for shunning it. The origin of the analysis used here for the conversation samples is a structural description (Quirk et al., 1985) which was later modified so that it could be applied to clinical language samples (Crystal, Fletcher and Garman, 1976, 1989). The clinical application, called the Language Assessment, Remediation and Screening Procedure (LARSP), was developed primarily for use by clinicians working with developmental language disorder. LARSP has since been extensively used in clinical settings to examine the language of children and adults with language disorders (Crystal, 1979). It is an essentially linear description of grammatical structure, based on an adult grammar with an extensive corpus and reference (Quirk et al., 1985). Does this use of a linear description restrict the analysis and any conclusions that we may make about elderly language? There is no doubt that it is not easy to translate this analysis into, for example, a generative description but, if we consider the research discussed in Chapter 2 on comprehension and production of left and right branching embedded clauses by the elderly, then it requires a relatively minor change in analysis to accommodate such structures and to compare the data here with that research.

The analysis allows us to look at the normal distribution of each grammatical structure, concentrating mainly on phrase and clause structures within sentences and the processes of coordination and subordination. Structures are examined in terms of length of each unit and grammatical complexity, with comparisons being made between these two distinct operations. We know relatively little about the incidence of clause structures and sentence types in adult grammatical form and any interactions between them. A 2-year-old child produces grammatical structures that are normally limited in both length and complexity of utterance and child language research suggests that interaction between these two aspects is variable (Crystal, Fletcher and Garman, 1976). Whereas the development of language in children is well documented, we have very little knowledge of the interactions between language processes in adult language: there are descriptions of language structures and explanations of how language is generated but the literature on language use is scarce (Crystal and Davy, 1976; Stubbs, 1983; Milroy, 1987).

LARSP has been modified for use with elderly language samples, mainly by the addition of certain specific complex structures and by extensions to the analysis of language errors and the addition of repair counts. Appendix I and Appendix II give the original LARSP chart (1981) and the modification used for this analysis.

In order that the analysis can be followed relatively easily, the description of each group of structures is preceded by an explanation of the grammatical analysis, and a glossary of terms is included in Appendix III. Further discussion of this method of grammatical analysis and the clinical applications can be found in Crystal, Fletcher and Garman (1981, 1989) and Crystal (1979, 1982). Each group of structures and processes is related to meaning and situational use, with comprehensive examples of the structures found in standard British and American English and in British dialect forms. The original grammar on which LARSP is based (Quirk et al., 1985) can be used for analysis of regional dialect forms but it does not include them. Most of the elderly people in the sample used dialect forms, and a number of sources were used to identify and verify them (Cheshire, 1982; Trudgill, 1983).

Language variation in the elderly

The approximate frequency with which each structure occurs is as important for a general description of the language of the elderly as which structures are used in conversation. The amount of variation in the frequency with which structures are used also needs investigation. The comparison of clause, phrase and grammatical word level development is important in child language because it shows the integration of language processes but the relevance of such findings for adult language is unclear. However, we know from psycholinguistic research that there are constraints on the individual's ability to process certain types of structures. Interactions between sentence length and complexity in language output will increase the overall processing load but the result of this increased load is not known. This aspect of language production therefore becomes of interest in the elderly, particularly as there is evidence that the elderly have difficulty in understanding complex sentence structures and larger chunks of text.

There are other phenomena of conversational language which are also important. Ellipsis, for example, is the process by which redundancy is curtailed in language use. It allows us to leave out words, phrases and clauses that are understood in that particular context. If asked why you are going home, you can reply *because I'm tired,* rather than *I'm going home because I'm tired.* Ellipsis requires a rule-based knowledge of what may and may not be deleted, yet we know very little about its use in normal adult language. The language we produce in everyday life may contain linguistic errors and disfluencies of various types. The literature on these errors and our ability to detect them is extensive but there is little specific research on the elderly and their disfluencies. The ability to monitor language for meaning and make changes, detect errors and correct them is termed repair (Levelt, 1983) but, again, there is very little information on this process among the elderly population. Ellipsis, errors and repair are described in Chapter 4, paying attention to such factors as context, length and grammatical complexity.

What is a sentence?

The analysis used here is based on sentences: that is, sentences are analysed into their constituent structures of clause elements, phrasal structures and word based grammatical information. The next six sections describe how sentences are defined, analysed and used. It is tempting to call the components of any spoken language sample *utterances*, but it is sentences and their internal structures that will be analysed: *utterance* has been used here to describe problem strings of words that cannot be analysed easily. All other sentence-like structures are counted as sentences. A *major sentence* is described as being composed of a main clause and, optionally, any number of subordinate clauses.

The man took his hat off because he was hot /
main clause subordinate clause

We might choose to describe this relationship in a different form, using brackets to define the relationship between the clauses, with one clause being embedded in another:

(The man took his hat off (because he was hot))

This definition of major sentences deliberately excludes clauses joined by coordination being considered as one sentence because of the difficulty in deciding how to differentiate between types of coordination. The decision on sentence boundaries is made using a hierarchy of six criteria. If the first criterion does not resolve the issue of sentence boundary, the next criterion is considered and this process continues until the boundary is defined. Using such a method approximately 98% of all the sentences in the data were found to have boundaries that could be defined.

- A full major or elliptical sentence has a main clause and optionally one or more subordinate clauses (1).

1. and she wouldn't believe me when I said how old I was / (Mrs S)
main clause
subordinate clause 1
subordinate clause 2

- Clauses that are connected by coordination and with a coordinator are considered to be separate sentences (2).

2. they'd get one/ *and* put him in a tent for bait / (Mrs C)
coordinator
Sentence 1 Sentence 2

The inclusion of a coordinator in this part of the definition is made so that clauses, joined by coordination but with no coordinator, can be considered as one sentence (3).

3. Mrs T, explaining the snooker room rules in her home:

we give the room up to men / you see / to play /
comment clause
main clause
subordinate clause

The only exception to this rule is made when subordinate clauses within a sentence are coordinated with a coordinator.

- A sentence which is repaired within the first clause element is considered to be one sentence, whatever the reason for repair (4).

4. *I . they* used to ring up sometimes to know if you're in / (Mr H)

- A sentence that is repaired after the first clause element is considered one sentence if the repair is one of grammatical structure only but it is considered two sentences if there has been a change of meaning (5).

5. but we're only trying to say what you've got to . / you can't get dressed yourself completely / (Mr R)

- Any sentence boundary that requires further clarification is analysed using prosodic criteria (6).

6. Kenya and all that. all around that part of the world / (Mr H)

The phrase *all that* could be a stereotyped utterance with the following phrase being a completely separate comment. The level tone on *all that* and increased speed of utterance on *all around* (not shown in the transcription above) suggest that a repair has occurred. The use of prosody is obviously helpful in isolating parenthetic sentences in the data (7).

7. then I went into the um . / the um / .
its a long time ago now / .
parenthetic sentence
those for the people in charge / (Mr R)

- Any other sentences remaining were analysed in terms of their contexts.If their immediate neighbour sentences could be defined, the resulting structure between the two defined sentences was considered to be a separate sentence (8).

8. and I'd say well I'm going fishing / or I'm doing this
sentence sentence
but now I don't suppose we . / it bin about one day / has it
neighbour defined sentence sentence
in time . of all the time / (Mr R)

The 2% of sentences that could not be resolved without reference to their contexts were almost exclusively sentences which had been abandoned or repaired (see Chapter 4, pp. 102, 111).

Sentence length: word measures

Sentence length measures have often been used in child language research and occasionally in comparison between the normal elderly and those with some form of dementia. Such measures are useful as an illustration of change brought about by disease. In this chapter we are more interested in the range of mean sentence lengths among elderly subjects in the study as a measure of variation in normal language production, rather than in establishing mean norms.

Two measures of sentence length have been used in the analysis:

- Mean sentence length (MSL) is defined as the mean number of words in a sentence when both major and minor sentences were taken into account.
- The mean number of words per sentence in major sentences only (MSL major sentences) was also counted. Major sentences include all elliptical and full major sentences. Incomplete/abandoned sentences and ambiguous sentences are also counted within this category.

This second count makes the very important division between usually short minor sentences and the longer major sentences. It might then be argued that the second definition of sentence length is also faulty because it combines both elliptical and full major sentences, which, by the inclusion of usually shorter elliptical major sentences, again might distort the perception of sentence length. The reasons for including elliptical major sentences are: (1) that these elliptical sentences are major sentences in grammatical terms and, given a choice of categorising them as either major or minor sentences, they can be defined only as major sentences; (2) because they are major sentences, a sentence length measure of only full major sentences would be a distortion of the general description, and it is exactly that kind of general descriptive statement which we want to make in this chapter; (3) the relatively small number of elliptical sentences in the data does not make any major overall difference to the mean number of words per sentence. Approximately 20% of all major sentences in this language sample are elliptical and, of all elliptical sentences, just under half are two or more clause elements in length. Elliptical sentences are discussed on pp. 70–72.

A wide range of sentences is produced in each 20-minute sample (from 308 to 749). Just two factors are usually responsible for the variation in the number of sentences produced. Because the range for major sentences was 8.3 words in length at its upper end, the number of sentences with 10 or more words per data sample was counted. On average just over 15% of sentences in each sample had 10 or more words and the mean number of these sentences produced by men and women in the sample did not differ significantly, although there was a slight difference in mean: men produced an average of just under 2% more long sentences than women. However, the number of 10+ word sentences and the MSL in each data sample showed some relationships, the data samples with larger MSLs generally having more 10+ word sentences (1, 2). The longest sentence in the data analysed was 36 words.

1. well I said . if you're going to modernize Brenda's I said / .
   when its finished I said / couldn't I move in there? /
   (Miss B)
2. mind you. going back about ten or fifteen years /
   when she was busy I used to very often go and do a lot of
   hard work / . you know . with tacking and all that kind of thing
   for her / (Mrs S)

The other factor that affects the number of sentences produced in each sample is speech rate, which varies considerably among samples but which is not discussed here. Speech rate is the dominant factor influencing the amount of language produced in the samples, and the number of long major sentences in each sample is the major secondary factor. Several other factors, such as the mean number of sentences per turn, were investigated for their possible influence on the number of sentences produced. Increased turn-taking might, for example, detract from the time available for producing sentences, and the numbers of minor sentences (including comment phrases) might limit the time available to produce major sentences but neither of these affected the total number of sentences produced. The other major factor in the number of sentences produced is the relative amount of subordination and coordination occurring in each data sample.

The MSL for major sentences only is 5.8 for both men and women, and MSL (all sentences) is 5.1 for both sexes. Both measures of MSL have almost the same range, although that of major sentences only is larger by approximately one word. In both ranges there is a large cluster of measures around the MSL, which represents approximately 80% of the data samples (in spite of similar ranges of 3.9–6.7 for all sentences and 4.3–8.3 for major sentences only). Sentence length measures and total number of sentences for each individual sample are given in Appendix V.

Perhaps a more reliable indicator of the homogeneity of the sample is the standard deviation range for the MSL of all sentences and for the MSL of major sentences only, which include 70% of the samples. Although there is homogeneity in length measures throughout the data samples there is a distortion in thinking of 5.8 word major sentences as being typical because they represent mean sentence length. The distribution of MSL is rather flat in the middle range of four to six words, with a peak at two-word sentences and ten or more-word sentences.

Examples are given below of typical conversations, showing turn-taking and sentence length (in numbers of words) in a monologue (3, Miss B; 4, Mrs S).

3. A. now I tell you what we do as regards the wool /	11 words
we go to rummage sales /	5 words
B. yes /	
A. and we unpick and wash	5 words
B. yes	
A. and knit it up again /	5 words
B. oh that's a good idea /	5 words
A. yeah /	1 words
that's what we do now /	6 words
would you like a cup of tea? /	7 words
4. and the doctor got us these. this flat for us then /	11 words
we'd only bin here /	5 words
we came here in the March /	6 words
my husband died in the May /	6 words
and he was rushed into hospital /	6 words
so I've been living on my own since see /	10 words
but I bin. I bin staying with me daughter and me son at Caversham but /	13 words

Mean number of sentences per turn

Table 3.2 shows the mean number of sentences per turn (MNSPT) for the whole data sample, as well as for men and women separately.

Table 3.2 Means and ranges for the number of sentences per turn

	Range	*Mean*
Women	3.8–37.4	9.6 (7.1)*
Men	3.1–11.3	7.7
Total	3.1–37.4	8.8 (7.3)*

*Values in parentheses are the means if one exceptional case of 37.4 sentences per turn is excluded.

The MNSPT was counted to check the homogeneity of the conversations in turn-taking, as a measure of the success of the inteviewer in regulating the type of output of the people interviewed. It was argued that, if roughly the same topics were introduced into each inteview at the same time then, even allowing for human invention, the language samples were more likely to be homogeneous. This conversational strategy worked for all the interviews except one which, due to the randomised system used in assigning data samples, fell into the wholly analysed group. In this one interview the conversational strategy did not work as planned – which resulted in an astonishing 37.4 mean number of sentences per turn.

Apart from this one case, there is remarkable homogeneity in the range and mean of sentences per turn, from just over three to just over 12 sentences, but the range is quite evenly spread with a peak around the mean and a positive skew towards higher MNSPT.

Sentence measures summary

In the sample of fully analysed interviews, the MSL for major sentences is 5.8 words, with the greatest portion of major sentences being 5–7 words in length. Men and women did not differ for either the MSL of all sentences or the MSL for major sentences only, but men have a narrower range of variability in both measures of MSL than women. The number of sentences that can be produced in a 20-minute interview was very variable: women again have a wider range but, on average, men produce fewer sentences than women as well as having a much narrower range. The mean number of major sentences per interview was 74 fewer for men than for women. To put this another way, men produced 18% fewer sentences than women in the same time, though their MSLs were almost the same. Men and women produced a similar range of mean number of sentences per turn. Men and women also had similar means for number of sentences per turn, apart from the one exception of 37.4. (The profile of this woman is discussed in Chapter 5.)

Sentence types and categories

Sentences are divided into major and minor sentence types. Major sentences are divided into:

- Functions:
  - statements
  - commands
  - exclamations
  - comment clauses
  - tag questions
- Sentence types:
  - full
  - response ellipsis
  - self-generated ellipsis

- Disfluencies
    - uncompleted and abandoned
    - repaired
    - grammatical errors
    - ambiguous or semantic errors

Minor sentences are divided into:

- Social sentences such as *yes* or *hello*
- Stereotyped sentences such as *good on you*

The comparative percentages of major and minor sentences are relevant because a large proportion of stereotyped minor sentences in a data sample might lead to doubt about the efficient cerebral functioning of the individual. Major sentences are categorised, according to the function of the sentence, into statements, questions, commands and exclamations. As quasi-sentence functions, comment clauses and tag questions are also considered. Major sentences are further subdivided into full and elliptical major sentences. Elliptical sentences are also divided into those ellipses that occur as a response to the interviewer's last utterance and those that are self-generated within the person's own monologue. Lastly, a category of sentences containing disfluencies was set up to measure the number of uncompleted and abandoned sentences, repaired sentences, sentences containing semantic or grammatical ambiguities and sentences containing grammatical errors.

Major and minor sentences

On average, major sentences make up 85.5% and minor sentences 14.5% of all sentences. Major sentences always make up the greater proportion of sentences in the interview samples, as might be expected in an interview where one person is contributing approximately eight sentences to the interviewer's one intervention. Of the 85% of major sentences, over 80% of the interview sample was within 5% of this average. When the results of the sentence function categories were analysed, a similar picture emerged, with statements being the largest category. The mean percentage of exclamations, questions and commands was under 5% of the total number of major sentences, making statements overwhelmingly the largest major sentence category. Questions, with a mean of 11 per data sample, were generally used more than commands (with a mean of just over two), whereas exclamations appeared infrequently and were absent from many of the data samples. Again, the small number of such sentence types is probably due to the interview format. In everyday life the proportion of sentence types produced would vary according to context and conversational style.

Apart from those sentence types already mentioned here, two structures appear quite frequently in the data and have been counted separately. The first is the tag question (1), which, although the mean for its use is lower than for the full question form, is used more than the full question when individual data samples are compared. Ten people used the tag more often than the full question form, eight reversed this order, and two used both forms equally. A high correlation between tag questions and sex means that women are the principal users of such question forms.

1. have you heard one of these baby dolls cry? /
   she's got one and it's just like a baby / isn't it? / (Mrs D)

Tag questions are analysed fully because their form is productive. However, this is not the case with the second structure, the comment clause, which occurs frequently (2, 3). On the LARSP chart, because they develop later in child language, comment clauses are counted separately from minor sentences. As stereotyped non-productive structures that have little scope for change, there is a strong argument for including them in the minor sentence category.

2. but next Monday / *you see* / I have to go to the C.W.S
   printing works over at Elgar works /. where I used
   to work . / cos I was a bookbinder see / (Miss B)
3. I've had a lot of nice friends in my life *you know* / (Miss B)

If minor sentences and comment clauses are added together, the ratio of minor to major sentences changes considerably, minor sentences being over 25% of the total number of sentences produced, as opposed to under 15% of the total number of sentences when comment clauses are counted as part of the major sentence to which they are attached by coordination. This form of coordination can be described as covert, i.e. there is no overt coordinating conjunction such as *and* or *but*. The coordination is signalled by the intonational contour which binds sentence and comment clause together.

Clause elements

Clause element functions

Within the LARSP analysis, clause elements are parts of a sentence or an utterance which function in a particular way. For example, a noun phrase *my elder daughter* can function as a subject (S), object (O) or complement (C) clause element, depending on where the noun phrase occurs in the structure (1, 2, 3).

1. *my elder daughter* lives in Ohio /
   S
2. he married *my elder daughter* /
   O
3. Mary is *my elder daughter* /
   C

Two other types of clause elements are identified by LARSP: the verb clause element (V) and adverbial clause element (A) (4, 5).

4. he *has been running* /
   V
5. I got a few plants *out there* /
   A

As we discuss clause elements and phrasal structure, it will become clear that the verb clause element is probably the most easy to identify while subject, object, complement and adverbial clause elements can be realised by a single word, a phrase or a subordinate clause, and there may be more than one adverbial clause element in any sequence (6).

6. I live *near my daughter in a flat* /
   A A

Clause elements describe how a component of a sentence functions but do not necessarily tell us about the type of structure or word class. Obviously, the verb clause element contains a verb phrase but in (7) the adverbial clause element is realised by a noun phrase rather than prepositional phrases as in (6).

7. I can't sleep *all the time* /
   A

We can say that a particular structure functions as a particular type of clause element but clause elements can be realised by a number of different structures. As we look at clause element structures, examples will be given of these varying realisations.

Clause element measures

Mean sentence length in the elderly is of some use when trying to produce a general picture of the language samples but clause (and phrase length) measures show less variability than mean sentence length and are therefore better descriptors. In clause length measures, the mean represents the largest group of structures. Clause length has been counted simply by using the number of clause elements within each clause.

Table 3.3 gives the five clauses and their constituent clause elements that together make up almost 75% of all clauses produced by the elderly people in conversation. All these clauses have very stable distributions and show no change in variation either with increasing age or between men and women.

Table 3.3 Clauses that constitute 75% of clauses produced by the subjects in the study

Clause elements	*Percentage of clauses produced*
SVC/O	25.5
SV	13.9
SVA	13.6
SVC/OA	12.8
SVAA	7.8

In most instances the S, V, C and O clause elements appear in the order shown in Table 3.3 but the adverbial clause elements can appear in any position in the sequence. Clause elements can, of course, be moved to provide emphasis and this type of change has been logged separately. Although the A clause element can appear in any position in clause structure, in the elderly language samples it most often appears as a single A initially, or more frequently as one or more As at the end of an SVC/O structure (8, 9).

8. now Nancy . *when you leaves work* you must join the club /
   A S V O
   (Miss F)

9. my mother came *here in the First World War*
   S V A A
   when my father joined the army / (Miss F)
   A
   S V O

Sentence (9) also shows how the clause elements in each sentence are counted. The main clause is SVAAA, the final adverbial clause element being an adverbial subordinate clause which is then analysed into its constituent clause elements of SVO. As Table 3.4 shows, almost every possible combination of clause elements occurs in the language samples but some are much more frequent than others, the most frequent being SVC/O with a mean of 108.5 per 100 sentences. The fact that SVC/O has a mean greater than 100 shows that the elderly use subordinate clauses. If all the clauses are added together, it is apparent that the elderly must use subordinate clauses extensively in their conversational language (see pp. 97–102).

Some of the clauses in Table 3.4 appear to violate the rules of grammatical structure but most of such clauses will be elliptical sentences. SCA, for example, appeared only once in the language samples and as an elliptical sentence.

Table 3.4 Clause element means per 100 sentences

One-element clauses		*Four-element clauses*	
N	13.9	SVCO/A	54.1
A	10.5	SVAA	32.9
V	6	SVOO	2.8
Other	8.8	VOAA	–1
		SVOC	–1
Two-element clauses		*Five-element clauses*	
SV	58.5	SVOAA	11.6
VC/O	14.8	SVOOA	1.5
SC/O	1.4	SVOCA	–1
AX*	16.9	VOAAA	–1
		SVAAA	–1
Three-element clauses		*Six-element clauses*	
SVC/O	108.5	SVOAAA	–1
VC/OA	5.8	SVOOAA	–1
SVA	57.4	SVAAAA	–1
AAX	1.7	SVOOAX	–1
VOO	1	*Seven-element clauses*	
VOX	–1†	SVAAAAA	–1
VAA	–1	SVOAAAA	–1
SOA	–1		
AAA	–1		
SCA	–1		
VOC	–1		
OCA	–1		

* X denotes any clause element. † –1 = mean of less than one per data sample.

Elliptical sentences

Ellipsis is the process by which constituent structures in a sentence can remain unsaid but are understood. The implication is that the person is able to produce the full sentence but has not done so because, usually, to do so would increase redundancy. In child language and in acquired language disorders such as aphasia, we must be careful when describing a sentence as having undergone ellipsis because the person may not be able to produce that particular structure or have an underlying representation of that sentence structure. In adult language, the assumption is that the underlying representation is present but has not been used.

For the grammatical analysis, ellipsis at sentence level is categorised into two broad groups:

- those elliptical sentences which have been produced as the first major sentence directly after the interviewer has spoken, as a response to the interviewer's language output;
- those elliptical sentences which are produced at any other time in the subject's monologue as a response to the subject's own language output.

On average, each data sample produced 68.6 elliptical sentences and 17% of all major sentences were elliptical. If we consider the mean number of sentences per turn to be just over eight, it would seem logical that most of these elliptical sentences would be produced in the 20% of sentences immediately preceding the interviewer's turn, but this is not the case. The number of self-generated ellipses (81.3%) is much greater than the number of discourse response generated ellipses (18.7%).

Less than 20% of all elliptical sentences are produced in response to the interviewer, i.e. only approximately one in every five conversational turns produces an elliptical response immediately after it. Ellipsis, then, is being used by elderly people predominantly as a strategy to limit redundancy in their own conversational monologues (1, 2).

1. every morning. I go across / ?
   get my newspapers / E
   I get my. I got some friends here in the flats here /
   I get their newspapers at the same time / ?
   pop it through their door E
   come back here / – – E
   have me breakfast / E
   clear. clear the place up / E
   I got all this to do you see /
   (Mr B)

2. he said Nancy. you have a cyst in your stomach /
   hospital at once/ E
   and I was in there in oh. within twelve day/ –
   and it was wonderful /
   (Miss B)

In example (1) two sentences look like ellipsis but are not necessarily, and they have not been counted as ellipsis in the analysis. In the first sentence, the possible ellipsis is not recoverable because it is the first sentence of a new topic and the context therefore does not clarify the missing elements. In the second doubtful sentence it is not necessarily ellipsis but only anaphoric reference, i.e. reference which points back to a previous item. In this example, *at the same time* could be said to refer back to *every morning I go across / get my newspapers* but equally it could be argued that *I get their newspapers at the same time* is an elliptical form of the underlying full form *I get their newspapers at the same time as I get mine*.

By far the most numerous examples of ellipsis are the one-clause element sentences, of which about 20% are response generated and 80% self-generated sentences. This pattern of relative percentages is repeated for all the clause element categories (see Table 3.5).

Table 3.5 Clause elements and ellipsis

	Clause element			
	1	*2*	*3*	*4 /4+*
Mean percentage of response ellipsis	23.4	15.7	15.8	11.1
Mean percentage of self-generated ellipsis	76.6	84.3	84.2	88.9

Conversely, the least numerous category is response elliptical sentences with four or more clause elements, which are entirely absent in the majority of data samples.

Clauses with one element

The majority of clauses with one element in the samples are elliptical, with a smaller percentage being subordinate clauses. In adult language it is usually less difficult to assign a structure to a one-element clause category than it would be in a child's developing language where the full structure may not yet have developed. If intonation patterns do not clarify the analysis, the context will usually provide the speaker's intention. Of approximately 420 clause element sequences per sample, just under 10% are one-element clauses.

Of these, 8% can easily be categorised into type of clause element, and 2% are ambiguous. In the analysis, the one-element clauses were divided into *V*, *A*, *N* and *Other* categories (see Table 3.4). The N category contains all counts of possible S, C or O clause elements while Other contains any element that cannot be categorised more specifically. In the S, C and O categories, instances occur in the data where the elliptical form is not directly recoverable and therefore it seemed sensible for the purpose of this analysis to have an umbrella N category rather than splitting it into S, C, O and Other.

The V category occurs in two particular contexts. It occurs as an elliptical one-element clauses (1) and as a form of subordinate clause, most commonly in a post-modifying clause (2).

1. I keep well / and I eat . and *drink* / (Mrs S)
2. there's nothing *wants doing* / (Mrs L)

A very small number of the Other category of one-element clauses are also possibly verbs but cannot be added to the category with any certainty. The ambiguity lies between N and V, usually due to the use of a participle form in an ambiguous context (3).

3. there's a long list I think / . *waiting* / (Mrs T)

The A category appears in the usual range and forms expected in elliptical adverbial usage, namely adverb, preposition or noun phrase and adverbial subordinate clauses (4, 5, 6).

4. A: where did she learn that? /
   B: *in Reading* / (Mrs S)

5. A: does your budgie talk? /
   B: *not a lot* / no / (Mrs S)

6 A: do you see your daughter quite often? /
   B: oh yes / *'cause she doesn't live very far* you see / (Mrs S)

Other instances of one-element clause ellipsis occurred, which, although analysed as ellipsis, would not be acceptable when expanded directly into a full sentence (8).

8. A: what do you have to be careful not to eat? /
   B: oh anything very heavy or solids /
   not an awful lot of meal / (Mrs S)

The N category is made up partly of S, C and O clause elements, which most commonly occur in an elliptical form not directly recoverable, and therefore these one-element clauses are difficult to categorise (9).

9. but anyway . I went out to work /
   housework / (Mrs S)

Over 86% of one-element clauses are elliptical, suggesting that there is little scope for them in full sentence structure. As in most elliptical structures, the mean for response ellipsis is smaller (7.8) than that for monologue ellipsis (28.6). Of the total number of clause element sequences, the non-elliptical one-element clauses account for only 1.3%. The non-elliptical one-element clauses are almost always in the V category, which accounts for 1.4% of the total element clauses. The V category is therefore almost totally composed of subordinate clauses.

Clauses with two elements

Whereas the one-element clauses are largely elliptical sentences, clauses with two elements occur far more frequently within completed sentence structure. The mean for full two-element clauses is 70.15 per data sample compared with a mean of 21.5 for elliptical two-element clauses.

The most frequently occurring two-element clauses is SV, with a mean of 58.5, which accounts for 63.8% of all two-element clauses. SV often occurs in the form of reported speech, as in *X said*. This particular SV clause occurs often in the data, attached by intonation and used within clauses (1), coordinated between preceding and following utterances (2) and between clauses (3).

1. and you don't pay the money down like you did
   because / *I said* / well if I sold the house like
   I could put a little more down / (Mrs R)

2. *I said* you tell me *I said* / I only moved in here
   yesterday / (Mrs L)

3. and if you wanted to go out. up the Meadway /
   he said / you can go across the park / (Mrs L)

It is used productively in that it is used as part of longer clauses, as in example (2) where it appears in an SVO sequence at first and then in an SV form, coordinated at the end of an SVO clause. The falling stress, noted on the tape recording, at the end of the intonation pattern, isolates it from the next utterance. SV does occur in other forms, of course: as a full sentence structure (4); as a subordinate clause structure (5); and as an elliptical structure (6).

4. well. *my mother died* / (Mrs L)

5. wherever *we go* we're going to be isolated / (Mrs L)

6. he said we've got no notification /
   oh I said / don't talk so stupid /
   of course *you have* / (Mrs L)

VO, VC and AX element clauses also appear as main clause structure, although obviously not as full sentence structure in statement form. They appear as full sentence structure in the form of commands and questions in small numbers throughout the data as subordinate clauses and as elliptical sentences. As subordinate clauses, VA, VO and VC occur most frequently in noun–phrase post-modifying clauses (7, 8). The VC example (9) was found in a rare sentential relative clause (see pp. 101–102).

7. and I had four and five doctors *come to me* / (Mrs L)
   V A

8. but of course as you get older you get . have all
   these things er . *help you* / (Mrs L)
   V O

9. I'm thinking ahead all the time and I'm
getting all agitated which *is the trouble* / (Mrs R)
V C

The AX category is made up of VA elliptical sentences and subordinate clause VA sequences largely, with smaller numbers of AC/O and AA elliptical sentences as in the examples below (10, 11).

10. A: how old are you? /
B: *seventy three this January* / (Mrs L)
C A

11. A: have you been in these flats long? /
B: *four years this September* / (Mrs L)
A A

The smallest category in two-element clauses is also perhaps the most puzzling and in the grammatical analysis created an analytical problem. SC/O element clauses are rare, with a mean of only 1.4 per data sample, and nine out of 20 of the fully analysed data samples contain these sequences. They almost always occurred in the same form of subject subordinate clause plus a complement subordinate clause with the copular omitted (12, 13).

12. but *what I mean . when I had a lot of them inside*
S C

I didn't trouble about this thing / (Mr S)

13. *what I think . Mrs Thatcher should go* / (Mr L)
S C

Because this copular deletion occurred regularly, though in very small numbers, it was thought that it might be part of the Reading dialect, although it is not mentioned in the literature (Cheshire, 1982). The small pause that occurred in many examples of SC in the place of the copular showed an understanding that there was a grammatical slot which was not being filled and for this reason this clause was not considered an error.

Although the majority of two-element clauses are part of full sentence structure rather than elliptical sentences, two-element clauses are still peripheral in the sense that they do not form a major part of full sentence structure. SV is often found in a semi-stereotyped or 'code' form and used at times like a comment clause (*I said, she says*) although its productivity sets it apart from comment clauses and stereotyped sentences. Other two-element clauses are found only in subordinate clause structure or as elliptical sentences. Although the comparative percentage of elliptical to full two-element clauses is 23.5% to 68.5%, elliptical two-element clauses make up approximately one-third of all elliptical sentences. Two-element clauses will therefore frequently be found as the main or only clause in elliptical sentences but are much less prominent in main clauses as part of full sentence structure.

Clauses with three elements

With three-element clauses, the structure of full sentences becomes more apparent. They represent 40.9% of all element clauses, the largest category in the analysis. Of the total number of three-element clauses, only 5.1% are elliptical sentences; all others occur in full sentence structure, in both main clause and subordinate clause forms. Not only do three-element clauses represent the largest category of element clauses but in each data sample these clauses comprise a stable percentage of all clauses.

The most prolific three-element clause is SVC/O (61.6%), with SVO occurring twice as often as SVC. SVC/O occurs commonly as a main clause (1, 2), as a main clause with a subordinate clause (3, 4, 5) and as a subordinate clause (3, 5).

1. Well *it do look nice* / he said / (Mrs L)
   S V C

2. *You want to have a little laugh* / (Mrs L)
   S V O

3. *I'm not going to say I might not have it* / (Mrs L)
   S V O
   S V O

4. *There's nothing wants doing* / (Mrs L)
   S V C
   V O

5. *I have been told that its very nicely decorated*/ (Mrs L)
   S V O
   SV C

SVC/O occurs very rarely with a subject subordinate clause but the elderly often use a noun–phrase post-modifying clause in the subject clause element (6).

6. *and Mrs um. er Williams who is living with me .*
   staying with me now for company she belongs to the club /
   (Mrs R)

The second largest category of three-element clauses is SVA, accounting for 32.6% of three-element clauses and 13.7% of all clauses.

Again this clause is a common main clause (7, 8) and also occurs with an adverbial subordinate clause, usually in final position (9).

7\. *I can't sleep all the time /* (Mrs R)
S V A

8\. *well . she had to go to work /* (Mrs R)
S V A

9\. *and they kept on about when they were going to move us /* (Mrs R)
S V A

Although A is a clause element which can move into any position within an SVA sequence, it occurs less frequently in first position (10). Here A is a subordinate clause.

10\. and *when my sister and that died they wouldn't come /* (Mrs R)
A S V

It might seem an obvious point, but SVA sequences without a subordinate clause are short, while SVA and SVC/O sequences with a subordinate clause are almost twice the length (11, 12).

11\. *Butlins have taken over some of Ranks /* (Mr W)
S V O

12\. *it was Danes and Picts who used to fight each other over here /*
S V C
V O A
(Mr H)

The most frequently occurring of the minor forms of three-element clauses are VCA and VOA which have a mean of 5.8 (13, 14, 15, 16). The constraints on their occurrence might be said to be frequency or stylistic constraints (i.e. these forms can occur in a large enough or stylistically 'friendly' sample).

13\. all they done was *pump you with pills /* (Mrs L)
S V C
V O A

14\. oh yes / well as a matter of fact I just run out there *to*
S A V A
have a little look at it / you know / (Mrs R)
A
V O A

15\. *and be just so at the table /* (Mrs S)
V C A

16. *keep you on your toes* / don't they? / (Mrs D)
V O A

Of the remaining minor three-element clauses, only AAX (17, 18, 19) and VOO (20, 21) occur with any frequency. Other three-element clauses occurred only once or twice in the whole study (22).

17. we were earning four pound a week then /
all day from eight to five / (Mrs D)
A A A

18. I sometimes wishes I could walk out the
house and *live near my daughter in a flat* / (Mrs M)
V A A

19. A: do you know the neighbours on both sides? /
B: yes / *not these very well since they've not been here very*
O A A
long / see / (Mrs M)

20. *showed us the post office and the paper shop* / (Mrs L)
V O O

21. and then we'd say well *give us the officer's name* / (Mr R)
V O O

22. and *when they came a bit er . slack what they done they said*
A S C
to me you'll have to go on hygiene / (Mr B)

Of the 20 fully analysed data samples, eight were found to have a restricted three-element clause list of SVC/O, SVA, VC/OA and VOO only, with no other three-element clauses in them. Three-element clauses are obviously useful structures in conversational language in the sense that they are used frequently and are readily combined with subordination processes to produce complex sentences.

Clauses with four elements

Clauses with four elements make up 21.7% of all element clauses and, like three-element clauses, they occur as full sentence structure and subordinate clause structure much more frequently than as elliptical sentences. There are fewer variations in four-element clause structure than in three-element clauses: they are more similar to two-element clauses in the number of forms in which they occur, although four-element clauses are almost all full structures whereas two-element clauses have a larger percentage of elliptical sentences. Table 3.6 shows the range of four-element clauses found in the elderly language samples.

Table 3.6 Means and ranges for four-element clauses

	Mean	*Range*	*Data samples*	*Percentage of all four-element clauses*	*Percentage of all clauses*
SVC/OA	54.1	36–83	20	59.5	13
SVAA	32.9	21–60	20	36.1	7.9
SVOO	2.8	0–9	16	3.1	–1
SVOC	–1	0–2	5	–1	–1
VAAA	–1	0–1	3	–1	–1
VOAA	–1	0–1	1	–1	–1
VOOA	–1	0–1	1	–1	–1

There are seven combinations of four-element clauses, the largest being SVC/OA which accounts for 59.5% of all four-element clauses and appears both as a main clause (1) and as a subordinate clause (2).

1. *I got a few plants out there /* (Mr W)
S V O A

2. but I don't know now because I've well
I don't. *I haven't got the patience perhaps /* (Mrs R)
S V O A

Apart from the V clause element, each clause element in SVC/OA appears as a subordinate clause (3, 4, 5) within the language samples. This combination of four-element clause with one or more clause elements being a subordinate clause shows that the elderly are able to produce complex grammatical structures in their conversation and is an important pointer to the intact language skills of the elderly population. Although subject subordinate clauses are rare in four-element clauses, complement, object and adverbial clause element subordinate clauses are quite common.

3. *what I do though is study up . learning song words /* (Mr B)
S A V C
subordinate clause

4. *oh it won't be long before you're up here* /
S V C
Stage 1V complement subordinate clause

because two or three are going out and all that business / (Mrs R)
A
adverbial subordinate clause

5. I don't know quite *who he's working for* / (Mr W)
S V A O
object subordinate clause

The second largest category in four-element clauses is SVAA (36.1%). Examples (6), (7), (8) and (9) show some of the variations in SVAA. SVAA clauses have potential for change in the order of the clause element sequence in statements but much more constrained potential for order change in question and command sentence types.

6. well she. *eventually she went to hospital* / (Mr W)
A S V A

7. oh he said *Vi's coming home today* / he said / (Mr W)
S V A A

8. then *I walk down to the shops / to do a little bit of shopping* / (Mrs L)
S V A A

9. *she just gets on with it* / (Mrs D)
S A V A

The last four-element clause that occurs with any regularity is SVOO (10, 11). This is found in 16 of the 20 fully analysed samples, with the greatest frequency of usage being nine in one data sample. Both direct and indirect objects in this sequence can take the form of subordinate clauses but in the data samples no indirect object subordinate clauses could be found. However, SVOO itself was found as a subordinate clause.

10. *people tell me it could be arthritis set in after the fall* / (Mrs S)
S V O O
direct object subordinate clause

11. and then *I don't think he could have told you what he had seen* /
clause 1 S V O
clause 2 S V O O
clause 3 S V
(Mrs S)

Four other four-element clauses are found infrequently in the data: SVOC, VAAA, VOAA, VOOA. SVOC appears as full sentence structures, and the last three are usually subordinate clauses or elliptical sentences. Four-element clauses occur quite frequently in the data, largely as the main clause in full sentence structure or as subordinate clauses, but rarely as elliptical sentences. As with three-element clauses, when four-element clauses appear in ellipsis, it is usually in-monologue ellipsis where they occur with a frequency of 1.7 per data sample (compared with 0.2 per data sample for response ellipsis). The infrequency with which these elliptical sentences are found is partly a facet of the analysis. If, for example, a *why* question is asked then the full response often contains a *because* subordinate clause. But if the response is in the form of a *because* subordinate clause, signalled by the subordinator, it is analysed as an A clause element and is recorded on the chart as a one-element clause elliptical sentence (12). If the subordinator is omitted then the utterance is analysed as full sentence structure because we cannot assume a subordinate clause without evidence for it (13).

12. A: why did he do it? /
    B: because he was suddenly frightened /
    A
    subordinator S V A C

13. B: he was suddenly frightened /
    S V A C

Four-element clauses have a more restricted range of element combinations than three-element clauses, but are found in all data samples. Of the range of four-element clauses, SVC/OA and SVAA occur in all the data samples and together make up just over 20% of all clauses.

Clauses with five or more elements

Clauses with five or more elements occur infrequently but consistently throughout the corpus. Adding together five, six and seven-element clauses, this group has a frequency of 23.4 per data sample and comprises 5.6% of all clauses. Seven-element clauses are the longest clauses found in the data. There are no elliptical sentences at all in this group and only one instance of a subordinate clause in VOAAA. The remaining clauses with five or more elements are main clause sequences. The frequency with which these are found in the data is often small: of the 11 categories, only four have means of over one per data sample and three of these are five-element clauses. SVOAA has the biggest mean and is found in all 20 data samples (1). It often contains one or more subordinate clauses, most commonly of an adverbial type (2).

1. yes / *down there all the. all the water from Dunsford and*
   A O
   Dunsford Abbots just . they used to have to fetch from a spring
   S V
   in the middle of the village / (Mr W)
   A

2. then *he took me round to Circuit Lane /*
   S V O A
   to show me where the doctor's surgery was / (Mrs L)
   A
   subordinate clause
   subordinate clause

The second and most frequent of this group is SVAAA, which is found in all data samples but one. Again, it occurs as main clause structure only and often contains an adverbial subordinate clause (3, 4).

3. well anyway / *if you go up the Gloucester Road from Cirencester*
   A
   subordinate clause
   it's down at the bottom on the left hand side / (Mr W)
   SV A A

4. but um *I did go down to him* / when was it? / *last Monday*
   S V A A
   cos my legs were so bad / (Mrs M)
   A
   subordinate clause

The position of the adverbial clause element is predominantly to the right of S and V, but in (1) the first A clause, a subordinate clause, is to the left. In Chapter 2 we considered the evidence for a deficit in processing left-branching subordinate clauses in the normal healthy elderly. Here is an example of the production of such a structure. Very rarely does an A clause element come between S and V and then it is usually an adverb. Both (3) and (4) illustrate one of the many problems in analysis of more complex language, especially conversational language. Whereas *down* usually functions as a preposition or a verb particle, in (3) its use in *down at the bottom* is bordering on that of an intensifier, emphasising the phrase. The intonation pattern on the tape firmly links *down* and *at*. In (4) *down* might be considered a particle in the verb phrase or part of the adverbial phrase *down to him*, but the intonation pattern gives it neither a separate identity as an adverbial clause element nor any guidance as to its placement. Because it does not have the movement ability usually found with verb particles it has been analysed as part of the adverbial phrase *down to him*, acting like an intensifier.

The last five-element clause with a mean of over 1 is SVOOA. As we saw in four-element clauses, SVOO occurs regularly in the data, although only 2–3 times per sample. In the same way SVOOA occurs regularly but infrequently, being found in 13 of the data samples (5).

5. *they'll give you a kiss when you're going* / (Mr H)
   S V O O A

Within the category of six-element clauses, only SVOAAA has a mean of over 1 and occurs in 14 of the data samples (6).

6. and *I've just this minute taken two um . something for my*
   SV A O A
   stomach because I keep on burping / (Mrs R)
   A

One six- and one seven-element clause with small means are found regularly in the data. SVAAAA is found in ten of the data samples (7) and SVOAAAA is found in seven (8).

7. and *nowadays women only play for three sets in a final* / (Mr H)
   A S A V A A

8. but *although I should have been . er happy that he was here he'd*
   A SV
   never done a bit of gardening in his life before he came here /
   A O A A (Mrs R)

Inevitably, the grammatical analysis of the clauses becomes more difficult as the number of clause elements increases because the possibilities for subordination in the combinations of clause elements are greater, particularly in the form of post-modification. In (6), for example, it could be argued that *for my stomach* is a post-modifying phrase to *something* but the stress on *for my stomach* implies a contrast with other aspects of the body.

In much the same way that grammatical analysis becomes more difficult with increased clause element length, there is also difficulty in deciding whether ellipsis has occurred because an adverbial may be omitted but the sentence can still look like a completed structure or a substitution may be made so that the sentence is complete (9).

9. A: sometimes I don't speak to a soul all day /
 B: really / it doesn't worry you? /
 A: no / ... *it would have done once upon a time /*
 if it wasn't for that . you know television to keep
 you company / (Mrs M)

Clause element summary

It is clear from the description of clause level structures that the elderly are able to produce a wide range of structures, in terms of both the number of clause elements and the variations in structures themselves. Five clauses (SVC/O, SV, SVC/OA, SVA, SVAA) make up 75% of all clauses in the data; all have stable distributions that do not change with increasing age or sex. Over 80% of elliptical sentences occur within monologues and help to limit redundancy. There is some indication that people over 80 years are more variable in their use of ellipsis than those in their 70s. Only people over 80 produced more ellipsis than the standard deviation range. The age characteristics of the young and older elderly in the study are discussed further in Chapter 5.

Phrasal structure

Phrase level analysis

Phrase level analysis describes both specific components of phrase structure and the number of elements. Not all possible combinations of phrase structure appear on the chart and those that do have a developmental significance. Because so little is known about language structure in the elderly, the LARSP chart was modified very little at this level. Phrasal structures generally do not show such stable distributions as clausal structures and more of the language samples fall outside the standard deviation ranges but, as with clausal structures, the relationship between the phrasal structures that represent the most frequently occurring phrase types and the most frequent length of phrase is strong.

The most common length for noun or adverbial phrases is two words, making up 58% of all such phrases. Within this category of two-word phrases, determiner + noun (DN) phrases are, perhaps not surprisingly, the most common, accounting for 25% of all phrases. The next most common phrase is preposition + determiner + noun (PrDN), which comprises 12% of all phrases. When phrase length is considered, two- and three-word noun and adverbial phrases comprise over 88% of all phrase structures. Unlike clause structure, these phrase structures are evenly distributed within phrase structure categories and within individual language samples. Less frequently used structures have a more variable distribution. In common with clause structure, phrase structure shows no significant variation with either the age or sex of the elderly person.

Two-word noun or adverbial phrases

The two-word noun or adverbial phrase is the most common noun or adverbial expanded phrase found in the data, accounting for 58.2% of the total number of phrases. The most common type is DN, with a mean frequency of just over 77 per data sample (1, 2).

1. now I . *the sister* . in the Cotswolds. she's got nothing to do at all / (Mrs S)
2. I . I was *a methodist* all my life till we came here / (Mrs S)

Adjective + noun (AdjN) is far less frequent than DN, with a mean of 21.94. Although this is only a subjective statement, adjectives do not appear as frequently as might be expected in the data, given the mean number of sentences in the conversational samples. They do, however, appear in all data samples. When they do occur in a noun or adverbial phrase, they are often of only a restricted number of types, particularly adjectives of size and value (3, 4).

3. he drives and all / but he has to have *extra mirrors* / (Mr B)
4. er well first of all of course I've always got *bad legs* / (Mrs S)

The last category of two-word phrases is noun + noun (NN), which appears only in half the data samples (5). It has a limited context in which it can appear, being confined to noun phrases denoting possession.

5. I said that's *Viviette's doll* / (Mrs D)

Three forms of two-word prepositional phrases appear in the data:

Preposition + noun (PrN) mean = 28.7
Preposition + pronoun (PrPron) mean = 22.5
Preposition + adverb (PrAdv) mean = 7.4

Each prepositional phrase occurs in every data sample (6, 7, 8).

6. ooh well. I've been – under a doctor *for years* / (Mrs S)
7. and er. I look after myself *except weekends* when I eat *with them* / (Mrs S)

8. I'm very often playing snooker *over here* / (Mrs T)

The 'other' category has a mean of 14.9 and is composed of phrases which include intensifier + noun, intensifier + adjective (9) or quantifier + noun (10).

9. you see my legs were *so swollen* / (Mrs S)

10. oh a little village where I was born . named Ilmington /. *eight miles* from Stratford-on-Avon / (Mrs S)

Categorising these phrases as noun or adverbial phrases is a descriptive measure that does not say anything of their function in the sentence, and in particular does not describe their function in the clause element structure. Certain noun phrases, for example, can appear as adverbial clause elements (11).

11. he will be twenty *next month* / (Mrs S)
S V C A
quantifier + noun

Three-word noun or adverbial phrases

These phrases occur less often than two-word noun or adverbial phrases, having a mean of 93 per data sample, but there is consistency in terms of the frequency with which the various types occur. Table 3.7 sets out the five phrase types in this category, with means.

Table 3.7 Means and ranges for three-word noun or adverbial phrases

	Mean	*Range*	*Number of samples*
Determiner + adjective + noun	23.3	14–40	20
Adjective + adjective + noun	1.1	0–4	11
Preposition + determiner + noun	36.6	18–84	20
Preposition + adjective + noun	3.8	0–12	13
Other	17.9	4–31	20

The two noun phrases, determiner + adjective + noun (DAdjN) and adjective + adjective + noun (AdjAdjN), have very different distributions, DAdjN occurring frequently whereas AdjAdjN is rare in the data (1, 2).

1. I got *lovely big bedrooms* / and I've got *a modern kitchenette* out
Adj + Adj + N D + Adj + N
there / (Mrs L)

2. It seems that . *the lazy person* that doesn't bother to look out for
D + Adj + N
their future or anything / you know /. can get away with murder / (Mr B)

The prepositional phrases preposition + determiner + noun (PrDN) and preposition + adjective + noun (PrAdjN) have frequencies similar to those of the noun phrases. PrDN occurs frequently whereas PrAdjN occurs in only 13 of the data samples; PrDN, however, is significant because it is the most common prepositional phrase in the data (3, 4).

3. I mean to say *at the time* when it's happening it's really unpleasant / Pr + D + N (Mrs S)

4. I put them *in the garden* in summer / (Mr B)
Pr + D + N

The 'other' category in such phrases is varied, with intensifiers (5) and initiators (6) occurring quite frequently. Some examples are given below (5, 6, 7, 8, 9).

5. I knew it was *an awful shock* in winter / (Mr B)

6. when I moved it made *all that difficulty* / you know / (Mr B)

7. and it was my number on it / but another lady's account / and that was *a mess up* / (Mr B)

8. they could have . built me a proper bedroom there and had this room *a little larger* / (Mr B)

9. of course she's had to hold *hard and fast* / (Mrs L)

Four- or more word noun or adverbial phrases

In total, four- or more noun and adverbial phrases account for 11.2% of the total number of noun phrases and adverbial phrases. However, four-word noun and adverbial phrases comprise 8.3% of the total whereas those with five or more words account for only 2.9%. Only one category of four-word phrase occurs frequently; preposition + determiner + adjective + noun (PrDAdjN), which has a mean of 7.8 and occurs in all but one data sample (1, 2).

1. I'm struggling *with the same chrysanthe . chrysanthemums* / (Mr B)
Pr + D + Adj + N

2. for quite a few years I lived at Hertford *with my first husband* /
Pr + D + Adj + N
(Mrs D)

The Other category of four-word phrase structures has a mean of 17.6 and a range of 1–32. Below are examples of PrepDNN, DAdjAdjN, IDAdjN and PrepPrepNP phrases, all of which have been found more than five times in the corpus (3, 4, 5, 6).

3. and when we've come by *in my son's car* . he used to say to me / .ooh I wouldn't want to live there / (Mrs D)

4. but on the other hand it's *an awfully lonely life* / (Mrs D)

5. well I don't want *all those silly steps* there if I can / (Mr B)

6. my son got it *out of a book* / (Mrs D)

Although five-word phrases occur with a mean of just under 8 and in every data sample (7), there are very few instances of phrases with six or more nouns and adverbs (8).

7. they came to me but I think she's talking *a lot of old twaddle* / (Mrs D)

8. I was trying to build up *quite a nice little bit of balance* / (Mr B)

One particular type of complex noun phrase (noun phrase coordination) was counted separately. It appears in all data samples and has a mean of 5.4. Noun phrase coordination describes any noun phrase containing coordination except those noun phrases containing overt simple coordination, as in *Tom and Jerry*. The most frequent type in the data is apposition (9, 10, 11).

9. well when you're getting on . *the journey it* was two buses see / (Mrs B)

10. now *my daughter* . we had *her* trained for the law / (Mrs R)

11. *those embossed plates* . *they* came from the same place/ (Mrs W)

Not counting postmodification structures or phrasal coordination as in (12), the longest noun or adverbial phrase structures found in the data were adverbial phrases. These were seven words in length, including a preposition, and were found in only three language samples.

12. see / . he must have got *one of the young clerks or girls or some one* to send one down / (Mr B)

At this stage on the LARSP chart, the emphasis changes from logging each word in the phrase to characterising the most salient aspects of the phrase. One development is that of post-modifying phrases following a noun phrase. This is logged as noun phrase + preposition + noun phrase (NPPrNP). This phrasal structure appears quite often in the data, having a mean of 14.4 per sample (13).

13. anything to get away from *the truth of the matter* / (Mrs D)

NPPrNP occurs in every sample, with a range of 3–27, and may be part of a prepositional or a noun phrase. In some instances, another post-modifying phrase is added to the basic structure (14).

14. and sometimes *a friend of mine over there* . she comes over/ (Mrs D)

The impression gained from looking at these longer structures is that pre- or post-modification in the noun phrase is possible but there are psycholinguistic constraints on both being present, suggested by their infrequent use.

Phrasal expansion

Phrasal expansion refers to expansion of phrases within clause element structure. The ability to expand a word into a phrasal structure in, for example, an SVO clause structure is an important stage for child language development. The elderly language samples show frequent use of phrasal expansion in sentences. Apart from the verb phrase discussed below, the complement and object clause elements were expanded most frequently, followed by the adverbial clause element and the subject clause element. The amount of expansion peaked at two-word phrases but even for those with five or more word phrasal expansion of S, C, O and A clause elements the mean per data sample was almost 9.

The verb phrase

The description here is not only of the verb phrase (VP), but also of the verb clause element. The analysis is different from that of the noun phrase and the adverbial phrase, with less emphasis on the number of words in the VP and more emphasis on the constituent parts such as verb particles [clean it *up*], auxiliaries [you *have washed*], modals [he *should* go], and catenative verbs [he is *going running*]. Because the units forming the verb phrase usually occur only within the verb phrase, word categories such as auxiliaries, copulars and inflectional morphemes are included so that all aspects of the verb phrase can be described at once.

The simple verb phrase

Of the approximately 377 verb phrases per data sample, the vast majority come under the category of simple verb phrases consisting of a main verb only, one or more auxiliaries and a main verb or catenative verbs (linked main verbs). It should be remembered that, although the mean number of sentences per conversational sample is over 400, a percentage of these sentences are elliptical structures which may not contain a verb clause element.

Over 95% of all verb phrases fall into this simple verb phrase category, although some do so only because they have undergone ellipsis. Within the simple verb phrase, many of the VPs are single-word VPs. The mean number of copulars (verbs of being, etc.) alone, most of which are single-word VPs, is 84 per data sample. Ellipsis also plays a large role in producing single-word VPs because it often occurs at the V clause element in an SV + other clause elements sequence, and also within the verb phrase, setting apart an auxiliary from the main verb. The conversation below (1) shows the processes.

1. and she *used to say*. now Nancy
   aux + main verb
   when you *leaves* work you *must join*
   1 word VP aux + main verb
   the club / which I *did* / and I *got* my old card upstairs /
   elliptical 1 word
   1 word VP VP
   and I*'ve been* there nine years this month /
   aux + main verb
   nine years this month / so . not bad going is it? /
   copular VP
   (Miss B)

Example (1) also illustrates the use of two-word verb phrases. These are, of course, not always of the auxiliary and main verb type, although most are. Strings of two or more catenatives without an auxiliary occur only a few times in each sample (2, 3).

2. and *I mean to say* I'm not lonely with all my commitments and all my friends / (Miss B)

3. well three years ago . this October a gentleman *called to see* me / (Miss B)

Other simple verb phrases contain verb particles (4) and more than one auxiliary (5). The additions that are possible in a simple VP, such as particles, auxiliaries and negation, can make the VP quite long (6) but it is not a complex VP until the combination of auxiliary + two main verbs is present*. This division, while possibly sound developmentally, creates artificial boundaries in the analysis of adult language where there is no reason for making such a division on the grounds of use or processing constraints.

4. and sometimes it's not always convenient for people to *ring me up* / (Miss B)

5. A: would you have carried on working /
B: I *could have done* / (Miss B)

6. so I *haven't got to see* him till the spring . if I take the tablets / (Miss B)

It is also in the simple VP that dialect forms often occur, as the third-person agreement morpheme deletion below shows (7), but these dialect forms are often not used consistently (as example (8) shows, taken from the same data sample as (7)). Dialect form usage has long been known to be variable and the interviewer's own standard English dialect may have caused some of this variability.

7. so. as I was saying. and in number sixteen *live* my niece / (Miss B)

8. cos my brother *lives* next door with his wife . you see / (Miss B)

The simple VP is, then, very wide ranging, from one-word VPs to four- or more word VPs. Although it is possible to have lengthy simple VPs which might include auxiliaries, a main verb plus particle and negation, this combination was not found in the data. The simple VP is a much more prevalent form than the complex VP.

The complex verb phrase

The complex verb phrase has a mean of only 16.5 per data sample or approximately 4.3% of the total percentage of verb phrases. However, it is used fluently, with only an exceptionally rare error occurring within it. It also occurs in two distinct forms, one of which could be described as a simple continuous complex verb phrase, with at least one auxiliary and two or more main verbs (1). Obviously the continuity is present in a statement but can be disrupted by a change of word order to produce a question or by the intrusion of a noun phrase between the last main verb in a sequence and its particle (2).

*There is a second type of complex word phrase which does not meet this criterion. See p. 92.

1. cos I wouldn't like to forget them / and be bad or anything / (Miss B)

2. but I *used to help make them up* like / (Miss B)

The second type of verb phrase can best be described as a discontinuous complex verb phrase*. It does not have the same definition as the simple continuous complex verb phrase, being made up of a minimum of two main verbs which are separated by a noun phrase. This type of verb phrase is not as numerous as the first complex type, which occurs approximately ten times in each data sample, but it does have a frequency of more than six per data sample. The discontinuous complex verb phrase (3) is not to be confused with a structure superficially the same where the last main verb is the beginning of a subordinate clause (4).

3. its no good *telling me to remember to remind* them of anything because I would never remind them / (Mrs R)

4. I . well . as a matter of fact I just *ran out* there
verb phrase
to have a little look at it / (Mrs R)
subordinate clause

Verb phrase morphemes

LARSP counts morpheme information under *word*. Here we are concerned only with those morphemes which are found within the verb phrase. Contractions of auxiliaries, modals and copulars (*he's gone, she'd have done it but for her foot, she's happy*) correlate highly (but negatively) with the use of phrasal expansion of the complement or object clause element. The negative correlation suggests that contraction of the auxiliary or copular is linked with short, unexpanded complements and object clause elements. Conversely, the full form of an auxiliary or copular is not more likely to appear before an expanded complement or object. Three other inflectional morphemes, ING, ED and EN, were counted, primarily to look at the content of the conversation in terms of past tenses. The simple past tense ED has a mean of 136.6 occurrences in each data sample, showing that at least one-third of all verb phrases used were in the past tense. The EN past participle had a mean of 29.1. When EN and ED are added together, the total number of verb phrases used in some form of past tense goes up to 43%. The ING morpheme has a much more restricted use, with a mean

*In this verb phrase the noun phrase is simultaneously object of the first V and subject of the second (Crystal, 1979).

of 24.2, and signifies only that the participle ending has been used, not whether the VP as a whole was past, present or future.

The interesting aspect of this information is that the majority of the verb phrases used were not in the past. A fair proportion of the conversation was not old information but must have been about present events and personal opinion. The elderly are often described as inhabiting a world where the past becomes increasingly important, but there was no significant correlation between use of the past tense and age in the correlation matrix; i.e. the older elderly in the study did not use past tense forms more than the younger elderly. However, the subjects in the study were all relatively healthy and mobile. A comparison with those in residential care might well suggest different trends in temporal use of verb forms.

Pronoun use

Pronouns are one of a small number of grammatical words which are counted on the LARSP chart. Pronoun use is frequent and consistent throughout all the conversational language samples. It is especially relevant to look at the pattern of use because some research has pointed to increased pronoun use in the normal, healthy elderly and the dementing elderly (Obler and Albert, 1981). Because this research is descriptive and not comparative, no conclusions can be reached as to the change in pronoun use with increasing age. It is, however, possible to describe the pattern of usage and to compare the frequency of pronoun use with some of the disfluency categories. By looking at the internal consistency of the sample, any relationship between, for example, an increased number of errors and an increase in pronoun use when compared with the whole corpus can be described.

Pronouns occur very frequently in the data, having a mean of 364.4 and a range of 214–594 occurrences in the data. All but four of the 20 data samples are within the standard deviation range. The total number of sentences used in a sample and the prevalence of pronoun use tend to increase in line with each other. The same is true, although not so strongly, for the mean number of sentences per turn compared with the use of pronouns. In other words, the greater the number of sentences produced in the sample as a whole and in each conversational turn, the greater the likelihood that pronouns will be used. Pronouns, like ellipsis, reduce redundancy but may give rise to difficulties in reference.

The context in which pronouns are likely to be used is not altogether clear. SV and SXY are highly correlated with pronouns, suggesting that pronouns are likely to be used in shorter clauses, but sentences containing an adverbial subordinate clause (and therefore likely to be quite long) also correlate highly with pronoun use. Pronouns and expanded verb phrases are highly correlated so pronouns are more likely to occur in longer verb phrases. It has been suggested that the verb phrase is particularly complex to produce and the fact that pronouns are more likely to be used in expanded verb phrases may point to a simplification of the noun phrase to aid the production of the verb phrase.

Lastly, there is a high correlation between increased production of ambiguous utterances and increased pronoun use. While over-use of pronouns in a sentence may well cause ambiguity, this is not necessarily the reason for the correlation. An equally valid reason for the correlation might be some underlying difficulty with reference and naming ability which could produce both over-reliance in the use of pronouns and the presence of semantically or grammatically ambiguous sentences.

Summary

The means for all structures counted in the analysis during the 20-minute sampling period are given in Appendix IV (p. 236). This is a relatively crude measure but allows for comparisons to be made about the frequency with which the structures appear in the samples. The means for all structures per hundred sentences are given in Appendix V (p. 239); this is a useful measure for comparison with individual language samples.

In this chapter we have attempted to describe clause element strucure, phrase structure and word information, with means and ranges. This has been a selective description of grammatical structures used in the conversational samples of elderly people. Perhaps the most interesting aspect of this preliminary view is the range of different structures produced. In Chapter 4, we go on to consider how the elderly in the study cope with the production of the complex structures of subordination. We also look at the types of errors produced and how the elderly use repair.

Chapter 4 Complex structures, errors and repair in the normal elderly

Introduction

In this chapter two areas of language production that are particularly important for ageing research and the clinical field will be reviewed. In Chapter 2, one of the main conclusions from experimental research was that the normal elderly have some difficulty in understanding complex sentences and there is even some evidence for that difficulty being present in language production (Kemper, 1990). More specifically, sentences containing subordinate clauses have often been reported difficult to process. We now look at the complex sentence production of the elderly in the study and consider whether their ability in complex sentence production is commensurate with the literature. Secondly, we look at the error types produced by the normal elderly in their conversations and consider how able they are to monitor their own language performance and make language repairs. Both grammatical and semantic problems are analysed for the error analysis. Error analysis and repair counts provide knowledge that might usefully be applied to clinical situations. In assessing older adults with aphasia or a dementing disease, there is very little age-appropriate evidence about normal error types and repair patterns. Finally, we consider the interactions between complex sentence production, errors and repairs.

Coordinators and coordination, subordinators and subordination

The processes of coordination and subordination are important for cohesive relations within language. In developmental terms coordination appears before subordination. For the child, the change from linking sentences with coordinators such as *and* to producing complex sentences is a major step. As well as describing these processes in the elderly, we need to describe the use of coordinators and subordinators.

In particular, coordination can be accomplished by the overt use of a coordinator or by the prosodic contour joining two structures but without a coordinator. We therefore need to look at these processes and how they occur.

Coordinators and coordination

The most common coordinator is *and*, which makes up 61% of all coordinator usage in the samples described in Chapter 3. Just over 70% of all coordination is carried out with the overt use of a coordinating conjunction but 30% of coordination has no overt coordinator and is realised by intonation contours. Coordinators are not used solely as coordinating conjunctions but also function as sentence initiators, and indicators of turn-taking and turn continuation. In particular, the most common coordinator *and* is often used in just these ways (1, 2). Taking the mean total of sentences produced in each sample, coordination by covert or overt means occurs between approximately 65% of all sentences, making coordination a common feature of elderly language.

1. Mrs L describing her move into a new home:
   he said . well I can't come straight away / *but* I'll be down
   shortly / *and* er he came down / *and* he brought us . me up
   and . / I opened the door and ooh / this looks nice /

2. A: how old are you Mrs R ?/
   B: seventy three /
   A: seventy three / yes /
   B: *and* that's why I suppose I'm finding it a little harder really
   / you know /

Although we can describe the grammatical structures used in coordination, it is important to bear in mind that the functions of coordinators can be analysed in a number of ways if we consider discourse aspects. In example (2), Mrs R uses *and* to extend (or even change) her topic of conversation but it is not functioning as a coordinating conjunction. Its use here is to signal at the discourse level that the previous conversational topic is being continued.

The use of other coordinators such as *so*, *or* and *but* is common although they are used less frequently than *and* (3.) They also may be used an initiators.

4. no / . we very seldom see them / yes / *but* they're very sociable
   when they do / *or* if they need any help I go and help them /
   but um they don't [si] they sort of seem to manage / (Mr B)

Other sentence-connecting structures are counted under adverbial connectivity (5).

5. and er we met / and er we had fell in love and like that / and *then* we got married / and *then* we went out back to Canada / (Mrs S)

A covert use of coordination is often found between comment clause and major sentences and between major sentences and tag questions. This coordination is identified by intonational contours (6, 7).

6. I *mean they got* their own lives to lead / (Mr B)
7. yeah but the daughter / . one daughter works / the other one hasn't got *any conveyance has she?* /

Subordinators and subordination

Subordination is used here as a synonym of the term *embedding*. Subordination occurs in approximately 19.5% of all major sentences in the language samples. As well as describing subordinate clauses that are clause elements, we describe noun–phrase post-modifying clauses which are only part of a clause element. The process of producing a complex multi-clause sentence using embedding is of interest. One of the few areas that has been well researched in elderly language is comprehension of complex sentences and their production under experimental conditions, but little is known of their use in conversation.

Apart from counting sentences with two or more subordinate clauses of different types, all other subordinate clauses were counted separately but certain clauses occur so seldom that they have been classed together.

Adverbial subordinate clauses

The largest category of subordinate clauses is that of sentences containing one or more adverbial subordinate clauses, which appear in 9.1% of all sentences. These adverbial subordinate clauses are the most prevalent and are also found in the greatest variety of forms and contexts because the adverbial clause element is so flexible in its position in the sentence. Because it is the most prevalent form of subordinate clause, it is also the dominant means of achieving sentence complexity in the conversational samples. Adverbial subordinate clauses appear in all positions in the clause element sequences (1, 2, 3), both with and without the use of a subordinator to introduce the subordinate clause (4).

1. well / you see / *when the babies were small* you did have to do it / (Mrs D)
2. and I told them *if they want somebody else* I can go and play the triangle / (Mrs K)

3. and then I well . I walk up to the shops *if I want anything* / (Mrs D)

4. and I walked up into Oxford Road *to get the 17 bus* / (Mrs D)

Adverbial subordinate clauses also occur infrequently as isolated clauses, having undergone ellipses, usually introduced by *because* (5).

5. A: do you go up to town with your daughter-in-law? /
   B: not very often / no /
   because when I go to town I don't like people with me / (Mrs K)

In fact, example (5) is an even more complex example because it is an elliptical utterance with two adverbial subordinate clauses. Sentences with two or more adverbial subordinate clauses occur with a mean frequency of 3.9 per data sample, i.e. they occur in almost 1% of all major sentences. These multiclause sentences occur in all the data samples but one, although this sample contains sentences with two subordinate clauses of different types, showing that two subordination processes within a sentence are possible. When two adverbial subordinate clauses occur in a sentence, they appear either as distinct subordinate clauses both linked to the main clause at the same level, or as a subordinate clause within another subordinate clause (6, 7). They can also appear as two coordinated adverbial subordinate clauses (8).

6. *when she talks to you* you've got to put your ear up to her mouth *to hear her* / (Mrs L)

7. then he took me round to Circuit Lane /
   to show me where the doctor's surgery was / (Mrs L)
   subordinate clause 1
   subordinate clause 2

8. *because I was a pensioner* and *didn't have to work*
   subordinate clause 1 subordinate clause 2
   they did the other one on the Wednesday of the following week / (Mr K)

The distribution of adverbial subordinate clauses is very constant, with 80% of the sample falling within one standard deviation. Of the 20 fully analysed samples, 13 contain 7–10% of sentences with one or more adverbial subordinate clauses. Low correlations between sentences with adverbial subordinate clauses and elliptical utterances suggest that few subordinate clauses are found in elliptical utterances.

Postmodifying subordinate clauses

Postmodifying clauses are the second most frequent type of subordinate clause in data, appearing in 5.3% of all major sentences. These clauses are probably most commonly known as relative clauses. The difference between these subordinate clauses and other types are that postmodifying clauses do not constitute a separate clause element. They are commonly found postmodifying a noun phrase in a subject, complement or object clause element. The frequency of this type of clause may have been due to the nature of the language sample collected (two strangers talking, requiring added information to some references) and, certainly in narrative, postmodification is used as an explanatory tool. While postmodifying clauses appear in both subject and complement or object clause elements most frequently (1, 2, 3), they can also appear as noun–phrase postmodifying clauses in an adverbial clause element. The grammatical analysis of postmodification in an adverbial clause element is often rather ambiguous because of the mobility of a subordinate clause in that position (4) and therefore the intonation pattern has been used here to disambiguate the example. Stress on *Tuesday* signals that word as the more important piece of information.

1. and Mrs um er Williams *who is living with me . staying with me now for company* / she belongs to the club / (Mrs R)
2. and the shock was so much for me *that I can't get over it* / (Mrs R)
3. and then I had this other son / you see / *that's in America* / (Mrs R)
4. and then my husband had um a fall on the Tuesday *after we came back* / (Mrs R)

The distribution of postmodifying clauses throughout the data samples is spread between 1.8% and 8.9% of the total number of major sentences, with the largest number of data samples at 3% of the total number of sentences, suggesting great variability in the distribution of postmodifying clauses within the sample. Postmodifying clauses appear only infrequently in elliptical utterances.

Complement and object subordinate clauses

Complement and object subordinate clauses (C/O subordinate clauses) occur in approximately 4.6% of all major sentences. As such, they are the third largest group of subordinate clauses. As with the other minor groups of subordinate clause, C/O subordinate clauses are constrained in their sentence position. Unlike the adverbial subordinate clauses which appear in any position in the clause, they must come after the verb clause element (1, 2).

1. we just don't know *what's aback of the moneyed people / do we ?* / (Mr K)
2. he said you do . drag that leg / don't you ? / I said look / this is *what I've been telling you for months* / (Mrs L)

Complement subordinate clauses occur less frequently in the data than object subordinate clauses. In nine of the fully analysed samples and ten of the partially analysed samples, instances of copular deletion with C/O subordinate clauses made the sentence elliptical because the V clause element was not present (3). This deletion also often occurred in the context of a subject subordinate clause together with the complement subordinate clause. There were also instances in which the copular was not deleted and, as in example (3), another element or pause is often present where the copular might have been.

3. well / you see / *then what happened* / you see / *my husband died suddenly* / (Mrs D)

Subject, comparative and sentential relative subordinate clauses

Each of these three types of subordinate clause appear only rarely in the 40 samples: sentential relative clauses, for example, appear in only seven. Nine of the samples contain none of these subordinate clauses and, on average, they appear in under 1% of major sentences. As discussed above, subject subordinate clauses often (but not always) appeared with a complement subordinate clause and the V clause element deleted (1, 2).

1. see *what they done* they just watch points / (Mr B)
2. you know / *what I do* though is study up. learning songs / (Mr C)

Comparative subordinate clauses appear in only 15 of the 40 samples. Their scarcity seems to be due partly to comparison being expressed in other ways and partly to some difficulty in using the structure itself, making errors rather common among these sentences (3, 4).

3. well you can carry on but you get *lesser and lesser* / you can't concentrate like you used . used / (Mr H)
4. well *there's not so many in Wokingham as there is in Reading* / (Mrs R)

Sentential relative clauses were found in seven samples and appear easier to produce. They do not contain errors (5), although they may be grammatically ambiguous (6).

5. I can't just think of just today *which is unfortunate* / (Mrs R)
6. so all he done was sat down and read a paper / or looked at the horses *which he loved* / (Mrs R)

Sentences with two or more subordinate clauses of different types

Just over 1% of all major sentences in any sample are likely to contain two or more subordinate clauses of different types. The most common combinations are adverbial subordinate clauses with object or post-modifying subordinate clauses (1, 2). All but one language sample contained these complex multiclause sentences.

1. and then *when the war was over* / *instead of coming home with*
   A (subordinate clause) A (subordinate clause)
   the Royal Berkshire Regiment which I belonged to /
   postmodifying clause
   I er went to the Fifty First Warwickshire Regiment /
   S V A (Mr K)

2. I said *because I went to her house and had some tea*
   S V O
   subordinate clause 1
   subordinate clause 2
   it don't follow that I was courting her /
   subordinate clause 2 continued
   subordinate clause 3 (Mr K)

Conclusions on subordination and coordination

In child language, the development of coordination followed by subordination processes takes the child from the simple one-clause element sentence to complex multiclause sentences. In adult language, where these two processes are well established, coordination and subordination tend to fulfil very different functions in conversation. In the language of elderly speakers, coordination functions as a device to maintain and signal the continuity of conversation. Words such as *and*, commonly used as coordinators, are often used to signal the continuation of discourse or to signal the beginning of a conversational turn where the topic is being continued by a different speaker. Subordination is often used as an explanatory device, particularly in the case of postmodifying clauses.

The elderly seem to have little difficulty in using subordination to create complex sentences and just under 20% of all major sentences contain a subordinate clause. Not only do they use these subordinate clauses but the most frequently used is the adverbial subordinate clause. These clauses are quite flexible in the position in which they can occur in a sentence. In processing terms, this might make them more difficult to produce because there is a greater opportunity for error. As discussed below, there is some evidence that the elderly do produce more errors in this subordinate clause type.

Sentences containing disfluencies

The term disfluencies is applied here to processing features present in the conversations of the elderly. Four categories of disfluencies have been counted:

1. Uncompleted and abandoned sentences
2. Sentences containing identifiable grammatical errors
3. Sentences containing semantic or grammatical ambiguities
4. Repaired sentences

Within these categories, the frequency of occurrence is very variable, but none appear frequently. These four categories need to be treated differently from grammatical structures because they measure disfluencies that are likely to have a greater variation than common grammatical structures. Categories 1–3 are counts of language processing or planning failure. The final category represents evidence of linguistic monitoring. The extensive literature on repair in normal language demonstrates that repair is pervasive in our language output: we not only repair errors but also clarify, elaborate and change the emphasis of what we have said with linguistic repair (Levelt,1983). Repair is a count of both error correction in sentence production and changes made to sentences for repairs of other kinds.

On average, approximately 4.5% of sentences in the language samples contained an error of some kind and 7.3% contained a repair. The relative proportions of the three categories, measuring linguistic failure and repair, are given in Tables 4.1 and 4.2. All error categories have been added together because the numbers for each of these categories are small.

Table 4.1 Simple and complex sentences with and without errors

	Percentage of sample
Complete simple sentences	76.7
Simple sentences with errors	2.5
Complete complex sentences	19.8
Complex sentences with errors	2.0
Total	100.0

Relatively few sentences in the conversational language of the elderly contain errors but there is a discrepancy between simple and complex sentences. Just over 3% of simple sentences contain errors whereas 9.1% of complex sentences contain errors, suggesting that complex sentences are more difficult to produce.

A few sentences contain both linguistic failures that have not been repaired and sentence repairs (approximately 1.5% of the failure sample, but for the purposes of this description these sentences have been counted in both categories). Sentences containing repairs comprise 7.3% of all major sentences. When repairs are added to linguistic failures, the total percentage of sentences with some form of disfluency is 11.8% There were no significant differences in the number of disfluencies made by men and women, or between the 70–79 and 80+ age groups.

Table 4.2 Sentences with and without repair

	Percentage of sample
Sentences with repair	7.3
All other major sentences	92.7
Total	100.0%

However, all eight of the data samples with sentence repairs outside the standard deviation range belong to people in the 80+ age group. When the 20 partially analysed samples are also taken into consideration, seven more samples from the 80+ age group are outside the standard deviation range, whereas only one sample (from a man of 79 years) in the 70–79 age group fell outside the standard deviation range. The people in the 80+ group therefore show much greater variability in their efficiency for monitoring their own linguistic output.

Errors and sentence repair are therefore both to be expected as a norm in the conversational language of elderly people but people in their 80s are more variable in their mean error production and their ability to repair than people in their 70s.

Uncompleted and abandoned utterances

There is no doubt that decisions about whether an utterance has been abandoned are rarely easy. Two main types of uncompleted and abandoned (UA) utterances appear in the data. *Type 1* often occur if there is some other processing difficulty in the same utterance. The utterance may have been abandoned because linguistic monitoring has shown it to contain an error or, if there is no error, because of change of intention (1, 2). These utterances are often abandoned quite early.

1. well when I got married my husband *used to / he was* a boiler erector and he was always away somewhere / (Mrs L)

2. they came to fetch me every Tuesday night / and I go *down him to / . he lives* at Three Mile Cross / (Mrs D)

The second type (*Type 2*) is abandoned much later on in the utterance and often only the last word is missing. There are usually no signs that the uncompleted utterance has been monitored, either by intonation or by reference in the following utterance. Type 2 utterances contain no other signs of processing difficulty apart from omission of the final word (3, 4).

3. um it wasn't quite so bad when it *first* / *it got* worse . seems to have got worse as the time has gone on / (Mrs R)

4. she do her teeth and all that like / see / it's not as if *I have to do* / *you have* to keep on at her though / (Mrs D)

Some utterances pose analytical problems (5).

5. and I feel I need to lean on *somebody that* / . *and really* / they must be fairly bright you know / (Mrs R)

Example (5) is a problem because it may contain an overshoot word *that* in the first utterance. There is a slight pause after the tone unit boundary, suggesting that Mrs R has realised that the utterance is incomplete but the next utterance gives no indication that the incompleteness has been recognised. It cannot, for example, be interpreted as a clarification repair although there is certainly an elaboration of the first idea but it is not repair elaboration.

Uncompleted and abandoned utterances have a mean of 8.9 per data sample or just over 2% of all major sentences. There are no differences between men and women in their incidence. However, 90% of the 80+ group fall below the mean, compared with 70% of the 70–79 group who are above the mean, suggesting that in this conversational context the number of UA utterances decreases with age. UA utterances are also more likely to be grammatically complex. Approximately 33% of UA utterances are complex, containing a subordinate clause, compared with a mean of 20% for other complex sentences.

Semantic and grammatical ambiguities

Errors or ambiguities of a semantic or grammatical kind occur with a mean of just under four per data sample or just under 1% of all major sentences. Of 40 data samples, ambiguities were found in 39. Variation of occurrence is relatively wide, with only 65% of the data samples being within one standard deviation.

How appropriate is the inclusion of both semantic and grammatical ambiguities in a single category? They occur relatively infrequently in the data but present analytical problems of rather different types. Grammatical ambiguities commonly cause problems of analysis for the linguist but do not cause problems for the listener in the conversation who can usually follow the context of the conversation (1, 2).

1. Mrs R: but they don't tell you too much / do they? / what they're thinking /
   B: no /
   Mrs R: no / *although nowadays it seems heart failure more*
   A S V ?
   than anything nowadays / doesn't it ? /

2. well / *they live the road down there that got the calf* / (Mrs L)
   S V A?

Examples (1) and (2) show omission errors of crucial grammatical information, making the sentence grammatically ambiguous, although the general meaning of the sentence is clear and we can make assumptions about the grammatical structure. In (2) the meaning is somewhat obscured by the incomplete structure.

Semantic ambiguities, however, are often no problem to analyse grammatically but may create grave difficulties for the listener in the conversation, if there is no help from the immediate context (3, 4). To add a further category of ambiguity, the discourse itself may be the source of the ambiguity (5).

3. he was going over there to see one of the sites.
   S V A A
   to see what it was there / (Mr W)
   A

4. *you're never alone without a telly* / (Mrs K)
   S V C A

5. Mrs T had worked as a nurse in France during the First World War:
   B: what kind of work did you do? / you said you had done a certain amount of work? /
   Mrs T: in the war years? /
   B: no / afterwards / have you always worked? /
   Mrs T: oh well I've never been out to any sort of work /

Example (5) shows a different type of problem, which we have called *discourse ambiguity*. The interviewer knew that Mrs T had been a nurse but Mrs T considered that she had never been out to work because her wartime nursing did not count as work for her. The interviewer had also been specific in asking for work experience after the war.

Some strings of utterances containing ambiguities, errors and uncompleted utterances occur as well as examples of ambiguity which can be isolated easily. These strings are rare and tend to occur more often in the language samples of the 80+ age group, as in (6) from Mr W who was 83 years old when the sample was taped.

6. Mr W, talking about his son's job:
so er . I can't visit his headquarters now /
well . Hemel Hempstead /
that's where he's actually mm / .
his business something actually goes to /
so he must be pretty busy in his / .
cos I suppose all the . caravan business
was all .. finished soon . now /

There were no significant differences between the number of ambiguities produced by men and women or the younger and older group, but the 80+ group showed greater variation in the percentage of ambiguous utterances produced. The number of ambiguities was between 0 and 2.1% of all major sentences over the whole sample.

A cluster of variables connected with the adverbial clause element is highly correlated with ambiguities: SVAA; sentences with one adverbial subordinate clause; two- and three-word phrasal expansion of the adverbial. These correlations suggest that the adverbial clause element may occur within the same sentence as an ambiguity. Certainly the adverbial clause element has greater mobility within sentence structure than the other clause elements and this mobility may cause an extra processing load, which in turn leads to a greater risk of error. This explanation, although only tentative, is supported by similar high correlations with elliptical utterances having two or more clauses, certain rare types of sentence with four clause elements, and post-modifying clauses, all of which are relatively complex grammatical constructions.

A more puzzling correlation is that between the morpheme ED, which represents past tense use, and ambiguities. ED occurs frequently in the data, unlike ambiguities. The elderly are often reported as being able to produce more fluent language when recalling remote past events (Obler, 1980; Ulatowska et al, 1985). The high correlation here may reflect the fact that most of the language in the samples is discussion of recent past events which have not been repeated and practised in the same way as more remote events.

Grammatical errors

Grammatical errors are the largest of the three error categories, with a mean of 12.4 errors per data sample. As a percentage of the total number of sentences, a mean of 3.1% of sentences contain grammatical errors with a range between 1.2% and 5.7%. There is no difference between the young and old elderly, nor between the men and women in the study. The grammatical errors fall mainly into five areas, all of which occur with approximately the same frequency (apart from word order errors, which are infrequent):

- verb phrase agreement within clauses;
- verb phrase agreement between clauses;
- prepositional, verb particle and subordinator errors;
- determiner and pronoun errors within the noun phrase;
- word order errors, including duplication.

Verb phrase errors occur in all 40 language samples, most commonly as errors of agreement between the auxiliary and main verb (1, 2). Omissions of the main verb, usually a copular verb, have been counted as errors although they may be unrecorded dialect forms (3, 4).

1. and we met / and we *had fell in love and like that* / (Mrs S)
2. there's lots of things *I'd would like* and that but . no good / (Mrs S)
3. cos *she nearer* there / you see / than she is here / (Mrs D)
4. then I moved to the Oxford Road /
and then *I . there* thirty eight years / (Mrs S)

Examples such as (1) might be appropriate in some dialects but Mrs S used the standard form often in her language. Example (2) shows a common type of error, which has been labelled *intrusion* in this analysis: an extraneous word is added to an otherwise well structured sentence. These intrusions may signal repair of an utterance but here there is no hesitation or change of pitch to mark the repair and therefore no evidence that it is repair.

Errors of agreement between clauses occur between subordinated and coordinated clauses as well as between utterances not linked by grammatical structure, although they may be linked by reference (5, 6, 7).

5. er now *Patty's been in a home* . they *they motor out* to her every Sunday / (Mrs R)
6. *it didn't* matter then / *didn't it* / (Mrs R)
7. *she said* to me when I was / . when I did have this interview with her / *she said* if I had my way / Mrs R / I'd engage you now *she says* / it must before . go before the committee / (Mrs R)

Some examples such as (6) are relatively easy to classify in terms of the error: in (6) it is failure to use the rule which opposes the negated verb in either the main clause or the tag question, with a non-negated verb in the coordinated clause. Example (5) is more complex because the context suggests that the second verb phrase is appropriate but the first is not. The first clause requires repair or completion before it can be linked to the main clause.

Example (7) is another type of analytical problem. It could be argued that Mrs R has reverted to a dialect form for the third *said*. Certainly there is evidence that switching between standard and dialect forms of English is likely to happen when one partner in the conversation speaks a standard form and the other partner does not, as was the case here (Labov, 1978). However, it is also true that, in certain standard and dialect forms of English, the present form of the verb can be used in narrating a past event. It has been counted as an error because the two forms coexist within the same grammatical structure, unlike (8) and (9).

8. well / say twenty years I *was* married the first time / then for the second husband I *were* married nearly twenty five years / (Mrs D)

9. *I got* lovely big bedrooms / ..
and *I've got* a modern kitchenette out there / (Mrs L)

Prepositional, verb particle and subordinator errors tend to be omissions or intrusions. Intrusions are either the wrong word for the context or extraneous words added into an otherwise appropriate sentence. The omission of words does not have a severe impact on the listener, perhaps because the listener adds the missing word themselves (10, 11, 12, 13). The possible missing elements have been inserted in square brackets.

10. a and *even Canada they were living / you know / soup kitchens* and all like that / (Mrs S)
b and *even [in] Canada they were living / you know / [off/from] soup kitchens* and all like that /

11. a what part *did you go?* / (Mr W)
b what part *did you go [to]?* /

12. a and then *he came the army* / and went back to Canada / (Mrs S)
b and then *he came [out of] the army* / and went back to Canada /

13. a it's all *according what* kind of book they are / (Mrs S)
b it's all *according [to] what* kind of book they are /

Unlike omissions, intrusion errors do sometimes interfere with the listener's ability to understand. Intrusions can be divided into those which are clearly extraneous to the utterance and those which are replacing the appropriate word for that context (14, 15, 16, 17).

14. and they're such a long way away *so that*
I haven't anybody close at hand at all for me / (Mrs R)

15. well I can't say much *of it* today / (Mrs T)

16. when you compare to . windows in the country /
green everywhere you know /
so / of course / we had this put *on* . when we
first came here / (Mr H)

17. I said / ***that's what*** they wanted me to have
a sink unit took out / (Mrs L)

Intrusions occur throughout sentence structure and with all word classes. Determiners intrude quite frequently but only affect the meaning within the clause (18, 19). Pronoun intrusions however, because of their common use in reference, often affect structures larger than the clause (20, 21, 22).

18. well / ***the*** unknown . complaint / (Mr H)

19. but if they wanted help I suppose I'd be
a fool enough to go to it / you know / (Mrs R)

20. oh mother she says / you are naughty / she says / after all
you've done for us kids when ***you*** were little / the sacrifices
you made / (Mrs R)

21. she said oh you don't want to worry over that / we'll get it
done / and um ***between 'em . we*** got it down / (Mrs L)

22. I think she's got two customers / you know / very old people
that they like her to make / you know / (Mrs S)

The last category of errors is that of word-order problems and duplication. Word-order errors are rare in the data samples (23) but duplications appear quite frequently. Duplications are the redundant use of a word, phrase or clause in an utterance where it is already present. Some duplication occurs in conversation for emphasis and is a normal part of language but the duplication here does not fit into that category (24, 25, 26, 27).

23. ***especially I'm lonely*** / see / (Mrs M)

24. I could / yeah / but ***I just feel now the way I feel*** that I
couldn't stand the upheaval of moving / (Mrs R)

25. now my father / ***the year I was born*** / he piloted
Queen Victoria up the Manchester Ship Canal to
open it ***the year I was born*** / (Mrs R)

26. well / she does it ***now*** only occasionally ***now*** / (Mrs S)

27. I said I've got to lift it all down / and put it .
wrap up all my china up / (Mr B)

Apart from the five main areas of error, other errors can usually be categorised as agreement, omission and intrusion errors but occur in rather different contexts. For example, sentence (28) shows an agreement error between the noun phrases in a split noun phrase, although it could also be argued that some form of repair has been attempted unsuccessfully. Example (29) shows duplication and intrusion into a stereotyped phrase. The intrusion is grammatical but, as the same word is not repeated, it can really only be called semantic duplication. The dialect used by this woman allows the deletion of the *ly* morpheme under certain conditions (30, 31) but the same deletion occurs in other contexts where it is probably an error (32).

28. it run in our family cos *my mother* / when her sisters were younger / *they* used to be kid glove makers / (Mrs S)

29. and *every now and again or so* . for some unknown reason it just stops and everything comes up this way / (Mrs S)

30. it was in a *terrible* rundown condition / (Mrs B)

31. and the laundry / really / it's gone up *enormous* / (Mrs V)

32. yes / but er *unfortunate* she hasn't got a lot of work / (Mrs S)

Although the errors themselves are important because they indicate the range of what might be called 'normal' errors made by an elderly person, the contexts in which they occur also need to be investigated. A gross division has been made here between simple sentences (one clause only) and complex sentences (more than one clause). Approximately half the errors fell in each sentence category but, as complex sentences account for only 20% of all sentences, errors occur far more often in complex sentences than in simple sentences.

We do not have a clear answer to the question of how far this is due to sentence length in words, rather than grammatical complexity but three times as many grammatical errors occur in sentences with two or more subordinate clauses as in sentences with one subordinate clause. However, the comparative mean sentence length of simple sentences differs from that of complex sentences by an average of only two words. It is therefore likely that grammatical errors and grammatical complexity, as measured by number of clauses, are related. This is perhaps not surprising when we consider that agreement of various types has to be made between clauses in a sentence and certainly errors occur frequently with this aspect of agreement in the language samples.

There is also a hierarchy of grammatical error likelihood in subordinate clause types. The figures below give the percentage of errors in the most common subordinate clause types:

- Sentences with one adverbial subordinate clause 4.5%

- Postmodifying subordinate clause 3.7%
- Object/complement subordinate clause 2.9%

Grammatical errors are highly positively correlated with filler syllables, sentences with two or more subordinate clauses of different types and negation. They are also negatively correlated with I clause elliptical other and SVOX element clauses.

Sentence repair and filler syllables

These two aspects of language processing have been included together because they both represent processes through which language monitoring by the speaker is made apparent to the listener. Sentence repairs have a mean of 29.4 and a range of 12–53 occurrences in the conversational samples. Approximately 7.3% of the mean total number of major sentences are repaired in the course of their completion. Filler syllables have almost the same mean, occurring with a mean of 29.7 per data sample and with a range of 5–74. As filler syllables occur within and between both major and minor sentences, a percentage is not useful to describe the frequency of their occurrence.

Sentence repairs are found in the data in many different forms but the most common are error repairs at phrase and clause level and repair of word-order problems (1, 2, 3, 4).

1. well what I think it is was during the first war he had malaria *very very ill . very bad* in Salonica / (Mrs R)
2. he was a curator at Birmingham Museum for the last ten years / but he died *about a year ago / . two years ago* / (Mr H)
3. well then *where breakfast . tier . what they call the tier* plant is three tiers high / (Mr C)
4. she says *it must before . go before* the committee / (Mrs R)

From these examples we can build up a picture of the range of repairs. Examples (1) and (2) show repair of lexical choices which would, if unrepaired, have left (1) linguistically incorrect and (2) factually incorrect, although of course the listener would have been unaware of the error in (2). Example (3) shows a repair at the clause element level and (4) a repair of word order or lexical omission.

Although repairs are relatively frequent in the data, the particularly striking fact about filler syllables is their rarity. Considering that the mean total number of sentences produced is 470 per data sample, the number of possible contexts for filler syllables is very large, but on average only about 30 filler syllables per conversational sample were found, suggesting relative fluency in the production of language. However, this obviously says nothing about the accuracy of the language itself (5, 6, 7, 8).

5. if they was good biscuits like / .you get *er* so much premium every night / (Mr C)
6. what I was trying to do was get them to *um* do away with those concrete steps / and make me a *er* slope up / (Mr B)
7. well the one thing was I was *um* . rather hoping I was going to get into a flat at the back here / (Mrs R)
8. if I say well I'm not going to be so *er* conservative / I'm going to be social / well then I came back to labour / well they're just the same as conservative in the end / (Mrs T)

Filler syllables occur more often in longer sentences and there are very high positive correlations between filler syllables and infrequently occurring types of four-clause element utterances and coordinating conjunctions apart from *and* but correspondingly high negative correlations with SVAA clauses, four or more element clauses and complex grammatical constructions.

Summary

The elderly in this study use complex language structures in their conversations but they do so with minor difficulties, shown by the higher percentage of sentences with a subordinate clause that contains errors. There is some evidence that the young elderly in the group are different from the older elderly in the numbers of disfluencies they produce. The older elderly produced fewer repairs and linguistic errors on average than the younger elderly and we might tentatively say that they are producing more fluent language. Some 75% of the elderly group fell below the mean percentage for repairs and linguistic errors. Support for this suggestion of fluency with increasing age comes from analysing the most frequently used stuctures in the sample. The older elderly used a higher proportion of the five most frequently used clause element structures than did the younger elderly. A crude measure of the ability to monitor language was calculated using the difference between the numbers of sentence repairs and linguistic failures. The difference was calculated on the percentage of these features appearing in each data sample. Using this difference, 40% of the elderly produced more linguistic errors than repairs and the elderly who had the highest difference were among the older members of the old elderly group. All the elderly in the study did, however, show that they could monitor their language by use of repairs.

Chapter 5
Language profiles of the normal elderly

Variation in performance among the elderly

This chapter illustrates the grammatical variation discussed in Chapters 3 and 4 by examining conversational samples from eight elderly people whose samples were also part of the normal elderly study. Their particular profiles have been chosen because they are representative of the whole sample or because they demonstrate variation from the study norms in different aspects of grammatical structure and conversational performance.

Eight grammatical performance profiles

A description was given in Chapters 3 and 4 of the grammatical structures found in the conversational language of a group of normal elderly people. This description was accomplished in a relatively economical way, partly by looking at the means per 20-minute language sample or the percentage of that particular structure appearing in 100 sentences and partly by giving examples of the structures themselves. However, this tells only part of the story. In order to consider certain aspects of elderly language, it is also useful to look at individual profiles from the group data and investigate profiles that illustrate the range of language performance among the people in the study. It is also possible to look more closely at the interaction between the analysis of grammatical structure, discourse features and error/repair data. A brief description of each subject, with any relevant vocal or sociolinguistic features, is followed by short sample transcriptions. The transcriptions include the main prosodic contour features, as described below. A chart of the main grammatical features also gives information on sentence measures, disfluency information and repairs.

The transcription of intonation

The intonation transcription used here gives much more information than the tone unit and pause marking that has been used in Chapters 3 and 4 but it is by no means exhaustive and only the information that captures significant aspects of the way language has been used by that particular person is included.

Tone Units

Tone units are shown by vertical lines |

Uncompleted tone units

Uncompleted tone units, i.e. where the contour suggests that the tone unit has not been completed, are shown by |....

Nuclear tones

These are shown by . /

Non-nuclear glides

/ means glide up.
\ means glide down.

Stresses

– is used for stressed syllables.
. is used for unstressed syllables.
() denotes a heavily stressed syllable.

Prolonged syllables

= is used for prolonged syllables

Pauses

Pauses are marked within the typed sentence:

_ is a beat of the speaker's rhythm.

. is less than one beat.

— is more than one beat.

Pitch variation

This is shown by the relative height of dots and dashes.

Width of pitch glide

Width of pitch glide is shown by the length and angle of tadpole tail.

Other suprasegmental features

Other suprasegmental features (e.g. fast, slow, loud , quiet) are marked in bold in the margin, their place in the sentence marked by *, + or #.

This is an impressionistic analysis which is meant to give visual information on prosody. A transcription with similar relative heights of dots and dashes corresponds to somewhat 'flattened' intonation, as will absence of pitch glides. Conversely, greater use of prosodic contours will mean an increase in pitch glide marks and varied heights of dots and dashes that signal pitch variation.

Conversational language samples

Mrs L

Mrs L, aged 73 years, lives with her brother in a second-floor council flat. She is healthy, apart from a back condition which restricts her mobility. She has been a widow for many years but she is in regular contact with her children who are married and live nearby. She also has a large extended family and knows many people locally. Her phonation is normal with good volume and her articulation is precise. She is one of the younger members of the study.

Mrs L, describing the move into her present accommodation:

S so . ((of)) course she got on the phone
she said . they said we haven't got any papers — *fast; †loud, high
now look she said
I gave them to you so don't have that excuse — *slow, creaky; *slow, wide
T mm
S so um _ she said but they . — *slow
you won't get moved today — *fast
((and)) we'd had the gas cut off — *loud
the electric cut off
T oh no
S oh _ and the house was — *ingressive whisper
well you know ((what 'ou)) when you're going to move
T mm
S and er _ _ so she said _ I'll see if I can get someone to — *low
move you tomorrow — *fast
well my son in the meantime is up here . waiting for the — *wide, hoarse
furniture to arrive _
T (laughs)

so . he comes down in his car *wide
he said Mum what's gone wrong _ †fast
oh don't ask me what's gone wrong _ * deep, wide, quiet
and um _ I told him _ *slow
*deep
so . then Mrs B come on up *fast
she said Mrs L I can get you moved tomorrow _
but it's not till three o' clock in the afternoon †wide
*quiet
I said oh charming _ *deep, wide,
quiet
I said I want to [put]up _with it [bleeped out]
well I had my _ son and his wife _
and they was expecting their first baby
after nine years you know _

T oh were they _ *slow

S and so er _ then my niece _ and her husband so _
so _ Diana [ku] she does a morning job *slow
*wide
she comes from work
and she said _ I said well you have a summat to eat *fast
because they're not coming till three and .
we'll get all ready .
so she said all right .
what . I said well I'll _ I've got a lot of stuff
I said I've got to lift it all down and put it .
wrap up all my china up _ *narrow
she said ooh you don't want to worry over that she said *fast
we'll get it done _ *deep
and er . between 'em _ we got it done

Mrs L 73 yrs Conversation

A **Unanalysed**: 1 Unintelligible 1 | 2 Symbolic Noise 49 | 3 Deviant 1

Problematic: 1 Incomplete 14 | 2 Ambiguous 4

B

	Normal Response						Abnormal		
	Elliptical Major				Full Major	Minor	Structural	ø	Problems
	1	2	3	4					
Response ellipsis	1	0	0	0					
In monologue ellipsis	29	19	11	2					
Totals	30	19	11	2	660	89			

Stage I

Minor: Responses | Vocatives | Other | Problems

Major: Comm. 'V' 6 | Quest. 'Q' 3 | Statement 'V' 9, 'N' 18, 'A' 2 | Other 0 | Problems

Stage II

Conn. | Clause | Phrase | Word

- VX 7 | QX 2 | SV 228 | SO, SC } 1 | AX 8 | VO, VC } 14 | Other
- DN 96 | Adj N 23 | NN 0 | PrN 21 | VV 59 | V part 28 | Int X 20 | PrepAdv 16 | Other 1
- Word: -ing 31 | pl 47

Stage III

X + S:NP 6 | X + V:VP 16 | X + O:NP 6 | X + A:AP 2

- VXY 3 | let XY | do XY 4 | QXY | VS(X) 5 | SVC, SVO } 126 | SVA 69 | VCA, VOA } 6 | VO_dO_i 4 | Other
- D Adj N 39 | Adj Adj N 3 | Pr DN 39 | Pron^P_O 594 | Cop 78 | Aux^M_O 169 | Prep Prn 31 | Other 22
- Word: -ed 317 | -en 25 | 3s 15

Stage IV

XY + S:NP 15 | XY + V:VP 83 | XY + O:NP 88 | XY + A:AP 54

- +S 2 | VXY + 1 | QVS 3 | QXY + 9 | VS(X+) 1 | tag 5
- SVOA, SVCA } 50 | SVO_dO_i 9 | SVOC 0 | AAXY 37 | Other: SVOAA 7, SVOOA 2, SVC/OAAA 2, SVOAAAA 1, SVAAA, SVAAAA 10
- NP Pr NP 14 | Pr D Adj N 4 | cX 1 | XcX 24 | Neg V 49 | Neg X 14 | 2 Aux 2 | Other 0
- Word: gen 5 | n't 40 | 'cop 41

Stage V

- and 67 | c 89 | s 61 | Other
- Coord. | Other | Coord. | Other | Coord. 276 | Subord. A 1 37, 1 + 2 | S 0 | C/O 23 | Comparative
- Postmod. clause 1 21, 1 + 0 | other (S+) 0 | Postmod. phrase 1 + 1
- Word: 'aux 59 | -est 0 | -er 3 | -ly 0

Stage VI

(+) NP | VP | Clause — (−) Conn. | Clause | Phrase | Word

- NP: Initiator 12 | Coord. 4
- VP: Complex 40
- Clause: Passive 2 | Complement. 9
- Conn.: and | c | s
- Clause: Element ø | ⇄ | Concord
- Phrase: NP — D, Pr, Pron^P; Dø, Prø; D⇄, Pr⇄ | VP — Aux^M, Aux^O, Cop: ø
- Word: N — irreg, reg | V

Other 34 | All errors 22 | Ambiguous 4

Stage VII

Discourse: A Connectivity 7 | it 3 | Repairs 38 | Comment Clause 10 | there 7 | Emphatic Order 2 | Other

Syntactic Comprehension

Style: No dialect forms

Total No. Sentences: 749 + minor sentences; 660 − " "	Mean No. Sentences Per Turn: 37.4	Mean Sentence Length: 4.5

LARSP Chart – Mrs L

There is some evidence that the younger members of the study produced more sentences within the 20-minute sampling period and Mrs L managed to achieve the greatest number of 660 major sentences. What contributed to this high figure? Her speech is highly fluent and intelligible, she has a very high mean number of sentences per turn of 37.4, and her mean sentence length of 4.5 is slightly lower than the average of 5.1. She also has a different two-element : three-element clause ratio from most of the members of the study, with two-element clauses making up 51% of the total (compared with a mean for the whole sample of 22%). Her large number of sentences was achieved by reducing the peak of clause element length from three- to two-clause elements. Phrasal length showed a similar trend with three/four-word phrases occurring in only 1.1% of her sentences compared with a mean of 8.3%. Her ability to use subordinate clause structures was within the standard deviation range, as were her disfluency scores.

Mrs R

Mrs R, also aged 73 years, has been recently widowed. She is depressed and finding it hard to cope on her own. Her only son lives in America and, although she is a regular visitor to a club for retired people, she feels isolated and lonely. She lives in a house which she owns, but she would like to move into sheltered housing for the elderly. She is aware that this move is likely to be difficult because she is fit apart from some arthritis (which does not restrict her mobility) and is well able to care for herself. Her language is usually fluent but her intonation patterns sound flattened or forced. The prosodic contours are on the whole wide ranging although there are some near monotone stretches, particularly when she is describing the death of her husband, as she is doing in this language sample:

T concorde *loud

S oh yes

((I. wonder if)) . matter of fact I just run out there *fast

to have a little look at it

you know

it er it fascinates me so much *wide

T yes

S because you see I have a son in America *fast

T oh do you

S oh and I feel I'd love to just go up there you know in that

T yes

S oh and of course I only just go over in erm . well . the

last one was a [m] [bo] . a jumbo *wide

T yes

S a seven four seven you know but er _ otherwise erm *fast *slow

I er would love to go over in that *fast

just to see what it's like

T yes /

S some people say it's very nice and some say it's a bit small

you know inside *high †wide

((but (2 syllables) I)) just don't know

T yes

when did you last go to America

S at Christmas *wide

last Christmas you see and then I came back

and then my husband had erm _ a fall *narrow

[o] on the er Tuesday after we came back

we came back on Sunday *wide, fast

then he had a fall in the bedroom *wide

he was dressed but he had a fall in the bedroom †fast

he was just going down to make a cup of tea _ *narrow

and I had to phone a lady and she came over *narrow

and we got him back into bed *narrow

and then I phoned the doctor *fast

and the doctor made him get out of bed straight away

and walk to the bathroom and then walk down four steps . stairs

and then back again and told him he you know get up †deep

told him he'd be alright *fast

well then on the following Thursday week .

he was . [j] out in the kitchen with me and we *slow †arhythmic

were doing the ironing

and he always ironed the er .

he used to say well now now I can do the handkerchiefs

and I can do the towels

and he done that and then I would carry on with the shirts and things

T right

S and then he said um afterwards that er he would um *high †slow

wash and shave ⊙falsetto

T mm

well he liked doing it downstairs so he done that

and he just finished washing and shaving *rhythmic † wide

and he turned round and he went down and he died

Mrs R produced very close to the mean number of sentences for the whole group but her mean number of sentences per turn was almost two sentences greater and her mean sentence length was just under one word shorter. She produced the largest number of sentential clauses (five) of anyone in the study, a clause type which appeared in only a small number of samples. Her analysis showed a higher than average number of sentences with subordinate clauses and an average error and repair rate. At times in the transcription, she uses a very restricted set of intonational contrasts, reflecting her depression and sadness.

Mr R

Mr R, 71 years old, lives with his wife in a council house. He left school at 15, was apprenticed and became an engineer. He worked in a power station for many years. He is fit but his wife has recently had a stroke and she now has a dense left hemiplegia and finds any household tasks very difficult. Before his wife's stroke, Mr R was a keen fisherman but he now feels unable to leave her for any length of time, even though he has been offered help. The couple have two daughters who are both married and live nearby. His speech sounds slightly disfluent, probably due to a combination of vocal harshness and abrupt, hard onset. He also uses elaboration repair quite frequently.

Mrs R 73 yrs Conversation

A

Unanalysed			Problematic	
1 Unintelligible 1	2 Symbolic Noise 25	3 Deviant 0	1 Incomplete 16	2 Ambiguous 8

B

	Normal Response: Elliptical Major 1	2	3	4	Full Major	Minor	Abnormal: Structural	ø	Problems
Response ellipsis	5	1	1	0					
In monologue ellipsis	22	19	8	1					
Totals	27	20	9	1		19			

Stage I

Minor: Responses, Vocatives, Other, Problems

Major	Comm.	Quest.	Statement			
	'V'	'Q'	'V' 8	'N' 7	'A' 10	Other 5

Problems

Stage II

Conn.	Clause				Phrase		Word
	VX 3	QX	SV 96	AX 23	DN 105	VV 41	-ing 34
			SO, SC 0	VO, VC 17	Adj N 12	V part 50	pl 31
				Other	NN 0	Int X 66; Prep Adv 4	
					PrN 43	Other 6	

Stage III

X + S:NP 11 — X + V:VP 50 — X + C:NP — X + O:NP 15 — X + A:AP 16

Conn.	Clause				Phrase		Word
	VXY	QXY 1	SVC, SVO 146	VCA, VOA 0	D Adj N 35	Cop 129	-ed 189
	let XY				Adj Adj N 0		-en 34
		VS(X) 2	SVA 81	VO_dO_i 4	Pr DN 58	Aux^M_o 163; PrepPron 30	3s 17
	do XY			Other 5	$Pron^P_o$ 566	Other 19	gen 2

Stage IV

XY + S:NP 14 — XY + V:VP 67 — XY + C:NP — XY + O:NP 89 — XY + A:AP 36

Conn.	Clause				Phrase		Word
	+ S	QVS 2	SVOA, SVCA 76	AAXY 49	NP Pr NP 14	Neg V 62	n't 50
		QXY +		Others SVC/OAA 24; SVOAAA 4; SVOAAAA 1; SVAAA 11; SVAAAA 1	Pr D Adj N 7	NegX 20	'cop 25
	VXY +	VS(X+) 1	SVO_dO_i 1		cX	2 Aux 5	
		tag 1	SVOCO; SVOCAO		XcX 21	Other 21	'aux 27

Stage V

Conn.	Clause			Phrase		Word
and 144	Coord.	Coord.	Coord. 260 1; 1 +	Postmod. clause 1 26	1 + 1	-est 2
c 107	Other	Other	Subord. A 1 52; 1 + 4		Other (4) 20	-er 4
s 94			S 2; C/O 54; O sentential relative		Other (S) 9	
Other			Comparative 2	Postmod. phrase 1 + 1		-ly 27

Stage VI

(+)

NP	VP	Clause
Initiator 16	Complex 28	Passive 1
Coord. 5		Complement. 11

(−)

Conn.	Clause	Phrase: NP			VP	Word: N	V
and	Element ø	D	Pr	Pron^P	Aux^M Aux^O Cop	irreg	
c	⇄	Dø	Prø		ø	reg	
s	Concord	D⇄	Pr⇄				

Other — All errors 17 — Ambiguous 8

Stage VII

Discourse		Syntactic Comprehension
A Connectivity 62	it 5	Repairs 37
Comment Clause 91	there 4	Style: Idiomatic phrases 9
Emphatic Order 8	Other	Reduplication 1

Total No. Sentences 531+ minor sentences; 512 − " "	Mean No. Sentences Per Turn 10.7	Mean Sentence Length 6.7

LARSP Chart – Mrs R

Mr R, describing his work life :

T how long ago did you retire

S um _ _ this is . um er I'm seventy one now
retired at sixty five *fast
that's six years _
that's [n] actually I've done . thirty four years. *narrow
.thirty four and a half years in the power station _ *fast

T mm

S and I had a couple of blackouts *fast
I was a charge engineer _ _
and _ I um _ ((in)) stead of going sick *slow *narrow
I could've had a period of twelve month I _ resigned †slow
because I felt well if I [sh] [k]. carry on shift work this is
going to be _ the ending,and I think _ _ it planned out
very well in the end you know _ _
what I . drew . paid for her house *slow
that saved us a lot of money _
and then I went in the civil service in customs and excise

T oh _

S and I came out of there with a small pension you know

T what did you do in customs and excise

S just ordinary .clerking [k] you know
proper change from engineering you know

T was that in Reading

S Reading power station yes *fast

T yes

S and Reading customs and excise in Friar Street *narrow

T ah /

I didn't know that Reading would have a customs and excise

S oh yes oh yes

*quiet, wide breathy

T what sort of things did they deal with then

S well they deal with [or . or] _ firms and then there's

Mars you know *wide, deep

I mean I think they pay a million pounds probably a *deep

T (laughs)

S a month you know or something like that

and er _ all the big breweries you see *narrow

all the sugar content's there

T mm

S there's all these things going abroad .

via the um _ coastal _ places *narrow

petrol you see

T yes yes

you don't really think about that

I mean I don't really think about that

S no *wide

ooh no

well I mean they had about ten officers

going round all the time _

T yes

S there's all the betting done you see there *deep

T yes

S betting levies

T yes/

S cars in and out the country

T yes yes

S it's quite an experience the short time *wide, fast
I had there you know

T (laughs)

S _ seeing the officers read the papers and. try and catch
these people that were sort of fiddling *narrow
_ perhaps sets that come in without being any payment on them †slow
you know customs on them

T mm

S customs on them _ –quite good *quiet

Mr R's conversation sounds disfluent, largely due to a higher than average number of repairs: whereas the mean for major sentence repairs is 7.3%, Mr R had repairs in over 11% of his sentences. There is no evidence that he produced more errors as such because his means for uncompleted and ambiguous sentences was close to the mean for the sample so it is possible that most repair was to clarify or elaborate what he had already said.

Filler syllables were close to the mean but he used comment clauses far more frequently.

Mrs T

Mrs T, aged 93 years, is the oldest woman in the study. She is fit, mobile and lives in sheltered accommodation. She trained as a nurse and worked in France during the First World War. She has been a widow for several years and none of her children live close but she has nieces nearby whom she visits and who visit her. Her speech is intelligible, her pragmatic skills are excellent but, impressionistically, well rehearsed language is much more fluent than more novel topics. Her voice sounds as if breath support is unreliable and there is a tendency towards giving each syllable equal length and sometimes equal loudness so that prosody has a 'syllable timed' effect.

Mr R 71 → Conversation

A

Unanalysed			Problematic	
1 Unintelligible 4	2 Symbolic Noise 23	3 Deviant 0	1 Incomplete 4	2 Ambiguous 4

B

	Normal Response						Abnormal		Problems
	Elliptical Major 1	2	3	4	Full Major	Minor	Structural	ø	
Response ellipsis	9	4	2	0					
In monologue ellipsis	27	6	12	3					
Totals	36	10	14	3	346	72			

Stage I

Minor: Responses; Vocatives; Other; Problems

Major: Comm. 'V'; Quest. 'Q'; Statement 'V' 4, 'N' 24, 'A' 7; Other 0; Problems

Stage II

Conn. | Clause: VX; QX; SV 23; SO, SC 0; AX 18; VO, VC 10; Other 0 | Phrase: DN 70; Adj N 16; NN 2; PrN 21; VV 17; V part 28; Int X 24; Prep Pron 17; Other 3 | Word: -ing 36; pl 53

Stage III

X + S:NP 1; X + V:VP 10; X + O:NP 5; X + A:AP 7

Clause: VXY; let XY; do XY; QXY; VS(X); SVC, SVO 97; SVA 44; VCA, VOA 11; VO_dO_i 2; Other 6

Phrase: D Adj N 22; Adj Adj N 4; Pr DN 36; $Pron^P_o$ 290; Cop 82; Aux^M_o 107; Other 24

Word: -ed 90; -en 32; 3s 12; gen 0

Stage IV

XY + S:NP 10; XY + V:VP 46; XY + O:NP 66; XY + A:AP 37

Clause: + S; VXY +; QVS; QXY +; VS(X+); tag; SVOA, SVCA 44; SVO_dO_i 4; SVOC; AAXY 22; Other: SVC/OAAA 10; SVOOA 2; SVAAA 6

Phrase: NP Pr NP 12; Pr D Adj N 11; cX 0; XcX 27; Neg V 31; Neg X 8; 2 Aux 6; Other 23

Word: n't 30; 'cop 25; 'aux 17

Stage V

Conn.: and 52; c 36; s 40; Other

Clause: Coord.; Other; Coord.; Other; Coord. 150; Subord. A 1 23, 1 + 4; S 3; C/O 20; Comparative 0

Phrase: Postmod. clause 1 29, 1 + 0; Other (S+) 13; Postmod. phrase 1 + 0

Word: -est 0; -er 1; -ly 18

Stage VI

(+) NP: Initiator 5; Coord. 4 | VP: Complex 8 | Clause: Passive 1; Complement 15; how; what

(−) Conn.: and; c; s | Clause: Element ø; ⇄; Concord | Phrase: NP D; Dø; D ⇄; Pr; Prø; Pr ⇄; VP $Pron^P$; Aux^M; Aux^o; Cop ø | Word: N irreg; reg; V

Other 7 | All errors 20 | Ambiguous 4

Stage VII

Discourse: A Connectivity 14; it 8; Comment Clause 67; there 7; Emphatic Order 8; Other 4; Repair 39

Syntactic Comprehension

Style

Total No. Sentences 418 + minor sentences; 346 − " "	Mean No. Sentences Per Turn 6.4	Mean Sentence Length 6.1

LARSP Chart – Mr R

Mrs T, describing her current life:

S you must keep the alertness going — †syllable-timing
or you'll go down straight away — •quiet, high

T yes

yes

S see we haven't got time here — •fast, getting louder
us three here — •loud, †slow, ⊙deep

T (laughs)

S (few syllables) we're always doing something ((see)) — •quiet
I haven't got a free moment when you go till tomorrow — •fast

T no no

S ((till)) I come in at half past ten tonight and then — •fast
I flop into bed (laughs _) — •slow

T well that's the best way to be isn't it

S oh yes — •deep
I [2 syllables] enjoy it too .
I wouldn't like it like a lonely miserable life
some people lead — †syllable-timing
. I wouldn't — •quiet
. and some people here they get the library come — •syllable-timing
and they get their books .
they go in their flat and they read from morning noon and night
. and then when there's anything on they — •wide
don't know that it's on . — †high
cos they're not interested

T yes

_ so there are some people here who shut themselves away

((rather than to))

S oh ((plenty)) *wide

yes *quiet

T yes

S cos they like reading you see

well I couldn't read to that extent . *fast, syllable-timing

T no † deep

S (laughs) I couldn't *quiet

T do you read at all

S only me paper *fast

well I haven't time for anything more *wide, loud

time I've done my flat each day and been out shopping *hoarse

and come back and . do the vegetables and cooking *wide

T yes

S ((there)) well the . morning's gone

then I've a rest after dinner *syllable-timing

till about three *deep

then Ray comes in are you ready for our snooker *fast

yes off we go for two to three hours upstairs *syllable-timing

snookering

Mrs T produced very few repairs, uncompleted sentences or ambiguous structures but she did produce more sentences containing grammatical errors than the mean. In terms of grammatical complexity, her counts for sentences with subordinate clauses was close to the mean for the sample. She was one of only a few people in the study to use no tag questions and her count for comment clauses was low.

Miss B

Miss B, 74 years old, is single and lives alone in a small flat. She worked as a bookbinder in the same firm all her working life. Her brother and his wife live next door. She belongs to the same club as Mrs R, often visits housebound friends and is in contact with old workmates. She is a cheerful, active woman who enjoys talking and who does not sound her age.

Mrs T 93 yrs Conversation

A

Unanalysed			Problematic	
1 Unintelligible 11	2 Symbolic Noise 34	3 Deviant —	1 Incomplete 2	2 Ambiguous 2

B

	Normal Response						Abnormal		
	Elliptical Major				Full Major	Minor	Structural	ø	Problems
	1	2	3	4					
Response ellipsis	6	2	1	0					
In monologue ellipsis	31	30	11	1					
Totals	40	32	12	1	401	97			

Stage I

Minor	Responses	Vocatives	Other	Problems

Major	Comm.	Quest.	Statement			Other	Problems
	'V' 2	'Q' 1	'V' 14	'N' 11	'A' 13	Other 16	Problems

Stage II

Conn.	Clause				Phrase		Word
	VX	QX	SV 53	AX 30	DN 67	VV 23	-ing 35
			SO / SC 11	VO / VC 20	Adj N 18	V part 62	pl 54
					NN 0	Int X 40	
				Other 0	PrN 50	Prep Pron 28; Other 45	

Stage III

Conn.	Clause				Phrase		Word
	X + S:NP 5	X + V:VP 26			X + C/O:NP 18	X + A:AP 15	-ed 69
	VXY	QXY	SVC / SVO 93	VCA / VOA 6	D Adj N 18	Cop 83	-en 32
	let XY				Adj Adj N 2	Aux^M_O 140	3s 19
		VS(X) 3	SVA 55	VO_dO_i 0	Pr DN 35		
	do XY			Other 7	$Pron^P_O$ 329	Other 19	gen 0

Stage IV

Conn.	Clause				Phrase		Word
	XY + S:NP 9	XY + V:VP 47			XY + C/O:NP 61	XY + A:AP 42	
	+ S	QVS	SVOA / SVCA 71	AAXY 33	NP Pr NP 12	Neg V 58	n't 55
		QXY + 4		Other: SVOAA 23, SVOAAA 1, SVAAA 1, SVAAAA 1	Pr D Adj N 5	Neg X 16	'cop 42
	VXY +	VS(X+) 4	SVO_dO_i 0		cX 0	2 Aux 16	
		tag 0	SVOC 0		XcX 23	Other 17	'aux 26

Stage V

Conn.	Clause			Phrase	Word
and 75	Coord.	Coord.	Coord. 115	Postmod. clause 1 33 1 + 3	-est 0
c 39	Other	Other	Subord. A 1 37 1 + 3	Other (S+) 9	-er 3
s 34			S 0 C/O 15		-ly 14
Other			Comparative 2	Postmod. phrase 1 + 6; Postmod other 17	

Stage VI

(+) | (−)

NP	VP	Clause	Conn.	Clause	Phrase		Word
				Element	NP	VP	N V
Initiator 9	Complex	Passive 4	and	ø	D Pr Pron^P	Aux^M Aux^O Cop	irreg
Coord. 6	16	Complement 9	c	=	Dø Prø	ø	reg
			s	Concord	D= Pr=		
Other 16			All errors 18		Ambiguous 2		

Stage VII

Discourse			Syntactic Comprehension
A Connectivity 16	it 7	Repair 12	
Comment Clause 20	there 13		Style
Emphatic Order 8	Other 12		

Total No. Sentences 498 + minor sentences; 401 − " "	Mean No. Sentences Per Turn 7.0	Mean Sentence Length 6.01

LARSP Chart – Mrs T

Miss B, talking about her work:

S we used to do all sorts of books .
um _ well like um . let me see _ _ grocery books
and all things like that
ledgers
course I didn't do that sort of work .
but I used to help make them up like fold 'em

s = slow
q = quiet
c = creaky
f = fast

T yes

S stitching machine

w = wide

T yes

S perforating

w = wide

T yes

S long stitcher

w = wide

T yes

S where you put the [g/r] . books over and they're all stitched
you see .
oh very interesting job if you like that sort of work
but everybody don't
and numbering

h = high

T mm /

w = wide

S number all the sheets on there .
oh yes
I went there when it first opened in nineteen thirty three

s = slow

T did you
but it obviously suited you

S oh yeah (. laughs)

q = quiet
w = wide

T yes

S I loved it _
well I think I'm easy going
I can always make friends quick you know

h = high
d = deep

T yes

S I have I've got plenty of friends .

and I've just had the phone put in you see this year _

because I used to get some phone calls . q = quiet
d = deep
c = creaky

from my sister in law _

and sometimes it's not always convenient for people to

ring me up n = narrow

so all on the spur of the moment I thought I'll

have it myself

T yes

S so . you('ve) got to save a bit harder for it but it's worth it f = fast
c = creaky
l = loud

really

T yes /

S well now once a week I have a dear friend . that .er .

she was my forelady _

and she's not enjoying very good health at the present moment

so I ring her up one Tuesday

and she rings me up the other / n = narrow
d = deep

Miss B produced a slightly lower number of sentences than the group mean and had a slightly higher percentage of repaired sentences and comment clauses but all her scores were otherwise close to the mean.

Mrs S

Mrs S, aged 85 years, has a duodenal ulcer but she is active and looks after herself. She worked from home as a dressmaker for many years. She originally moved in to sheltered accommodation with her husband who was ill but he died 6 years before this interview. Her daughter and son live nearby. She has a modified 'cockney' accent, i.e. a traditional urban London accent. Her chart shows large numbers of unintelligible utterances due to interruptions by her budgerigar.

Miss B 74 yrs Conversation

A

Unanalysed			Problematic	
1 Unintelligible 1	2 Symbolic Noise 17	3 Deviant 0	1 Incomplete 3	2 Ambiguous 3

B

	Normal Response						Abnormal		
	Elliptical Major				Full Major	Minor	Structural	ø	Problems
	1	2	3	4					
Response ellipsis	2	5	0	0					
In monologue ellipsis	14	12	5	1					
Totals	16	17	5	1	339	48			

Stage I

Minor — *Responses* / *Vocatives* / *Other* / *Problems*

Major — *Comm.* 'V' 1 | *Quest.* 'Q' 1 | *Statement* 'V' 3, 'N' 9, 'A' 6 | Other 0 | Problems

Stage II (Conn. | Clause | Phrase | Word)

- Clause: VX 1; QX 1; SV 45; SO, SC } 0; AX 12; VO, VC } 9; Other 0
- Phrase: DN 66; Adj N 21; NN 1; PrN 28; VV 17; V part 20; Int X 20; Prep Pron 13; Other 21
- Word: -ing 18; pl 49; -ed 114; -en 27; 3s 8; gen 4; n't 30; 'cop 40; 'aux 27; -est 0; -er 2; -ly 13

Stage III

- X + S:NP 2; X + V:VP 15; X + C/O:NP 12; X + A:AP 9
- Clause: VXY; let XY; do XY; QXY; VS(X) 10; SVC, SVO } 103; SVA 36; VCA, VOA } 4; VO$_d$O$_i$ 0; Other 3
- Phrase: D Adj N 22; Adj Adj N 2; Pr DN 39; Pron^P_O 323; Cop 90; Aux^M_O 96; Other 29

Stage IV

- XY + S:NP 9; XY + V:VP 39; XY + C/O:NP 71; XY + A:AP 26
- Clause: + S; VXY +; QVS; QXY +; VS(X+) 17; tag 10; SVOA, SVCA } 64; SVO$_d$O$_i$ 2; SVOC; AAXY 30; Other SVOOA 2; SVOAA 12; SVOAAX 2; SVAAA 9; SV(A4+) 2
- Phrase: NP Pr NP 16; Pr D Adj N 3; cX 0; XcX 13; Neg V 31; Neg X 3; 2 Aux 13; Other 21

Stage V

- Conn.: and 54; c 50; s 57; Other
- Coord; Other; Coord.; Other
- Clause: Coord. 108; Subord. A 126, 1 + 6; S 0; C/O 14; Comparative 0
- Phrase: Postmod. clause 1 11, 1 + 4; Other (s+) 6; Postmod. phrase 1 + 0

Stage VI (+) / (−)

- NP: Initiator 11; Coord. 5
- VP: Complex 14
- Clause: Passive 5; Complement. 9
- Conn.: and; c; s
- Clause Element: ø; =; Concord
- Phrase NP: D; Dø; D =; Pr; Prø; Pr =; Pron^P
- Phrase VP: Aux^M; Aux^O; Cop — ø
- Word: N irreg; reg; V
- Other 4; All errors 6; Ambiguous 3

Stage VII

- *Discourse*: A Connectivity 23; it 9; Repair 37; Comment Clause 31; there 5; Emphatic Order 9; Other 9
- *Syntactic Comprehension*
- *Style*

Total No. Sentences 387 + minor sentences; 339 − " "	Mean No. Sentences Per Turn 6·6	Mean Sentence Length 6·2

LARSP Chart – Miss B

Mrs S, describing her early married life:

S er well er I was bred and born in London
and then met my husband during the First World War *fast, quiet
and he was a Canadian *fast

T yes

S in the Canadian army

T oh

S and er _ and we met and . we had . fell in love ((and)) *fast
like that and er

T yes

S then we got married _ then went back out ((in)) to
Canada ((and that))

T oh did you d = deep

S yes oh yes went to Canada w = wide *fast
and my daughter was born in Canada w = wide *fast

T oh was she

S yes d = deep

T gosh but you didn't stay

S mm h = high

T you didn't stay in Canada

S no no h = high
well it was at at the end of the First World War and ʃ = fast h = high
it was er when the slump . the world was . everything was . f = fast

T oh

S everything was . even Canada
they were living on . on er . soup kitchens
and all like that

T yes

S you see it was terrible and England was the same n = narrow
so my husband said well dear so what are we going to n = narrow

do _

stay here and and freeze to death

or go to England and starve to death _

T (laughs)

S and we had a nice little bungalow and all — f = fast

T yes

so er luckily we was able to sell it for what we . paid for — f = fast

it _

so and then we came back to to England — w = wide, h = high

T yes

S yeah and all . all that and went went . went . to live with

a friend of mine — d = deep

because my mother had had died you know and that

before I went to Canada and that and _ so _ (sighs)

(laughs) _ — f = fast

we've bin living _ and so ((we've bin in Reading))

my [s] . son was born in Reading and

T yes — q = quiet

S he's . forty fifty. fifty six

T yes

S so I've bin in Reading ((fifty)) six years

and mostly . [t/] mostly Tilehurst you know — q = quiet

I lived in Reading for a few years

and then I went . got moved to the Oxford Road

Mrs S was one of the older members of the study and, by and large, her chart shows most of the trends found in older samples. Her mean sentence length for major sentences is the highest in the sample but she has a lower than average percentage of sentences with subordinate clauses. Her extra sentence length is largely due to intruded comment clauses such as *and that*. Her overall use of comment clauses is almost twice the mean in the study. Her discourse shows the extensive use of coordination and coordination conjunctions.

Mrs S 85yrs Conversation

A

Unanalysed			Problematic	
1 Unintelligible 21	2 Symbolic Noise 74	3 Deviant 0	1 Incomplete 15	2 Ambiguous 6

B

	Normal Response						Abnormal		
	Elliptical Major				Full Major	Minor	Structural	ø	Problems
	1	2	3	4					
Response ellipsis	5	2	1	2					
In monologue ellipsis	43	35	8	2					
Totals	48	37	9	4	318	162			

Stage							
Stage I	Minor	Responses		Vocatives	Other	Problems	
	Major	Comm. 'V' 2	Quest. 'Q' 1	Statement 'V' 6 'N' 21 'A' 11	Other 13	Problems	
	Conn.	Clause			Phrase		Word
Stage II		VX	QX 1	SV 39; SO, SC } 3	AX 27; VO, VC } 14; Other 0	DN 90; Adj N 26; NN 1; PrN 49	VV 19; V part 39; Int X 33; Other 8	-ing 17; pl 57
Stage III		X + S:NP 6	X + V:VP 18		X + O:NP 9	X + A:AP 15	-ed 117
		VXY; let XY; do XY	QXY; VS(X) 3	SVC, SVO } 117; SVA 59	VCA, VOA } 11; VO$_d$O$_i$ 1; Other 5	D Adj N 20; Adj Adj N 1; Pr DN 39; Pron° 348	Cop 108; Aux^M_O 110; Prep Pron 20; Other 45	-en 33; 3s 12; gen 9
Stage IV		XY + S:NP 19	XY + V:VP 58		XY + O:NP 66	XY + A:AP 60	n't 21
		+ S; VXY +	QVS 1; QXY + 1; VS(X+) 1; tag 3	SVOA, SVCA } 55; SVO$_d$O$_i$ 4; SVOC 0	AAXY 26; Other SVOOA 2; SVC/OAA 14; SVOAAA 2; SVOAAAA 1; SVAAA 8	NP Pr NP 14; Pr D Adj N 12; cX 0; XcX 52	Neg V 23; Neg X 13; 2 Aux 4; Other 29	'cop 23; 'aux 18
Stage V	and 106; c 51; s 56; Other	Coord.; Other	Coord.; Other	Coord. 265; Subord. A 129 1+3; S 0; C/O 14; O; Comparative 2		Postmod. clause 124 1+0; Other (S+) 16; Postmod. phrase 1+0		-est 0; -er 4; -ly 12

Stage VI	(+)			(−)				
	NP	VP	Clause	Conn.	Clause	Phrase		Word
					Element	NP	VP	N V
	Initiator 12; Coord. 6	Complex 14	Passive 2; Complement 7	and; c; s	ø; ⇄; Concord	D, Pr, Pron^P; Dø, Prø; D ⇄, Pr ⇄	Aux^M Aux^O Cop; ø	irreg; reg
	Other 2			All errors 16		Ambiguous 6		

Stage VII	Discourse		Syntactic Comprehension
	A Connectivity 40; Comment Clause 107; Emphatic Order 2	it 2; there 4; Other 5; Repairs 53	Style Idiomatic phrases 4; NB London dialect

Total No. Sentences 480 + minor sentences; 318 – " "	Mean No. Sentences Per Turn 7.8	Mean Sentence Length 5.9

LARSP Chart – Mrs S

Mr H

Mr H, 85 years of age, lives alone in his own home. He has been a widower for 30 years and his son died recently. He has a very structured life, with a group of mainly male friends. They go out to drink and eat together most days. He is fit and often visits friends who are ill or unable to leave home. His speech rate is quite slow and his voice is produced at low volume and low pitch. Articulation of /s/ is imprecise. Analysis of his language sample showed a low mean number of sentences per turn and a low mean number of sentences. He inhabits a largely masculine world and has done so for many years, which may have contributed to these low means. The researcher felt that his profile in particular might have changed dramatically with a male conversational partner.

Mr H, describing his son:

S well I I go to the doctors _ _
I well . woke up one day and I _ _ *wide
I couldn't do me _ collar up and that kind of thing _ *deep
and I went to the doctors and _ _ he had to look up my
records *wide
I hadn't been there for _ _ nine months _ _ _ *wide
you see er _ _ I've been a . a widower now for _ thirty *quiet
years _

T yes yes

S and er I had one son _ _ and _ he spent most of his time *quiet
abroad _
until he got a post in England _ _
he was a [k'u] curator at Birmingham . Museum
the last . ten years but _ he died about a year . two years ago

T oh he must have died quite young

S forty eight

T really what did he have

S well it's _ unknown _ complaint
they think . it might have . been . from when he was *arrhythmic
abroad

T oh really

S because _ when he first went abroad _ _ he joined the
World Health _

in Nigeria you see he was out there for . ten years _ *quiet
and this . post _ came in . Birmingham . Museum _
and he applied for it and got it you see *quiet

T m ... what was his training as _
S er . natural history
T oh
S he got his _ _ he got them in dribs and drabs _ *deep
BSc _ MSc _ and _ he was going on and have er _ _ *fast
be a doctor you see
T yes _ _ yes _ _ have you got relatives in Reading _
S no I've got a nephew . who lives just outside Reading _ *wide
T have you lived in Katherine Street for a long time _
S huh fifty years *quiet
T yes has it changed much
S no *quiet
T no
S but _ outside the [tow] . outside the town _ now _
if . when you go this way _ er . west _ _ when you come to
a pub _ _
then it was all country
all those council estates when I . first came here . came
here . I came here in nineteen hundred and eight
T oh did you
S yes _ _ it was all fields *quiet
there was no council estates or anything _
and the same with _ Caversham _ _
that was a little place on its own

Mr H produced one of the lowest number of sentences in the 20-minute sampling period and his percentage of sentences with repairs (4%) was much lower than the mean of 7.3%. The language sample had a larger number of conversational turns, shown by a low mean number of sentences per turn of 3.1, and he asked more questions than most people in the study.

Mr H 85yrs Conversation

A

Unanalysed			Problematic	
1 Unintelligible 2	2 Symbolic Noise 5	3 Deviant /	1 Incomplete 1	2 Ambiguous 5

B

	Normal Response						Abnormal		
	Elliptical Major				Full Major	Minor	Structural	Ø	Problems
	1	2	3	4					
Response ellipsis	7	6	3	1					
In monologue ellipsis	23	12	6	2					
Total	30	18	9	3	275	37			

Stage I

Minor	Responses	Vocatives	Other	Problems
Major	Comm. 'V'	Quest. 'Q'	Statement 'V' 4, 'N' 9, 'A' 8	Other 14 / Problems

Stage II

Conn.	Clause				Phrase		Word
	VX	QX 12	SV 20	AX 16	DN 59	VV 4	-ing 7
			SO	VO } 10	Adj N 19	V part 30	pl 1
			SC	VC }	NN 0	Int X 11	
			Neg X	Other	PrN 15	Other 31	

Stage III

Conn.	Clause				Phrase		Word
	X + S:NP 0		X + V:VP 9		X + O:NP 7	X + A:AP 6	-ed 119
	VXY	QXY	SVC } 57	VCA 4	D Adj N 14	Cop 64	-en 14
	let XY		SVO }	VOA	Adj Adj N 0	Aux^M_O 77	3s 2
	do XY	VS(X)	SVA 56	VO_dO_i 6	Pr DN 32		gen 0
			Neg XY	Other	$Pron^P_O$ 214	Other 25	

Stage IV

Conn.	Clause				Phrase		Word
	XY + S:NP 7		XY + V:VP 46		XY + O:NP 15	XY + A:AP 15	n't 21
	+ S	QVS	SVOA } 36	AAXY 28	NP Pr NP 12	Neg V 24	'cop 19
		QXY +	SVCA }	SVAAAS 5; Other SVAAAA 1	Pr D Adj N	Neg X	'aux 21
	VXY +	VS(X+)	SVO_dO_iA 2	SVOAAS; SVCAA 4		2 Aux 2	
		tag 4	SVOC 0	SVCAAA 1; CVCAAAA 1	XcX 26	Other 21	

Stage V

Conn.	Clause			Phrase		Word
and 30	Coord.	Coord.	Coord. 70 1 1+	Postmod. clause 14		-est 0
c 23	Other	Other	Subord. A 1 29 1+ 5		Other 21	-er 0
s 50			S 0 C 108			
Other			Comparative	Postmod. phrase 26		-ly 1

Stage VI

(+)			(−)				
NP	VP	Clause	Conn.	Clause	Phrase		Word
				Element	NP	VP	N V
Initiator	Complex	Passive 4	and	Ø	D, Pr, Pron^P	Aux^M, Aux^O, Cop } Ø	irreg
Coord 6	6	Complement 4	c	=	DØ, PrØ		reg
			s	Concord	D ⇄, Pr ⇄		
Other 2			All errors 11			Ambiguous 5	

Stage VII

Discourse		Syntactic Comprehension
A Connectivity 17	it 8 } Repairs 13	
Comment Clause 22	there 7 }	Style
Emphatic Order 5	Other	

Total No. Sentences 312 + minor sentences; 275 − minor sentences	Mean No. Sentences Per Turn 3.1	Mean Sentence Length 5.7

LARSP Chart – Mr H

Mrs D

Mrs D, 77 years old, lives on her own in a ground-floor flat. She has always lived in the same town and has a large circle of friends and family. She has twice been widowed but was married for over 20 years each time. She has some mobility problems due to arthritis but appears active and cheerful. Her voice quality contains some creak and breathiness, perhaps due to her arthritis, and she sounds elderly.

Mrs D, describing her granddaughter:

T does your granddaughter live in Reading

S no *quiet

no

she lives at um _ near Weston-super-Mare

she's up here for her holidays

she likes coming to her gran for her hol

but she's not coming any more †high

because as she says you have to work too hard (_ laughs) *wide

then you can see her working now can't you *wide

she's out . playing

. that's all her rubbish there by the way †loud

T is it

S yes she said gran that's not rubbish she said fast *wide

that's my do [der . der der] _ have you

. have you heard one of these baby dolls cry

T yes

S she's got one ((oh (whispered))) and it's just like

a baby isn't it *wide, quiet

T yes

S eh *quiet

T mm

S eh _

do you know dinner time I had some friends here

and . he said to me _ _ since when you had a baby *wide †fast

you know like

see I said – that's. Vivette's doll _ _ high, wide

so he said um _ _ is it really I said yes that's Vivette's doll †quiet *high

. but he thought perhaps somebody else was here like *quiet *wide

you know

T mm

S said that is Vivette's doll

T (laughs)

S eh _

T mm

S . kids really amuse you don't they

((and . sort of))keep you on your toes don't they ⊙wide

T yes

S eh

T yes

S they do me then but she's not a bad little kid ((is she))

T does she come to stay with you quite often *very quiet

S only once a year _ because you see . she's ((I can't . I . I [d]))

.do you know Weston at all

T little bit

S do you know . do you know Wirral

T _ yes

S just outside Weston

T mm

S well that's where they come from _ *quiet
come from Wirral just outside Weston see so she comes
. but this year she's coming for all her holidays *wide †quiet
sometimes she only comes for a fortnight _
but this time she wanted to come for five weeks *high

T uhuh

S . see so well just what can you do *high
oh I mean if I couldn't put hup . hup with her like *low
then someone would come and fetch her but _ as she's *fast
alright
I think there's no need for them to come and *quiet
fetch her they're coming and fetching her on the third
of September

Mrs D used large numbers of filler syllables and had the greatest number of tag questions of any person in the study. Tag questions are pervasive in her conversation. Her use of comment clauses is also greater than the mean. These two features make her conversational style very distinctive.

Profile variation among the elderly

A small number of the language samples from the main study produced profiles on the LARSP chart which were markedly different in some way from the rest of the profiles. These profiles seem to differ either because some structures are used far more or less often than usual among the data samples or because a generally infrequently occurring aspect of grammar is used relatively often. Most of these differences are illustrated in the eight profiles considered in this chapter. It is important to consider these variations in profiles because the imbalance of grammatical structures may affect the sample as a whole. Alternatively, those structures appearing far more frequently than in the sample as a

Mrs D 77 yrs Conversation

A **Unanalysed**

1 Unintelligible 5 2 Symbolic Noise 14 3 Deviant 0

Problematic

1 Incomplete 17 2 Ambiguous 5

B

	Normal Response: Elliptical Major 1	2	3	4	Full Major	Minor	Abnormal: Structural	Ø	Problems
Response ellipsis	3	4	2	0					
In monologue ellipsis	19	11	3	0					
Total	22	15	5	0	589	65			

Stage I

Minor: *Responses* · *Vocatives* · *Other* · *Problems*

Major: *Comm.* 'V' · *Quest.* 'Q' · *Statement* 'V' 6 'N' 7 'A' 16 · Other 0 · Problems

Stage II

Conn. · Clause · Phrase · Word

Clause: VX 5 · QX 1 · SV 55 · AX 10 · SO, SC 0 · VO, VC 10 · Other

Phrase: DN 95 · VV 43 · Adj N 33 · V part 33 · NN 7 · Int X 49 · PrN 40 · Other 15

Word: -ing 34 · pl 70

Stage III

X + S:NP 6 · X + V:VP 26 · X + C/O:NP 22 · X + A:AP 5

Clause: VXY 1 · let XY · do XY · QXY · VS(X) · SVC, SVO 144 · SVA 85 · VCA, VOA 8 · VO_dO_i 0 · Other 1

Phrase: D Adj N 29 · Adj Adj N 1 · Pr DN 45 · Pron^P_o 503 · Cop 106 · Aux^M_o 200 · Prep Pron 36 · Other 17

Word: -ed 135 · -en 41 · 3s 34

Stage IV

XY + S:NP 14 · XY + V:VP 68 · XY + C/O:NP 72 · XY + A:AP 51

Clause: + S · VXY + · QVS 2 · QXY + 8 · VS(X+) 8 · tag 44 · SVOA, SVCA 71 · SVO_dO_i 5 · SVOC 2 · AAXY 60 · Other SVOOA 5, SVC/OAA 8, SVOAAA 3, SV AAA 15

Phrase: NP Pr NP 11 · Pr D Adj N 10 · cX 0 · XcX 30 · Neg V 92 · Neg X 22 · 2 Aux 10 · Other 2

Word: gen 9 · n't 87 · 'cop 60 · 'aux 45

Stage V

Conn.: and 57 · c 73 · s 78 · Other 1

Coord. · Other let SVOC 1 · Coord. · Other · Coord. 284 · Subord. A 140 1 + 2 · S · C 10 · O 1 · Comparative 0 · 26 · Sentential relative 1

Phrase: Postmod. clause 1 8 · 1 + 0 · Other (5+) 24 · Postmod. phrase 1 + 1

Word: -est 0 · -er 0 · -ly 58

Stage VI

(+) NP: Initiator 8 · Coord. 2 · VP: Complex 32 · Clause: Passive 2 · Complement 9

(−) Conn.: and · c · s · Clause: Element Ø · = · Concord · Phrase: NP D · DØ · D= · Pr · PrØ · Pr= · Pron^P · VP Aux^M · Aux^o · Cop · Ø · Word: N irreg · V reg

Other 32 · All errors 12 · Ambiguous 5

Stage VII

Discourse: A Connectivity 36 · it 16 · Repairs 37 · Comment Clause 104 · there 7 · Emphatic Order 7 · Other

Syntactic Comprehension

Style NB tag questions, Complex phrase structures

Total No. Sentences 654 + minor sentences, 589 − " " · Mean No. Sentences Per Turn 7-8 · Mean Sentence Length 5.9

LARSP Chart – Mrs D

whole may point to other structures that are used infrequently. Those infrequently used structures, which may often occur in some profiles, are more likely to show stylistic variation than point to an alternative use of a structure.

The most obviously deviant profile on sentence measures is that of Mrs L, who produced 749 sentences in the 20 minutes of analysed language, 660 of them major sentences. Her mean number of sentences per turn was an astonishing 37.4, the next highest being 12 (see pp. 64–65). Her conversational style during the interview was to use reported speech extensively in narrative and she was a good communicator who could hold her audience. Her chart profile was similar to others in most aspects of grammar in terms of the percentages of each particular structure but her profile showed differences in just those structures which would allow her to produce greater numbers of sentences. Short clauses of two-clause elements made up 51% of all her clauses while the mean for the whole sample was 22%. Conversely, 20.3% of all her clauses were three-element clauses, far fewer than the mean of 40.9% (see pp. 76–78). Only 9.3% of her sentences contained subordinate clauses compared with the mean of 16.2%. Her large number of sentences was produced by a reduction in the peak of clause element length from a mean of three to a mean of two and a reduction in the amount of subordination processes. There is also some evidence that phrasal length was lower than the mean for the group. Two- and three-word phrases came within the standard deviation range, but three- and four-word phrases were found in only 1.1% of Mrs L's sentences, compared with the mean of 8.3% (see pp. 83–89).

These figures may suggest that Mrs L was using simpler grammatical structures and it must then be necessary to consider whether she has a problem in producing more complex structures. This does not seem to be the case because Mrs L produces the full range of subordinate clause types and her scores for four and four-plus element clauses falls within the standard deviation range. Mrs L's scores on incomplete utterances, ambiguous utterances and repairs are also within the standard deviation range. The only disfluency score outside this range is grammatical errors, but even here the mean percentage for the whole study is 3%, while grammatical errors were found in 3.3% of sentences in Mrs L's profile (see pp. 106–111). Mrs L's profile suggests that shifts in the relative frequency of use of certain structures can affect the profile while having little significance in terms of the overall profile. It might be argued that Mrs L's language sample is not a conversational sample because of the large mean number of sentences per turn score. Even with such a score, her overall profile was not markedly different from those of the rest of the study.

At the other end of the sentence production scale are Mrs L and Mr H, both in their 80s, who produced only 284 and 275 major sentences respectively, compared with the mean of 402 sentences in the 20-minute sampling period. Their mean number of sentences per turn scores were among the lowest in the sample, Mrs L's being 3.8 and Mr H's 3.1. With such low score, obviously more of the conversational time was spent in turn taking, but is there evidence that these two people merely produced language more slowly? When their profiles are investigated, they show remarkable similarity to the other study profiles for most variables. Mr H, however, produced marginally longer than average sentences. The only structure which showed a higher than average was five or more element clauses (see pp. 81–84). On many of the chart categories which can add to sentence length, he had produced the structures less frequently than the lower end of the standard deviation range. Structures such as phrasal expansion of the object, complement and verb showed a lower mean. Mr H therefore seemed genuinely to produce language more slowly. Mrs L showed very much the same profile but it is surprising that, although she has a low mean sentence length, she produced well above the mean number of repairs, uncompleted sentences, ambiguous utterances, grammatical errors or filler syllables, on either gross measurement or percentage measures. There is therefore no evidence that either person had any more difficulty than the rest of the sample in structuring their language.

Other chart profiles were different from the general sample because normally infrequently occurring structures were found more often than the standard deviation range. Some of these, such as Mrs S's greatly increased score on unintelligible utterances, reflect environmental factors: in Mrs S's case a budgerigar interrupted the tape recording. In most samples, increased scores on infrequently occurring structures were part of stylistic variation. Mrs D used tag questions approximately twice as often as the general sample. Her chart profile showed the second highest number of comment clauses and she also produced several sentential relative clauses, a type of subordinate clause with a mean occurrence of less than one per data sample (see Table 3.8).

Mrs D, like Mrs L, was an efficient producer of sentences, and her total number of sentences was second only to Mrs L's. She used tag questions and comment clauses to maintain closer contact with the interviewer (1).

1. see / now somedays I can sit here and knit perhaps
   two or three squares / and other days perhaps I
   won't even touch it / *you see* /
   but then wool's got so awfully expensive now /
   hasn't it? /

(Mrs D)

Comment clauses can be used with the same function as filler syllables such as *er*. Certainly Mrs D's symbolic noise count was low. Even so, there is no reason to suggest that she is using comment clauses as filler syllables to gain time for processing language, given the high total number of sentences she used, and her counts on sentence repair, semantically ambiguous utterances and grammatical errors (which are within one standard deviation). Her relatively frequent use of sentential relative clauses, on the other hand, has no predictive ability in terms of her use of subordination. She has a low percentage of subordinate clauses (see pp. 97–102), and even postmodifying clauses, which are most like sentential relative clauses, have a low occurrence in her language sample. This lack of subordinate clauses is balanced by a higher than average use of three-, four- and five-plus element clauses (see pp. 76–84).

A correlation matrix showed no significant correlation between mean sentence length and either amount of subordination or longer clause element strings. It is difficult to believe that there is no relationship between increased use of subordination processes and increased sentence length, but perhaps this is best illustrated by looking at individual data samples which have either a high mean sentence length for major sentences only or a high percentage of subordinate clause use. Mrs M (not profiled here) has, by a margin of over 8%, the highest percentage of sentences containing subordinate clauses. Over 34% of her sentences contain subordination compared with a mean of 16.2% for the rest of the elderly people in the study. Her mean sentence length for major sentences is 5.9, which is exactly the mean for the whole sample, in spite of such a high percentage of subordinate clause sentences. A reason for this may be the relatively low number of three, four, five and more word phrases in her language sample.

Mrs S, however, has the highest mean sentence length of 8.3 words, while producing 15% of sentences with subordinate clauses, just slightly lower than the mean of 16.2%. She shows no deviation from the mean percentage of clause element length for the whole sample, nor are her phrase length scores higher than average. She does, however, show higher than average scores on sentence repairs, with 16.6% of her sentences containing repairs compared with an average of 7.2%, and this may, in part, account for the extra sentence length.

From such samples, it is evident that individual scores differing greatly from the mean may affect other scores. The total number of sentences produced in any language sample may be affected by the relative percentage of different clause lengths but the profile as a whole is unlikely to be greatly affected. The main difference, which markedly increased or reduced scores made on certain structures, is on stylistic aspects of the language sample.

Conclusions

We have been asking questions about the nature of language use and comprehension in the elderly and about the possibility of language change with increasing age. In this chapter certain aspects of the conversational language of the normal healthy elderly person have been described and the similarities and variations between the language samples have been considered.

We have concentrated on a general description of language used by elderly people who have no known neurological or psychiatric disease. We can make comparisons between communicatively disordered elderly people and the normal, healthy elderly. The comparisons are useful for two reasons:

- first, any description of the language, and in particular the grammatical structure of the normal, healthy elderly, serves as the starting point for the assessment of those elderly people who have cerebral disease causing dementia or cerebral trauma which may cause a degree of aphasia;
- secondly, a comparison between the healthy elderly and other groups with different health or residential profiles may contribute towards the understanding of the structure of language and its relationship with perception and cognition.

The group of people whose language samples were used in this study are a random sample of the healthy elderly, defined by certain neurological and social parameters. They are thought to be representative of the healthy elderly population and are neither superior nor inferior in terms of ageing, although the sample may contain people towards either end of the normal elderly spectrum. In both neurological and behavioural reality, there is as yet no absolute dividing line between those who can be classified as normally ageing and those who show early signs of abnormal cerebral deterioration.

How homogeneous is the study sample?

Perhaps the most surprising finding of the study is how homogeneous the sample is in terms of the grammatical structures produced. Although the actual number of sentences produced in 20 minutes of conversation varied considerably, the grammatical structures showed little variation in distribution and frequency of occurrence throughout the samples. The most common clause element structure in the data is SVC/O which has a mean of 108 occurrences per data sample. Of the fully analysed samples, 18 had between 35% and 50% SCV/O clauses and 85% of the samples fell within one standard deviation. This stability is generally true for those structures which occur only a handful of times in each sample. For example, sentences with two or more subordinate clauses of different types have an occurrence of just under five per data sample, yet that distribution is even, with 85% of the samples falling within one standard deviation. There is certainly stylistic variation in the use of grammatical structures but this variation does not affect the overall profile of grammatical usage found among this particular population.

What comparisons can we make between the conversational language of healthy elderly and those with dementia?

Elderly people with dementia of Alzheimer's type (DAT) show signs of using a constrained grammatical system (see Chapter 6). The limits of the system seem to be the simple clause, and more complex structures are too difficult to produce or correct. Obviously the normal elderly are not so constrained and use many complex grammatical constructions in their conversational language. However, they show greater difficulty in producing error-free sentences containing one or more subordinate clauses. They also have some difficulty in maintaining grammatical agreement between main clauses as well as between clauses linked by coordination only.

Can we define a core grammar used by the elderly?

A core grammar can be defined by the frequency of occurrence of certain structures. The distribution measures of clause element structures peak at the three-element clause. This same pattern does not hold for phrase structures, which peak at one- and two-word phrases and decline thereafter for noun, verb and adverbial phrases. This core grammar is largely composed of simple sentences, without subordination. However, subordinate clauses, including postmodifying clauses, occur in almost 20% of all major sentences. Coordination between sentences is more common than subordination in sentences and both overt and covert coordination happen quite frequently. Another major aspect of the core grammar is ellipsis, which occurs in approximately 17% of all major sentences but is much more frequent within a monologue or conversational turn than in response to the participant in conversation. Perhaps the most controversial entry into the core grammar is disfluencies, which must be included if this is a performance core grammar because they occur in over 11% of all major sentences. However, this distribution is more variable than other core, frequently occurring structures.

What conclusions can be made about disfluencies and repairs in the conversational language of the elderly?

The core grammar is almost entirely made up of often used grammatical structures. It represents the fluent, efficiently produced language of the normal elderly in their 70s, 80s and even those over 90 years of age. Although disfluencies have been included in the core grammar to give it a performance dimension, the biggest group of disfluencies belongs to sentence repairs that show linguistic monitoring. Most of the normal elderly in this study produced more sentence repairs than linguistic failures, i.e. grammatical errors, ambiguous utterances and uncompleted sentences. There is therefore clear evidence of efficient language monitoring. There is also an age factor in sentence repairs, with those over 80 years being more variable in the number of repairs used, while the 70+ age group were all within the standard deviation range. An explanation of this might be that the very elderly can be split into two groups: the normally ageing who produce greater numbers of repairs because language becomes progressively more difficult to produce; and the abnormally ageing who produce fewer sentence repairs because they are not monitoring language as well. This latter group may resemble elderly people with DAT who are said to produce fluent language. There is some evidence for two such groups. The healthy elderly who used fewest repairs were among the very elderly and they also had below mean scores for linguistic failures. Conversely, the people who produced most repairs were also those who produced on or above mean scores on linguistic failures. One hypothesis about this division is that the elderly who were inefficient monitors and showed proportionately less repair than the mean might also show a lack of ellipsis because both sentence repairs and ellipsis might need increased linguistic vigilance. However, there is no evidence from this study to support such a hypothesis.

Does any evidence from this study support the word-finding difficulties that the elderly themselves often complain about?

The relationship between semantic and grammatical levels in language is brought out in the dysfluencies present in the language of the normal elderly, but there is no real evidence for either general or specific word-finding difficulties in conversational language. Certainly the elderly produce a small number of uncompleted sentences and some of these are abandoned with only the last word missing. A review of abandoned utterances shows that the missing words would probably not have been low-frequency words and therefore the fact that they are abandoned may be due to monitoring lapses on the part of the normal elderly rather than lexical accessing problems. In the discussion of grammatical errors, it was noted here that the normal elderly occasionally omit words, which causes grammatical error, but these omissions occur infrequently and seem to be due to brief monitoring lapses rather than retrieval difficulties. This study gives tentative support to Cohen and Faulkner's (1983) finding that the elderly make good use of contextual facilitation towards the end of a sentence or clause.

Apposition (for example, *the hospital down the road, St Leonard's*) is the only structure that seems to be used when there are specific lexical accessing difficulties. The absence of any significant number of word omissions may be due to the facilitation created by context in conversational language. The semantic system at the level of lexical representation works well in the conversational language of the elderly. Some problems with semantic relationships occur and occasionally semantically ambiguous sentences are produced. These are very rarely repaired, which suggests that there may well be difficulty in monitoring such utterances. This suggestion parallels findings (Cohen, 1979; Cohen and Faulkner, 1983) that the normal elderly have difficulty in anomalous sentence comprehension and in detection of lexical semantic change. The old elderly in the study show a tendency to produce more ambiguous utterances than the young elderly but this category is made up of both semantic and grammatical ambiguities so that it is difficult to draw conclusions.

Do certain sentence types or structures appear more difficult for the elderly to produce?

Sentences with subordinate clauses contain more linguistic failures than simple sentences, which may be due to the semantic as well as the grammatical complexity of the subordination process. The normal elderly find it more difficult grammatically to produce sentences con- taining two or more subordinate clauses, but when sentences are produced they will be no more ambiguous or uncompleted than sentences with only one subordinate clause. This suggests that grammatical efficiency may be confounded by length as well as complexity, whereas the incomplete or ambiguous status of a sentence is more likely to be due to complexity alone. This complexity may be grammatical, semantic, or both. Although no particular sentence types seem difficult for the elderly to produce, certain subordinate clause types do cause such difficulties. Many of the comparative subordinate clauses in the corpus contain errors. Sentences with adverbial subordinate clauses are more likely to contain errors than sentences with postmodifying or complement/object subordinate clauses. One of the few studies to look at the structure of language in the elderly is that of Kynette and Kemper (1986), who found that their normal elderly did not produce sentences with left-branching subordinate clauses. Although these sentences were not produced in large numbers in the study, they were found in almost all samples and did not contain any more errors than sentences with right-branching subordinate clauses. Kynette and Kemper also found that their subjects did not produce structures with modal auxiliary verbs, subject relative clauses and noun–phrase complement structures, which were all found in this study. The discrepancy between these studies is probably because Kynette and Kemper's study was an analysis of oral narratives whereas we have reported formal conversational language.

Filler syllables were described within the categories of disfluencies. They also show linguistic monitoring, but this occurs relatively infrequently in the language of the normal elderly. Other structures such as tag questions, comment clauses and coordinating conjunctions may fulfil the same role as filler syllables, which seem to occur more often in longer sentences. The idea that use of comment clauses increases with age has not found any support in this data, nor does filler syllable use increase with age. In fact, comment clause use varies considerably among the people in this study but the variation is mostly due to conversation style. There is some evidence that the normal elderly may find certain structures of language more difficult to produce than others but the disfluencies in their language conform to those described in the normal population (Buckingham and Kertesz, 1976; Nooteboom, 1980). They also show some adaptation to that difficulty by the increased use of a core grammar and linguistic monitoring. As a rule, their linguistic competence is functionally unimpaired.

In the next chapter, we will begin to consider the effects of pathological ageing on language processing and performance. The relationship between cognition and language in the dementias will also be discussed.

Chapter 6
Language pathology in non-Alzheimer dementias

Incidence and prevalence

Estimates vary considerably with the populations studied (Thal, Grundman and Klauber, 1988; Erkinjuntti et al., 1987) but Alzheimer's disease is by far the most common of the dementias, accounting for 50–70% of all dementias in western Europe and North America. Multi-infarct dementia is the next most prevalent and accounts for 20–25% of cases but is far more common in Japan than Alzheimer's disease. Other forms of dementia are extremely rare, few accounting for more than about 2% of the dementia population. To some extent, any consideration of incidence and prevalence is not entirely useful in a climate in which research is changing the map of aetiologies. For example, some people who would previously have been diagnosed as having Alzheimer's disease would now be classified as having cortical Lewy body disease, a distinct disease entity.

In the UK, approximately 750 000 people have some form of dementia and the vast majority live in the community. A communication impairment is frequently a common starting point for the disease process. In this chapter the language pathology in the non-Alzheimer dementias will be discussed, and the language pathology in dementia of Alzheimer type will be discussed in Chapter 7. We have been selective in our descriptions for two reasons: the incidence of some rare types of dementia such as normal pressure hydrocephalus is very low but, more importantly, we have not been able to find any studies that describe language functions in these dementias.

Pick's disease

Pick (1892), in his paper 'On the relation between aphasia and senile atrophy of the brain' emphasised the presence of dysphasia in his 71-year-old patient:

> In observing the speech disorder we lay greatest emphasis on the fact that we are not dealing with the disorder which can exclusively, or even primarily, be attributed to simple amnestic effects of the senile process, but rather, it more closely parallels those which are the result of focal lesions; it resembles those disorders which Wernicke-Lichteim described as transcortical sensory aphasia in so far as we could determine that the patient's primary symptoms were loss of understanding of speech and writing, paraphasia and partly retained ability to speak.

Few authors since have looked as closely at this disease, which often presents with a specific language impairment and relatively spared cognitive function. Pick's disease may be the cause of some cases of progressive aphasia (see pp. 154–156). Certainly there are a number of reports in the literature of patients whose language impairment deteriorates only slowly over many years, who are not reported as having gross behavioural changes and who are diagnosed as having Pick's disease at post mortem (Graff-Radford et al., 1990; Scheltens et al., 1990). Poeck and Luzzatti (1988) make the point that Pick's disease is now used to describe a condition in which altered behaviour is a prominent symptom and which has a distinct pathological picture, whereas Pick's original patient had a severe progressive language disorder and a different pattern of cortical damage.

Cummings and Benson (1992) describe the disease as having three stages. Patients present with personality changes such as lack of spontaneity and inactivity, and emotional changes such as inappropriate laughter. Impaired insight and judgement are also a feature, but language abnormalities are among the earliest intellectual deficits. As the disease progresses, language impairment increases, often with relative sparing of cognitive functions such as mathematical skills, memory and visuospatial skills. In the final stage of the disease, patients develop extrapyramidal disorders, intellectual decline in all areas, mutism and incontinence. The disease process commonly takes 7–10 years between diagnosis and death.

Wechsler et al. (1982) examined subjects with Pick's disease and compared them with patients with Alzheimer's disease. Those with Pick's disease initially presented with a more severe language disturbance and less severe cognitive difficulties. The authors therefore suggest that aphasia is a presenting symptom in Pick's disease, but not usually in Alzheimer's disease.

Pick's disease is not necessarily easy to diagnose even at post mortem and the literature suggests that a proportion of patients with Alzheimer's disease may have Pick's disease but Pick's disease usually begins at an earlier age than Alzheimer's disease, often in the 50s (Lishman, 1987). Diagnostic criteria on post mortem include the pre ence of Pick bodies and Pick cells in the brain matter. Cortical atrophy is most likely to be significant in the frontal and temporal lobes where one or both hemispheres may be affected. Rare reports of parietal, occipital and subcortical changes have been made (Wechsler et al., 1982; Munoz-Garcia and Ludwin, 1984; Holland et al., 1985).

Mutism is an often reported symptom, although this is not usually a presenting symptom, tending to appear in the middle stages of the disease process (unlike in Alzheimer's disease where it is common only in the final stages). Why people with Pick's disease become silent is not clear.

Case history: Mr E (Holland et al., 1985)

Mr E was heard to make non-speech sounds for 2 years after he stopped talking. Early on in the disease his speech was described as stumbling and he produced what might have been phonemic paraphasias but there is evidence that he might also have had dyspraxic difficulties.

Progressive dissociation of the semantic system from the phonological and assembly processes needed for spoken language may also account for the increasing mutism. For Mr E, this mutism was restricted to speech output. At first he was able to communicate well by writing and even in the later stages of the disease he could communicate meaning through single words, although he was unable to construct sentences correctly. He was able to produce a variety of written language constructions but not necessarily the appropriate structure at the right time (i.e. the problem in syntax appears to be one of access, with less and less becoming accessible as time goes on).

Mr E's writing samples suggest that he initially retained good access to his semantic lexicon for writing although low-frequency words were sometimes substituted for higher frequency ones. He was still able to understand most of the material he read until 1 year before he died. The most striking feature of his progressive language disorder is his auditory agnosia. Hearing acuity was good but he had difficulty in understanding spoken language. At first he could understand if the speaker slowed the rate of speech or repeated for him. He wrote that he understood better if the conversational context was known to him. Approximately 7 years after language changes were first noted, Mr E asked his family to write when they wished to communicate with him. He had also largely stopped talking at this point. A trial training period of Amerind was started about 18 months before he died. He learned 50 signs but could not combine or use them despite encouragement from his family. That he could learn shows some intact memory skills. Mr E showed no sign of echolalia, which is normally associated with transcortical sensory aphasia, the aphasic syndrome Pick used to describe his patient.

Case history: EK (Thompson, 1986)

Pick's disease is a rare form of dementia but should be considered if there are initial personality and/or specific language changes. The case of Mr E suggests that communication can be maintained until late on in the disease process because of specific modality sparing. However, the patient EK (a

78-year-old widow who lived alone) presented with marked behavioural changes and showed quite marked changes in language and cognition over a 1-year period. She was diagnosed as having Pick's disease after referral to a psychogeriatric assessment team. A CT scan demonstrated frontal atrophy but there was no evidence of vascular disease or metabolic disorders. She was well groomed, emotionally labile, with paranoid delusional thoughts, fair insight, mild cognitive impairment, a non-fluent dysphasia and organisational problems typical of frontal lobe dysfunction. Neuropsychological assessment indicated bilateral frontal and temporal lobe impairment. Her mother had had an undiagnosed form of dementia when she died at the age of 89 years.

EK had a history of 10 years' diminished socialisation, during which interaction with her sister and neighbours deteriorated and she developed suspicious thoughts about the local butcher. On assessment, she was found to have a moderate dementia, with disorientation in place and a poor knowledge of current events. She was not good at digit repetition either forwards or backwards and found sentence repetition even more difficult. She was able to identify objects by name and function without difficulty but her auditory comprehension was reduced to the 60th percentile on the Token test. EK produced some paraphasic errors such as *puckers* for *Tweezers, bolt* for *lock* and *shaving* for *razor*. Word fluency was also at the 60th percentile, with the patient giving responses outside the designated category. On sentence construction, EK performed poorly but showed evidence of semantic processing. Asked to formulate a sentence from the words *hot* and *summer*, she produced *playing down the beach; hair, water* and *girl* produced *shampoo*. Copying and automatic writing were at ceiling but dictation scored only at the 50th percentile. There was no evidence of any form of apraxia but calculation scored only at the 10th percentile.

EK was admitted to a psychogeriatric hospital 1 year later, having been found naked in the street at night. On reassessment she had almost no spontaneous verbal output. Her dementia score had deteriorated but she was still tidy and well groomed. She was somewhat euphoric and disoriented in time and place but managed to give the main points of a personal history when asked. Recent memory was reduced but automatic speech was retained and she was able to count and recite the days of the week in reverse. EK remained able to identify objects by their name and function but her scores on both the Token test and written sentence comprehension had fallen (see Table 6.1).

Although confrontation naming had shown deficits on initial assessment, at test 2 it showed only a marginal change but EK was dramatically less able to describe the function of objects. One response was jargon, one was a concrete association (*milk* for *cup*) and she gave one unrelated response (*gallop* for *spoon*).

The patient's word fluency had deteriorated and this time she produced perseverations as well as responses not within the specified category. Sentence construction remained poor. Scores on the reading tests remained at ceiling apart from written sentence comprehension, which fell to the 50th percentile. Writing tests were unchanged apart from automatic writing, which dropped from the 95th to the 5th percentile. There was no evidence of constructional apraxia apart from cube drawing and perspective.

Table 6.1 Language and cognitive skills profile: EK

	Percentile scores	
	Test 1	*Test 2*
Test showing deterioration		
Dementia Rating Scale	40	20
Raven's Matrices	50	15
Block Design	95	50
Token test	60	30
Sentence repetition	15	10
Sentence comprehension	95	50
Confrontation naming	30	20
Description of function	95	5
Gesture	95	20
Word fluency	60	25
Automatic writing	95	5
Calculation	10	5
Constructional praxis	90	80
Repeating digits forward	70	20
Repeating digits in reverse	50	30
Test scores showing deficit but stable		
Sentence construction	5	5
Written naming	70	70
Dictation	50	50
Tests stable at ceiling		
Object identification by name	95	95
Object identification by function	95	95
Automatic speech	95	95
Word reading	95	95
Word recognition	95	95
Sentence reading	95	95
Copying	95	95
Oral praxis	95	95
Ideomotor praxis	95	95

Although EK had little verbal output, there was no evidence of ideomotor or oral apraxia.

EK was older than the expected age range for Pick's disease but she had a long history of personality and behavioural disturbance. Her spontaneous language was severely reduced, particularly shown by her verbal fluency and description of object function.

EK had a long history of diminished socialisation but it is not clear whether this difficulty was part of the Pick's disease process or was a separate personality disorder. Like Mr E, her verbal output, and in particular her ability to initiate language, deteriorated while other modalities had some retained aspects but she does not demonstrate the same depth of specific modality sparing.

Diffuse Lewy body disease

Diffuse Lewy body disease was considered to be a rare form of dementia, but some authors now think it may be the second most common form of dementia after Alzheimer's disease (Homer et al., 1988; Burns et al., 1990). It is a primary degenerative dementia characterised by interneuronal inclusions similar in structure to the Lewy bodies found in Parkinson's disease. These inclusions reflect neuronal loss, and are found in the cortex and the subcortical nuclei in this disease.

Some overlap with Alzheimer-type pathology has been found in some studies, which might suggest that diffuse Lewy body disease is just a variant of Alzheimer's disease but a strong case is now being made for its distinction as a separate form of dementia (Dickson et al., 1992).

The clinical features of diffuse Lewy body disease have been consistently described: patients present with early fluctuation in cognitive state and with periods of acute confusion; cognitive impairment is less than would be expected in Alzheimer's disease in the early stage, but extrapyramidal and psychiatric symptoms, particularly visual hallucinations, are a common finding; the progress of the disease is variable but all patients develop dementia and have at least one extrapyramidal deficit (Byrne, 1992).

Galloway (1992) examined subjects with this disease and found a specific pattern of memory deficits and motor disturbances, and Fearnley et al. (1991) described a patient with features of hyperkinetic dysarthria and nominal dysphasia. As yet there are no detailed studies of speech and language functioning in patients with diffuse Lewy body disease.

The progressive aphasias

Language impairment may be an isolated, presenting feature in Alzheimer's and Pick's diseases, but signs of generalised cognitive impairment are usually quick to appear. However, some patients have been reported whose language impairment progresses slowly over a number of years without significant cognitive impairment (Mesulam, 1982; Chawluk et al., 1986; Poeck and Luzzatti, 1988; Tyrrell et al., 1990). This progressive language impairment may be a prolonged initial phase of Alzheimer's or other dementias and recent findings suggest that the great majority of these patients go on to develop a more generalised dementia in the final stages of the disease process. Poeck and Luzzatti (1988) concluded that only a few out of over 30 patients described in the literature maintained an isolated language impairment.

Most patients presented in the literature with progressive aphasia have a fluent form of language deficit and have been classified as having anomic, transcortical sensory or Wernicke-type aphasia, although Tyrrell et al. (1990) describe one patient with good auditory comprehension whose language impairment was non-fluent and who had a number of apraxias, and Weintraub et al. (1990) describe the longitudinal course of four other non-fluent patients. Most patients with progressive aphasia show left hemisphere focal atrophy and studies using positron emission tomography (PET) now suggest that in some patients there may be little or no functional disturbance in the right hemisphere (Chawluk et al., 1986; Tyrrell et al., 1990). Recently, Hodges et al. (1992) have described a group of five fluent patients with severe anomia, reduced vocabulary and difficulty in understanding single words. This study gives detailed information on neurological, cognitive and language testing which is useful in further defining the characteristics (and particularly the specific processing impairments) which may be found. They suggest that such patients should be termed *semantic aphasics* because of their prominent disorder in this area.

MH, a 63-year-old patient described by Poeck and Luzzatti (1988), was a businesswoman who presented with severe word-finding problems. All medical investigations for hypertension or cerebrovascular disease were negative. Her language was fluent but showed severe word-finding problems, empty phrases and semantic paraphasias. She attempted to repair her output errors but was not always successful. She was, at that time, still able to communicate adequately with little help from her conversational partner. IQ tests showed MH to be within the average range for the normal population. Over the next 3 years her language deteriorated to the extent that she had to stop work but she had an active social life. Subsequent assessment showed few attempts to self-correct and increased use of stereotypes, and conversation needed support from the examiner. Her IQ had dropped but it was still within the average range. All areas of testing on the Aachen Aphasia Test showed similar declines.

Mesulam and Weintraub (1992) reviewed the literature on the progressive aphasias and identified a specific condition, which they called *primary progressive aphasia*. They distinguished this from Alzheimer-type dementia and identified the syndrome as progressive decline in language, absence of deficits in other domains for at least 2 years, no disturbance of consciousness, no signs of a more generalised dementia syndrome and no systemic disorder or other brain disease that could account for the progressive deficits in language.

Many patients with progressive aphasia develop signs of language difficulty before their mid-60s and the disease progression is slow. If cognitive impairment occurs, then it either appears late in the disease process or is a minor component of the disorder, and cognitive deterioration is slower than language loss. Whether these patients form a distinct and separate type of dementia is not clear but their lack of significant cognitive impairment, retained functional language and daily living abilities suggest that they may benefit from management and advice different from that given to patients with more general cognitive decline.

Finally, there are also reports in the literature of other focal dementias, which include visual agnosia (Taylor and Warrington, 1971) and specific alexia in posterior dementia (Freedman et al., 1991; Freedman and Costa, 1992). Given the fact that atrophy can be localised and remain so, at least for a period, patients with specific impairments of language, praxis, visual processing and aspects of cognition should be an expected part of the range of dementias, although rare.

Vascular dementias

Multi-infarct dementia

Multi-infarct dementia (MID), sometimes called vascular dementia, is caused by multiple small infarcts which leave lacunae (small holes) in the white matter of the brain and the brainstem in about 70% of cases, and is often associated with hypertension. The infarcts are largely from the heart and atheromatous plaques in blood vessels outside the cerebrovascular system. Larger cortical infarcts may also occur in about 20% of cases and a mixture of cortical and subcortical lesions in the remaining 30% (Meyer et al., 1988). As with Alzheimer's disease, there is considerable debate as to whether the variation in symptoms and disease progresson in MID represents heterogeneity within a single disorder or a number of separate syndromes.

After Alzheimer's disease, MID is the second most common cause of dementia in North America, Europe and Australia but is the most common cause in Japan and China (Bannister, 1992). Hachinski et al. (1974) developed a 13-point ischaemia scale which helps to differentiate vascular dementias from primary degenerative dementia (see Appendix V). This scale is now used widely but not uncritically. High scores suggest MID whereas lower scores suggest Alzheimer's and other non-ischaemic dementias. Features that score most points and therefore make a diagnosis of MID more likely are abrupt onset, fluctuating course, history of strokes, and focal neurological symptoms and signs. The fluctuating course of MID often includes at least some recovery after an episode and it may be amenable to a range of treatments (Roth, 1981).

A complication of medical diagnosis in MID is the high incidence of both this and Alzheimer's disease in the same people. Tatemichi (1990) discussed the mechanisms of stroke related to dementia and outlined the ways in which dementia can result from cerebrovascular disease:

- The cerebral injury may be located in a region which can affect many cognitive functions, such as the association areas of the posterior cerebrum.
- The volume of the cerebral injury may reach a point where compensation is no longer possible.
- The number of injuries may have an additive or multiplicative effect.
- Alzheimer's disease and stroke may interact, with stroke adding to the effects of early Alzheimer's.

MID is marked by an abrupt onset with stepwise deterioration and a fluctuating progression. Early clinical features include weakness, slowness, dysarthria, dysphagia, small-stepped gait and emotional lability (Hachinski et al., 1974). Pseudobulbar dysarthria is the most common form of speech disturbance. Because of the focal nature of the damage, there is no characteristic pattern of behaviourial deficits in the earlier stages of the disease but language deficits may be present if there is specific left hemisphere damage, and dysprosody has been reported where there is right hemisphere damage (Ross, 1981).

Patients with lacunae infarcts who show cognitive deficits may also have decreased spontaneity, reduced initiative, response inhibition and mental set shifting deficits (Ishii, Hishahara and Imamura, 1986) while another group with presumed stroke-related white matter degeneration are more likely to exhibit decreased spontaneity, decreased speed of information processing and elaboration (Gupta et al., 1988; Junque et al., 1990). Loring et al. (1986) examined cognitive and language functioning in patients with MID and Alzheimer's disease and concluded that neuropsychological testing alone could not reliably distinguish between the two conditions although there is some evidence that more specific language testing may be able to do so (Kontiola et al., 1990; Sasanuma, Sakuma and Kitano, 1990). Sasanuma, Sakuma and Kitano (1990) carried out a longitudinal study of MID and Alzheimer's disease and found that those with MID had preserved recent memory, more diverse language profiles and less decline in their scores over time than those with Alzheimer's disease.

Despite the high incidence of MID, there have been very few studies of language impairment, perhaps because of the problem of reporting fluctuations in performance which may include partial recovery of function. Language impairment may be similar to specific aphasia syndromes (Benson, 1979) but there is also a co-occurring dysarthria. Lesser (1989) described a patient with MID whose language profile was similar to that of transcortical sensory aphasia. This man had preserved oral spelling and repetition but severe anomia and poor semantic comprehension. His spelling suggested a dissociation between his semantic system and his store of written word forms (graphemic output lexicon).

Group studies of language in MID suggest that there is simplification of structural aspects of sentence production with retained sentence content, and empty words are used less frequently than in Alzheimer's patients (Hier, Hagenlocker and Shindler, 1985; Mendez and Ashla-Mendez, 1991). With increasing severity, sentence length and syntactic complexity are further reduced and sentence fragments become more common. Powell et al. (1988) compared the language and speech characteristics of a group of subjects with MID with those of an age and severity matched group of Alzheimer's subjects. They concluded that MID was associated with a clinically distinguishable pattern of speech and language disturbances. Motor-speech disturbance was present in nearly all cases of MID but in few of Alzheimer's disease so that a diagnosis of Alzheimer's disease should be questioned in a patient with melodic or articulatory disturbance. Language abnormalities were not as evident in the patients with MID who had fewer characteristics of fluent aphasia. Instead, they produced fewer, shorter, less syntactically complex utterances than those with Alzheimer's disease.

MID produces heterogeneous deficits but depression is often a specific complicating feature which may not be amenable to medication (Kramer and Reifler, 1992). The patterns of language, cognitive deficits and behavioural changes are determined by the specific arteries affected and the location and extent of infarcted tissue (Mahler and Cummings, 1991). Because of the variability in motor speech, language and swallowing deficits, the possibility that control of hypertension may stop the deterioration in some patients and even produce a limited improvement in function, careful assessment of patients is necessary.

Case history: GC (Thompson, 1986)

GC, a 70-year-old woman who was referred to a neurology department with 'general deterioration', illustrates the potential for partial recovery. CT scanning showed changes associated with degenerative vascular disease, particularly in the right parietal region, and a diagnosis of MID was made.

On first assessment, the Dementia Rating Scale showed GC to have a moderate dementia but she gave a good personal history with unimpaired attention. Identifying objects by name was very poor but auditory comprehension on the Token Test was only mildly impaired and digit repetition was also near ceiling. There were no errors of expressive language, reading, writing, calculation or praxis. However, her word fluency and block design were mildly impaired.

On second assessment GC was orientated to person and place but not time. Digit recall was reduced to the 50th percentile but auditory comprehension on the Token Test had improved marginally to the 90th percentile. Confrontation naming had fallen sharply, with one semantic paraphasia, but word fluency showed only a marginal fall. Sentence construction had fallen from the 90th to the 70th percentile due more to word retrieval difficulties than to disturbance of syntax. Written sentence comprehension and written naming both showed deterioration but single-word reading tests remained near ceiling. Gestural ability, which had been near ceiling on first assessment, dropped steeply. Praxis remained intact except for constructional praxis which dropped sharply.

On the third assessment the patient remained disorientated in time and demonstrated impaired recent memory. Her score on the Dementia Rating Scale had fallen futher. However, most language tests had either remained stable or had improved percentiles. Word naming, written naming and written sentence comprehension were back at near ceiling and sentence construction remained unchanged. Word fluency had dropped marginally due to violations of the time constraint rather than inability to generate words. Gesture and constructional praxis had improved to near ceiling.

Despite a moderate dementia on the Dementia Rating Scale, this patient's language abilities were well preserved on the first assessment, showed evident deficits on the second assessment and had recovered on the third assessment (Table 6.2), illustrating the classic stepwise progression of MID rather than a steady progression in severity. This profile illustrates that patients with MID can improve their language, which is of considerable importance for their management (see Chapter 9).

Table 6.2 Language and cognitive skills profile: GC

	Percentile scores		
	Test 1	*Test 2*	*Test 3*
Dementia Rating Scale	50	40	30
Tests which change			
Object identification by name	10	95	95
Token test	85	90	95
Repeating digits forwards	90	50	50
Repeating digits backwards	95	50	95
Confrontation naming	95	50	95
Gesture	95	20	95
Word fluency	80	75	70
Sentence construction	90	70	70
Written sentence comprehension	95	70	95
Written naming	95	40	95
Calculation	95	60	60
Constructional praxis	85	40	85
Tests which remain near ceiling for all three assessments			
Object identification by function			
Sentence repetition			
Automatic speech			
Description of object function			
Single word reading			
Word recognition			
Sentence reading			
Automatic writing			
Dictation			
Copying			
Oral praxis			
Articulatory praxis			

Binswanger's disease

This is a form of vascular dementia caused by multiple infarcts of the white matter of the cerebral cortex with lacunar infarcts in the subcortical areas of the basal ganglia and the thalamus but sparing of the cortex and subcortical arcuate fibres. The clinical features of the disease are a history of hypertension, vascular disease and possibly acute strokes. There is then a gradual accumulation of neurological symptoms with prominent motor disturbances including pseudobulbar palsy with associated dysarthria and behavioural and mood changes including agitation, depression, irritability and euphoria. These symptoms predominate over a memory disorder which is difficult to assess due to inattention (Caplan and Schoene, 1978).

Interest in the disease has been renewed since the white matter infarcts have been clearly seen by MRI scanning. The disease is essentially progressive but, if treatment can control blood pressure and other factors associated with vascular disease, then patients can have periods of relative stability during which they may be able to benefit from treatment for speech and language deficits (Cummings and Benson, 1992).

Parkinson's disease

The dementia associated with Parkinson's disease has been described as subcortical but there is ample evidence that both cognition and language functions show deficits. Parkinson's disease is characterised by disturbance of motor function, in particular muscular rigidity and/or tremor. It is a common disease, with a prevalence of 108:100 000 in the UK, which is comparable to the average reported prevalence across other countries (Sutcliffe et al., 1985). It is most likely to begin in the 60s and affects men and women equally. The average prevalence of dementia in Parkinson's disease is thought to be just over 35% but, for idiopathic Parkinson's disease and adjusting for age-related cognitive changes, the figure is probably 15–20% (Brown and Marsden, 1984). The wide range of prevalence figures shows some controversy in this area: Cummings (1988), for example, suggests that 40% of these patients have dementia and that most have some neuropsychological deficits, but these figures must be viewed in the light of the individual patient's age, level of motor deficits and drug intake.

The pathology of Parkinson's disease has been associated with damage to the basal ganglia and related structures. There may be Lewy body damage in the cortex or cholinergic forebrain. Increasing knowledge of neurotransmitters and receptors has shown that the cortex, and in particular the frontal lobes, are sites for dopamine receptors. Research on language change in Parkinson's disease is equivocal in its conclusions. The pathology causing possible language deficits is equally inconclusive. Damage to subcortical structures may affect language processing, or the language deficit may be caused by reduced cortical functioning, as shown in more recent metabolic scanning studies (Kuhl, Metter and Reige, 1984).

There is no consensus concerning the possible co-occurrence of Alzheimer's and Parkinson's diseases. Alzheimer-type cortical changes have been found in neuropathological studies of patients with Parkinson's disease. Whether the two disease processes co-occur or development of one predisposes to development of the other is not known. Other studies have suggested that advancing age in a population with Parkinson's disease may account for the Alzheimer-type changes (Heston, 1981).

Cognitive function usually shows a discrepancy between performance and verbal IQ, with performance IQ showing a greater decrement, largely due to slow or abnormal motor function on tests requiring motor coordination or prompt responses. Depression is another common feature.

Before we consider the possibility of language deficits in Parkinson's disease, the features of parkinsonian dysarthria need to be described in detail because, by themselves, they may convey an impression of slowness of thought and cognitive dysfunction which is not necessarily confirmed on testing. Several studies have investigated whether increasing cognitive loads, while keeping motoric aspects of the task constant, cause difficulties for patients with the disease. Most of these studies show no evidence of processing decrements with increased cognitive load when age-matched groups of affected and normal subjects are used (Brown and Marsden, 1986; Rogers et al., 1987) although one study found a decrement in an older group of patients (Wilson et al., 1980). This slowing of the processing of auditory, visual and tactile sensory information is called *bradyphrenia* and should not be confused with another symptom commonly found in these patients (*bradykinesia*), which describes slowness of movement.

Bradykinesia may impact on language performance by one of three possible mechanisms:

- slowed initiation of motor acts (Leandersson, Meyerson and Persson, 1972);
- motor responses may be carried out slowly (Anderson and Horak, 1984);
- motor planning may be slowed (Brown and Marsden, 1991).

Muscle rigidity is another major component of most dysarthrias in Parkinson's disease, usually affecting all speech systems (respiratory, phonatory, resonatory, articulatory and initiation mechanisms). Parkinsonian speech is typically slow to be initiated, with reduced ability to control speed leading to a fast speech rate, reduced volume and pitch range and some articulatory imprecision. Gross movements of the orofacial musculature are often restricted while the fine movements for speech are often relatively intact. Single words may be quite intelligible but connected speech is usually less so. Because of difficulty in making pitch and volume changes, speech is often difficult to understand because it does not contain the normal range of intonation contrasts needed to signal structural, meaning and emotional features of language. In addition, perhaps because of muscular rigidity, these patients may have difficulty in using paralinguistic means of expression such as facial expression and gesture. Medication may alleviate some of these features, but there are highly complex patterns of drug response in patients with this disease: one study, for example, suggests that medication may be the cause of some learning impairment in Parkinson's disease which disappears when medication is withdrawn (Gotham, Brown and Marsden, 1988). With medication, improvement in general mobility, for example, does not necessarily carry with it any corresponding change in speech patterns and vice versa. Mr AL, a patient seen by one of the authors, had good general mobility and was able to play a round of golf but his speech was intelligible only in a quiet environment and he was often asked to repeat. When his drug regimen was changed because he developed tardive dyskinesia, his overall mobility was reduced but his speech intelligibility improved. Golf was important to him, however, and he requested another drug change.

Language skills in Parkinson's disease may show deficits in more complex areas of language processing. Most of the studies on language function have used relatively undifferentiated groups of patients and do not take into account effects of medication or lack of it. Scott, Caird and Williams (1984) found that their patients had difficulty in appreciating intonation and facial expression but showed no language deficits on a shortened aphasia test battery. They did, however, produce significantly more deviant utterances than the control group of normal elderly when describing facial expression. There were no hearing loss or auditory discrimination problems in the group with Parkinson's disease. The difficulty in interpretation of intonation and facial expression was not related to duration of the disease or specific medication.

There is some evidence of difficulty in interpreting linguistic information in this condition. Although Scott et al. (1984) found no impairment of auditory comprehension at single word, sentence or paragraph level, McNamara et al. (1992) suggested that patients are less able to monitor their own language errors. Using language produced when describing the Boston Cookie Theft picture (Goodglass and Kaplan, 1983), McNamara et al. found that patients corrected only 25% of their own errors, compared with a normal elderly group whose correction rate was over 82%. The group with Parkinson's disease, who had an average age of 61;3 years and had been screened to exclude dementia, had a correction rate similar to a group with Alzheimer's disease but there were qualitative differences. The Parkinson's group were able to correct single words and make reformulation repairs, i.e. corrections that alter the grammatical structure of the phrase or sentence in which the error occurs, but the Alzheimer's group used mainly reformulation-type repairs. This evidence corresponds to other evidence on word retrieval in Parkinson's disease. Patients can make single-word corrections because they have better access to their lexicon whereas naming disorder and specific-word retrieval deficits are pervasive in patients with Alzheimer's disease. McNamara et al. (1992) suggest that the Parkinson's group have monitoring difficulties due to frontal system dysfunction. Huber, Shuttleworth and Freidenberg (1989), using a group with an average age of 70;4 years and matched for cognitive function on the Mini Mental State Examination, replicated the findings of many studies (see Knight, 1992, for a review) that these patients are significantly worse at word fluency tasks than normals and found them to be worse than the Alzheimer group. Word fluency requires retrieval of as many words as possible in one category in a timed period, usually 1 minute. However, Hanley (1981) suggests that the significant difference in word fluency disappears if age and vocabulary scores are matched. On a naming test, the patients with Parkinson's disease performed significantly better than those with Alzheimer's, although they were significantly worse than the normal controls. Unfortunately the control group was on average 5–6 years younger than the group with Parkinson's disease, but other studies report similar findings (Matison et al., 1982). No deficits in comprehension of single words and commands were found in the group with Parkinson's disease who were tested on the Western Aphasia Battery.

Other studies suggest that there may be problems in both understanding and production of sentences, in particular syntax (Obler and Albert, 1981; Lieberman et al., 1989; Grossman et al., 1991). Both spoken and written language have been shown to be different from those of normal age-matched controls, having shorter phrase length in spoken language (Iles, 1989) but using more words per theme and more complex sentence structure in written language (Obler and Albert, 1981). Sentence comprehension seems to be impaired when syntax becomes more complex but increased length of sentence does not increase comprehension difficulty (Grossman et al., 1992). Patients appear to have more difficulty in understanding sentences containing relative clauses than sentences containing subordinate clauses in detection of an omitted grammatical morpheme, and seem to be helped by semantic constraints such as non-reversibility of sentences (Grossman et al., 1992). If we consider the possibility that some patients may have a form of dementia, these language findings suggest that the dementia in Parkinson's disease is not like that in Alzheimer's disease.

An alternative way to view some of the problems in Parkinson's disease to consider how these deficits arise. Disruptions to frontal lobe mechanisms, possibly caused by a reduction in dopamine level, has been put forward as the most likely explanation (Gotham et al., 1988; Huber et al., 1989; Taylor, Saint-Cyr and Lang, 1990). Below-normal scores on word fluency tests can be indicative of frontal lobe damage but equally can indicate poor generalised cortical functioning. One of the most interesting features of research into this disease is in the area of dual task performance and internal versus external cue processing. There is now a body of research suggesting that these patients show impairment on tasks which require them to use their own internal cues but perform much better when external cues are provided (Brown and Marsden, 1988). Tasks which require set shifting, i.e. the ability to learn a specific task and then switch to another, do appear more difficult for such patients than normal controls despite the absence of dementia (Taylor, Saint-Cyr and Lang, 1986) and whether or not they are taking L-dopa. Tweedy, Langer and McDowell (1982) found this same difficulty in the ability of their study group to utilise semantic cues as memory aids. Although most research in this area has concentrated on motor performance, there is some evidence that deficits in set switching or performance of dual tasks may also apply to language. This points to a possible deficit in a central cognitive mechanism which may affect language.

Depression is another aspect of the disease, which can be important in assessing language and communication deficits and in decision making on management. It has a reported incidence of up to 50% (Gotham, Brown and Marsden, 1986). Whether the depression is reactive or endogenous is not known but analysis of the literature suggests that the symptoms are closer to those of reactive depression. Depression is obviously not necessarily an abnormal reaction to a degenerative disease but it may require treatment. Some symptoms of Parkinson's disease, such as sleep disturbance, also appear in depression.

Therefore signs of dementia in Parkinson's disease may, for most clients, be no more than the sum of the parts, i.e. no more than an interaction between age, motor dysfunction and drug effects. Careful investigation of drug effects and patterns of performance during the day as well as cognitive performance need to be made before dementia is diagnosed. Finally, patients with this disease have consistently shown a good response to several forms of group therapy for their communication disturbance (Scott and Caird, 1981, 1983; Robertson and Thomson, 1983; Johnson and Pring, 1990).

Progressive supranuclear palsy

Alternatively called Steele–Richardson–Olszewski syndrome after the authors who first described it, progressive supranuclear palsy typically includes a gaze palsy, pseudobulbar palsy, dysarthria, dysphagia and dystonic rigidity of the neck and upper trunk, and may be diagnosed as Parkinson's disease at first because extrapyramidal signs are prominent and the age range for presentation is similar. The dementia of this disease has been described as consisting of forgetfulness, slow mentation, dysarthria, emotional or personality changes and impaired ability to manipulate acquired knowledge in the absence of dysphasia, agnosia and perceptual abnormalities (Maher and Lees, 1986). The disease is progressive and usually results in death within 6 years, unlike Parkinson's disease which is not necessarily life-threatening.

It has been classified as a subcortical dementia and most investigations of small groups of these patients have shown no definite signs of primary language difficulty although other deficits such as initiation problems and dysarthria may produce a communication disturbance (LeBrun, Devreux and Rousseau, 1986). A study by Maher, Smith and Lees (1985) examined cognitive deficits in subjects with this condition at the time of diagnosis and reported mild word-finding difficulty but no evidence of dysphasia or comprehension difficulties. Podoll, Schwarz and Noth (1991) have found evidence of language impairment secondary to other cognitive deficits including increased rates of repair and misnamings. Other deficits in reading and writing appear to be due to visual processing changes or to the gaze palsy. Sentences are well formed but syntactically simple, and memory function equals that of normal controls (Milberg and Albert, 1989). The dysarthria in progressive supranuclear palsy is characterised by a slow speech rate, low volume and restricted prosody due to poor pitch variation and difficulty in altering loudness for stress (Hanson and Metter, 1980). Palilalia is sometimes found but as the disease progresses speech is initiated less often and response latencies are great (Albert et al., 1974).

Huntington's disease

This progressive and familial disease, affecting both sexes, usually has a mean age of onset between 30 and 45 years, beginning with either involuntary movement or personality changes. It is inherited as an autosomal dominant and, because of the familial nature of the condition, it is not usually difficult to diagnose. Members of those families in which it is present are usually aware of the possibility that it may develop. It is associated with cortical and basal ganglia degeneration.

The motor speech disturbance is largely a hyperkinetic dysarthria with sparse speech, altered prosody, decreased phrase length and lack of speech initiation (Podoll et al., 1988; Ross et al., 1990): there may also be impairment of comprehension of prosody (Speedie et al., 1990). Language changes include simplified syntax and press of speech (Illes, 1989). Word-finding difficulties have also been reported but visual processing impairments rather than specific semantic impairment may contribute to the deficit (Hodges, Salmon and Butters, 1991; Bayles and Tomoeda, 1983).

Few studies have examined the progression of Huntington's disease in relation to language and cognitive functioning but a study by Butters et al. (1978) compared the neuropsychological deficits found in recently diagnosed subjects with those in advanced Huntington's disease. The recently diagnosed group had specific memory disorders associated with difficulty in acquiring new information and reduced verbal fluency, which was due to difficulty in retrieval from long-term memory rather than a specific language dysfunction as naming was intact on other tests. The advanced group showed generalised non-focal cognitive disturbance but picture naming was preserved, suggesting less widespread deterioration than in other dementia-producing disorders.

Creutzfeldt–Jakob disease

Creutzfeldt–Jakob disease is a rare degenerative disorder caused by a slow transmissible virus which principally affects the frontal and occipital lobes of the cortex, the brainstem and cerebellum. Hart and Semple (1990) give an excellent synopsis of the literature on the pathology and differential diagnosis of this and other, related, disorders. The disease has a mean age at onset of 60 years and can progress rapidly. Even in its chronic form, the average length of time from diagnosis to death is 2 years. A recent cause of this condition in young adults between 20 and 34 years has been virus contamination of growth hormone, given to stimulate physical growth in undersized children (*BMJ* Editorial, 1992).

In approximately one-third of patients, an initial diagnosis of psychiatric disorder is followed by aphasia, agnosia, apraxia, dysarthria and memory disturbance. The dysarthria is most likely to be a combination of cerebellar and extrapyramidal types. Motor disturbances include myoclonus (which may be an early feature of the disease), rigidity and tremor due to extrapyramidal involvement, cerebellar ataxia, visual disturbances and cranial nerve palsies (Bieliauska and Fox, 1987; Cummings and Benson, 1992). Patients may present with an isolated Wernicke's-type aphasia (Mandell, Alexander and Carpenter, 1989). Patients in the later stages become mute and may go into coma for some weeks before death.

Depression and dementia

Depression is a common symptom, cause and consequence of ill health in elderly people (Cooper, 1987). Estimates of depression among the elderly are varied but there is evidence of high rates of undiagnosed depression (Brayne, 1990). In addition, the complex interaction between depression and dementia has resulted in confusing terminology in the literature.

Communication in an elderly person with endogenous (i.e. of unknown origin) depression is often impaired, with reduced intonation range and slow response latency. Language is often impoverished, with the patient giving brief replies which are unlikely to lead on to further discussion. On specific tasks, however, depressed patients may do well. Descriptions of the Cookie Theft picture by depressed elderly people may be as good as, or better than, those given by the normal healthy elderly, with fewer errors and fewer repairs (Maxim, 1991) as in the example below from a depressed man, aged 72 years:

a boy a boy on a stool /
and he's trying to reach something off a off the shelf /
looks as if he's stealing something. I don't know /
and and the little girl's standing up /
and it might be his mother washing up /
and the water's overflowing /
she's got a plate in her hand /
and the boy's falling off his stool /
there's a window over the sink /
looks as if there might be sweets in that box I don't /
or it might be biscuits biscuits /
the lady's washing up /
and there's there's soup bowls on the sink and a plate /

Emery (1989) used the Western Aphasia Battery to show that depressed elderly subjects performed significantly better than patients with Alzheimer's disease on all measures and were scoring significantly lower than normal controls only on measures that involved errors on the most complex items.

Intellectual impairment associated with psychiatric disturbance has been given the name *pseudodementia*. The literature is confused in this field as the term has been applied to different populations:

- elderly individuals with depression whose dementia is reversed by drug treatment;
- elderly individuals who have a progressive dementia associated with an underlying psychiatric condition which in the elderly is almost always depression. This condition can be regarded as reversible but, even if the depression shows some response to drug treatment, the dementia continues to progress.

Whether the elderly people in this second category in fact have an organic underlying cause for their dementia is a matter of debate.

It has been estimated that there is a 30% chance of misdiagnosis of the clinically depressed elderly person who presents with a history of cognitive impairment, sleep disturbance, appetite loss, psychomotor slowing, depressed affect and poor memory (Jarvik, 1982; Cummings and Benson, 1992). The need for accurate diagnosis of the dementia syndrome of depression from organic causes is obviously essential because appropriate drug intervention and therapy may be successful (Grossberg and Nakra, 1988).

The terms ***dementia of depression*** and ***pseudodementia*** have also been applied to elderly patients who have been admitted to hospital because of acute illness or injury and who develop depressive symptoms with associated cognitive deficits after surgery or prolonged institutionalisation.

The syndrome of depressive dementia has been defined by a number of authors. The lists in Table 6.3 compare history, signs and symptoms between the depressive dementias and organic dementias, adapted from Wells (1979).

Table 6.3 Comparison of organic and depressive dementias

Depressive dementia	*Organic dementia*
History	
Onset can be dated fairly precisely	Onset vague
Rapid progression of symptoms after onset	Slow progression
Family aware of dysfunction and its severity	Family often unaware
History of psychiatric illness	No psychiatric history
Patient frequently complains of cognitive loss	Patient rarely complains
Patient communicates strong sense of distress	Patient appears unconcerned or 'explains' loss
Clinical features	
Patient unwilling to respond/ gives 'don't know' answers	Patient gives near miss answers/will guess if encouraged
Recent and remote memory loss severe	Recent memory more equally impaired
Variability in performance on tasks of similar difficulty	Consistently poor performance on tasks of similar difficulty

Depression can occur in association with dementing diseases, notably Alzheimer's and Parkinson's diseases, which makes differential diagnosis difficult. Early on in the course of Alzheimer's disease patients may have a co-occurring depression (Reifler, 1986) or may be referred with a diagnosis of depression, which is then found to be a primary dementing illness (Feinberg and Goodman, 1984), sometimes called pseudo-depression. Depression can also be a major feature in the dementias associated with subcortical damage such as Parkinson's disease and Huntington's disease.

Case history: DA (Thompson, 1986)

DA, a 68-year-old farmer, was referred to a neurology department with emotional lability and withdrawal of interest. A CT scan demonstrated no major infarcts and the EEG showed medium to low amplitude with mild slowing of the left temporal regions as the sole abnormality. His mental state suggested mild dementia. He was oriented in time, place and person and gave a clear account of his case history. He presented with no dramatic disturbances of comprehension, expressive language, reading, writing, calculation or praxis. Word fluency was at the 30th percentile but emotional lability was noted to affect his performance during testing. Written naming also showed moderate deficits at the 59th percentile.

A year later, DA showed no evidence of deterioration in his language and cognitive skills: in fact, his score on written naming had improved to the 80th percentile. His word fluency had increased to the 60th percentile but remained low in relation to his other scores. There was no dramatic decline on retesting of the kind that accompanies organic dementia. With encouragement from the clinician, he was able lift his scores, in spite of tearfulness when he met the clinician for the second time and throughout the assessment.

The emotional disturbance, good concentration, behavioural improvement with encouragement and general stability or improvement of scores all suggest the diagnosis of pseudo-dementia.

The AIDS–dementia complex

Bannister (1992) lucidly sums up the problem of describing neurological aspects of the acquired immune deficiency syndrome (AIDS):

> The neurological complications of AIDS are difficult to summarize, as they may occur at each different stage of the disease and present with different patterns of disease with differing time courses, frequency and pathology, and probably even different pathological mechanisms. (p. 519)

The AIDS–dementia complex can take a variety of forms but usually includes lethargy, progressive cognitive impairment and slowing of movement and speech. It may present as a sudden, focal or progressive aphasia as the following two patients, seen by one of the authors, suggest.

Patient A had been HIV positive for some years but gradually began to have difficulties with all aspects of language. At first, he had an isolated word-finding deficit which was restricted to language output. Language functions were progressively compromised but only in the last stages of the disease was there any evidence of cognitive deficit. From his reported onset of these language deficits to his death was approximately 18 months.

Patient B was initially diagnosed as having a brain tumour, having presented with a sudden onset of language problems. His language and cognitive functions both deteriorated rapidly and he died within 4 months of the initial diagnosis.

Navia, Jordan and Price (1986) also described two forms of dementia in AIDS, one being steadily progressive and at times punctuated by accelerated deterioration and the other occurring in 20% of cases, having a much slower and protracted course. In terms of speech and language functioning, in the early stage there may be motor problems with speech and writing. Mild word-finding problems are found in some subjects, and language is affected by slowness of thought and mood changes. As the dementia progresses verbal responses become slower and less complex with virtual mutism in the final stage of the disease. Most patients with AIDS develop dementia associated with an HIV encephalopathy but a smaller percentage develop a dementia before AIDS has been diagnosed (Cummings and Benson, 1992).

Wernicke's encephalopathy/Korsakoff's psychosis

Thiamine deficiency (most commonly due to chronic alcohol abuse) causes these conditions, which are characterised by an isolated loss of recent memory in an otherwise alert person with little other evidence of remote memory, immediate recall or other cognitive changes. Strictly speaking these conditions are therefore amnesias rather than dementias, but chronic alcohol abuse and associated head trauma can lead to alcoholic dementia. As head injury has a peak of incidence in old age, it is important for clinical management that these two conditions are understood to be linked and that an underlying or frank Korsakoff's psychosis may complicate subsequent recovery from head injury.

Communication ability is reduced because memory for recent events is poor but language remains intact. Murdoch (1990) describes the relationship between the two conditions as 'Wernicke's encephalopathy represents the acute stage of this process and Korsakoff's syndrome the residual mental deficit that usually occurs in the late stages of Wernicke's encephalopathy' (p. 172). The following patient was seen by one of the authors.

Mr M, aged 76 years, was admitted to hospital, having been knocked over by a car just after he had left a bar. He had no history of health problems but was known to drink heavily. He was referred for language assessment which showed he had moderate but non-specific language deficits. He processed language slowly and appeared to have difficulty in remembering anything he had done earlier in the same session. The overall impression was that of confusion. It was recommended that he be referred for psychometric testing if there was no significant improvement in communication abilities within a 10-day period. On assessment, Korsakoff's psychosis was diagnosed.

Alcoholic dementia has been described as being more severe in the elderly and clinically the progression is slow with impairment in abstracting ability, short-term memory and verbal fluency (Cutting, 1982). If the patient ceases to consume alcohol there is usually an improvement in cognitive abilities but return to pre-alcoholic levels is unusual (Grant, Adams and Reed, 1984).

Conclusions

Many conditions that cause dementia have language impairment as a component but the causal relationship between cognitive decline and decline in language performance must be viewed with caution, particularly in the light of evidence from the progressive aphasias. The overall picture of the causes and types of dementia appears to be constantly changing with better use of imaging techniques and neuropsychological and language investigation. Although the literature contains single case and small group studies, there are still far too few studies where language and communication deficits are described and compared adequately. The paucity of longitudinal studies makes it impossible to say why or even how language processes break down because studies often only give broad descriptions of language function.

Chapter 7
Language pathology in Alzheimer's disease

The Alzheimer's disease complex

Approximately 20% of people over the age of 75 will have some type of dementia, Alzheimer's disease being the most common form. In this chapter the effects of dementia of Alzheimer type (DAT) on language processing will be examined. DAT has been described as a temporal lobe disorder with neural loss in the temporal–parietal–occipital junction area. The hippocampus and amygdala may be the initial sites for the pathology, which then progresses to the posterior parietal and temporal lobes (Martin, 1990). Further pathology may spread to the frontal lobes and to subcortical sites.

There is no positive test for DAT and diagnosis is by exclusion criteria and examination of behavioural, cognitive and language data. Appendix VII gives the criteria used for diagnosis in *The Diagnostic and Statistical Manual of Mental Disorders* (DSM-III-R, American Psychiatric Association, 1987). Most patients discussed in this chapter should, therefore, rightly be called probable DAT patients.

Alzheimer himself paid great attention to language disturbance in his description of a 57-year-old patient in 1907 (Alzheimer, 1977):

> When shown objects she could name them relatively correctly. However, even her perceptions were disturbed. Immediately after naming the objects she would forget them. She drifted from one line to the next while reading – either enunciating the individual letters or speaking in meaningless tone. While writing, she repeated single syllables, omitting others and quickly became confused. She used perplexing phrases when speaking or made paraphasic errors (*mild pourer* instead of *cup*). She would hesitate during speech. She did not understand some of the questions put to her. She appeared to have forgotten the use of several objects.

Methodological issues associated with distinguishing between normal ageing, the effects of dementia and variables such as education were discussed in Chapter 1 (pp. 18–27) and need to be borne in mind when evaluating the research in this field. Research into language disturbance in DAT has been influenced by four separate research trends:

1. Group studies of the language characteristics in DAT, which describe symptom clusters and severity
2. Studies which have compared the language disturbance in dementia with that of aphasia, using the syndrome-based classification in the Wernicke–Lichtheim tradition.
3. Single case studies, which have looked closely at the underlying language deficits, sometimes longitudinally.
4. Small group studies, which have looked at patients who present with distinct subtypes of DAT.

Early group studies viewed the language disturbance in DAT as hypothetically only quantitatively distinct from normal ageing language but current research suggests that there are many qualitative differences (Appell et al., 1982; Bayles and Kaszniak, 1987). DAT, as the most common form of dementia, has been intensively researched but, although it is possible to describe general characteristics of the disorder in DAT, the underlying processes and the nature of the disruption to these processes is still only as clear as the current state of knowledge about the mechanisms involved in these processes, which might be described as rudimentary.

When looking at the research on DAT or when testing patients with possible DAT, the following questions need to be considered:

- Are language and cognition equally disordered or is there an imbalance between these two systems?
- Which language processes are disordered, which are spared and how are they disordered?
- What level of severity is present and does this knowledge help to illuminate the current processing deficits, i.e. are these deficits severity dependent or do they contribute to the severity?

Heterogeneity within DAT is now widely recognised but there is considerable debate as to why this variation occurs and its relationship to the neuropathology affecting brain structures. Hardy (1992) suggests that DAT does represent a single pathological entity that presents in different forms although recent genetic studies point to a number of aetiologies that eventually lead to DAT. Other researchers suggest that there are several different forms of the disease which are assumed to represent different pathological processes or varying patterns of occurrence of these processes. Examples of different forms of DAT are:

- late onset;
- familial Alzheimer's (Rossor, Kennedy and Newman, 1992);
- early onset (Faber-Langendoen et al., 1988);

- Alzheimer's associated with Down's syndrome (Johanson et al., 1991).

There is, however, also evidence of heterogeneity within these subgroups of the disease. For example, Rossor et al. (1992) found variation in the onset and progression of familial Alzheimer's disease within families which may reflect disease variation or variation in associated factors such as education and age.

Studies that have examined the symptomatology of DAT suggest that certain symptoms are associated with faster rates of decline (Chui et al., 1992) but whether these symptoms reflect a different biological basis to the disease is not known. Mayeux, Stern and Sano (1992) investigated symptoms such as extrapyramidal and psychotic disorder in DAT and suggested that the presence of these symptoms did not define different clinical entities, but rather that they were manifestations of different stages of disease progression. Joanette, Poisant and Beland (1992) also reject the notion of different forms of DAT. They suggest that different profiles of deficits and preserved abilities between individuals may be due to individual differences in brain organisation for cognition and normal age-related changes in this organisation.

Variation in the level of language dysfunction in DAT and its significance has been specifically studied for diagnosis and prognosis. Chui et al. (1985) suggest that prevalence and severity of aphasia correlate with duration of illness and that early onset DAT predicts the early development of language problems. Seltzer and Sherwin (1983) suggest that early onset DAT (before age 65) is associated with greater language problems than late onset and that these different onsets represent distinct subtypes of DAT, with early onset DAT being associated with increased vulnerability of the left hemisphere. Filley, Kelly and Heaton (1986) also found greater disruption in language processing in early onset DAT but interpreted this disruption as being due to variation in disease progression. However, Koss and Friedland (1987) express doubts over the conclusions drawn by such studies because other aspects of the disorder are not adequately assessed. They reject theories of a subtype of DAT in which the left hemisphere is particularly vulnerable on the grounds that studies have not examined subjects carefully enough for evidence of disorders usually associated with the right hemisphere such as visual perceptual problems.

This debate clearly illustrates the need for future research to examine language dysfunction in detail and to relate deficits to the underlying pathology. There is also a need to examine language in relation to other factors such as cognitive functioning, age, education and premorbid functioning. The concept of DAT language having a homogeneous progressive course of semantic deficit, syntactic deficit and finally phonological deficit is still prevalent but under siege.

Longitudinal profiles

There is now a consensus that the language symptomatology in DAT is heterogeneous and that, although it is possible to describe language and cognitive functions at different stages in the disease progression, it is more useful to investigate and compare the deterioration of specific processes. One of the main problems in group studies that use a profile approach is that very little can be said about what the individual patient can and cannot do. Single case studies of DAT have, to some extent, helped, particularly because they often point to specific deficits and dissociations between deficits that are unlikely to be found in group studies.

Unless single case studies are longitudinal, however, only a snapshot of a moment in the disease progression is possible. As an introduction to language and cognitive change in DAT, the longitudinal profiles of three patients with DAT are presented below. All were tested three times during a 3-year period on a number of conservative language and cognitive tasks, all of which have been standardised on a normal elderly population. These tests do not specify underlying impairments, although some suggestions are made. The first test was taken at the time of the patient's initial referral to hospital due to language/cognitive difficulties. Such profiles are inadequate for the description of specific language processing but they are able to provide some idea of the variation found as the disease progresses.

Profile 1 (Thompson, 1986)

BD, a 64-year-old railway worker, lived at home but was hospitalised when tested for the third time. Initial assessment showed that he had moderate dementia. He was disoriented in time and place but was able to give an accurate personal history. Memory for non-personal events and recent memory were impaired. Auditory comprehension on the Token Test was impaired but he was able to point to objects by name and function. Sentence and digit repetition both showed deficits. Apart from sentence repetition, language output tasks were well preserved, with word fluency being particularly impressive. There was no evidence of a disturbance of reading or writing, nor of oral or limb apraxia. A deficit in calculation was also evident. Raven's Matrices was within normal limits but his score on Block Design showed some impairment.

On the second assessment BD remained in the moderate dementia range on the Dementia Rating Scale although his score had dropped. He had difficulty in attending. Auditory comprehension on sentence and single-word tasks were unchanged. Language output skills overall remained well preserved but word fluency and sentence construction showed frank deficits. Written sentence comprehension fell sharply but all other reading tasks remained near ceiling. Both measures of cognitive function, Block design and Ravens matrices score showed deficits.

On the third assessment, BD had severe dementia and was disoriented in all but person. Auditory comprehension of sentences fell again, reflecting particular difficulty with the most complex parts of the Token Test but identification of objects to name and function remained good. His repetition of digits forwards improved to near ceiling but on reversed digit span his score fell to the 45th percentile, which is reflected in his inability to attend to auditory sentence comprehension tasks. Language output was well preserved apart from word fluency which fell again. Sentence construction also showed increased deficits but sentence repetition had improved. Automatic writing, copying and written naming all showed deficits for the first time and constructional apraxia became more evident. His Raven's Matrices score had dropped significantly but block design showed only a marginal drop.

BD showed a pattern of progressive deterioration of cognitive and more complex comprehension language skills. Written and auditory sentence comprehension both declined. There was a progressive loss of word fluency, sentence construction, calculation, constructional ability and writing. The ability to understand single words, to name objects and to describe objects by function was preserved. All single-word reading and writing tasks, apart from spelling which showed a small decrement, were also preserved, as was the ability to read sentences aloud.

Table 7.1 Language and cognitive skills profile: BD

	Percentile scores		
	Test 1	*Test 2*	*Test 3*
Dementia Rating Scale	50	30	10
Block Design	85	75	70
Language tests showing change			
Token test	70	70	40
Sentence repetition	60	50	90
Repeating digits forwards	70	70	95
Repeating digits in reverse	70	80	50
Word fluency	95	85	50
Sentence construction	90	70	50
Sentence comprehension	95	65	65
Automatic writing	95	95	10
Written naming	95	95	80
Copying	95	95	50
Calculation	50	50	10
Constructional praxis	90	90	50
Tests which remain at or near ceiling			
Identifying objects to name			
Identifying objects to description			
Automatic speech			
Confrontation naming			
Describing object function			
Gesture			
Word reading			
Word recognition			
Sentence reading			
Single-word dictation			
Oral praxis			
Ideomotor praxis			

Table 7.2 Language and cognitive skills profile: CB

	Percentile scores		
	Test 1	*Test 2*	*Test 3*
Dementia Rating Scale	59	20	5
Block Design	50	40	35
Tests which show change			
Token test	95	50	25
Sentence repetition	30	20	15
Repeating digits forwards	20	20	30
Repeating digits backwards	70	20	20
Automatic speech	95	95	30
Describing object function	95	95	50
Word fluency	55	25	5
Sentence construction	30	30	5
Word recognition	95	95	10
Written sentence comprehension	70	45	10
Automatic writing	95	95	10
Dictation	95	70	70
Calculation	95	60	60
Ideomotor praxis	95	95	50
Constructional praxis	90	80	30
Tests which are stable			
Copying	50	50	50
Tests which show preserved function			
Identifying objects to name			
Identifying objects to function			
Confrontation naming			
Gesture			
Word reading			
Sentence reading			
Written naming			
Oral praxis			

Profile 2 (Thompson, 1986)

CB was a 57-year-old woman who worked in an office. On initial assessment she was well oriented but had a deficit of recent memory. Short-term auditory memory on digit recall and sentence repetition were both impaired but auditory sentence comprehension on the Token Test was normal. Word fluency and sentence construction both showed deficits but confrontation naming, object function description and all single-word reading and writing tasks were well preserved. Her score on the Dementia Rating Scale suggested that she had a moderate dementia and her Block Design score was low but her Raven's Matrices score was within normal limits. Although conversational language sounded superficially normal, CB's medical notes commented on her avoidance of language, by use of such phrases as 'you've caught me on a bad day today' or 'I've been very busy with the children today and I don't feel like talking just now'.

On second assessment CB was disoriented but maintained long-term memory. Sentence repetition, digit recall, auditory and written sentence comprehension had all deteriorated further. Spoken language output remained free of naming errors but word fluency had continued to decline. Single-word reading tests remained at the 95th percentile, as did the ability to read sentences aloud. As her written sentence comprehension had continued to fall, CB could read aloud some material that she could not understand. Written naming remained good but writing single words to dictation now showed a deficit. Block Design and Raven's Matrices scores both fell further.

On the third assessment CB was disoriented to person, time and place and was unable to give a history. Auditory and written sentence comprehension scores continued to fall. Confrontation naming and object function description remained well preserved but word fluency and sentence construction fell further. All writing tests now showed deficits apart from written naming. The Block Design remained at the 35th percentile but CB's Raven's Matrices score fell again.

CB showed increasing disintegration of cognitive ability and there was an early loss of short-term memory. Although auditory and written sentence comprehension both showed reductions, identifying objects to name and function was preserved. Spoken and written object naming was retained but word fluency and sentence construction skills were reduced. Although CB could read single words and sentences aloud, even word recognition was poor by the third assessment. Constructional abilities and measures of non-verbal cognitive skills showed progressive decline although her score on the Block Design test was initially lower but deteriorated less than her Raven's Matrices score. Oral praxis and the ability to gesture was retained.

Profile 3 (Thompson, 1986)

VC was a 56-year-old housewife who presented with a disturbance of language. A CT scan was performed and showed no real abnormalities or focal lesions. The ventricular system was well defined with no displacements. On initial assessment VC was oriented in time and place but not person. She was unable to give a non-personal history or to recall information from recent memory. Her score on the Dementia Rating Scale was at the 30th percentile but Block Design and Raven's Matrices were much higher, suggesting relatively good cognitive function. VC had no difficulty in identifying objects by name or function or in written word comprehension but all other language tests were compromised. Confrontation naming and describing object function were particularly severe deficits. Auditory and written sentence comprehension were poor and auditory memory on digit span scored at the 30th percentile. Automatic speech was well preserved, scoring at the 95th percentile. VC's spontaneous language was marked by anomia, circumlocution, stereotyped utterances and gesture, which was good on initial testing. Initial attempts at sentence construction were poor but she was able to read some sentences, scoring at the 70th percentile. Her written sentence comprehension was low, showing that she was able to read some material which she did not understand. Initially, automatic writing and copying were preserved but VC was not able to write to dictation. She scored well on calculation and on constructional ability but tests of oral and ideomotor apraxia only yielded scores at the 10th percentile.

On the second assessment, VC showed a decline in all of her scores apart from those of automatic speech, automatic writing, Block Design and

Raven's Matrices.

On the third assessment, VC showed a further decline in language and cognitive abilities, scoring at almost floor level on all tests except digit span forwards (on which there was a marginal improvement), automatic writing, copying, constructional praxis, Block Design and Raven's Matrices (which fell drastically).

VC presented with quite severe language deficits with a marked drop in test scores from the first to second year but her cognitive skills on Raven's Matrices were well retained until a sudden deterioration from the second to the third testing. Automatic speech and automatic writing were more resistant to deterioration, as were drawing and calculation.

Table 7.3 Language and cognitive skills profile: VC

	Percentile scores		
	Test 1	*Test 2*	*Test 3*
Dementia Rating Scale	30	10	5
Block Design	85	80	80
Tests which show change			
Identifying objects to name	95	10	5
Identifying objects to function	95	5	5
Token test	10	5	5
Sentence repetition	15	10	5
Repeating digits forwards	30	20	30
Repeating digits backwards	30	20	5
Automatic speech	95	95	5
Gesture	20	10	5
Word fluency	10	5	5
Sentence construction	25	5	5
Word reading	10	5	5
Word recognition	95	10	5
Sentence reading	70	5	5
Written sentence comprehension	20	5	5
Automatic writing	95	95	5
Written naming	10	5	5
Copying	95	50	50
Calculation	90	10	5
Oral praxis	10	5	5
Ideomotor praxis	10	5	5
Constructional praxis	85	50	50
Tests with scores near floor level		5th percentile	
Confrontation naming			
Description of function			
Dictation			

All three profiles show deterioration in language and cognitive functions but they also show considerable variation between the patients in terms of the relationship between language and cognitive decline, the course of the progression on individual subtests and the areas of language function which are either spared or show deficits.

Language research

Deficits at the semantic level have received most attention in DAT because language changes are most apparent at this level. Descriptions of language produced by patients with DAT have, almost without exception, concentrated on investigating the reduction of available vocabulary and the breakdown of logical associations that are common in language produced by people with DAT. Some attention has also been given to the deteriorating quality of discourse that is shown in DAT and discourse analysis has been used to describe changes in conversational interactions (Hutchinson and Jenson, 1980; Ulatowska et al., 1981). Most studies of language in DAT look at different levels of breakdown as language deteriorates. These studies give a valuable overall view of the range of language behaviour that can be found among people with dementing illnesses. They do not, however, often look at the language as the reflection of a linguistic system undergoing change but rather as a reflection of cognitive or neurological processes in decline (Appel et al., 1982; Bayles, 1982). More recent single case studies have discussed the dissociations of impairment that can be found in DAT and the longitudinal aspects of language processing deficits (Funnell and Hodges, 1990; Chertkow and Bub, 1992; Joanette et al., 1992). The next six sections discuss some of the most relevant findings from the literature.

Lexical semantics

Difficulty in word finding is one of the most noticeable features of dementia and appears to have several causes. Howes (1964) found the word frequencies in the vocabulary of one patient to be within normal limits. Obler (1980) reported that word frequencies and the probability of co-occurrence between words affected subjects' ability to repeat sentences. There is some evidence that the lexical–semantic system breaks down differently, if not independently, from other cortical functions in a large subgroup of DAT (Martin, 1987).

Schwartz, Saffran and Williamson (1981), working with a group with DAT, suggested that under-selection of the semantic lexical item is a cause of naming problems in DAT. Given a series of four pictures and asked to identify one item, patients showed much greater difficulty in selecting the correct item from four items of the same class than in identifying one item from four different semantic classes. Although the group had difficulty in selecting the correct written word when given the word orally, they could match the spoken word more easily to conceptually related items. There was no correlation between naming and conceptual ability, and individuals who were able to name well might show gross conceptual problems when tested on other tasks, such as figure copying, in the absence of visual problems. Schwartz et al. also found that the naming and language comprehension scores of the group were similar. Most research reports that comprehension scores are better than naming scores so this finding is surprising (Bayles et al., 1992).

Auditory comprehension of words, sentences and paragraphs does show deficits in DAT but a close correlation between access to the semantic system and the ability to understand has been suggested. Although working memory may show deficits, increased length of sentence, for example, is less a factor in comprehension than semantic complexity (Hart, 1988). This may be a result of the tests used or of the homogeneity of diagnosis within the group. Early group studies occasionally used mixed populations because of the difficulty in making accurate diagnoses of dementia type, thus producing findings that do not accurately describe any particular type of dementia.

Schwartz, Marin and Saffran (1979), in a study of a single patient with suspected DAT, found evidence of a more intact but usually inaccessible semantic system. Their patient was able to name only one out of 70 items although the patient demonstrated by gesture that she did recognise some of the items. Asked to select the correct name from five written words, the patient's percentage of objects correctly recognised went up to more than 50%, which was much greater than chance. Of the errors, 51 out of the total of 140 made were of the semantic distractor item (e.g. item = cat, semantic distractor = dog). Out of 35 such word pairs, the patient was able to identify only four items correctly and frequently over-extended the choice to the semantic distracter item when selecting from the five-item test. This is interpreted as being caused by the gradual loss of semantic features for each item, with more specific semantic features lost before more general semantic features. Although the visual representations of the items may have been sufficiently similar to cause some of the patient's errors, it must be assumed that the patient's ability to show recognition by gesture ruled out this interpretation.

Whitaker (1976) provided further evidence that the semantic system in dementia can remain partially intact and accessible under certain conditions. Her possible DAT patient had no useful social language. When eye contact was made and the examiner spoke, the patient exhibited echolalia. Given a determiner + adjective + noun phrase which contained a phonemic error, the patient would correct the phrase when shown the actual object. Some of the phonemic substitutions created a semantically meaningful word, e.g. *pork* for *fork*, *wooden stable* for *wooden table*. The patient still corrected the items, showing that the word had been successfully related to the object. Only when she was shown no object did she repeat exactly what the examiner had said, even when the phonemic change created a nonsense word, e.g. *a yellow tencil.*

The literature, therefore, suggests that the semantic system at single-word level may remain at least partially intact in DAT up to a relatively late stage in the disease process. The semantic feature system may be susceptible to breakdown, with more specific features being lost first. Patients have difficulty in correctly selecting an item from others in the same semantic category and may confuse items sharing several of the same semantic features. In moderate to severe DAT, superordinate identification, in which a stimulus item has to be matched to an appropriate category, is more difficult than a spoken word to picture matching task, suggesting loss or inaccessibility of semantic categories (Bayles, Tomoeda and Trosset, 1992). The same study suggests that confrontation naming is an easier task than superordinate naming. Sorting objects by category was found to be easier than recognising the function or specific features of an object (Martin et al., 1985). However, patients with DAT have been widely reported to have difficulty on word fluency tasks and to generate fewer examples of category than controls (Troster et al., 1989; Kontiola et al., 1990).

Patients with DAT may be aware of their steadily diminishing semantic fields and will tag on descriptive phrases such as *cutting blade, hand bell, ink pen, drinking cup* to the object name or will replace it by a descriptive phrase. Such behaviour suggests that these patients have some ability to monitor and change their language behaviour. Bayles and Tomoeda (1983) found that over one-quarter of incorrect naming responses were correct contexts or functions. The concepts of under-selection and specific semantic feature loss, both postulated as reasons for incorrect recognition, are not necessarily synonymous and may point to different types or even stages of lexical–semantic breakdown. Although naming errors are more likely to be semantically associated with the target, these patients do produce phonemic paraphasias and even neologisms in the later stages, particularly in spontaneous language. They may also use words, phrases or even short sentences repeatedly in their conversational language, sometimes as perseverations and sometimes as markers when other lexical items are not available.

The naming deficit in DAT has largely been attributed to a semantically based deficit (Hodges et al., 1991) although there is some evidence for perceptual difficulties, particularly as the disease progresses. A longitudinal study by Funnell and Hodges (1990) of a single patient suggests that the phonological output lexicon, in which spoken word forms are stored, may also be disrupted. The patient, Mary, was followed over 2 years and initially spoke fluently although she had word-finding difficulties and circumlocutions. Her performance and verbal IQ were similar, with a much higher predicted premorbid IQ. On subsequent picture naming tests, her performance declined in line with word frequency and she could not name better when given semantic cues. She could, however, repeat the picture names accurately and read them aloud well but she had greater difficulty in repetition and reading of nonsense syllables.

This discrepancy between word and non-word repetition suggests that the store of word forms (phonological output lexicon) is intact. On the picture naming task, Mary could sometimes name when given a phonemic cue, having failed to name spontaneously. Phonemic cueing became less effective as overall naming scores decreased. Despite general word frequency effects, specific items were consistently named or not, suggesting that the problem was not one of access to the semantic system. If items had been named spontaneously on recent testing, then phonemic cueing sometimes produced the target name. Diesfeldt (1991) describes a similar patient whose diagnosis is given as primary degenerative dementia and who had some preserved semantic abilities with retained ability to name and read irregular words but difficulty in reading non-words and function words. Such in-depth single case studies point to other single-word processing deficits, such as difficulty accessing the phonological output lexicon, which are easily obscured by group studies.

Dick, Kean and Sands (1989) illustrate the interaction of naming skills with aspects of semantic memory. They investigated recall of self-generated words in patients with DAT and the normal elderly and found that the patients did not show increased recall with self-generated words as the normal elderly did. They suggested that this was due to a breakdown in semantic encoding as well as a deficit in semantic memory.

Loss of the use of lexical stock, then, is one of the most common features of language in DAT. Indeed, severity of object naming and overall dementia are highly correlated (Skelton-Robinson and Jones, 1984). This loss also affects language used in conversation and the semantic relationships between words, although there is evidence that semantic priming and cueing are possible (Herlitz et al., 1991).

Semantic and grammatical processes above single-word level

One of the most commonly reported areas of spared language in DAT is that of grammatical structure (Appell et al., 1982), but this may be disturded because of breakdown at the lexical–semantic level. Kempler, Curtis and Jackson (1987), using age-matched normal controls, found that subjects with DAT produced a normal range and frequency of structures, but Troster et al. (1989) suggest that such patients have particular difficulty in understanding and constructing complex grammatical structures. The correction of semantic anomalies, however, can be difficult for the person with DAT. Whitaker's (1976) patient would correct most simple sentences containing grammatical errors on repeating them but would merely echo sentences containing a semantic anomaly, without correction. This difficulty in recognition of semantic (but not grammatical) anomalies has also been found in the normal healthy elderly in text comprehension. However, Whitaker's patient could, at times, disambiguate some ambiguous utterances when reading them (e.g. *shooting hunters*). As Whitaker remarks, it is difficult to understand the process by which this disambiguation occurred. The patient was capable of deriving one form of a word from another (e.g. satisfy–satisfaction) and therefore showed that she was capable of some linguistic processing.

Whitaker explains the process of disambiguation with reference to Clark and Begun's (1971) finding that sentences with an animate subject are easier to process than those with an inanimate subject but it is equally feasible that her patient was using a 'most popular sentence type' way of disambiguating (Bever, 1970). This explanation would suggest that the linguistic system in dementia can only process such partial utterances at their most simple or most frequently occurring level. Many of these ambiguous utterances can be disambiguated in several different ways. Given the utterance *walking dogs*, the patient changed the utterance to *dogs walking*, also an ambiguous phrase but one that does resemble a fragment of a simple declarative sentence. The patient generally opted to produce this type of utterance unless the partial utterance strongly suggested a common and much-used phrase, when it would be repeated verbatim (e.g. *boiling water*).

The process of reduction to more simple semantic and grammatical forms also took place when Whitaker's patient was asked to read paragraphs containing grammatically complex sentences and to read a long anomalous sentence. From the paragraph reading, the patient produced simple declarative sentences, usually using words from the paragraph. Occasionally words derived from others in the paragraph would be produced, again showing possible use of the semantic system. A simple declarative sentence was produced from a semantically anomalous sentence which, in its written form, contained two embedded clauses, showing that the patient did have difficulty with retention of grammatical complexity.

Schwartz, Marin and Saffran (1979), although working with a patient whose language breakdown was less severe, nevertheless found close parallels between their patient and Whitaker's. To look at the relative sensitivity to semantic and syntactic context, three contextual conditions were devised which required a written response to disambiguate. The semantic context was most difficult for the patient, who had to listen to three words, all in the same grammatical category and all semantically related, and then write the last word (e.g. under, on, *in*; tavern, hotel, *inn*). The first two words were meant to act as a cue into the semantic context. Disambiguation of phrases and sentences was more difficult but the written responses that the patient gave were more than 50% correct, e.g. *a nose* versus *he knows; she blew out the candles* versus *she wore a blue suit*.

The grammatical framework in which a word appears may therefore be a much surer entry to the correct lexical item than is semantic cueing. The grammatical level in DAT, like the semantic system, appears to be modified but may remain partially intact. The inability to read embedded clauses points to difficulty with more complex syntax.

Williamson and Schwartz (1981) followed a patient over 4 years and found evidence from conversational samples that the grammatical organisation of language undergoes change. As the patient's language deteriorated, fragments of simple sentences, in the form of isolated noun and verb phrases, appeared more frequently. The number of complete, simple sentences declined as the number of fragmentary phrases went up. False starts to sentences and fillers decreased over the sampling period, thought to be due to an increasing inability to self-correct. Verbs of quotation, e.g. *think, feel*, increased at the same rate as sentence fragments because, it was suggested, they commonly appear in sentences with an embedded clause, which are difficult to construct. However, the number of grammatically complete sentences containing a subordinate clause remained small but constant.

Obler (1980) also points out that the language of Alzheimer's patients contains a large range of subordinating conjunctions but they are used inappropriately, and the grammatical function of these words (to signal the relationship between clauses) is not fulfilled. Tissot, Duval and de Ajuriaguerra (1967) found that their patients, who could correct morpheme agreement errors in simple sentences, could not correct errors of subordinating conjunctions. This is a predictable finding because these subordinating conjunctions have complex functions which are both grammatical and semantic, but it also suggests that research has concentrated too much on the most simple morphemic and grammatical levels while neglecting areas of grammar which are more complex. The fact that some grammatical processes continue to work, even in the very late stages of DAT, can be used as evidence that this system has some functional independence but to say that the grammatical level is intact is ignoring the complexity of language processing.

Whereas word frequency is an important variable in word retrieval, frequency of word co-occurrence is an important variable in sentence repetition and construction. Obler (1980) looked at the effect of word frequency on the ability to repeat sentences. Her group could repeat long sentences in which the words were both of high frequency in the general vocabulary and had a high ratio of co-occurrence, but both grammatical and semantic relationships were lost in much shorter sentences where the words were of low frequency and low co-occurrence. For example, the sentence *the spy fled to Greece* was repeated as *the fly fed to geese*.

These findings underline the possible dissociations between semantic and other linguistic levels in DAT but patients with DAT are able to continue some aspects of language processing. These on-line processes are dependent on spared aspects of the linguistic system, which appears to operate with such variables as word frequency and canonical structures. Whitaker (1976) regards the language used by the severely deteriorated DAT patient as automatic and non-volitional linguistic behaviour because the linguistic system is functioning with little back-up from the cognitive systems that give language its creative dimension and allow communication. Obler's research on frequency and co-occurrence reveals another aspect of the deteriorating system which leads to simplification in grammatical form and semantic content.

Many researchers have characterised spoken language in dementia as both redundant and elliptical (Critchley, 1964; de Ajuriaguerra and Tissot, 1975), with fluently produced language and sentence fragments. This is not necessarily a contradictory situation because it seems likely that certain features may predominate at one particular stage in the disease process. Certainly, utterances tend to become shorter as the degree of dementia becomes very severe and the initiative to use language is lost (Stengel, 1964).

However, the use of the terms *redundant* and *elliptical* is, perhaps, rather misleading, particularly the latter term which implies a knowledge of that part of the utterance that has undergone ellipsis. It also implies an integrated semantic and grammatical framework for the utterance on which the process of ellipsis is to occur. As some facets of both grammatical and semantic levels of language are not available in DAT, the extent to which ellipsis can take place is curtailed. Fragments of uncompleted utterances are a feature of fluently produced DAT language and may look like ellipsis (de Ajuriaguerra and Tissot, 1975; Rippich and Terrell, 1988; Maxim, 1991) but the mechanisms by which these fragments are produced are not clear. Some of the fragments may be the unfinished and abandoned attempts at constructing an utterance, but equally some may be examples of successful and unsuccessful elliptical processes.

Bayles (1981) tested the ability to correct auxiliaries and modals, using tag questions which require a knowledge that the tag is related to the main clause and that part of the process involves ellipsis. Although some tags were corrected, Bayles found a hierarchy of difficulty with *be* verb tags at the top but could find no explanation why. If *have* auxiliary tags were also difficult to correct, it might be that the lack of semantic content of *be* and *have* auxiliaries plays some part. Because they have less semantic content than modal verbs such as *would*, the *be* and *have* auxiliaries may give less stimulus to the semantic system than modal verbs which carry a greater semantic content. The ability to correct some tag question errors does show that relationships between clauses not connected by any formal conjunctions may remain partially intact in DAT, and suggests that other processes such as producing elliptical utterances may also be possible.

Fluent language in DAT is often due (at least partly) to the redundancies it contains (Obler, 1980) and to phonological and suprasegmental fluency. The use of adjectives and adjective strings that reduplicate aspects of each other or of the noun to which they are attached may also be a common feature (Sinclair, 1967; Obler, 1980). Exclamations also increase as the number of propositions decreases, showing a greater reliance on fixed form or stereotyped utterances, and may be inserted into declarative utterances, either appropriately or not, giving the language used the illusion of fluency.

Blanken et al. (1987) compared the spontaneous speech of subjects with DAT with that of Wernicke-type aphasics. They found no evidence of systematic syntactic disturbance in the DAT subjects and suggested that the fluent empty speech was due to a failure to form prelinguistic conceptual structures of speech act representations. These representations are assumed to control the content-related decisions of sentence production.

A study by Kern et al. (1992) found that normal elderly subjects and those with DAT produced verbal intrusions during a series of language and cognitive tests. The normal elderly tended to produce recall inaccuracies, whereas those with DAT produced novel intrusions. The recall inaccuracies involved information within the correct semantic category which enabled the elderly person to reach the required information and was therefore said to be a compensatory strategy. The novel intrusions of the subjects with DAT did not contribute to coherence of the language and were therefore considered pathological.

Research into language in DAT above single-word level has been hampered to some extent by the hypotheses used. Although it appears that grammatical processes may be more resistant to the disease process than the lexical–semantic system, there is ample evidence that grammatical structure does show deterioration. Just as single-word research has shown that both access and loss of lexical items is possible in DAT, so research above single-word level points to the need to consider how linguistic processes interact and how the disease progression impinges upon these processes.

Discourse, cohesion and repair

Pragmatic ability, the ability to use language in context, becomes more severely impaired as the disease progresses and overall cognitive function deteriorates. However, clinicians working with this population report some meta-awareness of appropriate communication. A patient seen by one of the authors was almost untestable on standard IQ and language assessments but retained the ability to make contextually appropriate (though somewhat stereotyped) statements and questions, with appropriate prosodic contours, e.g. *isn't this food delicious?* at lunch.

Hutchinson and Jenson (1980), comparing institutionalised normal elderly with a similar group who had dementia, found that those with dementia initiated topics more frequently than the normal group and also violated topic initiation rules more frequently by not signalling or explaining the change of conversational topic. The group with dementia also used twice as many commands, requests and questions as the normal group. Nearly 30% of dementia group utterances were classed as inappropriate to the conversational context in which they were spoken, compared with under 2% in the normal group.

Ripich and Terrell (1988) found that their group of DAT patients also used more words to discuss a topic but that the conversational turns were shorter than those used by the normal elderly. Further research by Ripich et al. (1991) on turn-taking and speech act patterns in DAT showed that these subjects used shorter turns and fewer assertive acts, but more requests and increased non-verbal information. Conversational partners also modified the discourse by using shorter turns. The authors conclude that the basic structure of the discourse is preserved and that the differences observed are compensatory. For example, shorter turns decrease the memory load in conversation, making it more likely that the conversation will continue.

The ability to use cohesion in discourse is another area of impairment in DAT. When we listen to spoken language, we can normally easily tell if the utterances are related to each other. Cohesion is the linguistic relationship between utterances. The research findings reflect the complexity of this area but suggest that both structural and semantic aspects of cohesion are disrupted (Alpert et al., 1990). The use of ellipsis and redundancy in DAT have already been discussed and we have seen that there is impairment in this relatively complex area of linguistic processing. Patients with DAT have difficulty in maintaining simple grammatical agreement across clauses within the same sentence. It is therefore perhaps not surprising that cohesion impairment occurs.

In a single case study of the written language of a probable DAT patient (Mrs W), Lahey and Feier (1982) found that lexical cohesion was the most stable form of cohesion but that Mrs W reiterated words across sentences rather than using related words. In particular, her ability to use pronouns as reference decreased across samples, as did both intra- and inter-sentence ellipsis. Absence of a clear referent has been reported as occurring far more frequently in the language of DAT than in the normal elderly (Ripich and Terrell, 1988). Similarly, absence of an appropriate topic is far more frequent in dementia groups than the normal elderly (Hutchinson and Jenson, 1980). The ability to use cohesive devices is likely to be dependent on the functioning of a number of linguistic processes, as well as working and other memory components, and its impairment will reflect the decline of these processes. Another pointer to the level of meta-awareness of language function is the ability to repair, either to correct errors or to change the emphasis of what is being said. This ability is impaired in DAT in comparison with the normal elderly and other diagnostic groups with dementia (Maxim, 1991; McNamara et al., 1992).

McNamara et al. found that their group with DAT made significantly more undetected errors than normal elderly or Parkinson's patients. The groups with DAT and Parkinson's disease repaired about 25% of their errors but the DAT group used mainly single-word substitutions while those with Parkinson's disease used both single-word substitutions and syntax reformulations.

Maxim (1991) examined the spontaneous speech used in picture description for patients with DAT, multi-infarct dementia, aphasia and depression and normal elderly subjects. The samples were analysed in terms of the grammatical structure and the errors made and repaired. For the group with dementia, the percentage of errors correlated positively with increasing severity of dementia. They produced significantly more linguistic errors and abandoned utterances (sentence fragments) than age-matched normal elderly and depressed elderly subjects. There was no difference between the normal elderly and the dementia group on repairs but, interestingly, there was a significant difference between the fluent aphasic group and the other groups, the aphasics producing repairs in 20% of their sentences. The normal elderly produced a greater percentage of sentences with linguistic errors in this picture description task than in the conversational language described in Chapters 3–5, but they did so less frequently than subjects with DAT. Below is an example of the Cookie Theft Picture description from a normal elderly woman of 76:

> well the woman is washing up /
> but the sink is overflowing / and the boy is on the stool / which is collapsing / he's getting cookies out of the jar / and he's going to fall because the the stool's collapsing /

Linguistic errors and abandoned utterances were a common feature of the picture descriptions produced by people with DAT. Below is an example from a man of 74 with DAT:

> a little girl there / (six unintelligible syllables) /
> a little girl / I don't know what that is /

whether that's whether that's a bowl /
there's a boy boy there standing on a stool /
a lady here / she looks / she's got a / bowl in her hand / (unintelligible) / look like some dishes there or bowls / I don't know which / there / there's a window there / curtains and a window again / I don't know what this is / this is a thin (unintelligible) /
oh that's a sink unit with taps on /
that look like to me / a boy with that's his hat /
that's (unintelligible) / his shoes cupboards /
can't think of nothing else /

Another picture description is from a man with DAT aged 72:

these are kids aren't they /
oh there's a mother there's a mother there / yeah /
and a younger one / suppose / oh there she is /
aha and there's a younger one there a younger one /
PROMPT: and what's happening in the picture? /
right well he's doing cookies for something or other /
I don't know what they are /
cookie jar don't know what that is /
that one well probably be this this one / and that one / across there / somewhere across there anyway /
I don't know that I can put anything else into that me /

Because the linguistic analysis for this study was crude, no division between grammatical and semantic errors was feasible but, given the extensive research on preservation of grammatical structure in DAT, these findings point to variations between the use of conversational and elicited language samples, which may need more constrained language skills. Although grammatical structure is present, higher level grammatical skills that need to be integrated with the semantic system for appropriate linguistic functioning show greater degradation in subjects with DAT than in normal elderly.

The above examples show that cohesive devices are being used but some of the utterances are not topic specific. Some are clear attempts at processing information that is difficult to access, e.g. *I don't know which*. Ripich and Terrell (1988) found that their DAT group used more words to discuss topics than the normal elderly and cohesion was disrupted twice as often. Cohesion also changes in DAT, which may be of diagnostic significance. Gloser and Deser (1990) found that measures of cohesion can discriminate between DAT and aphasia.

Agnosia and Alzheimer's disease

So dramatic is anomia in DAT that some authors have argued that it has an agnosic component; i.e. patients with DAT have difficulty in perceiving the nature of the object they are required to label. Aphasics, by contrast, have difficulty in finding the label. Others have argued that the degree of anomia parallels the severity of cognitive dysfunction and that naming tasks may assist in the differential diagnosis of dementia subtypes. Patients with DAT may also auditorily misperceive and therefore guess responses. Stevens (1985) has noted the tendency of such patients to misinterpret visual information in picture description tasks. Similarly, Rochford (1971) argues that semantic errors in dementia have an agnosic component, and Martin (1987) found that a specific subgroup of these patients showed visuospatial deficits. Errors in writing to dictation are often caused by misperception of the stimulus. The following sentences, written from dictation, suggest that certain words are not being processed through the semantic system but are being written via a non-word route:

Target: This is a very nice day
= This [ɪjəfɛrnes] day
Target: This brick building was built
= This brick [bɪldɪŋsəs bɪld]
Target: Last year
= last [rɪ]

Confirmed visual or auditory agnosia appears to be rare in anything but profound DAT: usually these patients are able to match objects and point to objects without error in the earlier stages of the disease. Auditory comprehension is frequently impaired in mild and moderate DAT but impaired working or short-term memory and language processing deficits may interact. The ability to repeat single words and short sentences accurately would suggest that auditory agnosia is not a significant component.

Visual processing problems are often cited as a possible cause of naming difficulty in DAT, but careful studies which analyse the errors made when naming have concluded that the errors are far more likely to be due to semantic processing deficits (Smith, Murdoch and Chenery, 1989). However, these patients do have far greater difficulty in recognising degraded letters or object pictures than the normal elderly, suggesting that their visual processing can be disrupted more easily or perhaps requires more complete information to facilitate processing (Corkin, 1982; Heindel, Salmon and Butters, 1990; Grist and Maxim, 1992).

Evidence points away from visual and auditory agnosia being part of the general picture of deficits in DAT but these deficits are sometimes present and need to be screened for (Warrington, 1975).

Reading, writing and spelling

It has been suggested that single-word reading is particularly well preserved in DAT (Nelson and O'Connell, 1978; Nebes, Martin and Horn, 1984). Reading, writing and spelling are, however, all part of language processing and therefore likely to be impaired at some stage in the disease process, but the ability to read single words aloud may be retained even in severe DAT. Nelson and O'Connell (1978) have used this knowledge in the National Adult Reading Test (NART), which gives a measure of premorbid IQ. It is useful in mild and moderate DAT and for patients who have had at least 12 years of education (Stebbins et al., 1990). Patients are asked to read a list of irregularly spelled words. Schwartz, Saffran and Marin (1980) have noted that patients with DAT are able to use regular spelling rules to assist reading but they are less able to read irregular and nonsense words. Fromm et al. (1991), in a group longitudinal study of DAT and patients and normal controls matched for age and education, found that oral word reading is sensitive to DAT and that this ability does decline with time. Both DAT and control groups attempted to read the NART irregular words using regular grapheme to phoneme conversion rules but the DAT group produced more phonetically impossible errors, suggesting that even regularisation rules may break down. Reading sentences aloud, however, is often impaired and may, in part, be due to scanning difficulties (Stevens, 1985; Hart, Smith and Swash, 1986).

In contrast to reading aloud, reading single words and sentences for comprehension does not show the same sparing (Schwartz et al., 1979; Appell et al., 1982). Bayles et al. (1992) report that their patients with mild DAT scored between 60% and 90% of the normal mean for reading comprehension. Their most severely affected patients scored very poorly, if at all, on reading comprehension.

Alzheimer described both dyslexia and dysgraphia in his original patients and recent reports have correlated impairment of writing to the severity of the disease (Bayles et al., 1992). Writing deficits may be characteristic of familial Alzheimer's disease. Rapcsak et al. (1989) studied spelling of regular and irregular words in DAT and normal elderly subjects. They found that spelling of irregular words was significantly worse in DAT and suggested that this was due to a loss or impaired access of word representations from the orthographic lexicon. Horner et al. (1988) used a writing proficiency score to rate written narrative description in patients with DAT and found a significant correlation between writing ability and severity of dementia.

Certainly writing and spelling are both vulnerable in DAT because of deficits in language processing, but disturbances of praxis and visuospatial processes may contribute in the later stages of the disease (Martin, 1987). Writing in DAT may therefore show spelling and language impairment but may also show difficulties in motor coordination, praxis and visuospatial orientation. Writing errors may be incomplete words, missed inflections, substituted letters and incomplete spelling. The ability to copy is better preserved than the ability to write spontaneously or to take dictation. The spelling to dictation errors of a patient with DAT shown below seem to reflect difficulty in acoustic and phonological analysis. The spellings suggest some use of phoneme to grapheme correspondence or phonological similarity with the spoken form but note that initial letters do not correspond well. The patient discussed below also produces two responses which are not real words, suggesting that the information is not being processed through either the semantic system or the orthographic output lexicon.

> ***bell*** written as ***dell***
> ***pipe*** written as ***bibe***
> ***torch*** written as ***rorch***

The same patient, 1 year later:

> ***bell*** written as ***tell***
> ***pipe*** written as ***bide***
> ***torch*** written as ***porck***

The dyspraxias and Alzheimer's disease

Dyspraxia is the inability to perform certain purposive movements and movement complexes, with the conservation of mobility, sensation and coordination. Ideomotor, ideational and constructional dyspraxia may all appear in DAT and these disorders will affect everyday demands of daily living. Whether these are discrete deficits or only a part of larger decrements is not clear, but some research suggests the latter (Foster et al., 1986; Miller, 1986; Kempler, 1988).

A patient seen by one of the authors illustrates the range of dyspraxias in DAT. Mrs L was described on referral as having a dressing dyspraxia, general reduction of IQ and language impairment. She did need help with dressing, particularly doing up buttons, but also had difficulty in opening her handbag and putting on make-up. The last activity is further complicated by the mirror image. She was able to copy orofacial and speech movements but could not do these same movements to command. Her ability to draw and copy were severely impaired but she had no difficulty manipulating cutlery when eating. She retained a remarkable ability to play the piano but made some mistakes and was not able to create the same level of interpretation that had been possible before her illness.

Oral and verbal apraxia are both rare in early DAT, unlike in Pick's disease where they may be a presenting feature. Reduced praxis may reflect the most probable area of cortical damage in each disease. Oral and verbal apraxia appears more frequently with lesions of the anterior cortex, as in Pick's disease, whereas other dyspraxias are a more common sequel to diseases of the posterior cortex, as in DAT. Findings from a PET scan study suggest that dyspraxia for oral commands and dyspraxia for imitation show different loci of cortical deficit (Foster et al., 1986).

Patients with DAT invariably have constructional difficulties on drawing tasks. Reichman et al. (1991) used a drawing test of increasing complexity to identify visuoconstructive deficits in DAT subjects. They also showed that constructional deficits are highly correlated with severity of dementia, memory and language deficits in DAT. However, they also noted that visuoconstructive deficits are present in some normal elderly people.

Conclusions

Language is compromised in all stages of DAT but there is an enormous variation in deficits among individuals. We have tried, in this chapter, to discuss some of the key issues in describing language deficits in DAT. It is common to present checklists of functions showing deficits and spared areas at different stages of the disease but such lists are meaningless without knowledge of the research on which they are based. For clinicians who wish to use such information in a clinical context, the most informed and accessible research is cited below. Bayles et al. (1992) provide extensive information on language functions linked to stages of the disease measured on the Global Deterioration Rating Scale (Reisberg et al., 1982) and compared with normal age- and education-matched controls. Boller et al. (1991) suggest that poor performance on language tests at initial diagnosis, particularly naming tests, may be a good predictor of rapid decline in DAT, rather than age or severity of dementia.

Equally important is the knowledge that we now have concerning the variation in presentation of DAT and the techniques for testing for deficits. For example, Joanette, Poissant and Valdois (1989) presented a multiple single case study which looks at contrasting patterns of language and cognitive presentation and which is a good model for the investigation of the underlying processing deficits and course of the disease.

Chapter 8
Current service provision for the elderly in the UK

Introduction

The previous chapters of this book have discussed issues relating to ageing (Chapter 1), the changes in language processing that occur with normal ageing (Chapters 2–5) and the ways in which the disease processes in dementia may affect language (Chapters 6 and 7). We now turn to the provision of services for the elderly and consider how well their needs are currently being met. Policy on service provision in the UK is primarily directed by central government and accessed through local health and social services but local policies on levels and types of provision vary dramatically if they are not directly tied to legislation.

A strong case has been made in this book for normal age-related change in language and cognitive processing to be considered on a developmental spectrum. It has been established that the vast majority of elderly people live independently and adjust well to these changes. Funding authorities might therefore have a vested interest in maintaining and facilitating this adjustment in order to promote independent living. In fact there is little provision in the field of language and cognition, although a few areas in the UK have specialised memory clinics that advise clients on how to compensate for their memory problems and some areas provide support services to new hearing-aid users. However, most services are provided for those clients with advanced, disease-related difficulties, with emergency admission to acute hospital services being the point at which many elderly people come to the notice of health professionals or care providers.

There are moves to change the situation in the UK with the introduction of the 1993 Community Care Act, which changes the emphasis in care for the elderly away from hospital-based central services to community-based local services. The potential impact of these changes on services such as speech and language therapy for elderly people will be discussed in Chapter 10.

In this chapter the current elderly care policies will be reviewed and service provision will be examined with an emphasis on speech and language therapy services.

Issues in service provision

There is a need to discuss access to therapy and the attitudes of professionals. The question 'should the elderly have equal access to interventions that are available to younger age groups?' sets out starkly the issue of equal opportunities and resource management.

The need for specialised services for the elderly has long been recognised and both geriatric medicine and psychogeriatric services have been developed to meet such needs. However, these developments also mean that the elderly are seen as a separate category with their own resources. Although medical specialties have certainly been helpful in terms of understanding illness in the elderly, they have also created some barriers. For example, most rehabilitation units in the UK have age limits above which they will not accept patients. Some units have been created especially to cope with elderly rehabilitation needs but these are not available in every health district. Provision of services, then, is varied and uneven.

A second issue is that of resource management. There are many ways to allocate resources but in rehabilitation the concept of ability to benefit from intervention is quite dominant for very practical reasons. Given limited resources, targeting those most likely to respond well is one way of making a decision about who should get treatment. Estimating the communication needs of an elderly population is not an easy task. Furthermore, the development of services to the elderly with swallowing disorders has changed the roles of members of the rehabilitation team in the UK, the USA, Canada and Australia (Riensche and Lang, 1992). In particular, speech and language therapists have seen their caseload and role in the care team radically altered to accommodate the need for acute assessment of the elderly dysphagic person. This change has come at a time when research into aphasia therapy is showing that carefully targeted therapy is beneficial and when increasing numbers of elderly people require careful diagnostic assessment if intervention is to be useful. Therefore the resources to serve an increasing communicatively impaired elderly population are limited.

The provision of such services is uneven in most developed countries and often lacking altogether in the developing world. The elderly communicatively impaired may fall within services for stroke-related disorders, progressive neurological disorder or within psychogeriatric care. Undoubtedly, in most countries, speech and language therapy services are most readily available within an acute hospital setting and least available in the community, where most of the elderly live.

With the recent introduction of a business structure and a 'market-led' approach within the UK National Health Service, intervention is coming under close scrutiny and measures of clinical audit are being developed. For the elderly, these measures need to encompass the perceptions of users and information relating to the influence of communication on the ability to cope with independent daily living, as well as more traditional measures of communication change. Although measuring outcome for clients has tended to be profession-specific, it can be argued that rehabilitation for the elderly is best looked at as a team outcome. The concept of needs assessment, which can be defined as the ability to benefit from health care, is particularly important in developing useful services but may be superseded by either what is asked for (demand) or what is provided (supply) (Stevens and Gabbay, 1991).

There has been some demand for screening of the elderly population for dementia for example (O'Connor et al., 1993), but there is no evidence that the elderly would benefit from such a service unless it was followed up by accessible management and support (McIntosh and Power, 1993). However, demand for health screening at a more general level has resulted in the revised (1990) GP contract including an offer for an annual check-up and home visit for those over 75 (O'Neill, 1991).

Other factors influence provision of health care although the implementation of this provision is seldom outlined. Projects such as the Department of Health's report on assessment of needs, which is epidemiologically based, suggests levels of service provision for stroke and dementia but does not provide models of how these might operate.

Current provision of care for the elderly

There is an implicit assumption that the needs of the elderly are different from those of younger people but how true is this? Certain diseases, such as stroke, arthritis and the dementias (major causes of disability, which particularly limit the ability to live independently) are far more prevalent among the elderly population but they do occur among younger populations. The difference in provision reflects a pragmatic need to deliver health care as economically and efficiently as possible to a relatively large group of elderly people, many of whom may have multiple health needs. This is particularly so in the 85+ age group, the fastest growing group. It is not uncommon for geriatric medicine wards to contain very few people in their 70s but many in their 80s and 90s, and this is also seen in residential homes for the elderly.

Elderly people needing health care are more likely to be referred to geriatric medicine if they fall into one of the following categories (Whitaker and Tallis, 1992):

- previously under the care of a consultant geriatrician;
- resident in a Local Authority Part III home, private rest home or

private nursing home (indicating a degree of physical and/or mental frailty);
- long-standing confusion, poor mobility, falls or incontinence;
- acute presentation with confusion, poor mobility, falls or incontinence;
- presentation with a specific condition requiring intensive rehabilitation (e.g. cerebrovascular accident).

Elderly people living at home who do not go into hospital have variable access to services. One of the most useful developments in elderly rehabilitation in the UK is that of the geriatric day hospital where patients may be referred by GPs or hospital doctors, but in many areas GPs under-refer (George and Young, 1989). Such units provide all the services of an acute geriatric medical ward on a daily basis without the need to enter residential care and are particularly suited to the frail elderly.

The multiplicity of agencies that provide clinical and other care for the elderly allows for flexibility of provision but may also cause problems of access to services. For example, if an elderly person is ill, he or she will normally visit the GP as a first step. The GP may then provide referral to specialist geriatric or psychogeriatric services, which are usually based at the district general hospital. Psychogeriatrics has been a recognised specialty in the NHS only since 1989 and, although services are usually structured in terms of a medical model with the consultant psychogeriatrician heading the service, there has always been a strong emphasis on a team-based approach and community outreach (Jolley and Arie, 1992).

If an elderly person needs help on returning home from hospital then he or she may either be put in touch with social services via their medical practitioner or contact the service themselves. If finance is a problem then social services (local authority) may act as mediators with social security (Department of the Environment) who provide the necessary benefits but the elderly person may also need to go back to the GP for help in getting certain benefits (e.g. a wheelchair or a mobility allowance).

Griffiths (1988) commented:

> At the other extreme one is immediately struck by the differences between the arrangements for provision of medical and non-medical care. If a person is in need of medical care he knows he has to contact his GP, who will then arrange for appropriate medical care to be given. It would be too elaborate and indeed inappropriate for a similar system to be set up for non-medical care. What is surprising however is that such a system involving the assignment of a person in need of support to an individual carer, so as to become his responsibility, is rarely made, even where it would be highly applicable, e.g. in the case of patients discharged from long stay hospitals. (p. iv)

Figure 8.1 shows the care options for the ill or disabled elderly within the state sector.

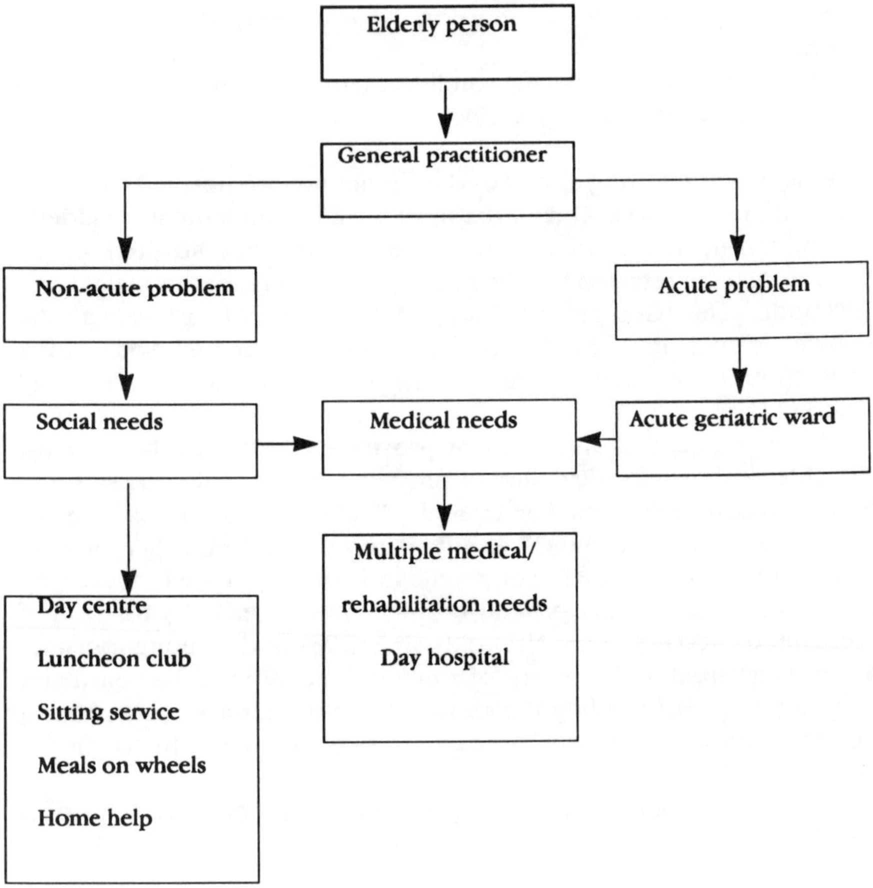

Figure 8.1 Care options for the ill or disabled elderly within the state sector

Rehabilitation needs of the elderly may also be provided via a number of different routes. Speech and language therapy is most commonly provided on a geriatric ward, in a day hospital, in a stroke unit for the elderly, by outpatient appointment to a rehabilitation department, via a domiciliary speech and language therapy service or via a hospital or community clinic group. Long-term care is provided in local authority, voluntary (i.e. non-profit-making and charitable) homes and in a decreasing number of NHS long-stay beds. However, most elderly people in long-term care are resident in the private sector, in either residential homes or nursing homes (Bosanquet, Laing and Propper, 1990).

How do people in long-term care outside the NHS access assessment and rehabilitation services? There is no clear picture, but access appears to depends to some extent on the initiative of the home manager, the elderly person or their relatives. Well run homes try to arrange some rehabilitation services on site but there is no statutory need for them to do so. Domiciliary rehabilitation is provided by the NHS in some areas but the extension of this service into private sector homes is rare. Elderly people in private care may access these services but may well have to go to a local hospital as an outpatient in order to do so. Given that approximately 330 000 people aged 60 and over live in residential homes or hospitals, a large number of elderly people who are most in need of rehabilitation services have under-developed and unclear routes of access to such services.

Current speech and language therapy provision for the elderly

In many ways current service provision for the elderly reflects the enormous variation in speech and language services for clients with acquired communication disorders. Rossiter and McInally (1989) highlighted the great variation in such services for adult clients with aphasia, and a study of language therapy provision for clients with aphasia across three different health districts showed that the number of therapists working with aphasic clients varied from 0.6 to 3.0 per 100 000 of population (a range of 4–7 full-time equivalent therapists) (Jordan, 1991). These figures represent a difference between an average of 59 minutes therapy per client per week and only 28 minutes per week. The number of elderly aphasic clients in each district was estimated to vary from 126 to 174 per 100 000 of the population aged over 65 years. This variation may be due to:

- different numbers of aphasic clients (the author rejects this as unlikely given that there were no major differences in population types across the two districts);
- different referral policies;
- presence or absence of other modes of therapy for elderly people (such as through community services).

It is therefore difficult to gauge exactly how much speech and language therapy time is being devoted to elderly clients.

A survey of Frenchay Health Authority conducted by Enderby and Davies (1989) indicated that, in addition to the elderly people catered for under the headings of stroke, head injury and progressive illness (up to 58 per 100 000), 46 new referrals with communication problems occurred each year per 100 000 of population within the specialty of care of the elderly. Enderby and Davies estimate that this number of elderly clients represents a workload equivalent to 1.1 therapists per 100 000 of population specifically for the elderly in addition to the provision for other acquired disorders. Bryan et al. (1991) have suggested that the provision formats used in this study to estimate the number of therapists needed may not reflect the heterogeneity of the client group or the need to tailor therapy to individuals in order to achieve their maximum communicative potential. The figure suggested by Enderby and Davies may therefore under-represent the speech and language therapy needs of the elderly population.

Speech and language therapy provision for the elderly appears to be dependent upon:

- the level of provision for acquired disorders across the whole adult population;
- the presence or absence of specialist services for the elderly;
- the presence or absence of community-based provision for adults;
- the presence or absence of specialist services for clients with dementia.

Where there is no specialist elderly or psychogeriatric service, the service for acquired disorders may have to exclude clients with dementia from their therapy provision. This exclusion leads to difficulty in assessing exactly the speech and language therapy services that are provided for elderly clients.

The College of Speech and Language Therapists commissioned a report on speech and language therapy for the elderly with dementia. A survey of the provision for this client group was conducted in 134 districts. The resulting working party report (College of Speech and Language Therapists, 1990) showed that 42 of 134 districts had no service for clients with dementia, and 29 offered a specialist service for the elderly mentally infirm, with the majority of the therapists working in psychiatric, geriatric or psychogeriatric teams. Of the individual clinicians who took part in the survey, 97% had contact with this client group varying from full-time involvement to an occasional 'on-request' remit. Between one and 20 clients with possible dementia were referred each month. This large range was again said to reflect the contrast between 'on-request' services and existing specialist services. The average annual referral rate for elderly mentally ill patients with dementia was 50, which is as frequent as other client groups such as those with dysphagia and acute medical conditions. The sources of referral were mainly geriatricians and other hospital specialists with psychogeriatricians ranked third. The emphasis on referrals from hospital specialists may reflect their access to current speech and language therapy provision. Referrals from general practitioners, community psychiatric nurses and relatives or clients were less common but much more numerous than those from other sources such as district nurses and voluntary organisations.

Most services to the elderly with dementia were offered in a hospital inpatient setting in acute geriatric (21%), geriatric rehabilitation (20%) and continuing care departments (20%). Psychogeriatric locations accounted for 17% of cases. Outpatient services were in day hospitals (29%), by domiciliary visits (20%) and in private and local authority homes (43%). This is perhaps an indication of the need for services to extend into the community. Districts that can offer only an 'on-request' service are probably not providing for the elderly in the residential care setting. Furthermore, suggestions for change within the NHS, such as the Tomlinson report (1992) on services in London, indicate that deployment of services into the community (with subsequent reduction in 'central' hospital provision) is to be encouraged. In many ways such a move could assist the provision of services to elderly people with communication problems who live in the community, although resource implications are obviously important limiting factors in the current national health service marketplace (see Chapter 10).

Therapists contributing to this survey were asked whether their elderly clients with dementia were routinely re-assessed: 48% answered yes and 52% answered no. Where clients were routinely re-assessed this was mostly within a 4–6 month period. This raises questions regarding the provision of ongoing services and monitoring of clients with what is essentially a progressive neurological disorder.

Approximately 60% of elderly clients with mild dementia were offered some form of management, reducing to only 10% for those with severe impairment. Individual treatment accounted for only 25% of clinician–patient contact time, with many clinicians specifically commenting on the need to work directly on neurological symptoms (e.g. dysarthria and dysphagia in multi-infarct dementia). Group therapy, counselling and advice, and education of carers and other professionals accounted for most of the therapy time. Only a small number of the therapists had a research commitment and most of these were self-initiated projects without outside funding. Therapists expressed a need for continued training in this field and requested information on differential diagnosis, assessment and management of dementia and research updates.

Speech and language therapists working with the elderly are acutely aware of the need for specialist knowledge in this area. Davies and Van de Gaag (1991) specified the core skills and knowledge base for speech and language therapy common to those therapists working with adult and elderly clients as well as those with learning difficulties and paediatric clients. However, the skills and knowledge base agreed for the particular needs of therapists working with adult and elderly clients showed some specific differences (taking the aspects deemed essential by more than 80% of clinicians). These are shown in Table 8.1.

Table 8.1 Core skills and knowledge base deemed essential for speech and language therapy

Common skills/knowledge base	*Specific elderly skills/knowledge*
Desire to learn and acquire new knowledge	Respect for the client
Flexibility	Professionalism
Empathy	Realism
Positiveness	Flexibility
Professionalism	Objectivity
Self-awareness	Sensitivity
Enthusiasm	Positiveness
	Empathy

Bebbington (1991) showed that speech and language therapists who worked with the elderly for at least 51% of their time were significantly more likely to have a positive attitude towards the elderly. Questionnaires were sent to therapists in 50 different health districts, with half of them going to therapists who worked with the elderly and half going to therapists who worked with other client groups. Several points were made: 77% of the therapists disagreed with the view that working with the elderly is depressing, 79% disagreed with the statement that older clients are poorly motivated towards treatment;. 77% agreed with the statement that elderly people were cared for in inadequate surroundings; 99% supported team working. This survey therefore supports the need for specialist services for the elderly and for newly qualified therapists to have the opportunity to work with the elderly in order to develop more favourable attitudes.

There is clearly a need for continuing education in this field. Short courses on research developments and clinical intervention techniques and postgraduate courses for clinicians who wish to specialise in working with the elderly need to be supported. Clinicians need to develop their skills and knowledge basis through experience and research. Furthermore, educational establishments need to promote and support more collaborative clinical research in the field of dementia.

All courses leading to qualification as a speech and language therapist in the UK include some teaching on language in the elderly and working with elderly clients. This teaching involves both speech pathology and medical input. There is a need to integrate this teaching and to extend the topics to reflect current practices, community work, the multidisciplinary team and the specific assessment and intervention procedures developed for clients with dementia. Ideally, students should have contact with both the normal elderly and the elderly with dementia and should observe speech and language therapists working with elderly clients.

Chapter 9
Speech and language therapy intervention with the elderly

Introduction

In the last chapter we outlined the great variation in service provision for the elderly. It is clearly somewhat problematic to try to give an account of what clinicians actually do with elderly clients when there is little consensus. A further problem is that of caseload variation. The literature on assessment of different client groups is clear but some intervention studies that refer to 'elderly' clients mean only older aphasics whereas others include clients with communication disorders secondary to dementia. Similarly 'dementia' may refer exclusively to Alzheimer's disease or to clients with a mixture of aetiologies. Where possible, in this chapter, these factors are specified, but the chapter inevitably reflects the lack of client definition.

Before we review assessment and treatment practices, the rationales behind intervention, including age as a prognostic factor, will be discussed.

Intervention studies with the elderly

Studies that look at the effects of age on recovery of speech and language functioning are equivocal in their findings, but there is some evidence that it is not age itself which hampers recovery but the presence of other health factors – and the elderly are more likely to have multiple health problems. It should be stressed that a fit elderly person may do as well in therapy as someone younger, all other things being equal (Sarno, 1980). This is perhaps an optimistic statement when the evidence on recovery from stroke is considered more closely, although more studies have concluded that age is either not a negative factor or that it is only weakly so (Rose, Boby and Capildeo, 1976; Basso, Capitani and Vignolo, 1979; Sarno, 1980) than have found age to be a poor prognostic sign (Sands, Sarno and Shankweiler, 1969; Holland and Bartlett, 1985).

However, other factors might make prognosis poorer in the elderly stroke patient. In Chapter 1 the relationship between type of aphasia and age was discussed and we concluded that older people are more likely to have Wernicke's aphasia with significant comprehension deficits. Older people tend to have more severe language disorders than younger people (Holland and Bartlett, 1985) and a large aphasia-producing lesion may reveal an underlying multi-infarct dementia which was not previously apparent.

Holland and Bartlett (1985) point out that, although the elderly may do as well given equality of circumstance, the context for recovery is rarely equivalent: elderly people are more likely to have co-occurring health problems and a more severe communication problem, their environment may not be as supportive as that of younger stroke patients and there may be less or no family support. Holland found that her elderly stroke patients received less therapy for communication disorders than younger aphasics, principally because it was not offered in residential nursing homes. However, it is clear that the elderly aphasic may recover spontaneously or respond to treatment as well as a younger aphasic. The oldest patient in Holland and Bartlett's study (93 years) made the greatest gain of anyone in the study and maintained it, so they stress that statistical trends do not preclude individual differences.

Another way of approaching this issue is to consider needs benefit by contrasting two people with aphasia following cerebrovascular accident.

DF was 45 years old when he had a stroke which resulted in a mild hemiplegia and aphasia. He was hospitalised for less than 3 weeks and was discharged from the hospital mobile but with a moderate Broca's type aphasia. He received speech and language therapy as an outpatient but the clinician was concerned about his lack of progress after a month and decided to devote a session to discussion of his situation. With help, DF told her that he really wanted more physiotherapy because, after a period of unemployment, he had recently got a manual job which he could return to if his limb function could be improved. He felt that therapy for language function was not a priority at that time because he could communicate quite well. His family confirmed his view and arrangements were made for him to be reassessed by physiotherapy but intervention for his language disorder was discontinued.

Mrs LM was a 78-year-old woman with a conduction-type aphasia who lived on her own. She had no mobility problems and a mild upper limb hemiparesis had quickly resolved. She wanted to improve her reading and writing skills in particular because she could use these to compensate for her poor spoken language output and therefore would be less dependent on neighbours for certain tasks such as shopping.

These examples underline two important aspects of intervention: it is important wherever possible (1) ask patients how they see their needs and (2) to plan intervention which takes these needs into account.

Holland (1980) starkly outlines the context of intervention for elderly aphasics:

> Being in an institution generally has depressing effects on language use. Being in an institution is more likely if one is old. Observations such as these serve to remind clinicians that treating aphasia without considering the social context is probably not much better than not treating it at all.
>
> (p. 187)

This statement is just as valid for elderly people with a range of communication disorders, including aphasia, dysarthria and language disorder secondary to dementia.

Reports of intervention aimed at improving or maintaining communication demonstrate the large number of different professions involved with the elderly, for example nurses, occupational therapists and psychologists (Wilson and Moffat, 1984; Holden and Woods, 1988). These professionals have, in turn, used many different interventions with the elderly, e.g. speech and language therapy (Gravell, 1988). This plethora of professionals and interventions reflects the varying membership of the care team and the demand that exists for help with communication.

Intervention for the elderly does not differ in its range or variety from that for any other age group but, because we know that the elderly may have multiple disorders, it is particularly necessary to assess carefully and disentangle the symptoms from the underlying causes. If a 52-year-old man is referred after a stroke there may be expectations of hypertension, but the same diagnosis in someone of 84 years should alert us to possible hypertension, as well as to the effects of normal ageing on test scores and the need to consider any abnormal cognitive changes that might suggest dementia.

Elderly people with specific communication problems need access to the same range of interventions and rehabilitation measures as younger people. One area of intervention in which elderly people have consistently shown a good response to therapy (i.e. they have responded specifically to the therapy itself and there has been a measure of generalisation and/or maintenance of therapy gains) is that of communication therapy for patients with Parkinson's disease (Johnson and Pring, 1990).

Bourgeois (1991) carried out an extensive review of the literature relating to the treatment of communication disorders in dementia. This literature was found in gerontology, social work, nursing and psychology journals but rarely in speech pathology journals. Many of the studies have design and methodological problems but Bourgeois states that

> the literature reviewed supports the potential for positive outcomes from communicative treatment and treatment research for individuals with dif-

> fuse degenerative neurological disease. Although the individuals treated do not constitute a homogeneous population, the fact that positive communication outcomes were reported in such a diverse population is encouraging. (p. 840)

There is clearly a need for more systematic research in this area. This issue will be discussed further in Chapter 10.

What speech and language therapists do with elderly clients

The role of the speech and language therapist in the care and management of elderly patients with communication disorders has been described by Gravell (1988), Baseby (1989) and Bayles and Kaszniak (1987). Several key roles are suggested:

- assessment;
- direct speech and language therapy intervention;
- group work;
- environmental manipulation;
- monitoring;
- working with carers, including those in the residential sector;
- referral to other agencies.

These types of interventions will be examined in more detail below.

Assessment of elderly clients

Initial assessment attempts to establish a differential diagnosis of the communication disorder but assessment is a continuous process, especially in clients with degenerative disorders. Working with an elderly population requires the ability to assess the communication abilities of the person and the communicative context, and to act upon those findings in a way which is useful for both the patient and the carers. It is a complex process requiring two different types of assessment at the same time: assessment of function and assessment for diagnosis and prognosis. The context in which the clinician is working may dictate the focus for the assessment and unfortunately this may be influenced by service resources rather than by client need.

The main components of a communication assessment include:

- peripheral sensory function – hearing and vision;
- motor speech function – including dental state;
- language skills;
- pragmatic skills;

- non-verbal communication skills;
- functional communication abilities;
- cognitive function – memory and orientation.

Communication between professionals is important. Most speech and language therapists tend to use assessment material which is designed specifically for their needs and which is often not familiar to other members of the care team. The exception to this is the use of the Mini-Mental State Examination (Folstein, Folstein and McHugh, 1975) and the Mental Test score (Hodkinson, 1972), both of which rate cognitive function.

Rating scales such as that in the Clifton Assessment Procedures for the Elderly (CAPE) (Pattie and Gilleard, 1979; Pattie, 1981) are widely used by other members of the care team. An adaptation such as the one shown in Table 9.1 might enable other professionals to be more aware of communication dependency and to be more confident in discussion with speech and language therapists.

Table 9.1 CAPE scale adapted for communication

Dependency category	*Interpretation*
A	No impairment in communication. Independent
B	Mild impairment of communication but can communicate most needs. May need to be asked questions for clarification
C	Moderate impairment. Medium dependency. Likely to require considerable help in conversation. Burden of communication is on the listener
D	Marked impairment. High dependency. Unable to communicate most needs. Language output very limited. May require non-language-based communication system
E	Severe impairment. Maximum dependency. Unable to communicate any needs. May express emotion by facial expression or intonation. Unable to use either language or non-language system

When assessing language and communication function in the elderly with possible dementia, speech and language therapists have traditionally resorted to the use of aphasia test batteries, using their own clinical experience to separate out those patients with focal lesions from those with progressive dementing conditions. Most aphasia test batteries are poorly standardised on the elderly population and even those which have been standardised often use what we would now consider young elderly populations. The cultural/familiarity factor is often not controlled for and tests such as the Boston Diagnostic Aphasia Examination (BDAE) (Goodglass and Kaplan, 1983) and the Western Aphasia Battery (Kertesz, 1980) have not been standardised on populations outside North America although there is now some useful information on the Boston Naming Test (Goodglass and Kaplan, 1983) for UK testing (Armstrong and Grieg, 1992). Whether we wish to continue using aphasia test batteries, which have other drawbacks and may not illuminate the underlying deficits, is perhaps another matter for debate. The aphasia test batteries do provide a repeatable measure of language function which can be used for comparison with the client's previous test results, with other client groups and with other disorders.

In testing for Alzheimer's disease, clinicians need to be aware that different patterns of impairment from those seen in focal aphasia are usually apparent. For example, clients with Alzheimer's disease are much more likely to be able to read single words aloud than aphasic clients even if their comprehension is severely compromised.

One of the first attempts to discover more about language function in the elderly using aphasia tests was that of Walker (1982) who tested normal, frail and elderly patients with dementia on the Minnesota Test for the Differential Diagnosis of Aphasia (MTDDA) (Schuell, 1965). She found levels of ability in her normal elderly group (age range 60–90) very different from Schuell's normal group (age range 19–72). Walker found that the MTTDA did not adequately discriminate between normal elderly, frail elderly, aphasics and a group with dementia. The normal elderly subjects made errors on all but three of 46 subtests and, on 22 of 46 subtests, more than 20% of the normal elderly group made errors.

More recently, Horner et al. (1992) have used the Western Aphasia Battery as a diagnostic tool to differentiate between focal aphasia and Alzheimer's disease. Appell et al. (1982) found that subjects with advanced Alzheimer's disease had higher fluency ratings but poorer comprehension scores than a group of aphasics with left hemisphere lesion with quite well preserved object naming. Horner's results did not replicate Appell's finding largely because their Alzheimer's group was less severely affected and did not show the poor comprehension suggested by Appell. They did, however, have difficulty in discriminating right hemisphere lesion patients from the Alzheimer's group: four out of ten of the Alzheimer's patients were classified as right-hemisphere damaged subjects and two of ten right-hemisphere damaged subjects were classified as having Alzheimer's disease. No subscores on the Western Aphasia Battery aphasia quotient showed significant differences between the patients with Alzheimer's disease and those with right-hemisphere damage. Using the aphasia, reading and writing quotients together, just under 75% of all subjects (but only 60% of DAT subjects) were correctly classified. Eight aphasics were correctly classified but two were misclassified as having Alzheimer's disease. The Western Aphasia Battery's use as a diagnostic tool is therefore somewhat limited, although Horner's subject groups were small and she used overall quotients rather than looking for subtests which might discriminate between groups.

Both Appell et al. and Horner et al. concluded that their Alzheimer's disease subjects did not produce what they term 'focal aphasic signs' of phonemic and semantic paraphasias or morphosyntactic deviations, but nor did the right hemisphere damaged subjects, which created a diagnostic problem.

The Western Aphasia Battery also offers a 'cortical quotient', which is made up of all the aphasia subtests plus reading, writing, construction, praxis tests and Raven's Progressive Coloured Matrices (Raven, 1965). Lower scores on the cortical quotient than on the aphasia quotient suggest more global cognitive damage but the combined procedures are quite lengthy which limits its potential for everyday clinical work.

Significant differences between focal aphasics and those with Alzheimer's disease as shown by Appell et al. (1982) and Horner et al. (1992) are shown in Table 9.2

Table 9.2 Differences between focal aphasia and Alzheimer's disease on the Western Aphasia Battery

Early stage DAT	Speech fluency better in DAT than in aphasia Naming better in DAT than in aphasia Repetition better in DAT than in aphasia
Late stage DAT	Higher fluency rating in DAT than in aphasia Poorer comprehension in DAT than in aphasia

From Appell et al. (1982) and Horner et al. (1992).

Other tests have been used for diagnostic purposes, such as Luria's Neuropsychological Investigation (Christensen, 1974), which can differentiate among normal people, Alzheimer's disease and alcoholic Korsakoff syndromes (Blackburn and Tyrer, 1985). This assessment contains sections on memory, orientation and intellectual processes in addition to language function tests. The Aphasia Screening Test (Whurr, 1974) is reported to be the test most widely used by British clinicians working with the elderly. It has been normed for an elderly population but its use is confined to investigation of language function and there is no literature on its diagnostic potential. The popularity of this test is largely due to its portable and clear pictorial format. Assessment on wards where light may be bad, or the client's spectacles not available, makes it a pragmatic choice for many clinicians.

A more rational approach is to bring together a number of tests that have been shown to discriminate between people with Alzheimer's disease and other groups. Such assessments do not use aphasia as the basis for assessment, nor do they necessarily exhaustively examine the language functioning of patients with dementia, but they do provide the clinician with an effective tool for diagnosis and severity rating.

Bayles et al. (1989, 1992) and Stevens (1992) have both taken this approach, although Stevens' test list is shorter and her procedure contains a weighted scoring system for each response, described in her paper. Stevens' screening test is specifically for discriminating between people with dysphasia and Alzheimer's disease, but Stevens acknowledges the need to extend the diagnostic range to multi-infarct dementia. The test does not classify aphasics according to syndromes, but would be a useful starting point for more detailed language testing because it allows the clinician to probe the possible underlying deficits by focusing on the quality of the response. Stevens' screening test consists of the following subtests:

- naming line drawings of common objects;
- written word/picture matching with syntactic and semantic distracters;
- action picture description: photographs;
- action picture description: line drawings;
- reading single SVO sentences;
- reading paired SVO sentences;
- written sentence/picture matching with syntactic and semantic distracters.

Bayles et al. (1989, 1992) have developed a Core Linguistic Battery consisting of the following subtests. These are fully described in their papers and are now published as the Arizona Battery for Communication in Dementia (1992):

- confrontation naming;
- auditory comprehension (word/picture matching);
- writing to dictation (single words);
- reading comprehension (word/picture matching);
- oral reading (single words);
- concept definition (word definition scored using WAIS (Wechsler, 1958) criteria);
- coordinate naming (give two other names in same category as object);
- superordinate naming (given object, name superordinate category)
- superordinate identification (words to superordinate category matching);
- pantomime expression (pantomime use of object pictures);
- pantomime recognition (gesture to picture matching).

There is also an additional set of subtests which includes sentence formulation and the Mini-Mental State Examination. Bayles et al. have used this battery to compare the performance of patients with Alzheimer's disease with their performance on the Global Deterioration Scale (Reisberg et al. 1982) which gives a severity rating largely independent of language function.

In a useful article on the response of small groups (10–14) of British young, normal elderly and elderly with unclassified dementia, Armstrong and Grieg (1992) discuss the Test for Reception of Grammar (Bishop, 1983), the Graded Naming Test (McKenna and Warrington, 1983) and the Boston Naming Test (Goodglass and Kaplan, 1983). The response norms and ranges for these groups are set out in Table 9.3.

Both normal and dementing elderly groups had mean ages above 74 years. They found that the normal elderly and the dementia group had different patterns of responses on the Test of Reception of Grammar but similar patterns on the Boston and Graded Naming Tests and concluded that the Test for Reception of Grammar and the Boston Naming Test were more useful for clinical application with the elderly than the Graded Naming Test, which aims to detect high-level word-finding difficulty and is IQ related.

Table 9.3 Response norms and ranges for the Test for Reception of Grammar, Boston Naming Test and the Graded Naming Test

	TROG	*BNT*	*GNT*
Total score possible	20	60	30
Young adult			
mean	19	Not tested	Not tested
range	18–20	Not tested	Not tested
Normal elderly			
mean	17.9	43	15.2
rangc	16–20	29–57	9–24
Dementing elderly			
mean	13.3	20.4	5.2
range	8–20	12–35	0–15

TROG, Test for Reception of Grammar; BNT, Boston Naming Test; GNT, Graded Naming Test.

Most aphasia test batteries and assessments have been rightly criticised for not providing the clinician with information on the patient's ability to communicate, or on the strategies which the patient may have available to facilitate communication, the honourable exception to this being the Boston Naming Test. The need to assess communication, as opposed to specific language function, is particularly important with the elderly, whose diagnosis may be of a disorder secondary to dementia where intervention is likely to be advice to carers on manipulating the communicative environment. More important still is the need to assess what the patient knows about his or her communicative performance and how well they are able to repair their communication. Rao

(1990) describes the necessary components for adequate functional assessment of the elderly. Despite the increased awareness of this need, few available assessments fulfil these criteria. Communicative Abilities in Daily Living (Holland, 1980) and The Functional Communication Profile (Sarno, 1969) both provide information on communicative abilities, the latter by a checklist procedure and the former by simulation of real life events. The Edinburgh Functional Communication profile (Skinner et al., 1990) is another useful tool. It is a profile-based procedure for describing communicative interactions, including the ability to repair and allows separate ratings for different response modalities. This is a comprehensive and theoretically sound procedure which is under-used in the research literature, probably because the clinicians must set up situations in which to collect the data although suggestions are given for this. It is possible, however, for clinicians to use the Functional Communication Profile or Communicative Activities in Daily Living contexts and the Edinburgh scoring schemes, or to score the Edinburgh profile using information from other sources (e.g. the family or carer) and by asking questions about the patient's behaviour in contexts other than the clinic.

Research protocols that have been used to collect information on pragmatic abilities are set out by Hutchinson and Jenson (1980) and Prutting and Kirchner (1987), who have developed a useful clinical appraisal of pragmatic function.

Short tests for aphasia, such as the Frenchay Aphasia Screening Test (Enderby, 1987), designed for use by professionals other than speech and language therapists, have been used with an elderly population to gain information on language function but their use is limited. Collin (1991) suggests that the Frenchay Screening Test is adequate for medical needs but that it does not provide the detailed information necessary for diagnosis and management of communication deficit. Certainly the estimation of language deficit, and in particular comprehension difficulties, can be difficult for doctors, nurses and relatives (McClenahan, Johnston and Densham, 1992), and referral to a speech and language therapist is the most appropriate course of action.

The following case studies illustrate possible assessment procedures, taking into account clinical context and time constraints.

Mr AD, aged 79 years, had one or possibly two strokes. He was seen as an outpatient referral from a clinical psychologist and speech and language therapist with relevant test details (Wechsler Adult Intelligence Scale and the Aphasia Screening Test). He was a very fit man who lived on his own and was very frustrated by his communication difficulty. He had a fluent aphasia with many neologisms and phonemic paraphasias in his language output. A language sample was collected via conversational interview and description of the Cookie Theft Picture and sentence repetition from the Boston Diagnostic Aphasia Examination. Naming and naming facilitation were tested with the Boston Naming Test. To look at the underlying causes of his language deficits, including auditory and written input processing, selected tests from Psycholinguistic Assessments of Language Processing in Aphasia (Kay, Lesser and Coltheart, 1992) were used. After assessment, he was offered an 8-week course of intensive therapy.

Mr BM was seen on the ward following a head injury. He had a history of persistent alcohol abuse and the clinical psychologist's assessment showed that he had Korsakoff's syndrome but speech and language assessment on the Aphasia Screening Test suggested that he also had a language impairment. The Aphasia Screening Test was used because he had attention problems and responded better to large single stimuli. As all modalities seemed equally but only mildly impaired, it was concluded that focal damage was unlikely and this was subsequently confirmed on CT scan. Management was confined to support and advice for the carers.

Miss HN had been diagnosed as having moderate Alzheimer's disease but the ward staff were having difficulty in communicating with her and she often refused food. They asked the speech and language therapist for strategies to help them. The speech and language therapist used a conversational interview, the Cookie Theft Picture description and the Boston Naming Test. She also used the Edinburgh Functional Communication Profile scoring procedure to look at communication and pragmatic abilities. Assessment showed that comprehension for daily activities was adequate if Miss HN was looking at the speaker and the speaker repeated the message at a slightly slower rate than normal. Compliance with requests was greater if the staff member maintained both eye and physical contact (e.g. held her hand).

Mrs KL was 74 years old when she was referred with a diagnosis of possible Alzheimer's disease with progressive aphasia. She was seen as an outpatient and repeated measures were taken on the Boston Diagnostic Aphasia Examination and the Boston Naming Test. At her third bi-yearly assessment, she began to exhibit a range of dyspraxias and the Dabul Apraxia Battery (Dabul, 1979) was used. Between the second and third assessments, her language function remained stable and she indicated that she wanted help to resume activities such as shopping which she had abandoned, largely through anxiety when her problems first became evident. She was referred to a local stroke group who took her reluctantly because of her diagnosis. However, apart from spoken output which deteriorated due to verbal dyspraxia, her language and communication skills remained stable for another 18 months and she gained enough confidence from the stroke group activities to return to doing her own shopping and using the bus.

Interventions with elderly clients

What specific interventions are commonly used with the elderly client group? A survey of speech and language therapists working with clients whose diagnosis included dementia (College of Speech and Language Therapists, 1990) found the following types of interventions reported, which accord well with the role of the clinician specified earlier (see p. 207):

- direct therapy intervention for aphasia and for focal impairments in MID;
- groups: communication, memory;
- environmental manipulation and adapting communication strategies;
- social skills and functional communication therapy with counselling;
- monitoring and maintenance strategies;
- working with carers;
- education of other staff.

Some of these interventions involve more direct work with communicatively impaired people while others are more likely to involve the carers in adaptation of the communicative environment.

Gravell (1988) summarises the questions that need to be asked in order to select an appropriate intervention, a major division being made between direct or clinician-delivered therapy and indirect therapy implemented by others. She stresses the need to ensure that impairment of sight, hearing and dentition are adequately compensated for, whether intervention is direct or indirect and before intervention begins. She suggests that barriers to direct intervention are factors such as reduced or absent insight, poor cooperation, low motivation, memory loss, cognitive impairment, unmanaged sensory impairment, fatiguability, physical illness and environmental factors but cautions that indirect interventions may be vital in encourageing communication. There is no doubt that some patients benefit from indirect therapy which gently encourages their involvement in communicative situations and can then progress to more direct therapies. Clinicians working with communication groups will recognise the picture of non-communicating clients who attend for some time before gradually attempting to interact. Depression is widespread in the ill or disabled elderly and, although reactive depression may spontaneously diminish, endogenous depression requires more direct intervention.

Other factors such as dehydration and constipation may interact with stroke to hinder attempts at rehabilitation. Isaacs (1978) describes a severely aphasic bedridden elderly man with a dense hemiplegia and a catheter who required careful rehydration by monitoring fluid intake and relief from constipation before he was able to benefit from physiotherapy and speech therapy input. The speech and language therapy input concentrated on finding routes to communication through gesture and contextual clues and on working with the nurses and relatives in using this information.

Direct therapy

Most direct therapy involves regular treatment sessions aimed at rehabilitating a lost or damaged skill such as auditory comprehension, language production, reading or writing, or at facilitating the use of compensatory mechanisms such as gesture. Walker and Williams (1980) worked with an elderly group of stroke patients who had a variety of communication disorders, using general verbal stimulation techniques with gradual elimination of clues. They found that 55% of their group achieved improved scores on language testing. Of these, 19% attained a functional level of communication by 3 months post onset on the Functional Communication Profile and another 22% achieved this level after the 3-month period. This period was selected as the re-assessment date because it represents the most widely accepted period of spontaneous recovery. Walker and Williams suggest that 12 months is the optimum period for intervention and that less may not provide maximum opportunity for a functional level to be achieved.

The CSLT survey (College of Speech and Language Therapists, 1990) found that speech and language therapists in the UK differentiated between Alzheimer's disease and multi-infarct dementia for the purposes of intervention. Although assessment and advice was the most common service provided for Alzheimer's disease, specific therapy for dysarthria and dysphagia was used with multi-infarct disease patients if any service was provided.

Speech and language therapy in elderly mentally infirm units in the UK is a slowly developing specialty which requires evaluation of its effectiveness. Griffiths and Baldwin (1989) describe individual case studies which demonstrate the service that a speech and language therapist might provide in such a setting and the need for cooperation between medical staff and the speech and language therapist in assessing effectiveness. The consultant had initially been sceptical of speech and language therapy involvement and the research had grown out of the need to assess the service.

Another service described in the survey is an innovative joint venture between a health authority and a county council, providing multidisciplinary management to elderly clients. After initial assessment, which is carried out wherever the elderly client is living at the time, each client is assigned to a key worker who is responsible for the client's individually designed care plan (which includes working with the family or other carers to increase their understanding of the client's communication abilities).

It appears to be particularly important for language therapy for the elderly client to focus on functional gains and supported use of communication skills. A survey of 68 stroke survivors (mean age 69 years) and their carers who were living at home asked the participants to state what improvements could be made to the treatment that they had received (Greveson and James, 1991). The results showed that, although only 5% of those interviewed wanted more rehabilitation, many commented that rehabilitation had concentrated only on essential activities of daily living and that they wanted help in resuming leisure and other such activities: 8% requested referral to a stroke club and 22% requested better post-discharge counselling and continuing support. The authors concluded that ongoing access to rehabilitation services is important for stroke survivors, with counselling and support being a primary requirement. Liaison between care providing agencies is also important, with the GP providing the first line of contact for patients who are no longer receiving hospital-based services.

A survey in Nottingham (Gladman, Albazzaz and Barer, 1991) showed that increasing numbers of disabled elderly stroke survivors are being discharged into private nursing homes. Of those who were admitted to private nursing homes (20% of the total), most were discharged to the home within 4 weeks of their hospital admission; marked dysphasia was one of the predictors of a poor outcome. Levels of subjective stress were noted to be high among those patients who could be assessed. The authors concluded that, as elderly patients with higher levels of disability are being discharged into private nursing homes, it is important that their rehabilitation potential is achieved before leaving hospital. These patients also need access to specialised services such as speech and language therapy, and nursing or care staff should be trained by professionals to participate in the residents' continued rehabilitation.

These surveys highlight the need for the extension of specialised services such as speech and language therapy into the residential sector and for professionals to adapt to the changing patterns of care provision for elderly people.

Group work

Group work encourages the use of existing or newly acquired skills and the generalisation of these skills to more everyday communicative settings. In residential settings, speech and language therapists may be involved in setting up and running groups with different aims: direct treatment groups, social groups, conversation groups and reminiscence groups. Communication might form only one of the aims of the group and the groups are often run by staff other than speech and language therapists.

Memory groups

Memory groups are an example of an intervention used by speech and language therapists. These are designed to improve specific memory problems, and should be differentiated from reminiscence therapy (which enables identification of common memories and interests) (Perotta and Meacham, 1981). Wilson and Moffat (1984) describe different types of memory intervention but caution that careful assessment is necessary to differentiate organic from non-organic problems: depression, for example, can be treated pharmacologically or with counselling. Borsley, in the survey initiated by the College of Speech and Language Therapists (1990), describes a memory line service run by a team working with the elderly mentally infirm with input from speech and language therapy. This telephone link provides an open referral service for any elderly person who is anxious about their memory function.

Reality orientation

Reality orientation is also often carried out as group work and is an approach to communication that research has shown can improve orientation in elderly people with dementia, but it needs to be continued if gains are to be maintained (Powell-Proctor and Miller, 1982; Holden and Woods, 1988). Holden and Woods (1988) describe this approach in detail, suggesting appropriate assessment procedures and different methods of implementation. They stress that reality orientation is most successful when it is used continuously by care staff or relatives. Speech and language therapists will recognise many of the communication strategies routinely used in this therapy because the strategies have been drawn from many sources: Lubinski (1981), for example, outlines a communication programme which incorporates aspects of reality orientation. Reality orientation requires careful planning and the cooperation of care staff to be successful. Interestingly, there is some evidence that implementing such a programme in residential homes may help to increase positive staff attitudes to elderly people (Smith and Barker, 1972; Barnett-Douglas, 1986).

Environmental manipulation

Advice on how to encourage and facilitate communication by altering the physical environment can be helpful. The effects of background noise (such as the television), seating arrangements that do not encourage social proximity and poor lighting can make communication impossible, particularly if it is already difficult for the elderly person. Additionally, in institutional settings the detrimental effects of an unstimulating environment on communication are well recognised (Lubinski et al., 1981). Increases in communicative behaviour have been demonstrated after altering ward routines in institutionalised settings (Melin and Gotestam, 1981).

Monitoring

Regular monitoring has been advocated for elderly clients with progressive diseases such as Parkinson's disease (Johnson and Pring, 1990) so that as the disease progresses the effects on speech and language skills can be made clear to the family and carers. Advice to the family and specific therapy provision can be made relevant to the client as and when it is needed rather than just at the stage of initial diagnosis. This was illustrated in the study of a patient with Pick's disease in which the patient's means of communication and the strategies that his family needed to adopt changed as the disease progressed (Holland et al., 1985) (see p. 151).

Bayles and Kasniak (1987) outline the value of monitoring patients with dementia in order to give accurate advice to carers, to evaluate any drug or other treatments being given and to accurately chart the disease progression.

Working with carers

Carers need to understand the effects of the disease process on speech and language, to have an exact picture of the abilities and difficulties of the person they are caring for and to have detailed guidance on how to promote communication and utilise compensatory strategies (such as gestures) to assist comprehension. This information needs to be presented in an accessible form; it may need to be repeated at intervals and the use of strategies to assist communication may need to be clearly demonstrated within a natural, familiar environment, ideally the patient's home.

The burden on care givers is well recognised (Jones and Peters, 1992); a survey by Rabins et al. (1982) showed that carers of patients with Alzheimer's disease reported problems with communication in 73% of cases and problems with eating meals in 55% of cases. Knight (1992) discusses the burden on the carers of patients with Alzheimer's disease and concludes that they require:

- education and counselling;
- group support;
- respite services.

A study by Riggans (1992) suggests that the relatives who are primary carers of people with dementia suffer symptoms of bereavement and that emotional support is vital to allow them to continue caring. A pilot project using a telephone helpline revealed large areas of unmet need among carers of the elderly mentally ill (O'Donovan, 1993). Speech and language therapists may be involved in offering emotional support if communication is a particular problem for the family. If community-based services with community resource teams are implemented, speech and language therapists may become key workers for certain clients and the provision of support would then be a recognised responsibility.

The cost of providing monitoring and continued support to carers both individually and via relatives support schemes is recognised as significant. However, a study by Brodaty and Peters (1991) showed that an intensive 10-day educational and support programme with continued follow-up for the carers of patients with dementia was cost-effective in terms of keeping the patients at home for longer and therefore saving on the cost of institutional care, as well as significantly reducing psychological stress in carers.

Written guides for carers of people with dementia can provide useful information (Toner, 1987), but the effectiveness of information specifically on communication has yet to be demonstrated. There is no doubt that the behaviour of someone with dementia can be distressing and that carers may need help in understanding that the behaviour is a reflection of the progressive brain damage. While face-to-face discussion is often the means for communicating information, written information can usefully remind and amplify what has been discussed.

Referral to other agencies

Referrals may need to be made to other medical and health agencies:

- dietician for advice on nutrition;
- medical social worker for advice on benefits;
- community services, e.g. day hospital or chiropody;
- voluntary sector agencies, e.g. speech-after-stroke clubs, day centres run by, for example, the Alzheimer's Disease Society or luncheon clubs for the elderly.

It is vital that clinicians are aware of the provision for the elderly in their local area and the referral procedures necessary to access such services.

Education of other staff

Education may be through reports, direct liaison at ward rounds and case conferences or direct educational programmes such as lectures and discussion groups. It is also important that speech and language therapists are seen in their work and can directly demonstrate therapeutic techniques. For example, with feeding, talks and videos can be helpful, but a demonstration of the techniques advocated may be necessary to convince busy nursing staff that these techniques can easily be incorporated into nursing routines with beneficial results.

It is also important for speech and language therapists to be involved in educating agencies who may be the first contact for elderly patients and upon whom they are dependent for referral, for example GPs and health visitors. As services for the elderly move away from hospital-based settings to the community, it is becoming more and more important for speech and language therapists to work with staff in residential homes.

Working in the residential care sector

Working in the residential care sector combines the skills that a clinician needs in working with carers and in educating other staff. Many elderly people with chronic illness are now admitted to private-sector residential and nursing homes or to local authority residential homes. Gosney and Edmond (1991) showed that 93% of residents in Part III homes in the central and southern area of the Liverpool Health District had at least one significant medical diagnosis of chronic disease: 13% had neurological disease; 5% deafness; 19% chronic confusion/dementia and 12% depression. Many of these residents could be predicted to have communication problems and the combined figure for neurological disease, dementia or deafness (49%) compares well with the incidence of communication problems found in a survey of one residential home in Bristol. Here 53% of the residents were found to have problems on the Western Aphasia Battery, on an assessment battery which indicated language problems associated with dementia, or both (Bryan and Drew, 1989). The residents were consistently rated by the care staff on a modified Functional Communication Profile (Sarno, 1969) as poor communicators, indicating that the staff were very aware of the communication difficulties encountered by these residents. Brodie (1986) also reported a significant proportion of elderly people in a residential home with communication problems.

Although there is such a high proportion of dependency among elderly care residents and many require a high level of personal care, including nursing (Gosney and Edmond, 1991), there has been little increase in staff ratios or training opportunities.

In a survey of 17 local authority homes within one health district (which asked the officers in charge to state what input they would like from the speech and language therapy service), 14 requested staff training (Bryan and Drew, 1987). A project followed this survey to try to establish service provision for the residential sector, and a programme of staff training was included. This was well received but needed to be very basic and, more importantly, to address the specific problems that each group of staff was experiencing. Examples of the type of input needed are given in handbooks specifically designed for care assistants working with the elderly (Maxim and Bryan, 1989; Bryan and Maxim, 1991).

Staff training was part of an overall increase in the speech and language provision for elderly people within one health district. As well as the training sessions, residents who were listed by the officers as causing particular concern were seen for assessment, advice was given, and in a few cases further therapy input was given as appropriate. This enabled staff to see that speech and language therapy was useful and effective, which was important in establishing future work that needed much more active input from the care staff.

It is vital to the success of work within the residential sector that:

- the managers of a home are fully committed to the input from the professional and are prepared to allocate time for training, talking to the speech and language therapist and joint assessments;
- the speech and language therapist is fully aware of how the home runs: the shift system, the eating arrangements, the allocation of staff to residents (key worker or care group systems) so that visits can be timed to cause minimum disruption to the routine;
- the clinician facilitates joint working (for example by demonstrating the best way to communicate during an activity such as tidying a resident's room). Advice needs to be tailored to the exact situation that the resident is experiencing;
- ongoing work (e.g. running a group) involves a link officer so that arrangements such as room allocation are dealt with. Practical requirements need to be mutually negotiated and then put in writing;
- frequent follow-up meetings regarding ongoing work are held so that the care staff remain closely involved and begin to see themselves as instrumental. Only at this point can the speech and language therapist reduce input, but even then close liaison and monitoring of activities, staff input and resident input are required.

An experimental group work project in two residential homes was set up by Bryan and Drew (1987). This aimed primarily to address the problem of residents who were able to communicate but rarely did so. The groups contained residents nominated by the care staff, with only those with very severe visual or hearing losses being excluded. A speech and language therapist and a care assistant from the homes ran each group. The aim was to encourage communication through discussion, quizzes, reminiscence and activities based around seasonal events. The sessions were planned by the speech and language therapist but run jointly by the speech and language therapist and the care assistant. In retrospect, it would have been better to have made a time allowance for planning to involve the care assistant.

The groups were evaluated by the managers of the homes and, as well as the obvious benefits during the sessions, the officers reported:

- more spontaneous conversation between residents, and more response from those who did not actually initiate conversation;
- increased conversation between care staff and residents, with topics extending beyond self and illness;
- more tolerance of those residents with specific speech problems because people realised that they had interesting things to say.

Overall it was interesting that staff were almost shocked by the level of conversation and activity achieved during the groups (although this did not seem unusual to the speech and language therapists), indicating that levels of expectation are extremely low within the care sector. Residents are frequently not given the opportunity to utilise the skills they have.

More controlled research is clearly needed to evaluate the effects of such communication work within the care sector and to compare the effects of speech and language therapist input with those of a group run only by care staff in order to justify expansion of therapy provision into the residential care sector.

Successful intervention with the elderly communicatively disabled is heavily dependent on the speech and language therapist working as part of the care team, as opposed to accepting referrals from them. Change, according to Griffiths and Baldwin (1989) and Walker and Williams (1980), is most possible when the clinician is allowed to work directly with other professionals and carers to demonstrate strategies for facilitating communication, and when direct therapy is used with the elderly person.

Chapter 10
Future directions

Proposed models of care in the UK

In 1989 the government published *Caring for People*, a document which described community care 'in the next decade and beyond'. Its main thrust was the improvement of community care and the establishment of areas of responsibility for community care to enable people to live as independently as possible in their own homes or in appropriate settings in the community. Four key components for provision of care in the community were specified in the document (p. 5):

1. Services that respond flexibly and sensitively to the needs of individuals and their carers
2. Services that allow a range of options for consumers
3. Services that intervene no more than is necessary to foster independence
4. Services that concentrate on those with the greatest needs.

The move from hospital to community-based care has been under way for some time for people with psychiatric illness. There have long been services to help the elderly and/or physically handicapped living in the community (e.g. meals on wheels and home care) and the government aim is to move emphasis away from hospital based care for the elderly population. One of the consequences of this is to reduce further the diminishing supply of long-stay geriatric beds (Kellett, 1993).

The principal change in policy involves local authorities having lead agency responsibility for assessing need, designing packages of care and ensuring that services are delivered. A unified community care budget will be in the control of the local authorities, providing for all forms of community care, including that for the elderly. Assessment of need will be managed through social services via consultation with the elderly person concerned, health workers and formal and informal carers. At present there are no guidelines for user participation so that a professionally dominated system is likely to prevail (Walker, 1992). The professionally dominated system is likely to prevail (Walker, 1992). The final decision on placement will be made by social services. This last proposal has been fiercely debated by GPs who would have a duty to inform social services of the possible community care needs of any patients on their lists but who could not determine the outcome of the needs assessment (Millard and Higgs, 1989). GPs are required to screen the health of all elderly patients with annual check-ups for those over 75 and initiatives have been proposed to provide support for carers and to increase day-care services in order to facilitate independent living. In theory, this change in emphasis may benefit the elderly but there must also be pessimism given that it is not clear whether the government's proposals are prompted by the desire to cut costs and reduce the emphasis on 'state provision' in favour of private sector care. It is difficult to judge the effect of the community-care legislation on service provision for the elderly at this early stage, and in many ways the pace of change and local variations in implementation make any consensus invalid. The provision of health care to the increased numbers of elderly living in the community has not been adequately addressed. Although occupational therapists have been working within social services for some time and a few services provide physiotherapy, there is no uniform access to rehabilitation and other health care services.

An example of how the community-care legislation will be implemented has been set out for services to the elderly mentally ill in Southwark by Thornicroft, Ward and James (1993), where both health professionals and social services personnel will be able to complete screening assessments using standard forms. If necessary, the local social services department will carry out a full needs assessment, but questions remain as to who will prioritise services, upon what basis and what will happen to clients whose needs cannot be met due to financial restrictions.

Care in the USA, Canada, Japan and France

Care in other countries may provide useful models for the UK.. There is remarkable similarity among types of services offered to the elderly, but differences emerge in the proportions of elderly people using the services and in the way that they are accessed (Tout, 1993). Even within the UK there are differences in, for example, the proportion of elderly people in long-stay NHS beds in England and Scotland, Scotland having retained long-stay beds to a far greater extent.

USA

In the USA some states provide home health care programmes for supportive medical services. These are defined as nursing, physical, occupational and speech therapy aspects of home health care (Brody,

1977). The programmes are organised by health care agencies who are participating in Medicare, the government insurance programme for the elderly. The elderly may also be eligible for funds from the Medicaid programme, if Medicare does not cover the cost of their needs. Medicaid is a welfare assistance scheme available to those in need on a means-tested basis (Hendricks and Calasanti, 1986). Rehabilitation services are available on medical prescription and require a treatment plan and regular re-evaluation. Some types of nursing home (e.g. skilled nursing facilities) have a statutory duty to provide some rehabilitation services.

Dowling (1981) sums up the US care context as follows:

> ... the real health care delivery world ... is a tripartite world, comprising, in addition to recipients and providers, 'third party' insurers or payers of health care costs who, under the banners of cost effectiveness and quality assurance, impose standards of participation on recipients and providers alike.
>
> (p. 307)

Because health insurance is neither national nor compulsory, the elderly American citizen may have restricted access to rehabilitation services.

The Clinton administration plan for an employer-led health care scheme with managed competition, purchasing pools for patients and more primary care doctors may lead to greater flexibility of entry to the health system for older American (Roberts, 1993).

Canada

In Canada, funding for health care is via compulsory insurance and, although health care is provided within the private sector, availability is more uniform. Health care and rehabilitation services for the elderly in Canada are more comparable to the provision in the UK.

France

France has historically had a larger proportion of elderly people in its population than other European countries and, according to EC information, allows less of its national budget for the elderly than most of its neighbours. In the last decade services for the elderly, including home help schemes, meal schemes and clubs for the elderly, have mushroomed but Guillemard (1986) describes the situation bleakly as a set of dispersed, circumstantial actions with very variable provision.

Japan

While the percentage of people over 65 in the population between 1980 and 2010 will remain relatively stable in the UK and the USA,

France and Canada will see a rise in numbers. In Japan, the percentage of people aged 65 and overwill double in the same period (OECD, 1988). Japan has a compulsory national health insurance programme and people over 65 are eligible for free medical care. Long-term care in Japan is provided either by the person's family or within three different types of health facility: hospitals specifically for the elderly; special nursing homes, staffed by nurses and trained nurse assistants; and residential rehabilitation units with stays limited to 3 months. Japan has a chronic nursing shortage, which has led to many elderly inpatients becoming bedridden (Okamoto, 1992).

Several factors emerge from this brief view of services, across several countries, for the elderly:

- the elderly as a group vary enormously in their health and social care needs so a range of services have evolved;
- access to services is often restricted, but the nature of the restrictions vary from country to country;
- demand for services is great and can create a de facto policy for care in the absence of government policy.

Aims for future speech and language therapy provision in the UK

Following the advent of 'care in the community' and recent changes in NHS structure, it is difficult even to speculate about how speech and language therapy services for the elderly may develop in the future. However, a number of reports have outlined what services should aim to achieve. *The Statement of Intent for Health Care Services in Old Age*, issued by the British Geriatric Society in 1988, advocates an integrated approach to service requirements. The specific aims relevant to rehabilitation services are that:

- all persons should have access to domiciliary services provided by the local authority to support them at home for as long as they wish;
- no person on account of disability should be confined to institutional care without having the benefit of rehabilitation and assessment by a multidisciplinary team;
- the quality of life within institutions should be of a high level so that elderly persons and their carers may regard such care as an acceptable way of spending the rest of their lives when remaining at home becomes impossible;
- age–sex registers should be established in every general practice and used to supervise the care of the vulnerable elderly;

- community services should be constantly reviewed so that they can be increased or decreased according to need, a key worker to be allocated to each elderly person receiving support in the community;
- adequate transport to be provided to support outpatient clinics, day hospitals, day centres and GPs' surgeries.

(See Appendix VIII for a full copy of the statement.)

These guidelines provide some useful indications for the future development of speech and language services for the elderly. *Communicating Quality,* the guidelines for service delivery issued by the College of Speech and Language Therapists (1990), states the aims and principles of service delivery for the elderly client group as:

- to provide a timely, effective and appropriate service to elderly people with communication difficulties in the context of multidisciplinary rehabilitation;
- to provide an integrated service to the elderly population with communication difficulties in a range of locations;
- to identify specific areas of speech and language difficulty;
- to assist the medical team in the overall diagnosis of the client's disorder;
- to ensure that the communication needs of the client are fully considered in their day-to-day management;
- to provide guidance and support to staff on how to maximise their interaction with clients during everyday activities and how to utilise strategies to aid communication;
- to at all times respect the rights and dignities of the elderly person, valuing them for the life experiences they hold.

A report commissioned by the NHS Management Executive on epidemiologically based needs assessment of services for people with dementia was published in a provisional form in May 1992 and sets out the major issues that health service purchasers should consider in specifying services for people with dementia. The following issues are relevant for speech and language therapy services.

- Early recognition is advocated and, following the introduction of new contracts for GPs, regular general health surveillance (which includes a mental state examination) is offered to those under 75 every 3 years and to those over 75 annually.

  Clearly a specialist service such as speech and language therapy could link to this surveillance process with referral of those patients who are found to be experiencing communication difficulties. At this stage advice and explanation will be important to the client and their carers, and will be vital in preventing maladaptive strategies such as avoidance of situations that involve communication. It would also be important to evolve a system of continued monitoring or regular re-referral in order to provide further therapy as and when the client experiences further deterioration in his or her speech and language abilities so that communication can be preserved for as long as possible. This could enhance the role of speech and language therapists in preventive care and management of elderly clients in order to maintain communicative functioning and to facilitate independent living.

- Multidisciplinary assessment throughout the course of the illness is advocated with community resource teams involved. The introduction of 'care management' will formalise the drawing up of a care plan where appropriate for the client, with the appointment of a case manager. The lead agency for these arrangements will be social services although the case manager may come from any agency. It may be necessary for the speech and language therapist to form part of the community resource team when communication problems are an important factor in an individual client's management. The need to liaise more closely with social services is also obvious. If the proposals for increased community care are fully implemented in the future, speech and language therapists and other health professionals may be employed by social services to deal specifically with elderly clients in a variety of community- and home-based settings.
- The value of specialist services to community-based services is highlighted in the report but speech and language therapy is not listed as one of the services currently available. It was apparent in the report of the College of Speech and Language Therapist (see pp. 214–218) that most speech and language therapists working with the elderly currently are working within hospital-based, medically led teams. There is a clear need for the role of speech and language therapists to be more widely publicised and to be extended into community care more often. Jolley, Kondratowicz and Wilkin (1980) outlined the merits of speech and language therapy involvement in psychogeriatric teams, and a recent report by Griffiths and Baldwin (1989) outlined the role developed by a speech and language therapist who joined a psychogeriatric team. The paper highlights the value of such a team member from both the speech and language therapist's and the psychogeriatrician's point of view. There is an urgent need for more research defining the specific role of speech and language therapy with elderly clients. It is also vital that speech and language therapists publish such research in journals with a wide range of professional readership.

The draft NHS report on services for elderly people with dementia concludes that:

> Assessment and specification of services for the special needs of groups of people with dementia is a complex task. Any specification must make the necessary links to the general services for the elderly. Within the specific services, in many areas little research is available to guide decision making. Nevertheless, there are clear, important and achievable objectives. Purchasers of services should examine the various choices carefully, both in terms of quantities of each service category, but also of the quality of service provided. It is likely that considerable gains in quality of life for both sufferers and carers, including the reduction of often enormous burdens of care can be achieved.
>
> (p. 29)

Future directions for research

Watson (1992) suggests that research into Alzheimer's disease will foster improvement in care and therapeutic strategies for patients with dementia. Throughout this book aspects of both normal and pathological ageing that require more research have been highlighted, particularly those which impinge on clinical management of elderly people with language difficulties. Methodological issues in this field are discussed by Bourgeois (1991) and Holland (1990).

The following programme of future research is suggested:

- A theoretical framework is needed, within which to understand cognitive ageing. This needs to be flexible enough to incorporate variables such as biological status, health, education and life experience. This would enable a clearer picture of normal ageing and its interrelationship with environmental factors to be elucidated. This might be expected to enable researchers to generate hypotheses that would distinguish between normal and pathological aspects of ageing.
- Longitudinal studies of language and cognition in ageing subjects and single case studies which examine the relationship of language and cognitive skills in both normal and pathological ageing should be carried out.
- Single-case longitudinal studies are needed, using neuropsychological approaches to language processing. These would contribute detailed descriptions of the dissolution of language in the dementias and could examine the interaction between different linguistic levels; for example, how much do single-word deficits contribute to deficits at the discourse level?
- Detailed descriptions of the language of patients with this disease may contribute to the debate over whether Alzheimer's disease represents one or several entities. The possibility of variation in onset and severity of language problems being an indicator of different forms of Alzheimer's disease provides some impetus to illustrating

the value of language assessment and may even lead to recognition of different management strategies for clients with different forms of dementia.

- The role of the speech and language therapist within the psychogeriatric team needs to be validated and the changes in working practices that may accompany community care need to be evaluated. Detailed descriptions of the clinician's role could fuel studies on the efficacy and cost-effectiveness of therapy for elderly clients with dementia.
- The effectiveness of monitoring and carer support for elderly clients with communication disorders needs to be proved.
- Efficacy studies also need to be conducted in the residential care sector to ascertain exactly what value speech and language therapy has and to examine the most effective ways of training residential care staff and the cost-effectiveness of joint initiatives between care staff and professional staff.
- The potential value of specialist services such as speech and language therapy to the maintenance of communicative functioning in the normal elderly needs to be explored.

Appendix I: Original LARSP chart

Name	Age	Sample date	Type

A	**Unanalysed**			**Problematic**		
	1 Unintelligible	2 Symbolic Noise	3 Deviant	1 Incomplete	2 Ambiguous	3 Stereotypes

				Normal Response						Abnormal		
				Major								
				Elliptical								
B	Responses Stimulus Type	Totals	Repetitions	1	2	3+	Reduced	Full	Minor	Structural	ø	Problems
	Questions											
	Others											
C	Spontaneous											

D	Reactions		General	Structural	ø	Other	Problems

Stage							
Stage I	Minor	Responses		Vocatives	Other	Problems	
	Major	*Comm.* 'V'	*Quest.* 'Q'	*Statement* 'V'	'N'	Other	Problems

Stage	Conn.	Clause				Phrase		Word
Stage II		VX	QX	SV SO SC Neg X	AX VO VC Other	DN Adj N NN PrN	VV V part Int X Other	-ing pl -ed
Stage III		VXY *let* XY *do* XY	QXY VS(X)	SVC SVO SVA Neg XY	VCA VOA VO_iO_d Other	D Adj N Adj Adj N Pr DN $Pron^P_O$	Cop Aux^M_O Other	-en 3s gen
Stage IV		+ S VXY +	QVS QXY + VS(X+) tag	SVOA SVCA SVO_iO_d SVOC	AAXY Other	NP Pr NP Pr D Adj N cX XcX	Neg V Neg X 2 Aux Other	n't 'cop 'aux
Stage V	*and* c s Other	Coord. Other	Coord. Other	Coord. 1 1 + Subord. A 1 1 + S C O Comparative		Postmod. clause 1 1 + Postmod. phrase 1 +		-est -er -ly

	(+)			(−)					
Stage VI	NP	VP	Clause	Conn.	Clause	Phrase			Word
					Element	NP		VP	N V
	Initiator Coord.	Complex	Passive Complement. *how* *what*	*and* c s	ø ⇄ Concord	D Dø D⇄	Pr Prø Pr⇄ $Pron^P$	Aux^M Aux^O Cop ø	*irreg* *reg*
	Other					Ambiguous			

Stage VII	*Discourse*		*Syntactic Comprehension*
	A Connectivity	*it*	
	Comment Clause	*there*	*Style*
	Emphatic Order	Other	

Total No. Sentences	Mean No. Sentences Per Turn	Mean Sentence Length

Appendix II: Modified LARSP chart

Name:　　　　Age:　　　　Conversational Sample

A	Unanalysed			Problematic	
	1 Unintelligible	2 Symbolic Noise	3 Deviant	1 Incomplete	2 Ambiguous

B	Normal Response						Abnormal		Problems
	Elliptical Major				Full Major	Minor	Structural	ø	
	1	2	3	4					
Response ellipsis			–						
In monologue ellipsis									
Totals									

Stage								
Stage I	Minor	Responses		Vocatives	Other	Problems		
	Major	Comm. 'V'	Quest. 'Q'	Statement 'V'	Statement 'N'	Other	Problems	
	Conn.	Clause				Phrase		Word
Stage II (6–2;0)		VX	QX	SV, SO, SC	AX, VO, VC, Other	DN, Adj N, NN, PrN	VV, V part, Int X, Other	-ing, pl
Stage III		X + S:NP		X + V:VP		X + C/O:NP	X + A:AP	-ed
		VXY, let XY, do XY	QXY, VS(X)	SVC, SVO, SVA	VCA, VOA, VO_iO_d, Other	D Adj N, Adj Adj N, Pr DN, $Pron^P_O$	Cop, Aux^M_O, Other	-en, 3s, gen
Stage IV		XY + S:NP		XY + V:VP		XY + C/O:NP	XY + A:AP	n't
		+ S, VXY +	QVS, QXY +, VS(X+), tag	SVOA, SVCA, SVO_iO_d, SVOC	AAXY, Other	NP Pr NP, Pr D Adj N, cX, XcX	Neg V, Neg X, 2 Aux, Other	'cop, 'aux
Stage V	and, c, s, Other	Coord., Other	Coord., Other	Coord., Subord. A 1 1 +, S C, Comparative		Postmod. clause 1 1 +, Postmod. phrase 1 +		-est, -er, -ly

Stage VI	(+)			(–)				
	NP	VP	Clause	Conn.	Clause	Phrase		Word
					Element	NP	VP	N V
	Initiator, Coord.	Complex	Passive, Complement.	and, c, s	ø, ⇄, Concord	D, Dø, D ⇄; Pr, Prø, Pr ⇄; $Pron^P$	Aux^M, Aux^O, Cop, ø	irreg, reg
	Other			All errors		Ambiguous		

Stage VII			
	Discourse		Syntactic Comprehension
	A Connectivity, Comment Clause, Emphatic Order	it, there, Other	Repair
			Style: Dialect features

Total No. Sentences (+ minor sentences / – minor sentences)	Mean No. Sentences Per Turn	Mean Sentence Length (all) MSL – minor sentences

Appendix III: Glossary of LARSP abbreviations

A	adverbial
Adj	adjectival
Aux	auxiliary
'aux	contracted auxiliary form
c	coordinator
C	complement
Comm	command sentence type
conn	connectivity marker
cop	copula
'cop	contracted copula form
D	determiner
Det	determiner system (errors)
-ed	past tense
-en	past participle
-er	comparative
-est	superlative
Excl	exclamatory sentence type
I	initiator
-ing	present participle
Int	intensifier
-ly	adverb marker
Mod	modal verb
N	noun
'N'	noun-like element Stage I
N Irreg	irregular noun inflections (errors)

Neg	negation
n't	contracted negative form
O	object
O_d	direct object
O_i	indirect object
part	particle
pl	plural
postmod clause	postmodifying clause
postmod phrase	postmodifying phrase
Pr	preposition
Pron	pronoun
Q	question word
Quest	question sentence type
s	subordinator
S	subject
v	main verb (at phrase structure level)
V	verb
'V'	verb-like element at Stage I
X, Y, Z	cover symbols for elements of structure
3s	third person singular
/	tone-unit boundary
´	nuclear tone – rising
`	nuclear tone – falling
–	nuclear tone – level
ˇ	nuclear tone – falling-rising
ˈ	indicates following syllable is stressed
.	brief pause
–	unit length pause
— —	double length pause
— — —	treble length pause
?	indicates doubt about transcriptional accuracy
(...)	uninterpretable speech
((...))	brief or incomplete utterance
*	utterance overlap

Appendix IV: Means for structures counted during the 20-minute sampling period

Sections A, B, C and sentence information, expressed as frequencies per 100 sentences

<table>
<tr><td>A Unanalysed utterances
Unintelligible 3.5 Filler syllables 29.7</td><td colspan="6">Problematic utterances
Uncompleted 8.9 Ambiguous 3.9</td></tr>
<tr><td rowspan="3">B Response ellipsis</td><td colspan="6">Elliptical major utterances</td></tr>
<tr><td>1</td><td>2</td><td>3</td><td>4+</td><td>Total</td><td>Total</td></tr>
<tr><td>7.6</td><td>3.3</td><td>1.3</td><td>0.2</td><td>12.4</td><td rowspan="2">68.1</td></tr>
<tr><td>C In monologue ellipsis</td><td>28.6</td><td>18.1</td><td>7.3</td><td>1.7</td><td>55.7</td></tr>
<tr><td>Minor sentences 68.1</td><td colspan="3">Full major sentences 402.1</td><td colspan="3">Elliptical major utterances 68.1</td></tr>
</table>

	Clause	Phrase	Other grammatical units	Word
Stage I	A 10.5 N 13.9 V 6 Other (1) 8.4			
Stage II	SV 58.8 AX 16.7 VC/O 14.8 SC/O 1.4	DN 77.1 PrN 28.7 PrepPron 22.5 AdjN 21.9 PrepAdv 7.4 NN 1.0 Other (2) 14.9	Vpart 30.6 VV/VV+ 25.0 Intensifier 24.5	
Stage III	SVC/O 108.5 SVA 57.4 VC/OA 5.8 AAX 1.7 VO_iO_d 1.0 Other (3) 2.2	PrDN 36.6 DAdjN 25.3 PrAdjn 3.8 AdjAdjN 1.1 Other (3) 17.9	Pron 364 Aux 127 Cop 84.1 Neg 51	ED 136.6 EN 29.5 ING 24.2 n't 38.6
Stage IV	SVC/OA 54.1 SVAA 32.9 SVO_iO_d 2.8 Other (4) 1.0	PrDAdjN 7.8 Postmodifying phrases 27.5 Other (4) 17.6	Phrasal expansion C/O 79.4 V 70.7 A 49.1 S 17.4	'aux/ 'cop 58.7
Stage V	SVOAA 11.6 SVO_iO_dA 1.5 Other (5) 1.0	Other (5) 7.9		
Stage VI	SVOAAA 2.1 Other (6) 0.5	Other(6+) 1.0	NP coord 5.4 VP complex 15.5	
Stage VII	Other (7) 0.5		Adverbial connectivity 23.4	

Stage V	Connectivity	Statement: Clause		Statement: Phrase
	AND 66.3 c 41.5 s 54.2	Coordination 153.3 Clause: A 36.5 Clause: C/O 18.6 Clause: S 0.9 Comparative Clause: S+Y 0.5 Sentential relative clause 0.5	It 3.6 A conn. 23.4 Tag questions 8.3 Comment clause 40.5	Postmodifying clause 21.4

Stage VI	Complex grammatical constructions: NP	Complex grammatical constructions: VP	Complex grammatical constructions: Clause	Complex phrasal grammatical constructions	Grammatical errors
	Initiator 6.7 Coordinator 5.1	Complex 16.5	Passive 3.2 Complement 7.7	5.3	12.4
	Other 3				

Stage VII		
	Sentence repair	29.4
	Emphatic order	6.2
	It	7.2
	There	7.2
	Phrasal ellipsis	0.5

Total number of sentences 470.2	Mean number of sentences per turn 8.4	MSL (all) 5.1 MSL – minor sentences 5.8

Appendix V: Means for structures per 100 sentences

<table>
<tr><td>A Unanalysed utterances
Unintelligible 0.2 Filler syllables 6.2</td><td colspan="6">Problematic utterances
Uncompleted 2.2 Ambiguous 0.9</td></tr>
<tr><td rowspan="3">B Response ellipsis</td><td colspan="6">Elliptical major utterances</td></tr>
<tr><td>1</td><td>2</td><td>3</td><td>4+</td><td>Total</td><td>Total</td></tr>
<tr><td>1.8</td><td>0.8</td><td>0.3</td><td>0.05</td><td>3</td><td rowspan="2">17</td></tr>
<tr><td>C In monologue ellipsis</td><td>7.1</td><td>4.5</td><td>1.8</td><td>0.4</td><td>13.8</td></tr>
<tr><td>Minor sentences 14.4</td><td colspan="3">Full major sentences 68.6</td><td colspan="3">Elliptical major utterances 17</td></tr>
</table>

	Clause		Phrase		Other grammatical units		Word	
	A	2.5						
	N	3.3						
Stage I	V	1.4						
	Other (1)	2						
			DN	25.3				
	SV	13.9	PrN	9.4				
Stage II	AX	4	PrepPron	7.4	Vpart	8.1		
	VC/O	3.5	AdjN	7.2	VV/VV+	6.6		
	SC/O	0.3	PrepAdv	2.4	Intensifier	6.1		
			NN	0.3				
			Other (2)	4.9				
Stage III	SVC/O	25.8	PrDN	12			ED	36.2
	SVA	13.6	DAdjN	8.3	Pron	90.6		
	VC/OA	1.3	PrAdjn	1.2	Aux	33.7	EN	7.7
	AAX	0.4	AdjAdjN	0.3	Cop	22.3		
	VO_iO_d	0.2	Other (3)	5.8	Neg	12.6	ING	9.6
	Other (3)	1.1						
Stage IV	SVC/OA	12.8	PrDAdjN	2.5	Phrasal expansion		n't	9.6
	SVAA	7.8	Postmodifying		C/O	36.2		
	SVO_iO_d	0.6	phrases	6.8	V	41.2	'aux/	
	Other (4)	0.3	Other (4)	5.7	A	34.4	'cop	15.5
					S	8.2		
Stage V	SVOAA	2.7						
	SVO_iO_dA	0.3	Other (5)	2.6				
	Other (5)	0.5						
Stage VI	SVOAAA	0.5			NP coord	1.3		
	Other (6)	0.5	Other(6+)	0.3	VP complex	4.3		
Stage VII	Other (7)	0.3			Adverbial			
					connectivity	4.9		

Stage V, VI and VIII information, expressed as frequencies per 100 sentences

	Connectivity		Statement				
			Clause				Phrase
Stage V	AND	16.4	Coordination	32.6	It	0.9	Postmodifying clause 5.3
	c	10.3	Clause: A	8.1	A conn.	4.9	
	s	13.4	Clause: C/O	4.6	Tag questions	2	
			Clause: S	0.2	Comment clause	8.6	
			Comparative	0.1			
			Clause: S+Y	1.1			
			Sentential relative clause	0.01			

	Complex grammatical constructions			Complex phrasal grammatical constructions	Grammatical errors
	NP	VP	Clause		
Stage VI	Initiator 1.7	Complex	Passive 0.8	3	3.1
	Coordinator 1.3		Complement 1.9		
	Other 3				

Stage VII	Sentence repair	7.3
	Emphatic order	1.5
	It	1.3
	There	1.3
	Phrasal ellipsis	0.1

Total number of sentences 100	Mean number of sentences per turn 8.4	MSL (all) 5.1 MSL – minor sentences 5.8

Appendix VI: Hachinski Ischaemia Score

Feature	*Score*
Abrupt onset	2
Stepwise deterioration	1
Fluctuating course	2
Nocturnal confusion	1
Relative preservation of personality	1
Depression	1
Somatic complaints	1
Emotional incontinence	1
History of hypertension*	1
History of strokes	2
Evidence of associated atherosclerosis	1
Focal neurological symptoms	2
Focal neurological signs	2

*Defined as either a history of present or previous hypotensive therapy or a current and consistent blood pressure of 170/110 or more.
From Hachinski et al. (1975).

Appendix VII: DSM-III-R criteria for diagnosis of dementia

A. Demonstrable evidence of impairment in short- and long-term memory. Impairment in short-term memory (inability to learn new information) may be indicated by inability to remember three objects after 5 minutes. Long-term memory impairment (inability to remember information that was known in the past) may be indicated by inability to remember past personal information (e.g. what happened yesterday, birthplace, occupation) or facts of common knowledge (e.g. past presidents, well-known dates).

B. At least one of the following:
   (i) impairment in abstract thinking, as indicated by inability to find similarities and differences between related words, difficulty in defining words and concepts, and other similar tasks.
   (ii) impaired judgement, as indicated by inability to make reasonable plans to deal with interpersonal, family and job-related problems and issues.
   (iii) other disturbances of higher cortical function such as aphasia (disorder of language), apraxia (inability to carry out motor activities despite intact comprehension and motor function), agnosia (failure to recognize or identify objects despite intact sensory function) and 'constructional difficulty' (e.g. inability to copy three-dimensional figures, assemble blocks, or arrange sticks in specific designs).
   (iv) personality change, i.e. alteration or accentuation of premorbid traits.

C. The disturbance in A and B significantly interferes with work or usual social activities or relationships with others.

D. Not occurring exclusively during the course of delirium.

E. Either (i) or (ii):
   (i) there is evidence from the history, physical examination, or laboratory tests of a specific organic factor (or factors) judged to be aetiologically related to the disturbance.
   (ii) in the absence of such evidence, an etiological organic factor can be presumed if the disturbance cannot be accounted for by

any non-organic mental disorder, e.g. Major Depression accounting for cognitive impairment.

Criteria for severity of dementia:

- Mild: although work or social activities are significantly impaired, the capacity for independent living remains, with adequate personal hygiene and relatively intact judgement.
- Moderate: independent living is hazardous and some degree of supervision is necessary.
- Severe: activities of daily living are so impaired that continual supervision is required, e.g. unable to maintain minimal personal hygiene; largely incoherent or mute.

Appendix VIII: British Geriatrics Society Statement of Intent (1988)

1. All persons irrespective of age to have access to the primary health care team and the health care services to support them at home on a daily basis and extra support at times of crisis, including support required at the time of acute illness, when it is the stated wish of the person to be treated at home.
2. All persons irrespective of age to have access to domiciliary services provided by the local authority to support them at home as long as it is their wish. These services to be adequate, and to provide a basis to make a choice between remaining at home or considering other forms of living either in sheltered housing or the more institutional living of a residential home.
3. Any awards of public money paid to elderly people should allow the person to have a multidisciplinary assessment and advice given on the most appropriate care for that person. If it is deemed that residential care is not the most appropriate form of care then the monies should still be given but used to allow the person to buy the care that is necessary to support them in their own home.
4. All persons irrespective of age and means to have access in the event of acute illness to a general hospital with full range of diagnostic facilities
5. All persons irrespective of age and means to have access without undue delay to first-class facilities for elective surgical procedures required to maintain quality of life.
6. No person on account of disability to be confined to institutional care without having the benefit of rehabilitation and assessment by a multidisciplinary team. Only those persons requiring 24-hour care by medical and nursing staff to remain in hospital.
7. The quality of life within institutions should be of high level so that elderly persons and their carers may regard such care as an acceptably way of spending the remainder of their lives when staying at home becomes impossible. Ready access to such care should also

be available in order to ensure that carers are not exposed to excessive stress but are guaranteed adequate respite.

8. Local directories of all available services to be available, to include health services, local authorities, voluntary bodies. Clear instructions to be given concerning contact points and individuals' telephone numbers.
9. Age–sex registers to be established in every general practice and to be used to supervise the care of the vulnerable elderly, the general practitioner to be responsible for notifying the non-health care needs of their patients to the local authority.
10. All health and local authority services to be readily available 24 hours a day, 365 days a year.
11. Constant review of community services so that they can be increased or decreased according to need, a key worker to be allocated to each elderly person receiving support in the community.
12. Every elderly person and their carers to have the right to have their case reviewed by the local authority in order that they may receive the support of their choice.
13. The expenditure of public money to finance care to be subject to the same degree of scrutiny as that within the NHS.
14. Adequate transport to be provided to support out-patient clinics, day hospitals, day centres and GPs' surgeries.
15. Provisions of effective registration and monitoring of standards in private and statutory residential and nursing homes, this is to be performed by an independent team of professionals experienced in the care of the elderly. Evidence should be obtained from elderly residents and their friends and relatives where appropriate.
16. Institute monitoring to ensure that health and social services are run cost-effectively to meet the full range of needs of the community in each locality.
17. There to be arrangements made by central Government to make sure that a full range of services is available and that health and local authorities are aware of the facilities needed to support people in hospital or the community.
18. In addition, we would like to register our concern about health maintenance organisations. They have not proved effective in providing comprehensive medical care for elderly people in the United States and thus it would seem highly unlikely that they would be of any benefit to elderly people in the United Kingdom.

References

Adams, C., Labouvie-Vief, G., Hobart, C.J. and Dorosz, M. (1991). Adult age group differences in story recall style. *Journal of Gerontology: Psychological Sciences* **45**, 17–27.

Ajuriaguerra, J. and Tissot, R. (1975). Some aspects of language in various forms of dementia. In: Lenneberg, E. and Lenneberg E. (Eds), *Foundations of Language Development: A Multidisciplinary Approach*, Vol. 1. New York: Academic Press.

Albert, M.L. (1980). Language in normal and dementing elderly. In: Obler, L.K. and Albert, M.L. (Eds), *Language and Communication in the Elderly*. Lexington, MA: Lexington Books.

Albert, M.L., Feldman, R.G. and Willis, A.L. (1974). The 'subcortical dementia' of progressive supranuclear palsy. *Journal of Neurology, Neurosurgery and Psychiatry* **37**, 121–130.

Allport, D.A. (1985). Distributed memory, modular subsystems and dysphasia. In: Newman, S. and Epstein, R. (Eds), *Current Perspectives in Dysphasia*. New York: Churchill Livingstone.

Alzheimer, A. (1977). A unique illness involving the cerebral cortex: A case report from the mental institution in Frankfurt am Main. Translated in: Rottenberg, D.A. and Hochberg, F.H. (Eds), *Neurological Classics in Modern Translation*, pp. 41–44. New York: Hafner.

American Psychiatric Association (1987). *Diagnostic and Statistical Manual of Mental Disorders*, 3rd edn. Washington: American Psychiatric Association.

Anderson, M.E. and Horak, F.B. (1984). Motor effects produced by disruption of basal ganglia output from the globus pallidus. In: McKenzie, J.S., Kemm, R.G. and Wilcock, L.N. (Eds), *The Basal Ganglia: Structure and Function*. New York: Plenum Press.

Andreason, N.C. (1975). Do depressed patients show thought disorder? *Journal of Nervous and Mental Disease* **163**, 186–192.

Appell, J., Kertesz, A. and Fisman, M. (1982). A study of language functioning in Alzheimer's patients. *Brain and Language* **17**, 73–91.

Armstrong, L. and Grieg, L. (1992). Assessment review: elderly patients. *CSLT Bulletin* **August**, 6–7.

Austin, D.R. (1985). Attitudes towards old age: A hierarchical study. *The Gerontologist* **45**, 431–434.

Australian Bureau of Statistics. (1982). *Australia's Age Population (Catalogue No. 4109.0)*. Canberra: Commonwealth Government Printing Office.

Ball, K.K., Beard, B.L., Roenker, D.L., Miller, R.L. and Griggs, D.S. (1988). Age and visual search: expanding the useful field of view. *Journal of the Optical Society of America* **5**, 2210–2219.

Bannister, R. (1992). *Brain and Bannister's Clinical Neurology*, 7th edn. Oxford: Oxford University Press.

Barnett-Douglas, H. (1986). Communication needs of the elderly in the community. *CST Bulletin* **May**, 6–9.

Baseby, A. (1989). The role of the speech therapist in care of the elderly. *Care of the Elderly* **1**, 87–88.

Basso, A., Capitano, E. and Vignolo, L.A. (1979). Influence of rehabilitation on language skills in aphasic patients. *Archives of Neurology* **36**, 190–196.

Basso, A., Capitano, E., Liacona, M. and Luzzati, C. (1980). Factors influencing type and severity of aphasia. *Cortex* **16**, 631–636.

Bayles, K.A. (1981). Comprehension deficits in several dementing diseases. Paper given at The 56th Annual Meeting of the Linguistic Society of America, New York.

Bayles, K.A. (1982). Language functioning in senile dementia. *Brain and Language* **16**, 265–280.

Bayles, K.A. (1991). Age at onset of Alzheimer's disease: relation to language dysfunction. *Archives of Neurology* **48**, 155–159.

Bayles, K.A. (1992). *Arizona Battery for Communication in Dementia*. Tucson, AZ: Communication Skills Builders.

Bayles, K.A. and Boone, D.R. (1982). The potential of language tasks for identifying senile dementia. *Journal of Speech and Hearing Disorders* **47**, 204–210.

Bayles, K.A. and Kaszniak, A.W. (1987). *Communication and Cognition in Normal Aging and Dementia*. Boston, MA: Little Brown.

Bayles, K.A. and Tomoeda, C.K. (1983). Confrontation naming impairment in dementia. *Brain and Language* **19**, 98–114.

Bayles, K.A., Tomoeda, C.K. and Caffrey, J.T. (1982). Language and dementia producing diseases. *Communicative Disorders* **7**, 131–146.

Bayles, K.A., Tomoeda, C.K. and Trosset, M.W. (1992). Relation of linguistic communication abilities of Alzheimer's patients to stage of disease. *Brain and Language* **42**, 454–472.

Bayles, K.A., Boone, D.R., Tomeoda, C.K., Slauson, T.J. and Kaszniak, A.W. (1989) Differentiating Alzheimer's patients from the normal elderly and stroke patients with aphasia. *Journal of Speech and Hearing Disorders* **54**, 74–87.

Bebbington, D. (1991). Speech therapy and elderly people: a study of therapists' attitudes. *Health Trends* **23**, 9–11.

Beech, J.R. and Harding, L. (1990). *Assessment of the Elderly*. Windsor: NFER-Nelson.

Bell, B., Wolf, E. and Bernholz, C.D. (1972). Depth perception as a function of age. *Aging and Human Development* **3**, 77–81.

Benson, D.F. (1979). Neurologic correlates of anomia. In: Whitaker, H. and Whitaker, H.A. (Eds), *Studies in Neurolinguistics, Vol.4*, pp. 293–328. New York: Academic Press.

Berwick, R. and Weinberg, A. (1984). *The Grammatical Basis of Linguistic Performance*. Cambridge, MA: MIT Press.

Bever, T.G. (1970). The cognitive basis for linguistic structures. In: Hayes, J.R. (Ed.), *Cognition and the Development of Language*. New York: John Wiley & Sons.

Bieliauska, L.A. and Fox, J.H. (1987). Early cognitive data in a case of Creutzfeldt–Jakob disease. *Neuropsychology* **1**, 49–50.

Bishop, D.V.M. (1983). *Test for the Reception of Grammar*. Abingdon: Leach.

Blackburn, M. and Tyrer, G.M.B. (1985). The value of Luria's neuropsychological investigation for the assessment of cognitive dysfunction in Alzheimer's type dementia. *British Journal of Clinical Psychology* **24**, 171–179.

Blanken, G., Dittman, J., Haas, J-C. and Wallesch, C-W. (1987). Spontaneous speech in senile dementia and aphasia: Implications for a neurolinguistic model of language production. *Cognition* **27**, 247–274.

Boller, F., Becker, J.T., Holland, A.L., Forbes, M.M., Hood, P.C. and McCougle-Gibson, K.C. (1991). Predictors of decline in Alzheimer's disease.

Bosanquet, N. (1978). *A Future for Old Age*. London: Temple-Smith/New Society.

Bosanquet, N., Laing, W. and Propper, C. (1990). *Elderly Consumers in Britain: Europe's Poor Relations*. London: Laing and Buisson.

Botwinick, J. (1978). *Aging and Behaviour*. New York: Springer.

Botwinnick, J. and Storandt, M. (1974). Vocabulary ability in later life. *Journal of Genetic Psychology* **16**, 95–96.

Botwinnick. J., West, R. and Storandt, M. (1975). Qualitative vocabulary responses and age. *Journal of Gerontology* **30**, 574–577.

Bourgeois, M.S. (1991) Communication treatment for adults with dementia. *Journal of Speech and Hearing Research* **34**, 831–844.

Bowles, N.L. and Poon, L.W. (1985). Ageing and retrieval of words in semantic memory. *Journal of Gerontology* **40**, 71–77.

Brayne, C.E.G. (1991). *A Study of Dementia in a Rural Population*. Thesis, University of Cambridge.

British Geriatric Society (1988). *Statement of Intent: Geriatric Nursing and Home Care*. London: British Geriatric Society.

British Medical Journal Editorial (1992). Families of victims of Creutzfeldt–Jacob disease to sue government. *British Medical Journal* **305**, 73.

Brodaty, H. and Peters, K.E. (1991). Cost effectiveness of a training program for dementia carers. *International Psychogeriatrics* **3**, 11–23.

Brodie, J.K. (1986). Communication defects in a residential home for the elderly: their prevalence and staff perceptions of them. *Journal of Clinical and Experimental Gerontology* **8**, 13–25.

Brody, E. (1977). *Long-Term Care of Older People*. New York: Human Sciences Press.

Brown, J.W. and Jaffe, J. (1975). Hypothesis on cerebral dominance. *Neuropsychologia* **13**, 107–110.

Brown, R.G. and Marsden, C.D. (1984). How common is dementia in Parkinson's disease. *Lancet* **ii**, 1262–1265.

Brown, R.G. and Marsden, C.D. (1986). Visuospatial function in Parkinson's disease. *Brain* **109**, 987–1002.

Brown, R.G. and Marsden, C.D. (1988). Internal versus external cues and the control of attention in Parkinson's disease. *Brain* **111**, 323–347.

Brown, R.G. and Marsden, C.D. (1991). Dual task performance and processing resources in normal subjects and patients with Parkinson's disease. *Brain* **114**, 215–231.

Bryan, K.L. and Drew, S. (1987). The benefits of therapy for elderly people in care. *Speech Therapy in Practice* **September**, 6–8.

Bryan, K.L. and Drew, S. (1989). A survey of communication disability in an elderly population in residential care. *International Journal of Rehabilitation Research* **12**, 330–333.

Bryan, K.L. and Maxim, J. (1991). Talking and Listening. In: Benson, S. and Carr, P. (Eds). *The Care Assistant's Guide to Working with the Elderly Mentally Infirm*. London: Hawker.

Bryan, K.L., Maxim, J., McIntosh, J., McClelland, A., Wirz, S., Edmundson, A. and Snowling, M. (1991). The facts behind the figures: A reply to Enderby and Davies. *British Journal of Disorders of Communication* **26**, 253–261.

Buckingham, H.W. (1980). On correlating aphasic errors with slips-of-the-tongue. *Applied Psycholinguistics* **1**, 199–220.

Buckingham, H.W. and Kertesz, A. (1976). *Neologistic Jargon Aphasia*. Amsterdam: Swets and Zeitlinger.

Burke, D.M. and Harrold, R.M. (1990). Automatic and effortful semantic processes in old age: Experimental and naturalistic approaches. In: Burke, D.M. and Light, L.L. (Eds), *Language, Memory and Ageing*. Cambridge: Cambridge University Press.

Burke, D.M., Worthley, J. and Martin, J. (1988). I'll never forget what's her name: Ageing and the tip of the tongue experience. In: Gruneberg, M.M., Morris, P. and Sykes, R.N. (Eds). *Practical Aspects of Memory: Current Research and Issues,* Vol. 2, pp. 113–118. Chichester: John Wiley & Sons.

Burns, A., Luthert, P., Levy, R., Jacoby, R. and Lantos, P. (1990). Accuracy of clinical diagnosis of Alzheimer's disease. *British Medical Journal* **301**, 1026.

Butler (1969). Age-ism: Another form of bigotry. *The Gerontologist* **9**, 243–246.

Butters, N., Sax, D., Montgomery, K. and Tarlow, S. (1978). Comparison of the neuropsychological deficits associated with early and advanced Huntington's disease. *Archives of Neurology* **35**, 585–589.

Byrne, E.J. (1992). Diffuse Lewy body disease. In: Arie, T. (Ed.). *Recent Advances in Psychogeriatrics*. Edinburgh: Churchill Livingstone.

Caplan, L.R. and Schoene, W.C. (1978). Clinical features of subcortical arterio-sclerotic encephalopathy (Binswanger's disease). *Neurology* **28**, 1208–1215.

Caramazza, A. and Zurif, E.B. (1978). Comprehension of complex sentences in children and aphasics: a test of the regression hypothesis. In: Caramazza, A. and Zuriff, E.B. (Eds), *Language Acquisition and Language Breakdown*. Baltimore: Johns Hopkins University Press.

Cattel, R.B. (1963). The theory of fluid and crystallized intelligence: a critical experiment. *Journal of Educational Psychology* **54**, 1–22.

Cavanaugh, J.C. (1983). Comprehension and retention of television programs by 20- and 60-year olds. *Journal of Gerontology* **38**, 190–196.

Central Statistical Office (1973). *Social Trends, 4*. London: HMSO.

Cerella, J., Poon, L.W and Fozard, J.L. (1981) Mental rotation and age reconsidered. *Journal of Gerontology* **36**, 620–624.

Charness, N. (Ed.) (1985). Ageing and problem-solving performance. In: *Ageing and Human Performance*. Chichester: John Wiley & Sons.

Chawluk, J.B., Mesulam, M.M., Hurtiz, H., Kushner, M., Weintraub, S., Saykin, A., Rubin, N., Alavi, A. and Reivich, M. (1986). Slowly progressive aphasia without generalized dementia: studies with positron emission tomography. *Annals of Neurology* **19**, 68–74.

Chertkow, H. and Bub, D. (1992). Semantic memory loss in Alzheimer-type dementia. In: Schwartz, M.F. (Ed.), *Modular Deficits in Alzheimer-Type Dementia*. Cambridge, MA:

Cheshire, J. (1982). *Variation in an English Dialect. A Sociolinguistic study*. Cambridge: Cambridge University Press.

Chomsky, N. (1965). *Aspects of the Theory of Syntax*. Cambridge, MA: MIT Press.

Chomsky, N. (1977). On Wh-movement. In: Culicover, P.W., Wasow, T. and Akmajian, A. (Eds). *Formal Syntax*. New York: Academic Press.

Chomsky, N. (1980). *Rules and Representations*. New York: Columbia University Press.

Christensen, A.L. (1974). *Luria's Neuropsychological Investigation*. Copenhagen: Munksgaard.

Chui, H.C. (1989). Dementia: A review emphasizing clinicopathologic correlation and brain–behaviour relationships. *Archives of Neurology* **46**, 806–814.

Chui, H.C., Teng, E.L., Henderson, V.W. and Moy, A.C. (1985). Clinical subtypes of dementia of the Alzheimer type. *Neurology* **35**, 1544–1550.

Chui, H.C., Lyness, S., Sobel, E. and Schneider, L.S. (1992). Prognostic implications of symptomatic behaviours in AD. In: Florette, F., Khachaturian, Z., Poncet, M. and Christen, Y. (Eds), *Heterogeneity of Alzheimer's Disease*. Berlin: Springer.

Chylack, L.T. (1979). Aging and cataracts. In: Man, S.S. and Coons, P.M. (Eds), *Special Senses in Ageing: A Current Biological Assessment*. Ann Arbor: University of Michigan.

Clark, E.O. (1980). Semantic and episodic memory impairments in normal and cognitively impaired elderly adults. In: Obler, L.K. and Albert, M.L. (Eds), *Language and Communication in the Elderly*. Lexington, MA: D.C. Heath and Co.

Clark, H.H. and Begun, J.S. (1971). The semantics of sentence subjects. *Language and Speech* **14**, 34–36.

Clark, H.H. and Clark, E.V. (1968). Semantic distinctions and memory for complex sentences. *Quarterly Journal of Experimental Psychology* **20**, 129–138.

Clark, E.V. and Clark, H.H. (1977). *Psychology and Language: An Introduction to Psycholinguistics*. New York: Harcourt Brace Jovanovich.

Code, C. and Lodge, B. (1987). Language in dementia of recent referral. *Age and Ageing* **16**, 366–372.

Code, C. and Rowley, D. (1987). Age and aphasia type: the interaction of sex, time since onset and handedness. *Aphasiology* **11**, 339–345.

Cohen, L.D. (1959). The WAIS performance of an aged sample: the relationship between verbal and performance IQs. *Journal of Gerontology* **14**, 197–201.

Cohen, G. (1979). Language comprehension in old age. *Cognitive Psychology* **11**, 412–429,

Cohen, G. and Faulkner, D. (1981). Memory for discourse in old age. *Discourse Processes* **4**, 253–265.

Cohen, G. and Faulkner, D. (1983). Word recognition: age differences in contextual facilitation effects. *British Journal of Psychology* **74**, 239–251.

Coleman, P.D. and Flood, D.G. (1987). Neuron numbers and dendritic extent in normal aging and Alzheimer's disease. *Neurobiology of Aging* **8**, 521–545.

College of Speech and Language Therapists (1990). *Communicating Quality*. London: College of Speech and Language Therapists.

Collin, C. (1991). Clinical standards to assist audit in medical rehabilitation. *Health Trends* **23**, 18–20.

Colsher, P.L. and Wallace, R.B. (1990). Are hearing and visual dysfunction associated with cognitive impairment? A population based approach. *Journal of Applied Gerontology* **9**, 91–105.

Constantinidis, J. (1978). Is Alzheimer's disease a major form of senile dementia? Clinical, anatomical and genetic data. In: Katzman, R., Terry, R.D. and Bick, K.L. (Eds), *Alzheimer's Disease: Senile Dementia and Related Disorders, Aging, Vol.7*, pp. 15–25. New York: Raven Press.

Copeland, J.R., Prilipko, L. and Sartorius, N. (1992). The World Health Organization Collaborative Study: development of evaluation instruments for assessment of dementia. *Clinical Neuropharmacology* **15** (Suppl 1), 491–492.

Coppens, P. (1991). Why are Wernicke's aphasia patients older than Broca's? A critical view of the hypotheses. *Aphasiology* **5**, 279–290.

Cooper, B. (1987). Psychiatric disorders among elderly patients admitted to general hospital wards. *Journal of the Royal Society of Medicine* **80**, 13–26.

Corkin, S. (1982). Some relationships between global amnesias and the memory impairments in Alzheimer's disease. In: Corkin, S., Davis, K.L., Growdon, J.H., Usdin, E. and Wurtman, R.J. (Eds), *Alzheimer's Disease: A Report of Progress in Research. Aging,* Vol. 19, pp. 149–164. New York: Raven Press.

Corso, J.F. (1981). *Aging Sensory Systems and Perception*. New York: Praeger.

Craik, F.I.M. (1984). Age differences in remembering. In: Squire, L.R. and Butters, N. (Eds), *Neuropsychology of Memory*. New York: Guilford.

Craik, F. and Jennings, J. M. (1992). Human memory. In: Craik, F. and Salthouse, T. (Eds), *The Handbook of Aging and Cognition*. New Jersey: Lawrence Erlbaum Associates.

Craik, F.I.M. and Lockhart, R.S. (1972). Levels of processing: a framework for memory research. *Journal of Verbal Learning and Verbal Behaviour* **11**, 671–684.

Craik, F.I.M. and Rabinowitz, J.C. (1985). The effects of presentation rate and encoding task on age-related memory deficits. *Journal of Gerontology* **40**, 309–315.

Craik, F.I.M. and Simon, E. (1980). Age differences in memory: The roles of attention and depth of processing. In: Poon, L.W., Fozard, J.L., Cermak, L.S., Arenberg. D. and Thompson, L.W. (Eds), *New Directions in Memory and Ageing: Proceedings of the George Talland Memorial Conference*. Hillsdale, NJ: Lawrence Erlbaum.

Critchley, M. (1964). The neurology of psychotic speech. *British Journal of Psychiatry* **40**, 353–364.

Crystal, D. (1979). *Working with LARSP*. London: Edward Arnold.

Crystal, D. (1982). *Profiling Linguistic Disability*. London: Arnold.

Crystal, D. and Davy, D. (1976). *Advanced Conversational English*. London: Longman.

Crystal, D., Fletcher, P. and Garman. M. (1976). *The Grammatical Analysis of Language Disability*. London: Edward Arnold.

Crystal, D., Fletcher, P. and Garman, M. (1981). *Revised LARSP Chart*. University of Reading.

Crystal, D., Fletcher, P. and Garman, M. (1989). *The Grammatical Analysis of Language Disability*, 2nd edn. London: Whurr.

Cummings, J.L. (1988). Intellectual impairment in Parkinson's disease: clinical, pathologic and biochemical correlates. *Journal of Geriatric Psychiatry and Neurology* **1**, 24–36.

Cummings, J.L. and Benson, D.F. (1992). *Dementia: A Clinical Approach*. Boston: Butterworth.

Cummings, J.L., Benson, D.E., Hill, M.A. and Read, S. (1985). Aphasia in dementia of the Alzheimer type. *Neurology* **35**, 394–397.

Cummings, J.L., Miller, B., Hill, M.A. and Neshkes, R. (1987). Neuropsychiatric aspects of multi-infarct dementia and dementia of Alzheimer type. *Archives of Neurology* **44**, 389–393.

Cutting, J. (1982). Alcoholic dementia. In: Benson, D. and Blumer, D. (Eds). *Psychiatric Aspects of Neurologic Disease. Vol 2*. New York: Grune & Stratton.

Dabul, B. (1979). *Apraxia Battery for Adults*. Oregon: CC Publications.

Darley, F., Aronson, A. and Brown, J. (1975). *Motor Speech Disorders*. Philadelphia: Lea & Febiger.

Davis, A. (1983). The epidemiology of hearing disorders. In: Hinchcliffe, R. (Ed.), *Hearing and Balance in the Elderly*.Edinburgh: Churchill Livingstone.

Davis, S. (1979). *An Investigation into the Language of the Elderly*. MSc thesis, University of London.

Davis, P. and Van de Gaag, D. (1991). Determining the professional competence of speech therapists: Stage one findings of a Department of Health Project on the use and value of speech therapy assistants. (Unpublished report)

De Ajuriaguerra, J. and Tissot, R. (1975). Some aspects of language in various forms of senile dementia. In: Lenneberg, E. and Lenneberg, E. (Eds), *Foundations of Language Development*, Vol. 1. New York: Academic Press.

Dementia Working Party Report (1990). London: College of Speech and Language Therapists.

Department of Health (1989). *Caring for People*. Cmnd 849. London: HMSO.

Dick, M.B., Kean, M-L. and Sands, D. (1989). Memory for internally generated words in Alzheimer-type dementia: breakdown in encoding and semantic memory. *Brain and Cognition* **9**, 88–108.

Dickson, D., Wu, E., Crystal, H., Matthiace, L., Yen, S. and Davies, P. (1992). Alzheimer's disease and age-related pathology in diffuse Lewy body disease. In: Florette, F., Khachaturian, Z., Poncet, M. and Christen, Y. (Eds), *Heterogeneity of Alzheimer's Disease*. Berlin: Springer.

Diesfeldt, H.F. (1991). Impaired phonological reading in primary degenerative dementia. *Brain* **114**, 1631–1646.

Dixon, R.A., Simon, E.W., Nowak, C.A. and Hultsch, D.F. (1982). Text recall in adulthood as a function of level of information, input modality and delay interval. *Journal of Gerontology* **37**, 358–364.

Dobbs, A.R. and Rule, B.G. (1989). Adult age differences in working memory. *Psychology and Aging* **4**, 500–503.

Dowling, R.J. (1981). Federal health insurance for the elderly. In: Beasley, D.S. and Davis, G.A. (Eds), *Aging, Communication Processes and Disorders*. New York: Grune and Stratton.

Edwards, B. (1991). Time to evolve. Paper presented at the MSD Foundation Symposium, London, September.

Eisdorfer, C. and Wilkie, F. (1972). Auditory changes. *Journal of the American Geriatric Society* **20**, 377–382.

Eisdorfer, C., Busse, E.W. and Cohen, L.D. (1959). The WAIS performance of an aged sample: The relationship between verbal and performance IQs. *Journal of Gerontology* **14**, 197–201.

Emery, O.B. (1989). Language deficits in depression: comparisons with SDAT and normal aging. *Journal of Gerontology* **44**, M85–M92.

Enderby, P. (1987) *Frenchay Aphasia Screening Test*. Windsor: NFER Test Publications.

Enderby, P. and Davies, P. (1989). Communication disorders: Planning a service to meet the needs. *British Journal of Disorders of Communication* **24**, 301–331.

Erkinjuntti, T., Sulkava, R., Kovanen, J. and Palo, J. (1987). Suspected dementia: evaluation of 323 consecutive referrals. *Acta Neurologica Scandinavica* **76**, 359–364.

Etholm, B. and Belal, A. (1974). Senile changes in the middle ear joints. *Annals of Otology, Rhinology and Laryngology* **83**, 49–54.

Faber-Langendoen, K., Morris, J.C., Knesevich, J.W., LaBarge, E., Miller, J.P. and Berg, L. (1988). Aphasia in senile dementia of the Alzheimer type. *Annals of Neurology* **23**, 365–370.

Falconer, J. (1986). Aging and hearing. *Physical and Occupational Therapy in Geriatrics* **4**, 3–20.

Fearnley, J.M., Revesz, D.J., Frackowiak, R.S.J. and Lees, A.J. (1991). Diffuse Lewy body disease presenting with a supranuclear gaze palsy. *Journal of Neurology, Neurosurgery and Psychiatry* **54**, 159–161.

Feinberg, T. and Goodman, B. (1984). Affective illness, dementia and pseudo-dementia. *Journal of Clinical Psychiatry* **45**, 99–103.

Filley, C.M., Kelly, J. and Heaton, R.K. (1986). Neuropsychologic features of early and late onset Alzheimer's disease. *Archives of Neurology* **43**, 574–576.

Fisch, L. (1978). Special senses: the ageing auditory system. In: Brockhurst, J.C. (Ed.), *Textbook of Geriative Medicine and Gerontology*. New York: Churchill Livingstone.

Folstein, M.F., Folstein, S.E. and McHugh, P.R. (1975). 'Mini-mental state': A practical method for grading the cognitive state for the clinician. *Journal of Psychiatric Research* **12**, 189–198.

Foster, N.L. and Chase, T.N. (1983). Diffuse involvement in progressive aphasia. *Annals of Neurology* **13**, 224–225.

Foster, N.L., Chase, T.N., Patronas, N.J., Gillespie, M.M. and Fedio, P. (1986). Cerebral mapping of apraxia in Alzheimer's disease by positron emission tomography. *Annals of Neurology* **19**, 139–143.

Fozard, J.L. (1990). Vision and hearing in aging. In: Birren, J.E. and Shaie, K.W. (Eds). *Handbook of the Psychology of Aging*. New York: Academic Press.

Franks, J.J. and Beckman, N.J. (1985). Rejection of hearing aids: attitudes of a geriatric sample. *Ear and Hearing* **6**, 161–166.

Frazier, L. and Fodor, J.D. (1978). The sausage machine: a new two stage parsing model. *Cognition* **6**, 291–325.

Freedman, L. and Costa, L. (1992). Pure alexia and right hernia chromatopsia in posterior dementia. *Journal of Neurology, Neurosurgery and Psychiatry* **55**, 500–502.

Freedman, L., Selchan, D.H., Black, S.E., Kaplan, R., Garnett, E.S., and Nahmias, C. (1991). Posterior cortical dementia with alexia: neurobehavioural, MRI and PET findings. *Journal of Neurology, Neurosurgery and Psychiatry* **54**, 443–448.

Fromm, D., Holland, A.L., Nebes, R.D. and Oakley, M.A. (1991). A longitudinal study of word-reading ability in Alzheimer's disease: evidence from the National Adult Reading Test. *Cortex* **27**, 367–376.

Funnell, E. and Hodges, J.R. (1990). Progressive loss of access to spoken word forms in a case of Alzheimer's disease. *Proceedings of the Royal Society*.

Galloway, P.H. (1992). Visual pattern recognition memory and learning deficits in senile dementias of Alzheimer and Lewy body types. *Dementia* **3**, 101–107.

Garman, M. (1990). *Psycholinguistics*. Cambridge: Cambridge University Press.

Garrett, M.F. (1975). The analysis of sentence production. In: Bower, G. (Ed). *The Psychology of Learning and Motivation: Advances in Research and Theory*. New York: Academic Press.

Gawel, M.J. (1981). The effects of various drugs on speech. *British Journal of Disorders of Communication* **16**, 51–57.

George, J. and Young, J.B. (1989). General practitioners and the geriatric day hospital. *Health Trends* **1**, 24–25.

Gioella, E.C. (1983). *Healthy Aging Through Knowledge and Self Care*. New York: Haworth.

Gladman, J., Albazzaz, M. and Barer, D. (1991). A survey of survivors of acute stroke discharged from hospital to private nursing homes in Nottingham. *Health Trends* **23**, 158–160.

Glen, A.I.M. and Christie, J.E. (1979). Early diagnosis of Alzheimer's disease: working definition for clinical and laboratory criteria. In: Glen, A.I.M. and Whalley, L.J. (Eds), *Alzheimer's Disease*. Edinburgh: Churchill Livingstone.

Gloser, G. and Deser, T. (1990). Patterns of discourse production among neurological patients with fluent language disorders. *Brain and Language* **40**, 67–88.

Goodglass, H. (1978). Acquisition and dissolution of language. In: Caramazza, A. and Zurif, E.B. (Eds), *Language Acquisition and Language Breakdown*. Baltimore: Johns Hopkins University Press.

Goodglass, H. and Kaplan, E. (1983). *The Boston Naming Test*. Philadelphia: Lea & Febiger.

Goodglass, H. and Kaplan, E. (1983). *Assessment of Aphasia and Related Disorders*, 2nd edn. Philadelphia: Lea & Febiger.

Gordon, K., Hutchinson, J.M. and Allen, C.S. (1976). An evaluation of selected discourse characteristics among the elderly. Research Laboratory Report. Department of Speech Therapy and Audiology, Idaho State University, Pocatello.

Gosney, M. and Edmond, E. (1991). The burden of chronic illness in local authority residential homes for the elderly. *Health Trends* **22**, 153–157.

Gotham, A.M., Brown, R.G. and Marsden, C.D. (1986). Depression in Parkinson's disease. A quantitative and qualitative analysis. *Journal of Neurology, Neurosurgery and Psychiatry* **49**, 79–89.

Gotham, A.M., Brown, R.G. and Marsden, C.D. (1988). 'Frontal' cognitive function in patients with Parkinson's disease 'on' and 'off' Levadopa. *Brain* **111**, 299–321.

Graff-Radford, N.R., Damasio, A.R., Hyman, B.T., Hart, M.N., Tranel, D., Damasio, H., Van Hoesen, G.W. and Rezai, K. (1990). Progressive aphasia in a patient with Pick's disease: a neuropsychological, radiologic and anatomic study. *Neurology* **40**, 620–626.

Grant, I., Adams, K.M. and Reed, R. (1984). Aging, abstinence and medical risk factors in the prediction of neuropsychologic deficit among long-term alcoholics. *Archives of General Psychiatry* **47**, 710–718.

Gravell, R. (1988). *Communication Problems in Elderly People*. London: Croom Helm.

Gravell, R. and France, J. (1991). *Speech and Communication Problems in Psychiatry*. London: Chapman & Hall.

Greveson, G. and James, O. (1991). Improving long-term outcome after stroke – the views of patients and carers. *Health Trends* **23**, 161–162.

Griffiths, R. (1988). *Community Care: Agenda for Action*. London: HMSO.

Griffiths, H. and Baldwin, R. (1989). Speech therapy for psychogeriatric services. Luxury or necessity? *Psychiatric Bulletin* **13**, 57–59.

Grist, E. and Maxim, J. (1992). Confrontation naming in the elderly. The Build up Picture Test as an aid to differentiating normals from subjects with dementia. *European Journal of Disorders of Communication* **27**, 197–207.

Grossberg, G.T. and Nakra, R. (1988). The diagnostic dilemma of depressive pseudodementia. In: Strong, R. (Ed.), *Central Nervous System Disorders of Aging: Clinical Intervention and Research*. New York: Raven Press.

Grossman, M., Carvell, S., Gollomp, S., Stern, M.B., Vernon, G. and Hurtig, H.I. (1991). Sentence comprehension and praxis deficits in Parkinson's disease. *Neurology* **41**, 1620–1626.

Grossman, M., Carvell, S., Stern, M.B., Gollomp, S. and Hurtig, H.I. (1992). Sentence comprehension in Parkinson's disease: The role of attention and memory. *Brain and Language* **42**, 347–384.

Guillemard, A.M. (1986). Social policy and ageing in France. In: Phillipson, C. and Walker, A. (Eds), *Ageing and Social Policy. A Critical Assessment*. Aldershot: Gower.

Gupta, S.R., Naheedy, M.H., Young, J.C., Ghobrial, M., Rubino, F.A. and Hindo, W. (1988) Periventricular white matter changes and dementia: clinical neuropsychological, radiological and pathological correlation. *Archives of Neurology* **45**, 637–641.

Hachinski, V.C., Lassen, N.A. and Marshall, J. (1974). Multi-infarct dementia. A cause of mental deterioration in the elderly. *Lancet* **ii**, 207–210.

Hanley, I.G. (1981). The use of signposts and active training to modify ward disorientation in elderly patients. *Journal of Behaviour Therapy and Experimental Psychiatry* **12**, 241–247.

Hanson, W. R. and Metter, E. J. (1980). DAF as instrumental treatment for dysarthria in progressive supra-nuclear palsy: A case report. *Journal of Speech and Hearing Disorders* **45**, 268–276.

Harasyieu, S.Y., Halper, A. and Sutherland, B. (1981). Sex, age and aphasia type. *Brain and Language* **12**, 190–198.

Hardy, J. (1992). Alzheimer's disease: many aetiologies; one pathogenesis. In: Florette, F., Khachaturian, Z., Poncet, M. and Christen, Y. (Eds), *Heterogeneity of Alzheimer's Disease*. Berlin: Springer.

Harris, A. (1971). *Handicapped and Impaired in Great Britain*. London: HMSO.

Harris, R.J. and Monaco, G.E. (1978). Psychology of pragmatic implication: information processing between the lines. *Journal of Experimental Psychology: General* **107**, 1–22.

Hart, G. (1980). The hearing of residents in homes for the elderly (South Glamorgan). University Hospital of Wales.

Hart, S. (1988). Language and dementia: a review. *Psychological Medicine* **18**, 99–112.

Hart, S. and Semple, J.M. (1990). *Neuropsychology and the Dementias*. London: Taylor and Francis.

Hart, S., Smith, C.M. and Swash, M. (1986). Intrusion errors in Alzheimer's disease. *British Journal of Clinical Psychology* **25**, 149–150.

Hasher, L. and Zacks, R.T. (1979). Automatic and effortful processes in memory. *Journal of Experimental Psychology: General* **108**, 356–388.

Haxby, J.V., Grady, C.L., Ungerleider, L.G. and Horwitz, B. (1991). Mapping the functional neuroanatomy of the intact human brain with brain work imagery. *Neuropsychologia* **29**, 538–555.

Heindel, W.C., Salmon, D.P. and Butters, N. (1990). Pictorial priming and cued recall in Alzheimer's and Huntington's disease. *Brain and Cognition* **13**, 282–295.

Hendricks, J. and Calasanti, T. (1976). *Grammars of Style and Styles of Grammar*. Amsterdam: North-Holland.

Hendricks, J. and Calasanti, T. (1986) Social policy and ageing in the United States. In: Phillipson, C. and Walker, A. (Eds). *Ageing and Social Policy. A Critical Assessment*. Aldershot: Gower.

Herbst, K.G. (1983). Psycho-social consequences of disorders of hearing in the elderly. In: Hinchcliffe, R. (Ed.), *Hearing and Balance in the Elderly*. Edinburgh: Churchill Livingstone.

Herlitz, A., Adolfson, R., Backman, L. and Wilson, L-G. (1991). Cue utilization following different forms of encoding in mildly, moderately and severely demented patients with Alzheimer's disease. *Brain and Cognition* **15**, 119–130.

Hertzhog, C. (1989). Influences of cognitive slowing on age differences in intelligence. *Developmental Psychology* **25**, 636–651.

Heston, L. (1981). Genetic studies of dementia with emphasis on Parkinson's disease and Alzheimer's neuropathology. In: Mortimer, J. and Schuman, L. (Eds), *The Epidemiology of Dementia*. Oxford: Oxford University Press.

Hier, D.B., Hagenlocker, K. and Shindler, A.G. (1985). Language disintegration in dementia: effects of aetiology and severity. *Brain and Language* **25**, 117–133.

Hodges, J.R., Salmon, D.P. and Butters, N. (1991). The nature of the naming deficit in Alzheimer's and Huntington's disease. *Brain* **114**, 1547–1558.

Hodges, J.R., Patterson, K., Oxbury, S. and Funnell, E. (1992). Semantic dementia. Progressive fluent aphasia with temporal lobe atrophy. *Brain* **115**, 1783–1806.

Hodkinson, H.M. (1972). Evaluation of a mental test score for assessment of mental impairment in the elderly. *Age and Ageing* **1**, 233–238.

Holden, U.P. and Woods, R.T. (1988). *Reality Orientation: Psychological Approaches to the 'Confused' Elderly*. Edinburgh: Churchill Livingstone.

Holland, A. (1980). *Communicative Abilities in Daily Living*. Baltimore: University Park Press.

Holland, A.L. (1990). Research methodology I. Implications for speech-language pathology. *ASHA Reports* **19**, 35–39.

Holland, A.L. and Bartlett, C.L. (1985). Some differential effects of age on stroke-produced aphasia. In: Ulatowska, A.K. (Ed.), *The Aging Brain. Communication in the Elderly*. London: Taylor and Francis.

Holland, C.A. and Rabbitt, P.M. (1991). Ageing memory: Use versus impairment. *British Journal of Psychology* **82**, 29–38.

Holland, A.L., McBurney, D.H., Moossy, J. and Rernmirth, O.M. (1985). The dissolution of language in Pick's disease with neurofibrillary tangles: A case study. *Brain and Language* **24**, 36–38.

Homer, A., Honovar, M., Lantos, P., Hastie, I., Kellett, J. and Millard, P. (1988) Diagnosing dementia: do we get it right? *British Medical Journal* **297**, 894–896.

Honjo,I. and Isshiki, N. (1980). Laryngoscopic and voice characteristics of aged persons. *Archives of Otolaryngology*, **106**, 149.

Hopkins, S., Brayne, C., Melzer, D., Pencleon, D. and Williams, R. (1992). *Epidemiologically Based Needs Assessment*. London: NHS Management Executive.

Horner, J., Heyman, A., Dawson, D. and Rogers, H. (1988). The relationship of agraphia to the severity of dementia in Alzheimer's disease. *Archives of Neurology* **45**, 760–763.

Horner, J., Dawson, D.V., Heyman, A. and McGorman, A. (1992). The usefulness of the Western Aphasia Battery for the differential diagnosis of Alzheimer's disease and focal stroke syndromes: preliminary evidence. *Brain and Language* **42**, 77–88.

Howard, D.V., Shaw, R.J. and Heisey, J.G. (1986). Aging and the time course of semantic activation. *Journal of Gerontology* **41**, 195–203.

Howes, D. (1964). Application of the word frequency concept to aphasia. In: de Rueck, A.V.S. and O'Connor, M. (Eds). *Disorders of Language. Ciba Foundation Symposium*. London: Churchill.

Huber, S.J., Shuttleworth, E.C. and Freidenberg, D.L. (1989). Neuropsychological differences between the dementias of Alzheimer's and Parkinson's diseases. *Archives of Neurology* **46**, 1287–1291.

Hulicka, I.M. and Grossman, J.L. (1967). Age group comparisons for the use of mediators in paired associate learning. *Journal of Gerontology* **22**, 274–280.

Hultsch, D.F. and Dixon, R.A. (1983). The role of pre-experimental knowledge in text processing in adulthood. *Experimental Ageing Research* **9**, 17–22.

Humes, L.E. (1984) Noise-induced hearing loss as influenced by other agents and by some physical characteristics of the individual. *Journal of the Acoustical Society of America* **76**, 1318–1329.

Hutchinson, J.M. and Jenson, M. (1980). A pragmatic evaluation of discourse communication in normal and senile elderly in a nursing home. In: Obler, L.K. and

Albert, M.L. (Eds), *Language and Communication in the Elderly*. Lexington, MA: D. Heath and Co.

Illes, J. (1989). Neurolinguistic features of spontaneous language dissociate three form of neurodegenerative disease: Alzheimer's, Huntington's and Parkinson's. *Brain and Language* **37**, 628–642.

Irigaray, L. (1973). *Le Langage des Demants*. The Hague: Mouton.

Issacs, B. (1978). Treatment of the irremediable elderly patient. In: Carver, H. and Liddiard, P. (Eds), *An Ageing Population*. London: Hodder and Stoughton.

Ishii, N., Hishahara, Y. and Imamura, T. (1986) Why do frontal lobe symptoms predominate in vascular dementia with lacunes? *Neurology* **36**, 340–345.

Ivy, G.O., MacLeod, C.M., Petit, T.L. and Markus, E.J. (1992). A physiological framework for perceptual and cognitive changes on aging. In: Craik, F. and Salthouse, T. (Eds), *The Handbook of Aging and Cognition*. New Jersey: Lawrence Erlbaum.

Jakobson, R. (1968). *Child Language, Aphasia and Phonological Universals. Janua Linguarum, Series Minor 72*. The Hague: Mouton.

Jarvik, K. (1962). Biological differences in intellectual functioning. *Vita Humana* **5**, 195–203.

Jarvik, L.F. (1982). Pseudodementia. *Consultant* **22** 141–146.

Jerger, J., Jerger, S., Oliver, T. and Pirozzolo, F. (1989). Speech understanding in the elderly. *Ear and Hearing* **10**, 79–89.

Joanette, Y., Poissant, A. and Valdois, S. (1989). Neuropsychological dissociations in dementia of the Alzheimer type: a multiple single case study. *Journal of Clinical and Experimental Neuropsychology* **11**, 91.

Joanette, Y., Ska, B., Poissant, A. and Beland, R. (1992). Neuropsychological aspects of Alzheimer's disease: evidence for inter and intra-function heterogeneity. In: Florette, F., Khachaturian, Z., Poncet, M. and Christen, Y. (Eds), *Heterogeneity of Alzheimer's Disease*. Berlin: Springer.

Johanson, A., Gustafson, L., Brun, A., Risberg, J., Rosen, I. and Tideman, E. (1991). A longitudinal study of dementia of Alzheimer type in Down's syndrome. *Dementia* **1**, 159–168.

Johnson, J.A. and Pring, T.R. (1990). Speech therapy and Parkinson's disease: a review and further data. *British Journal of Disorders of Communication* **25**, 183–194.

Jolley, D.J., Kondratowicz, T. and Wilkin, D. (1980). Helping the disabled in old people's homes. *Geriatric Medicine* **Nov**. 74–77.

Jolley, D. and Arie, T. (1992). Developments in psychogeriatric services. In: Arie, T. (Ed.), *Recent Advances in Psychogeriatrics*. Edinburgh: Churchill Livingstone.

Jones, D.A. and Peters, T.J. (1992) Caring for elderly dependants: effects on carer's quality of life. *Age and Ageing* **21**, 421–428.

Jordan, L. (1991). A profile of aphasia services in three health districts. *British Journal of Disorders of Communication* **26**, 293–316.

Junque, C., Pujol, J., Vendrell, P., Bruna, O., Jodar, M., Ribas, J.C., Vinas, J., Capdevila, A. and Martin-Villalta, J.L. (1990). Leuko-araiosis on magnetic resonance imaging and speed of mental processing. *Archives of Neurology* **47**, 151–156.

Kahane, J.C. (1981). Anatomical and physiological changes in the aging peripheral speech mechanism. In: Beasley, D.S. and Davis, G.A. (Eds). *Ageing Communication Processes and Disorders*. New York: Grune and Stratton.

Kahane, J.C. (1983). A survey of age-related changes in the connective tissue of the human larynx. In: Bless, D.M.H. (Ed.). *Vocal Fold Physiology*. San Diego: College Hill Press.

Kahn, H.A., Leibowitz, H.M., Ganley, J.P., Kim, M.M., Colton, J., Nickerson, R.S. and

Dauber, T.R. (1977). Framlington eye study 1. Outline and major prevalence findings. *American Journal of Epidemiology* **106**, 17–32.

Kaufman, A.S., Reynolds, C.R. and McLean, J.E. (1989). Age and Wais-R intelligence in a national sample of adults in the 20 to 74 year age range: A cross-sectional analysis with educational level controlled. *Intelligence* **13**, 235–253.

Kausler, D.H. (1989). Comments on aging memory and its everyday operations. In: Poon, L.W., Rubin, D.C. and Wilson, B.A. (Eds), *Everyday Cognition in Adulthood and Late Life*. Cambridge: Cambridge University Press.

Kausler, D.H. and Hakami, M.K. (1983). Memory for topics of conversation: Adult age differences and intentionality experiments. *Ageing Research* **9**, 153–157.

Kay, D.W.K., Beamish, P. and Roth, M. (1964). Old age mental disorders in Newcastle upon Tyne. Part 1, A study of prevalence. *British Journal of Psychiatry* **110**, 146–158.

Kay, D.W.K., Foster, E.M. and McKechie, A.A. (1970). Mental illness and hospital usage in the elderly: A random sample followed up. *Comprehensive Psychiatry* **11**, 26–32.

Kay, J., Lesser, R. and Coltheart, M. (1992). *Psycholinguistic Assessments of Language Processing in Aphasia*. Hillsdale, NJ: Lawrence Erlbaum.

Kellett, J. (1993). Long term care on the NHS: a vanishing prospect. *British Medical Journal* **306**, 846–848.

Kemper, S. (1990). Geriatric psycholinguistics: syntactic limitations of oral and written language. In: Light, L.L. and Burke, D.M. (Eds), *Language, Memory and Aging*. Cambridge: Cambridge University Press.

Kempler, D. (1988). Lexical and pantomime abilities in Alzheimer's disease. *Aphasiology* **2**, 147–159.

Kempler, D., Curtis, S. and Jackson, C. (1987) Syntactic preservation in Alzheimer's disease. *Journal of Speech and Hearing Research* **30**, 343–350.

Kent, A. (1989). Hearing difficulties and deafness. In: Benson, S. (Ed.), *Handbook for Care Assistants*. London: Hawker.

Kern, R.S., VanGorp, W.G., Cummings, J.L., Brown, W.S. and Osato, S.S. (1992). Confabulation in Alzheimer's disease. *Brain and Cognition* **19**, 172–182.

Kertesz, A. (1980). *Western Aphasia Battery*. London, Ontario: University of Western Ontario.

Kertesz, A. and Sheppard, H. (1981). The epidemiology of aphasia and cognitive impairment in stroke: age, sex, aphasia type and laterality differences. *Brain* **104**, 117–128.

Kiloh, L.G. (1981). Depressive illness masquerading as dementia in the elderly. *Medical Journal of Australia* **2**, 550–553.

Kimura, R.S. (1973) Cochlear vascular lesions. In: deLorenzo, A.J.D. (Ed.), *Vascular Disorders and Hearing Defects*. Baltimore: University Park Press.

Kirshner, H.S., Tanridag, O., Thurman, L. and Whetsell, W.O. (1987). Progressive aphasia without dementia: two cases with focal spongiform degeneration. *Annals of Neurology* **22**, 527–533.

Knight, R.G. (1992). *The Neuropsychology of Degenerative Brain Diseases*. London: Lawrence Erlbaum.

Kontiola, P., Laaksoner, R., Sulkawa, R. and Erkinjuntti, T. (1990). Pattern of language impairment in Alzheimer's disease and multi-infarct dementia. *Brain and Language* **38**, 364–383.

Koss, E. and Friedland, R.P. (1987). Neuropsychological features of early and late onset Alzheimer's disease. *Archives of Neurology* **44**, 797.

Kramer, S.I. and Reifler, B.V. (1992). Depression, dementia and reversible dementia. *Clinical Geriatric Medicine* **8**, 289–297.

Kuhl, D.E., Metter, E.J. and Reige, W.H. (1984). Patterns of local cerebral glucose utilization determined in Parkinson's disease by [F18] fluorodeoxyglucose method. *Annals of Neurology* **15**, 419–424.

Kynette, D. and Kemper, S. (1986). Aging and the loss of grammatical forms: a cross-sectional study of language performance. *Language and Communication* **6**, 65–72.

Labov, W. (1978). *Sociolinguistic Patterns*. Oxford: Basil Blackwell.

Lahey, M. and Feier, C.D. (1982). The semantics of verbs in dissolution and development of language. *Journal of Speech and Hearing Research* **25**, 81–95.

Lakowski, R. (1973). Effects of age on 100 time scores of red–green deficient subjects. *Modern Problems in Ophthalmology* **13**, 124–129.

Larson, G.W., Hayslip, B. and Thomas, K.W. (1992). Changes in voice onset time in young and older men. *Educational Gerontology* **18**, 285–297.

Leandersson, R., Meyerson, R. A. and Persson, A. (1972). Lip muscle function in parkinsonian dysarthria. *Acta Otolaryngologica* **74**, 271–278.

Le Brun, Y., Devreux, F. and Rousseau, J.J. (1986). Language and speech in a patient with a clinical diagnosis of progressive supranuclear palsy. *Brain and Language* **27**, 247–256.

Lesser, R. (1989). Selective preservation of oral spelling without semantics in a case of multi-infarct dementia. *Cortex* **25**, 239–250.

Levelt, W.J.M. (1983). Monitoring and self-repair in speech. *Cognition* **14**, 41–104.

Lewis, R.R. (1979). Macular degeneration in the aged. In: Han, S.S. and Coons, D.H. (Eds), *Special Senses in Aging: A Current Biological Assessment*. Ann Arbor: University of Michigan.

Lieberman, P., Friedman, J. and Feldman, L.S. (1990). Syntax comprehension in Parkinson's disease. *Journal of Nervous and Mental Disease* **178**, 360–366.

Light, L.L. (1992). The organization of memory in old age. In: Craik, F. and Salthouse, T. (Eds), *The Handbook of Aging and Cognition*. New Jersey: Lawrence Erlbaum.

Light, D.M. and Albertson, S.A. (1990). Comprehension of pragmatic implications in young and older adults. In: Burke, D.M. and Light, L.L. (Eds), *Language, Memory and Aging*. Cambridge: Cambridge University Press.

Light, L.L. and Burke, D.M. (1990). Patterns of language and memory in old age. In: Burke, D.M. and Light, L.L. (Eds), *Language, Memory and Aging*. Cambridge: Cambridge University Press.

Light, L.L. and Zelinski, E.M. (1982). Adult age differences in reasoning from new information. *Journal of Experimental Psychology: Learning, Memory and Cognition* **8**, 435–447.

Light, L. L., Zelinski, E.M. and Moore, M. M. (1982). Adult age differences in reasoning from new information. *Journal of Experimental Psychology: Learning, Memory and Cognition* **8**, 435–447.

Lipowski, Z.J. (1983). Transient cognitive disorders (delirium, acute confusional states) in the elderly. *American Journal of Psychiatry* **140**, 1426–1436.

Lishman, W.A. (1987). *Organic Psychiatry: The Psychological Consequences of Cerebral Disorder*, 2nd edn. Oxford: Blackwell Scientific.

Loring, D.W., Meador, K.J., Mahurin, R.K. and Largen, J.W. (1986). Neuropsychological performance in dementia of the Alzheimer type and multi-infarct dementia. *Archives of Clinical Neuropsychology* **1**, 335–340.

Lorso, J. (1977). Sensory processes and age effects in normal adults. *Journal of Gerontology* **26**, 90–105.

Lovelace, E.A. (1990). Basic concepts in cognition and aging. In: Lovelace, E.A.

(Ed.), *Aging and Cognition: Mental Processes, Self-Awareness and Interventions*. Amsterdam: Elsevier Science.

Lubinski, R. (1981). Programs in home health care agencies and nursing homes. In: Beasley, D.S. and Davis, G.A. (Eds), *Aging, Communication Processes and Disorders*. New York: Grune & Stratton.

Lubinski, R., Morrison, E.B. and Rigrodski, S. (1981). Perception of spoken communication by elderly chronically ill patients in an institutional setting. *Journal of Speech Hearing Disorders* **46**, 405–412.

Luria, A. (1973). Towards the mechanism of naming disturbance. *Neuropsychologia* **2**, 417–421.

Lynne-Davis, P.(1977). Influence of age on the respiratory system. *Geriatrics* **32**, 57–60.

McClenahan, R., Johnston, M. and Densham, Y. (1992). Factors influencing accuracy of estimation of comprehension problems in patients following CVA by doctors, nurses and relatives. *European Journal of Disorders of Communication* **27**, 209–220.

McGlone, J., Gupta, S., Humphrey, D., Oppenheimer, S., Miosen, T. and Evans, D.R. (1990). Screening for early dementia using memory complaints from patients and relatives. *Archives of Neurology* **47**, 1189–1193.

MacKay, D.G. and Burke, D.M. (1990) Cognition and aging: a theory of new learning and the use of old connections. In: Hess, T.M. (Ed.), *Aging and Cognition: Knowledge Organisation and Utilization*. Amsterdam: Elsevier.

McKenna, P. and Warrington, E.K. (1983). *The Graded Naming Test*. Windsor: Nelson.

McKhann, G., Drachman, D., Folstein, M., Katzman, R., Price, D. and Stadlan, E.M. (1984). Clinical diagnosis of Alzheimer's disease:a report of the NINCDS-ADRDA Work Group. *Neurology* **34**, 939–943.

McNamara, P., Obler, L.K., Au, R., Durso, R. and Albert, M.L. (1992). Speech monitoring skills in Alzheimer's disease, Parkinson's disease and normal aging. *Brain and Language* **42**, 38–51.

McIntosh, I.B. and Power, K.G. (1993). Elderly people's views of an annual screening assessment. *British Journal of Clinical Practice* **43**, 189–192.

Maccoby, E.E. (1971). Age changes in the selective perception of verbal materials. In: Horton, D. and Jenkins, J. (Eds), *The Perception of Language*. Columbus, OH: Charles E. Merrill.

Maher, E.R. and Lees, A.J. (1986). The clinical features and natural history of the Steele–Richardson–Olszewski syndrome (progressive supranuclear palsy). *Neurology* **36**, 1005–1008.

Maher, E.R., Smith, E.M. and Lees, A.J. (1985). Cognitive deficits in the Steele–Richardson–Olszewski syndrome. *Journal of Neurology, Neurosurgery and Psychiatry* **48**, 1234–1239.

Mahler, M.E. and Cummings, J.L. (1991). Behavioural neurology of multi-infarct dementia. *Alzheimer Disease Association Disorders* **5**, 122–130.

Mandel, A.M., Alexander, M.P. and Carpenter, S. (1989). Creutzfeldt–Jakob disease prescribing as an isolated aphasia. *Neurology* **39**, 55–58.

Marslen-Wilson, W.C. and Welsh, A. (1978). Process interactions and lexical access during word recognition in continuous speech. *Cognitive Psychology* **10**, 29–63.

Marsden, C.D. and Harrison, M.J.G. (1972). Outcome of investigations of patients with presenile dementia. *British Medical Journal* **2**, 249–252.

Martin, A. (1987). Representations of semantic and spatial knowledge in Alzheimer's patients: implications for models of preserved learning in amnesia.

Journal of Clinical and Experimental Neuropsychology **9**, 121–124.

Martin, A. (1990). Neuropsychology of Alzheimer's disease. The case for subgroups. In: Schwartz, M. F. (Ed.), *Modular Deficits in Alzheimer-Type Dementia*, pp. 143–175. Cambridge, MA: MIT Press.

Martin, A. Brouwers, P., Cox, C. and Fedio, P. (1985). On the nature of the verbal memory deficit in Alzheimer's disease. *Brain and Language* **25**, 323–341.

Matison, R. Mayeux, R., Rosen, J. and Fahn, S. (1982). 'Tip-of-the-tongue' phenomena in Parkinson's disease. *Neurology* **32**, 567–570.

Mayeux, R., Stern, Y. and Sano, M. (1992). A comparison of clinical outcome and survival in various forms of Alzheimer's disease. In: Florette, F., Khachaturian, Z., Poncet, M. and Christen, Y. (Eds), *Heterogeneity of Alzheimer's Disease*. Berlin: Springer.

Mayeux, R., Stern, Y., Rosen, J. and Benson, D.E. (1983). Is 'subcortical dementia' a recognizable clinical entity. *Annals of Neurology* **14**, 278–283.

Maxim, J. (1982). Language change with increasing age. In: Edwards, M. (Ed.), *Communication Changes in Elderly People*, Monograph No. 3. London: College of Speech Therapists.

Maxim, J. (1985). A grammatical analysis of the language of the senescent. PhD Thesis, Reading University.

Maxim, J. (1991). Can elicited language be used to diagnose dementia? *Work in Progress* **1**, 13–21. London: NHCSS.

Maxim, J. and Bryan, K.L. (1989). Talking and Listening. In: Benson, S. (Ed). *Handbook for Care Assistants*. London: Hawker.

Melin and Gotestam, K.G. (1981) The effects of rearranging ward routines on communication and eating behaviours of psychogeriatric patients. *Journal of Applied Behaviour* **14**, 47–51.

Mendez, M.F. and Ashla-Mendez, M. (1991) Differences between multi-infarct dementia and Alzheimer's disease on unstructured neuropsychological tasks. *Journal of Clinical and Experimental Neuropsychology* **13**, 923–932.

Mesulam, M.M. (1981). A cortical network for directed attention and unilateral neglect. *Annals of Neurology* **10**, 309–325.

Mesulam, M. (1982). Slowly progressive aphasia without generalized dementia. *Annals of Neurology* **11**, 592–598.

Mesulam, M.M. and Weintraub, S. (1992). Primary progressive aphasia: sharpening the focus on a clinical syndrome. In: Florette, F., Khachaturian, Z., Poncet, M. and Christen, Y. (Eds), *Heterogeneity of Alzheimer's Disease*. Berlin: Springer.

Meyer, B.J.F. and Rice, G.E. (1981). Information recalled from prose by young, middle and old adult readers. *Experimental Aging Research* 7, 253–268.

Meyer, B.J.F. and Rice, G.E. (1983) Learning and memory from text across the adult life span. In: Fine, J. and Freddle, R.O. (Eds), *Developmental Studies in Discourse*. Norwood, NJ: Ablex.

Meyer, B.J.F., Young, C.J. and Bartlett, B.J. (1989). *Memory Improved: Reading and Memory Across the Lifespan Through Strategic Text Structure*. Hillsdale, NJ: Lawrence Erlbaum.

Meyer, J.S., McClintic, K.L., Rogers, R.L., Sims, P. and Mortel, K.K. (1988) Aetiological considerations and risk factors for multi-infarct dementia. *Journal of Neurology, Neurosurgery and Psychiatry* **51**, 1489–1497.

Midwinter, T. (1989). A healthy old age. In: Benson, S. (Ed.), *Handbook for Care Assistants*. London: Care Concern.

Milberg, W. and Albert, M. (1989). Cognitive differences between patients with progressive supranuclear palsy and Alzheimer's disease. *Journal of Clinical and Experimental Neuropsychology* **11**, 605–614.

Millard, P.H. and Higgs, P.H. (1989). The future of care for the elderly. *Care of the Elderly* **1**, 284–285.

Milroy, L. (1987). ***Observing and Analysing Natural Language***. Oxford: Blackwell.

Miller, N. (1986). ***Dyspraxia and its Management***. London: Croom Helm.

Moscovitch, M.M. and Winocur, G. (1992). The neuropsychology of memory and aging. In: Craik, F. and Salthouse, T. (Eds), ***The Handbook of Aging and Cognition***. Hillsdale, NJ: Lawrence Erlbaum.

MRC Report (1977). ***Senile and Presenile Dementia. A Report of the MRC Subcommittee***. London: Medical Research Council.

Munoz-Garcia, D. and Ludwin, S.K. (1984). Classic and generalized variants of Pick's disease: a clinicopathological, ultrastructural and immunocytochemical comparative study. *Annals of Neurology* **16**, 467–480.

Murdoch, B.E. (1990). ***Acquired Speech and Language Disorders. A Neuroanatomical and Functional Approach***. London: Chapman and Hall.

Nance, W.E. and McConnell, E.E.(1973). Status and prospects of research in hereditary deafness. *Advances in Human Geriatrics* **4**, 173–250.

National Centre for Health Statistics (1980). Basic data on hearing levels of adults 25–74 years. US 1971–75 series U, No. 215. US Department of Health, Education and Welfare.

Navia, B.A., Jordan, B.D. and Price, R.W. (1986). The AIDS dementia complex: I. Clinical features. *Annals of Neurology* **19**, 517–524.

Nebes, R.D., Martin, D.C. and Horn, L.C. (1984). Sparing of semantic memory in Alzheimer's disease. *Journal of Abnormal Psychology* **93**, 321–330.

Nelson, J. and O'Connell, P. (1978). Dementia: the estimation of premorbid intelligence levels using the New Adult Reading Test. *Cortex* **14**, 234–244.

Nooteboom, S.G. (1980). Speaking and unspeaking: Detection and correction of phonological and lexical errors in spontaneous speech. In: Fromkin, V.A. (Ed.). ***Errors in Linguistic Performance. Slips of the Tongue, Ear, Pen and Hand***. New York: Academic Press.

Nussbaum, J.F., Thompson, T. and Robinson, J.D. (1989). ***Communication and Aging***. New York: Harper and Row.

Oakley, A. (1975). ***The Sociology of Housework***. London: Martin Roberton.

Obler, L.K. (1980). Narrative discourse style in the elderly. In: Obler, L. and Albert, M. (Eds), ***Language and Communication in the Elderly***. Lexington, MA: D.C. Heath and Co.

Obler, L. (1983). Language and brain dysfunction in dementia. In: Segalowitz, S.J. (Ed.), ***Language Functions and Brain Organisation***. New York: Academic Press.

Obler, L. and Albert, M. (1981). Language and aging: a neurobehavioral analysis. In: Beasley, D. and Davis, G.A. (Eds), ***Aging Communication Processes and Disorders***. New York: Grune and Stratton.

Obler, L.K. and Albert, M.L. (1985). Language skills across adulthood. In: Birren, J.E. and Schaie, K.W. (Eds), ***Handbook of the Psychology of Aging***. New York: Van Nostrand Reinhold.

Obler, L.K., Mildworf, B. and Albert, M. (1977). ***Writing Style in the Elderly***. Montreal: Academy of Aphasia Abstracts.

Obler, L., Albert, M., Goodglass, H. and Benson, D.F. (1978). Aphasia type and aging. *Brain and Language* **6**, 318–322.

Obler, L., Fein, D., Nicholas, M. and Albert, M.L. (1991). Auditory comprehension and aging: decline in syntactic processing. *Applied Psycholinguistics* **12**, 433–452.

O'Connor, D.W., Grande, M.J., Hyde, J.B., Perry, J.R., Roland, M.O., Silverman, J.D. and Wraight, S.K. (1993). Dementia in general practice: the practical consequences of a more positive approach to diagnosis. *British Journal of General Practice* **43**, 185–188.

O'Donovan, S. (1993). Call for help. *Nursing Times* **89**, 30–33.

OECD (1988). *Ageing Populations: The Social Policy Implications: Demographic Change and Public Policy*. Paris: OECD.

Office of Population Censuses and Surveys (1973). *General Household Survey*. London: HMSO.

Office of Population Censuses and Surveys (1981). *General Household Survey*. Introductory Report. London: HMSO.

OPCS (1988). *Surveys of Disability in Great Britain*, Report 1, September.

Okamoto, Y. (1992). Health care for the elderly in Japan: medicine and welfare in an aging society facing a crisis in long term care *British Medical Journal* **305**, 403–405.

O'Neill, D. (1991). Dementia and the GP. *Practitioner* **235**, 644–648.

Palmore, E.B. (1982). Attitudes towards the aged: what we know and need to know. *Research on Aging* **4**, 333–348.

Pattie, A. M. (1981). A survey version of the Clifton Assessment Procedure for the Elderly (CAPE). *British Journal of Clinical Psychology* **20**, 173–178.

Pattie, A.M. and Gilleard, C.J. (1979). *Manual of the Clifton Assessment Procedures for the Elderly*. Sevenoaks: Hodder and Stoughton.

Perlmutter, M. (1979). Age differences in the consistency of adult's associative responses. *Experimental Aging Research* **5**, 549–553.

Perrotta, P. and Meacham, J. A. (1981). Can a reminiscing intervention alter depression and self esteem? *International Journal of Aging and Human Development* **14**, 23–40.

Peterson, R.C., Smith, G., Kokmen, E., Ivnik, R.J. and Tangalos, E.G. (1992). Memory function in normal aging. *Neurology* **42**, 396–401.

Pick, A. (1892). Ueber die beziehungen der senilen hirnatrophie zur aphasie. *Praeger Med Wochenschr* **17**, 165–167.

Pitt, B. (1982). *Psychogeriatrics: An Introduction to the Psychiatry of Old Age*. Edinburgh: Churchill Livingstone.

Plude, D. J. and Doussard-Roosevelt, J. A. (1989). Aging, selective attention and feature integration. *Psychology and Aging* **4**, 98–105.

Plude, D.J. and Hoyer, W.J. (1985). Attention and performance: Identifying and localising deficits. In: Charness, W. (Ed.), *Aging and Human Performance*. Chichester: John Wiley & Sons.

Podoll, K., Schwarz, M. and Noth, J. (1991). Language functions in progressive supranuclear palsy. *Brain* **114**, 1457–1472.

Podoll, K., Caspary, P., Large, H.W. and Noth, J. (1988). Language functions in Huntington's disease. *Brain* **3**, 1475–1503.

Poeck, K. and Luzzatti, C. (1988). Slowly progressive aphasia in three patients. The problems of accompanying neuropsychological deficit. *Brain* **3**, 151–168.

Powell, A.L., Cummings, J.L., Hill, M.A. and Benson, D.F. (1988). Speech and language alterations in multi-infarct dementia. *Neurology* **38**, 717–719.

Powell-Proctor, L. and Miller, E. (1982). Reality orientation: a critical appraisal. *British Journal of Psychiatry* **140**, 457–463.

Prutting, C.A. and Kirchner, D.M. (1987). A clinical appraisal of the pragmatic aspects of language. *Journal of Speech and Hearing Disorders* **52**, 105–119.

Quirk, R., Greenbaum, S., Leech, G. and Svartvik, J. (1972). *A Grammar of Contemporary English*. London: Longmans.

Rabbitt, P. (1965). An age decremant in the ability to ignore irrelevant information. *Journal of Gerontology* **20**, 233–238.

Rabbitt, P. (1979). Some experiments and a model for changes in attentional selectivity with old age. In: Hoffmeister, F. and Muller, C. (Eds), *Brain Function in Old Age*. New York: Springer-Verlag.

Rankin, J. and Collins, M. (1985). Adult age differences in memory elaboration. *Journal of Gerontology* **40**, 451–458.

Rao, P. (1990). Functional communication assessment of the elderly. *ASHA Reports* **19**, 28–36.

Rapcsak, S.Z., Arthur, S.A., Blicken, D.A. and Rubens, A.B. (1989). Lexical agraphia in Alzheimer's disease. *Archives of Neurology* **46**, 65–68.

Raven, J.C. (1965). *Guide to Using The Coloured Progressive Matrices*. London: H.K. Lewis.

Reichman, W.E., Cummings, J.L, McDaniel, K.D., Flynn, F. and Gornbein, J. (1991). Visuoconstructive impairment in dementia syndromes. *Behavioural Neurology* **4**, 153–162.

Reifler, B. (1986). Mixed cognitive–affective disturbances in the elderly: a new classification. *Journal of Clinical Psychiatry* **47**, 354–356.

Reisberg, B., Ferris, S.M., de Leon, M. and Crook, T. (1982). The global deterioration scale for assessment of primary degenerative dementia. *American Journal of Psychiatry* **139**, 1136–1139.

Riegel, K. (1959). A study of verbal achievements of older persons. *Journal of Gerontology* **14**, 453–458.

Riensche, L.L. and Lang, K. (1992). Treatment of swallowing disorders through a multidisciplinary team approach. *Educational Gerontology* **18**, 277–284.

Riggans, L. (1992). Living with loss. *Nursing Times* **88**, 34–35.

Ringel, R. and Chodzho-Zaigo, W. (1987). Vocal indices of biological age. *Journal of Voice* **1**, 31.

Ripich, D.N., Vertes, D., Whitehouse, P., Fulton, S. and Ekelman, B. (1991). Turn-taking and speech act patterns in the discourse of senile dementia of the Alzheimer's type patients. *Brain and Language* **40**, 330–343.

Ripich, D.N. and Terrell, B.Y. (1988). Patterns of discourse cohesion in Alzheimer's disease. *Journal of Speech and Hearing Disorders* **53**, 8–15.

Rissenberg, M. and Glanzer, M. (1986). Picture superiority in free recall: the effects of ageing and primary degenerative dementia. *Journal of Gerontology* **41**, 64–67.

Roberts, J. (1993). Clinton's outline plan to fix the American health system. *British Medical Journal* **307**, 819–820.

Robertson, S.J. and Thompson, F. (1983). Speech therapy and Parkinson's disease. *Bulletin of the College of Speech and Language Therapists* **370**, 10–12.

Robinson,R.A. (1980). Treating confusion. *Geriatric Medicine* **November**, 10–15.

Rochford, G. (1971). A study of naming errors in dysphasic and in demented patients. *Neuropsychologia* **9**, 437–443.

Rogers, D., Lees, A.J., Smith, E., Trimble, M. and Stern, G.M. (1987). Bradyphrenia in Parkinson's disease and psychomotor retardation in depressive illness: An experimental study. *Brain* **110**, 761–776.

Ron, M.A. (1990). Suspected dementia: psychiatric differential diagnosis. *Neuropsychiatric practice and opinion* **2**, 214–219.

Rose, C., Boby, V. and Capildeo, R.A. (1976). A retrospective survey of speech disorders following stroke, with particular reference to the value of therapy. In: LeBrun, Y. and Hoops, R. (Eds), *Recovery in Aphasics*. Amsterdam: Swets and Zeitlinger.

Ross, E.D. (1981). The aprosodias: functional organization of the affective components of language in the right hemisphere. *Archives of Neurology* **38**, 561–569.

Ross, G.W., Cummings, J.L. and Benson, D.F. (1990). Speech and language alterations in dementia syndromes: characteristics and treatment. *Aphasiology* **4**, 339–352.

Rossiter, D. and McInally, K. (1989). Aphasia services: provision or privation? *CST Bulletin* **September**, 4–6.

Rossor, M. (1987). Dementia. *British Journal of Hospital Medicine* **July**, 46–50.

Rossor, M.N., Kennedy, A.M. and Newman, S.K. (1992). Heterogeneity in familial Alzheimer's disease. In: Florette, F., Khachaturian, Z., Poncet, M. and Christen, Y. (Eds), *Heterogeneity of Alzheimer's Disease*. Berlin: Springer.

Roth, M. (1981). The diagnosis of dementia in late and middle life. In: Mortimer, J.A. and Schuman, L.M. (Eds), *The Epidemiology of Dementia*. New York: Oxford University Press.

Roth, M. (1983). Depression and affective disorders in later life. In: Angst, J. (Ed.). *The Origin of Depression: Current Concepts and Approaches*. New York: Springer Verlag.

Roth, M., Tym, E., Mountjoy, C.Q., Huppert, F.A., Hendrie, H., Verma, S. and Goddard, R. (1986). Camdex. A standardised instrument for the diagnosis of mental disorder in the elderly with special reference to the early detection of dementia. *British Journal of Psychiatry* **149**, 698–709.

Royal College of Physicians Committee on Geriatrics (1981). Organic mental impairment in the elderly. *Journal of the Royal College of Physicians* **15**, 142–167.

Rumelhart, D.E. and McClelland, J.L. (1986). *Parallel Distributed Processing: Exploration in the Microstructure of Cognition*, Vol. I. Cambridge, MA: MIT Press.

Ryan, W.J. and Burk, K.W. (1974). Perceptual and acoustic correlation of aging in the speech of males. *Journal of Communication Disorders* 7, 181–192.

Ryff, C.D. (1986). The failure of successful aging research. Paper presented at the annual meeting of the Gerontological Society of America, Chicago.

Sasanuma, S., Sakuma, N. and Kitano, K. (1990). Longterm course of cognitive abilities of patients with probably Alzheimer type dementia and multi infarct dementia. Presented at the 4th International Aphasia Rehabilitation Congress, Edinburgh, September.

Salthouse, T.A. (1984). Effects of age and skill in typing. *Journal of Gerontology* **113**, 345–371.

Salthouse, T.A. (1985). Speed of behaviour and its implications for cognition. In: Birren, J.G. and Schaie, K.W. (Eds), *Handbook of the Psychology of Aging*, 2nd edn. New York: Van Nostrand Reinhold.

Salthouse, T.A. (1990). Cognitive competance and expertise in aging. In: Birren, J.E. and Schaie, K.W. (Eds), *Handbook of the Psychology of Aging*, 3rd edn. San Diego: Academic Press.

Salthouse, T.A. (1991). *Theoretical Perspectives on Cognitive Aging*. Hillsdale, NJ: Lawrence Erlbaum Associates.

Salthouse, T.A., Mitchell, D.R., Skovronek, E. and Babcock, R.L. (1989). Effects of adult age and working memory on reasoning and spatial abilities. *Journal of Experimental Psychology: Learning, Memory and Cognition* **15**, 507–516.

Sands, E., Sarno, M. and Shankweiler, D. (1969). Long-term assessment of language function in aphasia due to stroke. *Archives of Physical Medicine and Rehabilitation* **50**, 202–207.

Sarno, M.T. (1969). *Functional Communication Profile. Institute of Rehabilitation Medicine*. New York: University Medical Center.

Sarno, M.T. (1980). Language rehabilitation outcome in the elderly aphasic patient. In: Obler, L. and Albert, M. (Eds), *Language and Communication in the Elderly*. Lexington: D.C. Heath.

Schaffer, G. and Poon, L.W. (1982). Individual variability in memory training with the elderly. *Educational Gerontology* **8**, 217–229.

Schegloff, E.A. (1979). The relevance of repair to syntax-for-conversation. In: Givon, T. (Ed.), *Syntax and Semantics: Vol. 12. Discourse and Syntax*. New York: Academic Press.

Scheltens, P., Hazenberg, G.J., Lindeboom, J., Valk, J. and Wolters, E.C. (1990). A case of progressive aphasia without dementia: 'temporal' Pick's disease? *Journal of Neurology, Neurosurgery and Psychiatry* **53**, 79–80.

Schoenberg, B. S. (1986). Epidemiology of Alzheimer's disease and other dementing illnesses. *Journal of Chronic Diseases* **39**, 1095–1104.

Scholes, R.J. (1978). Syntactic and lexical components of sentence comprehension. In: Caramazza, A. and Zurif, E.B. (Eds), *Language Acquisition and Language Breakdown*. Baltimore: Johns Hopkins University Press.

Schonfield, D., Trueman, V. and Kline, D. (1982). Recognition tests of dichotic listening and the age variable. *Journal of Gerontology* **27**, 487–493.

Schuell, H. (1965). *Differential Diagnosis of Aphasia with the Minnesota Test*. Minneapolis: University of Minnesota Press.

Schwartz, M.F., Marin, O.S. and Saffran, E.M. (1979). Dissociation of language function in dementia: A case study. *Brain and Language* **7**, 277–306.

Schwartz, M.F., Saffran, E.M. and Marin, O.S.M. (1980). Fractionating the reading process in dementia: Evidence for word specific print-to-sound associations. In: Coltheart, M., Patterson, K.E. and Marshall, J.C. (Eds), *Deep Dyslexia*. London: Routledge.

Schwartz, M.F., Saffron, E.M. and Williamson, S. (1981). The breakdown of lexicon in Alzheimer's dementia. Paper given at Lingusitic Society of America 56th Annual Meeting, New York.

Scott, S. and Caird, F.I. (1981). Speech therapy for patients with Parkinson's disease. *British Medical Journal* **283**, 1088.

Scott, S. and Caird, F.I. (1983). Speech therapy for Parkinson's disease. *Journal of Neurology, Neurosurgery and Psychiatry* **46**, 140–144.

Scott, S. Caird, F.I. and Williams, B.O. (1984). Evidence for an apparent sensory speech disorder in Parkinson's disease. *Journal of Neurology, Neurosurgery and Psychiatry* **47**, 840–843.

Selkoe, D.J. (1992) Aging brain, aging mind. *Scientific American* **Sept**, 97–03.

Seltzer, B and Sherwin, I. (1983). A comparison of clinical features in early and late onset primary degenerative dementia. One entity or two? *Archives of Neurology* **40**, 143–146.

Sinclair, H. (1967). Conduites verbales et deficits operatoires. *Acta Neurologica et Psychiatrica Belgica* **67**, 852–860.

Skelton-Robinson, M. and Jones, S. (1984). Nominal dysphasia and the severity of senile dementia. *British Journal of Psychiatry* **145**, 168–171.

Skinner, C., Wirz, S., Thompson, I. and Davidson, J. (1990). *Edinburgh Functional Communication Profile*. Buckingham: Winslow Press.

Slater, P. E. (1964). Cross-cultural views of the aged. In: Kastenbaum, R. (Ed.), *New Thoughts on Old Age*. New York: Springer.

Smith, A.D. and Fullerton, A.M. (1981). Age differences in episodic and somatic memory: Implications for language and cognition. In: Beasley, D.S. and Davis,

G.A. (Eds), *Aging Communication Processes and Disorders*. New York: Grune and Stratton.

Smith, B.J. and Barker, H.R. (1972). Influence of a reality orientation training programme on the attitudes of trainees towards the elderly. *Gerontologist* **12**, 262–264.

Smith, S.R., Murdoch, B.E. and Chenery, H.J. (1989). Semantic abilities in dementia of the Alzheimer type: 1. Lexical semantics. *Brain and Language* **36**, 314–324.

Sonies, B. and Caruso, A. (1990). The aging process and its potential impact on measures of oral sensorimotor function. *ASHA Reports* **19**, 114–124.

Sorsby, A. (1966). *The Incidence and Causes of Blindness in England and Wales 1948–1962*. Reports on Public Health and Medical Subjects #144. London: HMSO.

Speedie, L.J., Brake, N., Folstein, S.E., Bowers, D. and Heilman, K.M. (1990). Comprehension of prosody in Huntington's disease. *Journal of Neurology, Neurosurgery and Psychiatry* **53**, 607–610.

Spiraduso, W.W. (1980). Physical fitness, aging and psychomotor speed: A review. *Journal of Gerontology* **35**, 850–865.

Stebbins, G.T., Wilson, R.S., Gilley, D.W., Bernard, B.A. and Fox, J.H. (1990). Use of the NART to estimate premorbid IQ in dementia. *Clinical Neurologist* **4**, 18–24.

Stengel, E. (1964). Neuropathology of dementia. *Proceedings of the Royal Society of Medicine* **54**, 911–914.

Stevens, A. and Gabbay, J. (1991). Needs assessment needs assessment. *Health Trends* **23**, 20–23.

Stevens, S.J. (1985). The language of dementia: a pilot study. *British Journal of Disorders of Communication* **20**, 181–190.

Stevens, S. J. (1992). Differentiating the language disorder in dementia from dysphasia: the potential of a screening test. *European Journal of Disorders of Communication* **27**, 275–288.

Stine, E.A. and Wingfield, A. (1990). The assessment of qualitative age differences in discourse processing. In: Hess, T.M. (Ed.). *Aging and Cognition: Knowledge Organization and Utilization*. Amsterdam: Elsevier Science Publishers.

Strehler, B.L. (1976). Introduction: Theories of aging. In: Platt, D. (Ed.), *Third Geissen Symposium on Experimental Gerontology*. Stuttgart: Schattauer.

Stubbs, M. (1983). *Discourse Analysis*. Oxford: Blackwell.

Sutcliffe, R.L., Prior, R., Mawby, B. and McQuillan, W.J. (1985). Parkinson's disease in the district of the Northampton Health Authority, UK. A study of prevalence and disability. *Acta Neurologica Scandinavica* **72**, 363–379.

Tatemichi, T.K. (1990). How acute brain failure becomes chronic. A view of the mechanisms of dementia related to stroke. *Neurology* **40**, 1652–1659.

Taylor, A.M. and Warrington, E.K. (1971). Visual agnosia: a single case report. *Cortex* **7**, 152–161.

Taylor, A.E., Saint-Cyr, J.A. and Lang, A.E. (1986). Frontal lobe dysfunction in Parkinson's disease: the cortical focus of neostriatal outflow. *Brain* **109**, 845–883.

Taylor, A.E., Saint-Cyr, J.A. and Lang, A.E. (1990). Memory and learning in early Parkinson's disease: Evidence from a 'frontal lobe syndrome'. *Brain and Cognition* **13**, 211–232.

Thal, L.J., Grundman, M. and Klauber, M.R. (1988). Dementia: Characteristics of a referral population and factors associated with progression. *Neurology* **38**, 1083–1090.

Thompson, I.M. (1983). BMV Language Scales. *Bulletin of the College of Speech and Language Therapists* **378**, 1–4.

Thompson, J. M. (1986). *Language Pathology in Alzheimer's-Type Dementia and associated Disorders*. PhD thesis, University of Edinburgh.

Thorndike, R.L. and Gallup, G.H. (1944). Verbal intelligence of the American adult. *Journal of General Psychology* **30**, 75–78.

Thornicroft, G., Ward, P. and James, S. (1993). Care management and mental health. *British Medical Journal* **306**, 768–771.

Till, P.E. and Walsh, D.A. (1980). Encoding and retrieval factors in adult memory for implicational sentences. *Journal of Verbal Learning and Verbal Behaviour* **19**, 1–16.

Tissot, R., Duval, R.J. and de Ajuriaguerra, J. (1967). Quelques aspects du language des demances degeneratives du grand age. *Acta Neurologica et Psychiatrica Belgica* **67**, 911–923.

Tomlinson, B.E. (1977). The pathology of dementia. In: Wells, C.E. (Ed.), *Dementia: Contemporary Neurology Series*. Philadelphia: E.A. Davies.

Tomlinson, B. (1992). *Report of the Inquiry into London's Health Services, Medical Education and Research*. London: HMSO.

Toner, H.L. (1987). Effectiveness of a written guide for carers of dementia sufferers. *British Journal of Clinical and Social Psychology* **5**, 24–26.

Tout, K. (1993). *Elderly Care: A World Perspective*. London: Chapman and Hall.

Troster, A.I., Salmon, D.P., McCullough, D. and Butters, N. (1989). A comparison of the category fluency deficits associated with Alzheimer's and Huntington's disease. *Brain and Language* **37**, 500–513.

Trudgill, P. (1983). *On Dialect: Social and Geographical Perspectives*. Oxford: Blackwell.

Tulving, E. (1972). Episodic and semantic memory. In: Tulving, E. and Donaldson, W. (Eds), *Organization of Memory*, pp. 381–403. New York: Academic Press.

Tulving, E. (1983). *Elements of Episodic Memory*. New York: Oxford University Press.

Tweedy, J.R., Langer, K.G. and McDowell, F.H. (1982). The effect of semantic relations on the memory deficit associated with Parkinson's disease. *Journal of Clinical and Experimental Neuropsychology* **4**, 235–247.

Tyrell, P.J., Warrington, E.K., Frackowiak, R.S.J. and Rossor, M.N. (1990). Heterogeneity in progressive aphasia due to focal cortical atrophy. *Brain* **113**, 1321–1336.

Ulatowska, H., North, A.J. and Macaluso-Haynes, S. (1981). Production of narrative and procedural discourse in aphasia. *Brain and Language* **13**, 345–371.

Ulatowska, H.K., Cannito, M.P., Hayashi, M.M. and Fleming, S.G. (1985). Language abilities in the elderly. In: Ulatowska, H.K. (Ed.), *The Aging Brain: Communication in the Elderly*. London: Taylor & Francis.

Valenstein, E. (1981). Age-related changes in the human central nervous system. In: Beasley, D.S. and Davis, G.A. (Eds), *Aging Communication Processes and Disorders*. New York: Grune and Stratton.

Wade, D.T., Langton-Hewer, R. and Wood, V.A. (1984). Stroke: The influence of age upon outcome. *Age and Aging* **13**, 357–362.

Walker, A.C. (1992). Towards greater user involvement in the social services. In: Arie, T.A. (Ed.), *Recent Advances in Psychogeriatrics*. Edinburgh: Churchill Livingstone.

Walker, S. (1982). Communication as a changing function of age. In: Edwards, M. (Ed.). *Communication Changes in Elderly People*. Monograph No.3. London: College of Speech Therapists.

Walker, S. and Williams, B.O. (1980). The response of a disabled elderly population to speech therapy. *British Journal of Disorders of Communication* **15**, 19–30.

Walsh, D.A. and Prasse, M.J. (1980). Iconic memory and intentional processes in the aged. In: Poon, L.W. et al. (Eds), *New Direction in Memory and Aging*. Hillsdale, NJ: Lawrence Erlbaum.

Walsh, K.W. (1978). *Neuropsychology: A Clinical Approach*. Edinburgh: Churchill Livingstone.

Warren, R.M. and Warren, R.P. (1966). A comparison of speech perception in childhood, maturity and old age by means of the Verbal Transformation Effect. *Journal of Verbal Learning and Verbal Behavior* **5**, 142–148.

Warrington, E.K. (1975). The selective impairment of semantic memory. *Quarterly Journal of Experimental Psychology* **27**, 635–657.

Watson, R. (1992) Alzheimer's disease: does it exist? *Nursing Standard* **43** 29–30.

Wechsler, D. (1958). *The Measurement and Appraisal of Adult Intelligence*. New York: Baillière, Tindall and Cox.

Wechsler, A.F., Verity, M.A., Rosenschein, S., Fried, I. and Scheibel, A.B. (1982). Pick's disease: a clinical computed tomographic and histologic study with Golgi impregnation observations. *Archives of Neurology* **39**, 287–290.

Weintraub, S., Rubin, N.P. and Marsel-Mesulam, M.M. (1990). Primary progressive aphasia: Longitudinal course, neuropsychological profile and language features. *Archives of Neurology* **47**, 1329–1335.

Weinstein, B.E. and Amsel, L. (1986). Hearing loss and senile dementia in the institutionalised elderly. *Clinical Gerontologist* **4**, 3–15.

Weinstein, E.A. and Kahn, R.L. (1952). Non-aphasic misnaming (paraphasia) in organic brain disease. *Archives of Neurology and Psychiatry* **67**, 72–79.

Welford, A.T. (1962). On changes of performance with age. *Lancet* **i**, 335–339.

Welford, A.T.(1985). Changes of performance with age: An overview. In: Charness, N. (Ed), *Aging and Human Performance*. Chichester: John Wiley & Sons.

Wells, C.E.W. (1971). *Dementia: Definition and Description*. Philadelphia: F.A. Davis.

Wells, N.E. (1979). *Dementia in Old Age*. London Office of Health Economic.

Wells, N. and Freer, C. (1988). *The Ageing Population. Burden or Challenge*. London: Macmillan Press.

Wertz, R.T. and Dronkers, N.F. (1990). Effects of age on aphasia. *ASHA Reports* **19**, 88–98.

Whitaker, H. (1976). A case of the isolation of the langauge function. In: Whitaker, H. and Whitacker, H.A. (Eds), *Studies in Neurolinguistics 2*. New York: Academic Press.

Whitaker, J. and Tallis, R. (1992). Misplaced elderly patients in hospital: clarifying responsibilities. *Health Trends* **24**, 15–17.

Whurr, R. (1974). *An Aphasia Screening Test*. London: Whurr.

Wilkin, E., Mashiah, T. and Jolley, D.J. (1978). Changes in behavioural characteristics of elderly populations of local authority homes and long-stay hospital wards. *British Medical Journal* **ii**, 1274–1276.

Williamson, S. and Schwartz, E.M. (1981). The dissolution of discourse in Alzheimer's dementia. Paper given at the Linguistic Society of America, 56th Annual Meeting, New York.

Willott, J.F. (1991). *Aging and the Auditory System: Anatomy, Physiology and Psychophysics*. London: Whurr.

Wilson, B.A. and Moffat, N. (1984). *Clinical Managemant of Memory Problems*. London: Croom Helm.

Wilson, R.S., Kasniak, A.W., Klawans, H.L. and Garron, D.G. (1980). High speed memory scanning in parkinsonism. *Cortex* **16**, 67–72.

Wilson, R. S., Rosenbaum, G., Brown, G., Rourke, D., Whitman, D. and Grisell, J. (1978). An index of premorbid intelligence. *Journal of Consulting and Clinical Psychology* 46, 1554–1555.

Worthington, E.L., Heath, M., Lunn, L.E. and Catlin, F.J. (1973). *Index-handbook of Ototoxic Agents*. Baltimore: Johns Hopkins University Press.

Yairi, E. and Clifton, N. (1972). Disfluent speech behaviour of preschool children, high school seniors and geriatric persons. *Journal of Speech and Hearing Research* **15**, 714–719.

Yesavage, J.A., Rose, T.L. and Bower, G.H. (1983). Interactive imagery and affective judgements improve face-learning in the elderly. *Journal of Gerontology* **38**, 197–203.

Zacks, R.T. and Hasher, L. (1990). Capacity theory and the processing of inferences. In: Burke, D.M. and Light, L.L. (Eds), *Language, Memory and Aging*. Cambridge: Cambridge University Press.

Zelinski, E.M. (1990). Integrating information from discourse: Do older adults show effects? In: Burke, D.M. and Light, L.L. (Eds), *Language, Memory and Aging*. Cambridge: Cambridge University Press.

Author index

Adams, C., 43
Adams, K.M., 172
Adolfson, R., 184
Alavi, A., 155–156
Albazzaz, M., 218
Albert, M.L., 20, 22, 22, 30, 34, 39, 41, 42, 44, 45, 47, 49, 51, 163–164, 166, 190
Albertson, S.A., 39–40
Alexander, M.P., 167
Allen, C.S., 41–42
Allport, D.A., 23
Alpert, M., 113
Alzheimer, A., 173
American Psychiatric Association, 18, 173
Amsel, L., 9, 15
Anderson, M.E., 162
Appell, J., 21, 29, 174, 181, 184, 193, 210, 211
Armstrong, L., 210, 213
Arthur, S.A., 193
Ashla-Mendez, M., 159
Au, R., 41, 45, 163–164, 190
Austin, D.R., 4
Australian Bureau of Statistics, 2

Babcock, R.L., 32
Backman, L., 184
Baldwin, R., 217, 224, 230
Ball, K.K., 32
Bannister, R., 157, 170
Barer, D., 218
Barker, H.R., 219
Barnett-Douglas, H. 14, 219
Bartlett, B.J., 33
Bartlett, C.L., 22, 205, 206
Baseby, A., 208
Basso, A., 22, 205
Bayles, K.A., 21, 23, 29, 49, 50, 167, 174, 181, 182, 183, 187, 193, 208, 212, 220
Beamish, P., 16
Beard, B.L., 32
Bebbington, D., 204
Becker, J.T, 195
Beckman, N.J., 11
Begun, J.S., 185
Belal, A., 11
Beland, R., 175, 181
Bell, B., 12
Benson, D.F., 21, 22, 47, 51, 151, 158, 159, 161, 166, 167, 169, 171
Berg, L., 174
Bernard, B.A., 193
Bernholz, C.D., 12, 19
Berwick, R., 37
Bever, T.G., 34, 185
Bieliauska, L.A., 167
Bishop, D.V.M., 213
Black, S.E., 157
Blackburn, M., 211
Blanken, G., 188
Blicken, D.A., 193
BMJ Editorial, 167
Boby, V., 205
Boller, F., 195
Borsley, D., 219
Bosanquet, N., 200
Botwinick, J., 14
Botwinnick, J., 29, 32, 45
Bourgeois, M.S., 207, 231
Bower, G.H., 33
Bowles, N.L., 33, 44

Brake, N., 166
Brayne, C.E.G., 167
British Geriatric Society, 228
Brodaty, H., 221
Brodie, J.K., 222
Brody, E., 227
Brouwers, P., 183
Brown, G., 25
Brown, J.W., 22, 47
Brown, R.G., 161–165
Brown, W.S., 188
Brun, A., 175
Bruna, O., 158
Bryan, K.L., 14, 202, 222, 223
Bub, D., 181
Buckingham, H.W., 48, 149
Burk, K.W., 8
Burke, D.M., 28, 31, 44, 45, 52
Burns, A., 155
Busse, E.W., 29
Butters, N., 167, 183, 184, 192
Byrne, E.J., 155

Caffrey, J.T., 21, 33
Caird, F.I., 163, 165
Calasanti, T., 227
Cannito, M.P., 42, 44
Capildeo, R.A., 205
Capildevila, A., 158
Capitano, E., 22, 204
Caplan, L.R., 161
Caramazza, A., 30
Carpenter, S., 167
Caruso, A., 8
Carvell, S., 164
Caspary, P., 166
Catlin, F.J., 10
Cattell, R.B., 29
Cavanaugh, J.C., 14
Cerella, J., 32
Charness, N., 33
Chase, T.N., 22, 194, 195
Chawluk, J.B., 155–156
Chenery, H.J., 192
Chertkow, H., 181
Cheshire, J., 58
Chodzo-Zajko, W., 2
Chomsky, N., 30, 49
Christensen, A.L., 211
Chui, H.C., 7, 175
Chylack, L.T., 12, 20
Clark, E.O., 29, 31
Clark, E.V., 35, 36
Clark, H.H., 35, 36, 185
Clifton, N., 41, 42
Code, C., 22
Cohen, G., 30, 31, 34, 37–39, 45, 49, 50, 51, 148
Cohen, L.D., 29
Coleman, P.D., 7
College of Speech and Language Therapists (CSLT), 202, 215, 217, 219, 229
Collin, C., 214
Collins, M., 14
Colsher, P.L., 11
Colton, J., 12
Constantinidis, J., 21, 33
Cooper, B., 167
Coppens, P., 22
Corkin, S., 192
Corso, J.F., 10
Costa, L., 157
Cox, C., 183
Craik, F.I.M., 14, 29, 33
Critchley, M., 52, 187
Crook, T., 195, 213
Crystal, D., 57, 58
Crystal, H., 155
Cummings, J.L., 16, 21, 151, 159, 161, 166, 167, 169, 171, 188, 195
Curtis, S., 183
Cutting, J., 172

Dabul, B., 215
Damasio, A.R., 151
Damasio, H., 151
Daubber, T.R., 12
Davidson, J., 214
Davies, P., 155, 201, 202, 203
Davis, A., 9
Davis, S., 42, 51
Davy, D., 58
Dawson, D., 193, 210, 211
De Ajuriaguerra, J., 30, 50, 186, 187
de Leon, M., 195, 213
Densham, Y., 214
Deser, T., 191
Devreux, F., 166
Dick, M.B., 184
Dickson, D., 155
Diesfeldt, H.F., 184

Dittman, J., 188
Dixon, R.A., 39
Dobbs, A.R., 32
Dorosz, M., 43
Doussard-Roosevelt, J.A., 31, 32
Dowling, R.J., 227
Drachman, D., 18
Drew, S., 14, 222, 223
Dronkers, N.F., 15, 25
Durso, R., 41, 163–164, 190
Duval, R.J., 50, 186

Edmond, E., 222
Edmundson, A., 202
Eisdorfer, C., 11, 29
Ekelman, B., 189
Emery, O.B., 168
Enderby, P., 201, 202, 214
Erkinjuntti, T., 150, 158, 183
Etholm, B., 11
Evans, D.R., 3

Faber-Langendoen, K., 174
Fahn, S., 164
Falconer, J., 11
Faulkner, D., 31, 34, 37–39, 45, 49, 148
Fearnley, J.M., 155
Fedio, P., 183, 194, 195
Feier, C.D., 189
Fein, D., 39
Feinberg, T., 170
Feldman, L.S., 164
Feldman, R.G., 20, 166
Ferris, S.M., 195, 213
Filley, C.M., 175
Fisch, L., 1
Fisman, M., 21, 29, 174, 181, 184, 193, 210, 211
Fleming, S.G., 42, 44
Fletcher, P., 57, 58
Flood, D.G., 7
Flynn, F., 195
Fodor, J.D., 37
Folstein, M., 18, 166
Folstein, M.F., 209
Folstein, S.E., 209
Forbes, M.M., 195
Foster, N.L., 194, 195
Foster, N.L., 22
Fox, J.H., 167, 193
Fozard, J.L., 12, 32

Frackowiak, R.S.J., 155–156
France, J., 16
Franks, J.J., 11
Frazier, L., 37
Freedman, L., 157
Freer, C., 4
Fried, I., 151, 152
Friedenberg, D.L., 164–165
Friedland, R.P., 175
Friedman, J., 164
Fromm, D., 193
Fullerton, A.M., 14, 23
Fulton, S., 189
Funnell, E., 24, 181, 183

Gabbay, J., 198
Galloway, P.H., 155
Gallup, G.H., 29
Ganley, J.P., 12, 20
Garman, M., 23, 37, 57, 58
Garnett, E.S., 157
Garrett, M.F., 48
Garron, D.G., 162
Gawel, M.J., 9
General Household Survey, 57
George, J., 199
Ghobrial, M., 158
Gilleard, C.J., 209
Gillespie, M.M., 194, 195
Gilley, D.W., 193
Gioella, E.C., 9
Gladman, J., 218
Glanzer, M., 33
Gloser, G., 191
Goodglass, H., 22, 30, 47, 51, 54, 209, 210, 213
Goodman, B., 170
Gollomp, S., 164
Gordon, K., 41–42
Gornbein, J., 195
Gosney, M., 222
Gotestam, K.G., 219
Gotham, A.M., 163–165
Grady, C.L., 7
Graff-Radford, N.R., 151
Grande, M.J., 198
Grant, I., 172
Gravell, R., 16, 25, 207, 208, 216
Greenbaum, S., 57, 58
Greveson, G., 218
Grieg, L., 210, 213

Griffiths, R., 199
Griffiths, H., 217, 224, 230
Griggs, D.S., 32
Grisell, J., 25
Grist, E., 192
Grossberg, G.T., 17, 169
Grossman, J.L., 33
Grossman, M., 164
Grundman, M., 150
Guillemard, A.M., 227
Gupta, S., 3, 158
Gustafson, L., 175

Hagenlocker, K., 159
Hachinski, V.C., 157–158
Hakami, M.K., 14, 22
Hanley, I.G., 164
Hanson, W.R., 166
Hardy, J., 174
Harris, R.J., 40
Harrison, M.J.G., 17, 27
Harrold, R.M., 44
Hart, G., 9
Hart, M.N., 151
Hart, S., 24, 167, 182, 193
Hasher, L., 32, 34
Hass, J-C., 188
Hastie, I., 155
Haxby, J.V., 7
Hayashi, M.M., 42, 44
Hayslip, B., 8, 13
Hazenberg, G.J., 151
Heath, M., 10
Heaton R.K., 175
Heilman, K.M., 166
Heindel, W.C., 192
Heisey, J.G., 33
Henderson, V.W., 175
Hendricks, J., 227
Herbst, K.G., 11
Herlitz, A., 184
Hertzhog, C., 8
Heston, L., 162
Heyman, A., 193, 210, 211
Hier, D.B., 159
Higgs, P.H., 226
Hill, M.A., 16, 159
Hindo, W., 158
Hishahara, Y., 158
Hobart, C.J., 43
Hodges, J.R., 24, 167, 181, 183
Hodkinson, H.M., 209
Holden, U.P., 207, 219
Holland, A.L., 22, 152, 193, 195, 205, 206, 207, 214, 220, 231
Holland, C.A., 33
Homer, A., 155
Honjo, I., 8
Honovar, M., 155
Hood, P.C., 195
Horak, F.B., 162
Horn, L.C., 193
Horner, J., 193, 210, 211
Horwitz, B., 7
Howard, D.V., 33
Howes, D., 181
Hoyer, W.J., 13, 31, 32
Huber, S.J., 164–165
Hulicka, I.M., 33
Hultsch, D.F., 39
Humes, L.E., 10
Humphrey, D., 3
Hutchinson, J.M., 41–42, 51, 181, 189, 190, 214
Hurtig, H.I., 164
Hurtiz, H., 155–156
Hyde, J.B., 198
Hyman, B.T., 151

Illes, J., 20, 164, 166
Imamura, T., 158
Irigaray, L., 47, 49
Isaacs, B., 216
Ishii, N., 158
Isshiki, N., 8
Ivnik, R.J., 14
Ivy, G.O., 11

Jacoby, R., 155
Jackson, C., 184
Jaffe, J., 22, 47
Jakobson, R., 30
James, O., 218
James, S., 226
Jarvik, L.F., 29, 55, 169
Jennings, J.M., 14, 22
Jenson, M., 41–42, 51, 181, 189, 190, 214
Jerger, S., 10
Joanette, Y., 175, 181, 195
Jodar, M., 158
Johanson, A., 175

Johnson, J.A., 165, 207, 220
Johnston, M., 214
Jolley, D.J., 14, 199, 230
Jones, D.A., 220
Jones, S., 184
Jordan, B.D., 171
Junque, C., 158

Kahane, J.C., 2, 8
Kahn, H.A., 12
Kahn, R.L., 17
Kaplan, E., 47, 54, 209, 210, 213
Kaplan, R., 157
Kaszniak, A.W., 162, 174, 208, 212, 220
Katzman, R., 18
Kaufman, A.S., 5
Kausler, D.H., 14, 33
Kay, D.W.K., 184
Kellett, J., 155, 225
Kelly, J., 175
Kemper, S., 95, 149
Kempler, D., 184, 194
Kennedy, A M., 20, 174, 175
Kent, A., 11
Kern, R.S., 188
Kertesz, A., 15, 21, 29, 48, 149, 174, 181, 184, 193, 209, 210, 211
Kiloh, L.G., 16
Kim, M.M., 12
Kimura, R.S., 10
Kirshner, D.M., 214
Kirshner, H.S., 22
Kitano, K., 158
Klauber, M.R., 150
Klawans, H.L., 162
Kline, J., 32
Knesevich, J.W., 174
Knight, R.G., 164, 220
Kokmen, E., 14
Kondratowicz, T., 230
Kontiola, P., 158, 183
Koss E., 175
Kovanen, J., 150
Kramer,S.I., 159
Kuhl, D.E., 162
Kushner, M., 155–156
Kynette, D., 149

Laaksoner, R., 158, 183
LaBarge, E., 174
Labouvie-Vief, G., 42
Labov, W., 56, 57, 109
Lahey, M., 189
Laing, W., 200
Lang, A.E., 195
Lang, K., 197
Langer, K.G., 165
Lakowski, R., 12
Langton-Hewer, R., 16
Lantos, P., 155
Large, H.W., 166
Largen, J.W., 158
Larson, G.W., 8
Lassen, N.A., 157–158
Leandersson, R., 162
Lebrun, Y., 166
Leech, G., 57, 58
Lees, A.J., 155, 162, 166
Leibowitz, H.M., 12
Lesser, R., 158
Levelt, W., 59, 102
Levy, R., 155
Lewis, R.R., 13
Liacona, M., 22
Lieberman, A., 189
Lieberman, P., 164
Light, L.L., 14, 28, 31, 37, 39–40
Lindeboom, J., 151
Lipowski, Z.J., 16
Lishman, W.A., 151
Lockhart, R.S., 29
Loring, D.W., 158
Lovelace, E.A., 33
Lubinski, R., 14, 219
Lucas, M., 220
Ludwin, S.K., 152
Lunn, L.E., 10
Luthert, P., 155
Luzzatti, C., 17, 22, 151, 155–156
Lyness, S., 175
Lynne-Davis, P., 8
Macaluso-Haynes, S., 42, 107, 181
McBurney, D.H., 152, 220
McClelland, A., 202
McClelland, J.L., 32
McClenahan, R., 214
McClintic, K.L., 157
McClone, J., 3
Maccoby, E.E., 31
McConnell, E.E., 10
McCullough, D., 183, 184
McDaniel, K.D., 195

McDowell, F.H., 165
Mace, N., 220
McGonigle-Gibson, K.C., 195
McGorman, A., 210, 211
McHugh, P.R., 209
McInally, K., 201
McIntosh, I.B., 198
McIntosh, J., 202
MacKay, D.G., 44
McKenna, P., 213
McKhann, G., 18
McLean, J.E., 5
MacLeod, C.M., 11
McNamara, P., 41, 45, 163–164, 190
McQuillan, W.J., 161
Maher, E.R., 166
Mahler, M.E., 159
Mahurin, R.K., 158
Mandell, A.M., 167
Marin, O.S., 23, 24, 30, 182, 185, 193
Markus, E.J., 11
Marshall, J., 157–158
Marsden, C.D., 17, 161–165
Marsel-Mesulam, M.M., 22, 155
Marslen-Wilson, W.C., 39
Martin, A., 173, 181, 183, 192, 194
Martin, D.C., 193
Martin, J., 45, 52
Martin-Villalta, J.A., 158
Mashiah, T., 14
Matison, R., 164
Matthiace, L., 155
Maxim, J., 34, 35–36, 38, 50, 51, 168, 187, 190, 192, 202, 222
Mawby, B., 161
Mayeux, R., 164, 175
Meacham, J.A., 219
Meador, K.J., 158
Melin, L., 219
Mendez, M.F., 159
Mesulam, M., 23, 155
Metter, E.J., 162, 166
Meyer, B.J.F., 33, 39
Meyer, J.S., 157
Meyerson, B.A., 162
Midwinter, T., 4
Milberg, W., 166
Mildworf, B., 22, 42
Millard, P.H., 155, 226
Miller, B., 16
Miller, E., 219
Miller, J.P., 174
Miller, N., 194
Miller, R.L., 32
Milroy, L., 58
Miosen, T., 3
Mitchell, D.R., 32
Moffat, N., 207, 219
Monaco, G.E., 40
Moore, M.M., 37
Moossy, J., 152, 220
Morris, J.C., 174
Morrison, E.B., 14
Mortel, K.K., 157
Moscovitch, M.M., 7
Moy, A.C., 175
Munoz-Garcia, D., 152
Murdoch, B.E., 171, 192

Naheedy, M.H., 158
Nahmias, C., 157
Nakra, R., 17, 169
Nance, W.E., 10
National Census, 3, 55
National Centre for Health Statistics, 9
Navia, B.A., 171
Nebes, R.D., 193
Nelson, J., 193
Neshkes, R., 16
Newman, S.K., 20, 174, 175
Nicholas, M., 39
Nickerson, R.S., 12
Nooteboom,S.G., 149
North, A.J., 42, 106, 181
Noth, J., 166
Nowak, C.A., 39
Nussbaum, J.F., 4, 5

Oakley, A., 56
Oakley, M.A., 193
Obler, L.K., 22, 22, 30, 34, 39, 41, 42, 43, 44, 45, 47, 49, 51, 106, 163–164, 181, 185, 188, 190
O'Connell, P., 193
O'Connor, D.W., 198
O'Donovan, S., 220
OECD, 228
Okamoto, Y., 228
Oliver, T., 10
O'Neill, D., 198
OPCS, 2
Oppenheimer, S., 3

Osato, S.S., 188

Palmore, E.B., 4
Palo, J., 150
Patronas, N.J., 194, 195
Pattie, A.M., 209
Perlmutter, M., 33
Perotta, P., 219
Perry, J.R., 198
Persson, A., 162
Peters, K.E., 221
Peters, T.J., 220
Peterson, R.C., 14, 22
Petit, T.L., 11
Pick, A., 150
Pirozzolo, F., 10
Pitt, B., 16
Plude, D.J., 13, 31, 32
Podoll, K., 166
Poeck, K., 17, 151, 155–156
Poissant, A., 175, 181, 195
Poon, L.W., 32, 33, 44
Powell, A.L., 159
Powell-Proctor, L., 219
Power, K.G., 198
Prasse, M.J., 13, 21
Price, D., 18
Price, R.W., 171
Pring, T.R., 165, 207, 220
Prior, R., 161
Propper, C., 200
Prutting, C.A., 214
Pujol, J., 158

Quirk, R., 57, 58

Rabbitt, P., 29, 31, 33
Rabinowitz, J.C., 14, 22
Rabins, P., 220
Rankin, J., 14, 22
Rao, P., 213
Rapcsak, S.Z., 193
Raven, J.C., 211
Reed, R., 172
Reichman, W.E., 195
Reifler, B.V., 159, 170
Reige, W.H., 162
Reisberg, B., 195, 213
Reivich, M., 155–156
Rernmirth, O.M., 152, 220
Revesz, D.J., 155
Reynolds, C.R., 5
Rezai, K., 151
Ribas, J.C., 158
Rice, G.E., 39
Riegel, K., 45
Riensche, L.L., 197
Riggans, L., 220
Rigrodsky, 14
Ringel, R., 2
Ripich, D.N., 187, 189, 190, 191
Risberg, J., 175
Rissenberg, 33
Robertson, S.J., 165
Robinson, J.D., 4, 5
Rochford, G., 192
Roenker, D.L., 32
Rogers, D., 162
Rogers, H., 193, 210
Rogers, R.L., 157
Roland, M.O., 198
Ron, M.A., 16, 26
Rose, C., 205
Rose, T.L., 33
Rosen, A., 189
Rosen, I., 175
Rosen, J., 164
Rosenbaum, G., 25
Rosenschein, S., 151, 152
Ross, E.D., 158
Ross, G.W., 166
Rossiter, D., 201
Rossor, M.N., 17, 20, 155–156, 174, 175
Roth, M., 16, 157
Rourke, D., 25
Rousseau, J.J., 166
Rowley, D., 22
Royal College of Physicians Committee on Geriatrics, 17
Rubens, A.B., 193
Rubin, N.P., 22, 155–156
Rubino, F.A., 158
Rule, B.G., 32
Rumelhart, D.E., 32
Ryan, W.J., 8
Ryff, C.D., 5

Saffran, E.M., 23, 24, 30, 181, 182, 185, 193
Saint-Cyr, J.A., 165
Sakuma, N., 158
Salmon, D.P., 167, 183, 184, 192

Salthouse, T.A., 6, 29, 31, 32, 33, 55
Sano, M., 175
Sands, D., 184, 205
Sarno, M.T., 205, 214, 222
Sasanuma, S., 158
Saykin, A., 155–156
Schaffer, G., 33
Schankweiler, D., 205
Schegloff, E.A.,. 41
Scheibel, A.B., 151, 152
Scheltens, P., 151
Schneider, L.S., 175
Schoenberg, B.S., 2
Schoene, W.C., 161
Scholes, R.J., 30, 34, 35, 50
Schonfield, D., 32
Schwartz, M.F., 23, 24, 30, 52, 181, 182, 185, 186, 193
Schwarz, M., 166
Scott, S., 163, 165
Selchan, D.H., 157
Selkoe, D.J., 7
Seltzer, B., 175
Semple, J.M., 24, 167
Shankweiler, D., 205
Shaw, R.J., 33
Sheppard, H., 15, 25
Sherwin, I., 175
Shindler, A.G., 159
Shuttleworth, E.C., 164–165
Silverman, J.D., 198
Simon, E., 29
Simon, E.W., 39
Sims, P., 157
Sinclair, H., 188
Slu D., 175, 181
Skelton-Robinson, M., 184
Skinner, C., 214
Skovronek, E., 32
Slater, P.E., 4
Slauson, T.J., 212
Smith, A.D., 14
Smith, B.J., 219
Smith, C.M., 193
Smith, E., 162, 166
Smith, G., 14
Smith, S.R., 192
Snowling, M., 202
Sobel, E., 175
Sonies, B., 8
Sorsby, A., 13
Speedie, L.J., 166
Spiraduso, W.W., 13
Stadlan, E.M., 18
Stebbins, G.T., 193
Stengel, E., 187
Stern, G.M., 162
Stern, M.B., 164
Stern, Y., 175
Stevens, A., 198
Stevens, S.J., 192, 193, 212
Stine, E.A., 39, 42
Storandt, M., 29, 32, 44
Strehler, B.L., 10
Stubbs, M., 58
Sulkava, R., 150, 158, 183
Sutcliffe, R.L., 161
Svartvik, J., 57, 58
Swash, M., 193

Tallis, R., 198
Tangalos, E.G., 14
Tanridag, O., 22, 34
Tatemichi,T.K., 157
Taylor, A.E., 165
Taylor, A.M., 157
Teng, E.L., 175
Terrell, B.Y., 187, 189, 190, 191
Thal, L.G., 150
Thomas, K., 8
Thompson, F., 165
Thompson, T., 4, 5
Thompson, I.M., 8, 152, 159–160, 170, 176, 178, 179, 214
Thorndike, R.L., 29
Thornicroft, G., 226
Thurman, L., 22
Tideman, E., 175
Till, P.E., 45
Tissot, R., 30, 50, 186, 187
Tomlinson, B.E., 2
Tomlinson, B., 203
Tomoeda, C.K., 21, 167, 182, 186, 187, 212
Toner, H.L., 221
Tout, G., 226
Tranel, D., 151
Trimble, M., 162
Trosset M.W., 182, 183, 193, 212
Troster A.I., 183, 184
Trudgill, P., 58
Trueman, V., 32

Tulving, E., 23, 32
Tweedy, J.R., 165
Tyrer, G.M.B., 211
Tyrrell, P.J., 155–156

Ulatowska, H., 42, 44, 107, 181
Ungerleider, L.G., 7

Valdois, S., 195
Valenstein, E., 47
Valk, J., 151
Van de Gaag, A., 203
Van Hoesen, G.W., 151
VanGorp, W.G., 188
Vendrell, P., 158
Verity, M.A., 151, 152
Vernon, G., 164
Veroff, 76
Vertes, D., 189
Vignolo, L.A., 205
Vinas, J., 158

Wade, D.T., 16
Walker, A.C., 225
Walker, S., 18, 210, 217, 224
Wallace, R.B., 11
Wallesch, C-W., 188
Walsh, D.A., 13, 45
Walsh, K.W., 15
Ward, P., 226
Warren, R.M., 43–44
Warren, R.P., 43–44
Warrington, E.K., 155–157, 193, 213
Watson, R., 231
Wechsler, A.F., 151, 152
Wechsler, D., 29, 212
Weinberg, A., 37
Weinstein, B.E., 9
Weinstein, E.A., 17
Weintraub, S., 22, 155–156
Welford, A.T., 31, 42
Wells, C.E.W., 47
Wells, N.E., 4, 169
Welsh, A., 39
Wertz, R.T., 15
West, R., 29, 45
Whetsell, W.O., 22
Whitaker, H., 23, 47, 49, 50, 52, 182, 185, 198
Whitehouse, P., 189
Whitman, D., 25
Whurr, R., 211
Wilkie, F., 11
Wilkin, D., 230
Wilkin, E., 14
Williams, B.O., 217, 224
Williamson, S., 52, 181, 182, 186
Willis, A.L., 20, 166
Willott, J.F., 10
Wilson, B.A., 207, 219
Wilson, L-G., 184
Wilson, R.S., 25, 162, 193
Wingfield, A., 39, 42
Winocur, G., 7
Wirz, S., 202, 214
Wolf, E., 12
Wolters, E.C., 151
Wood, V.A., 16, 25
Woods, R.T., 207, 219
Worthley, J., 45, 52
Worthington, E.L., 10
Wraight, S.K., 198
Wu, E., 155

Yairi, E., 41, 42
Yen, S., 155
Yesavage, J.A., 33
Young, C.J., 33
Young, J.B., 199
Young, J.C., 158

Zacks, R.T., 32, 34
Zelinsky, E.M., 37, 40, 42
Zurif, E.B., 30

Subject index

abandoned utterances, 103–104
acquired immune deficiency syndrome, 19, 170–171
acute confusional state, 15, 16
acute injury, 25, 171, 200
ageing, 1–4, 24,
  age changes and communication, 7–18, 34–41, 41–46
  biological age, 2
  chronological age, 2
  and dementia, 16, 19, 46–53
  the elderly, 1–2, 3–4, 55–57
  expectations of the elderly, 4–5
  neurocognitive changes, 3, 5–7, 31–33, 190
  senescence, 2–3
  senility, 3
  successful ageing, 5
agnosia, 192–193
AIDS–dementia complex, 19, 170–171
alcohol, 171–172
Alzheimer's disease, 15, 19, 149, 173–195, 210–213
  agnosias, 192–193
  definition, 174–176
  discourse, cohesion and repair,188–191
  dyspraxias, 194–195
  heterogeneity, 174–176
  incidence and prevalence, 150
  language breakdown, 46–53, 181–195
  language profiles,176–180
  lexical semantics,181–184
  and normal ageing, 46, 146
  reading, writing and spelling, 193–194
  semantic and grammatical processes, 184–188, 191
aphasia, 21–23, 46–53, 158–159, 163, 167, 170
  and dementia, 21–23, 46–53, 209–215
  and normal ageing, 46–53, 205–207
  progressive, 155–157
assessment, 25–26, 208–215
  tests not designed for the elderly, 25, 209–210
  multidisciplinary, 230
attention, 13, 31–32
auditory system, 9–11, 192–193, 208

Binswanger's disease, 19, 161
biological age, 3
British Geriatric Society, 228
  statement of intent, 228–229

carers, 220–221
chronological age, 2, 3, 6
clause elements, 59–61, 67–70, 72–84
cognitive ageing, 8, 10, 31–33
  theoretical frameworks, 5–7
College of Speech and Language Therapists, 202, 215, 229

communication, 7–18
assessment, 209, 213–214
between professionals, 209
disorders and disease processes 15–18, 171–172, 207
reduced mobility,13
community care, 196, 225–226,
conversational language, 146–149, 188–191
coordination, 95–97, 101–102
coordinators, 96–97
core grammar, 146–147
cortical dementia, 19, 20
Creutzfeldt–Jakob disease, 19, 167

dementia, 19, 150–172, 173–195
and ageing, 18–21, 146
AIDS–dementia complex, 19, 170–171
Alzheimer's disease,15, 19, 173–195
and aphasia, 21–23, 155–157
assessment, 209–215
Binswanger's disease, 19, 161
and cognition, 23–24
Creutzfeldt–Jakob disease, 19, 167
and depression, 15, 167–170
diffuse Lewy body disease, 19, 155
Huntington's disease, 15, 19, 166–167
incidence and prevalence, 150
Korsakoff's psychosis, 19, 171–172
multi-infarct, 15, 19, 157–160
Parkinson's disease, 15, 19, 161–165
Pick's disease, 15 19, 150–154
progressive supranuclear palsy, 19, 165–166
Steele–Richardson–Olszewski syndrome, 19, 165–166
unconfirmed diagnosis, 25
vascular, 19, 157–161
Wernicke's encephalopathy, 19, 171–172
depression,15, 159, 167–171
diffuse Lewy body disease, 155
disfluencies,102–112, 147, 163–164
grammatical errors, 106–111, 186
repair and filler syllables, 111–112, 147, 149, 186
semantic and grammatical ambiguities, 104–106, 185
uncompleted and abandoned utterances, 103–104
dyspraxia, 194–195
dysphagia, 155, 197

elliptical sentences, 70–72, 187
encephalitis, 30

filler syllables, 111–112

general practitioners, 199–200, 228–229
geriatric services, 198–201, 203, 228–230
grammatical structure, 54–94
in Alzheimer's disease, 184–188
ambiguities, 104–106
errors, 106–111
in normal ageing, 59–94

head injury, 15, 201
Huntington's disease, 15, 19, 166–167

institutionalisation,14, 219
intonation, 113–115

Korsakoff's psychosis, 19, 171–172

language, 28–36, 113–149
analysing elderly language, 57–58, 113–115, 146–147
change in the elderly, 28–30
comprehension, 34–41, 164
in dementia, 150–172, 174, 181–195
grammatical structure, 4–94, 95–102, 146–149, 184–188
with increasing age, 3–34
production, 41–46, 145–149, 164
profiles of normal elderly, 115–141

language (contd)
research, 30–31, 55–57, 175, 181, 203, 231–232
transcription, 113–115
variation, 59, 140–144
language profiles, 115–141, 152–154, 160, 176–180
language profiles (contd)
Alzheimer's disease, 176–180
normal elderly, 115–141
multi-infarct dementia, 160
Pick's disease, 152–154
Lewy body disease, 155
lexical semantics, 181–184

major sentences, 65–67
medication, 26–27, 163, 165
memory, 13–14, 32–33, 155, 161, 165–166, 169–170, 171–172, 195
minor sentences, 65–67
motor processing, 7, 162, 171, 208
multi-infarct dementia, 19, 157–160
language profile, 160
multiple sclerosis, 19

neurocognitive changes, 3, 5–7, 31–33
neurosyphilis, 19

Parkinson's disease, 15, 19, 161–165, 207
performance variation, 141–144, 209
phrasal structure, 84–93
analysis, 84–85
noun or adverbial phrases, 85–89
expansion, 89
verb phrase, 89–93
Pick's disease, 15, 19, 150–154
language profiles, 152–154
premorbid abilities, 25, 28–30
presbycusis, 10
private sector care, 198–201
profile variation, 242
pronoun use, 93–94
progressive aphasia, 21–22, 155–157
progressive supranuclear palsy, 19, 165–166
pseudodementia, 26, 27, 168–170
psychiatric illness, 15, 16, 167–170
psychogeriatric services, 197, 198–201, 203, 228, 230

reading, 193–194, 210
repair, 111–112, 147, 149, 186
residential care, 198, 199, 222–224
restricted mobility, 21

semantic ambiguities, 104–106, 185
senescence, 3
senility, 3, 4, 15
sensory deficits, 26
sentences, 59–84, 95–97, 101–112, 148–149
clause elements, 67–70, 72–84
complex, 95–102
coordination, 95–97, 101–102
definition, 59–61
disfluencies, 102–112
elliptical, 70–72
length, 62–64
major, 66–67
minor, 66–67
mean number per turn, 64–65
phrasal structure, 84–93
subordination, 97–102
types, 65–67, 148–149
service provision, 196–204, 228–231
in Canada, 227
current UK provision, 198–201
in France, 227
issues, 197–198
in Japan, 227
proposed UK provision, 225–226
speech and language therapy, 201–204, 228–231
in the USA, 226–227
single case studies, 151, 155–156, 158, 174, 185–186, 189, 195
single word processing, 43–46, 181–184
social services, 198–201, 226
speech production, 8–9
speech and language therapy, 201–204, 205–224
assessment, 203, 208–215, 230
CSLT survey, 202–203
direct therapy, 203, 217–218
education, 204, 221–222
environmental manipulation, 219–220
group work, 203, 218–219, 223–224
intervention studies, 205–208

speech and language therapy (contd)
interventions, 215–224
monitoring, 203, 220, 229–230
provision, 201–204
reality orientation, 219
service variation, 201–204
settings, 203
therapist's skills, 203–204
working with carers, 203, 220–221
working in the residential sector, 222–224
spelling, 193–194
spinocerebellar degeneration, 19
Steele–Richardson–Olszewski syndrome, 19, 165–166
stroke, 15, 19
subacute sclerosing panencephalitis, 19
subcortical dementia, 19, 20
subdural haematoma, 19
subordinate clause, 97–102

transcription, 113–115

uncompleted utterances, 103–104

vascular dementias, 19, 157–161
verb phrase, 89–91
verb phrase morphemes, 92–93
visual system, 10–11, 192–193, 208
voluntary sector, 221

Wernicke's encephalopathy, 19, 171–172
word-finding difficulties, 4, 148, 156, 158, 166, 171, 181, 184
writing, 171, 189, 193–194, 210